The
Religious
History
of American
Women

The Religious History of American Women

REIMAGINING THE PAST

Edited by

Catherine A. Brekus

The University of
North Carolina Press

Chapel Hill

Designed by Jacquline Johnson
Set in Minion by Keystone Typesetting, Inc.

This volume was published with the assistance of the
University of Chicago Divinity School and of the Greensboro
Women's Fund of the University of North Carolina Press.
Founding Contributors of the fund: Linda Arnold Carlisle,
Sally Schindel Cone, Anne Faircloth, Bonnie McElveen Hunter,
Linda Bullard Jennings, Janice J. Kerley (in honor of Margaret
Supplee Smith), Nancy Rouzer May, and Betty Hughes Nichols.

Portions of chapter 9 appeared previously in Ann Braude, "A
Religious Feminist, Who Can Find Her?: Historiographical
Challenges from the National Organization for Women,"
Journal of Religion 84, no. 4 (October 2004): 555–72, copyright
2004 by The University of Chicago Press; portions of chapter 12
appeared previously in Kristy Nabhan-Warren, *The Virgin of El
Barrio: Marian Apparitions, Catholic Evangelizing, and Mexican
American Activism* (New York: New York University Press, 2005).

The paper in this book meets the guidelines for permanence
and durability of the Committee on Production Guidelines
for Book Longevity of the Council on Library Resources.

Library of Congress Cataloging-in-Publication Data
The religious history of American women : reimagining the past /
edited by Catherine A. Brekus.
p. cm.
Includes bibliographical references and index.
ISBN 978-0-8078-3102-1 (cloth: alk. paper)
ISBN 978-0-8078-5800-4 (pbk.: alk. paper)
1. Women and religion—United States—History. 2. United
States—Religion. I. Brekus, Catherine A.
BL2525.R4698 2007
200.82'0973—dc22   2006102058

cloth   11 10 09 08 07   5 4 3 2 1
paper   11 10 09 08 07   5 4 3 2 1

For Claire and Rachel

Contents

The
Religious
History
of American
Women

Introduction

Catherine A. Brekus

Searching for Women in Narratives of American Religious History

Recently I was so eager to read a new dissertation on American religious history that I ordered an online copy from my university's library. Given the author's topic, I assumed that this new work would help me with my own research on early American women. Hoping for a preview, I typed the word "women" into the search engine so that I would not have to scroll through four hundred pages of text. Almost immediately, a message flashed on my screen: "Search term not found." Surprised, I tried other words—female, feminine, gender, woman—but always with the same results. My "search term," the subject of almost all of my historical research, could not be found.

More than thirty years after the rise of women's history alongside the feminist movement, it is still difficult to "find" women in many books and articles about American religious history. Although few scholars ever explain their choice to exclude women, many seem to assume that women's stories are peripheral to their research topics, whether Puritan theology or church and state. They do not seem hostile to women's history as much as they are dismissive of it, treating it as a separate topic that they can safely ignore. Since "women's historians" are devoted to writing women's history, those who identify themselves simply as "American religious historians" can focus on topics that seem more important to them.

This book is a collaborative attempt to explain why women's history should be an integral part of American religious history. Each of the twelve contributors to this volume has tried to answer the same simple and yet revolutionary question: What difference does it make to include women in our narratives of American religious history? Or to ask the same question a different way, why should American religious historians study the lives of women as well as of men? Rather than treating the answer to that question as self-evident, as if the recovery of women's stories should automatically lead to new narratives, the contributors to this volume have tried to offer concrete

1

models for how women's history transforms our understanding of America's religious past. All have been inspired by Ann Braude's influential 1997 essay, "Women's History *Is* American Religious History," which argues that serious attention to women's history undermines three of the most important "plots" that structure current interpretations of American religious history: declension, feminization, and secularization. When seen through the eyes of women, religion does not appear to have "declined" during the eighteenth century; it did not become newly "feminized" in the nineteenth century; and it did not completely lose its authority to "secularization" in the twentieth century.[1] How might other "plots" shift if American religious historians include women in their narratives?

Building on Braude's insights, the historians in this volume (including Braude herself) have turned their attention to detailed studies of particular groups and events, and they have asked challenging questions about traditional narrative frameworks. How would historians write about Puritans if they explored the lives of women as well as of men? What would be their main themes? How would historians tell the story of Judaism? Witchcraft? Mormonism? The origins of the Catholic Church in the United States? The women's rights movement? While some of the contributors argue for changes in emphasis and others for more significant revisions, all agree that women's history leads to an altered vision of America's religious past.

Since the religious history of American women is a vast topic, this book offers only a glimpse of what it might mean to "reimagine the past." What we offer in the following pages is not a comprehensive introduction to all of women's religious history but rather a set of provocative case studies that will hopefully inspire future work. By directly confronting the question of women's historical significance, we hope to encourage greater conversation about what is at stake when women are excluded from American religious history—or included in it.

Women's History and American Religious History

Since the rise of women's history in the 1960s and 1970s, thousands of articles and books have been published about women in American religious history. This literature is so enormous that it virtually defies categorization. Historians have published insightful studies of female religious leaders as diverse as Frances Willard (1839–1898), the founder of the Woman's Christian Temperance Union; Kateri Tekakwitha (1656–1680), a Native American convert to Catholicism; Jarena Lee (1783–?), the first African American female preacher; Ann Lee (1736–1784), the founder of the Shakers; and Fanny Crosby (1820–

1915), a popular hymnist.[2] They have written about women's religious activism in home and foreign missions, temperance societies, and antislavery organizations.[3] They have explored the religious beliefs of enslaved women, Catholic women, Jewish women, Mormon women, Holiness and Pentecostal women, African American Protestant women, and many others.[4] They have examined how religion has influenced women's political commitments, their personal lives (for example, their understanding of childrearing and marriage), and their attitudes toward gender roles.[5] Women who were rarely mentioned in the pages of books published before 1970 now have books dedicated to them alone: Catholic sisters, African American Baptist women, Protestant female preachers, immigrant Jewish women, Black Muslim women, Native American women, and Spiritualist female mediums.[6] There has been relatively little research on women who practice world religions in America—for example, Hinduism or Islam—but more studies will almost certainly appear as the American religious landscape grows increasingly pluralistic.[7] Because of the sheer richness of the field, Susan Hill Lindley was able to publish the first comprehensive textbook on women and religion in America, *You Have Stept Out of Your Place.*[8]

The history of women and religion in America has also gained a significant institutional presence in the academy. Many colleges, universities, and seminaries offer courses on American women and religion, and a few offer special master's or doctoral programs in women's studies in religion, including Harvard, Smith, Claremont, and the United Theological Seminary in Minneapolis. (In addition, Vanderbilt offers a graduate certificate in gender studies.) The Hadassah International Research Institute at Brandeis University and the Women's Studies in Religion Program at Harvard University Divinity School were each founded for the sole purpose of encouraging research on women's religious history. (The Hadassah Institute funds scholarship on Jewish women, while Harvard's program is nondenominational.)[9] In addition, the American Society of Church History established the Jane Dempsey Douglass Prize in 1989, which is awarded annually for the best essay on women in Christian history.[10] Many of the prize's winners have been American religious historians.

Yet despite the number of books published, degrees awarded, and prizes given, women's history has not yet gained full acceptance within the fields of either religion or history. While Judith M. Bennett, a historian, has expressed concern about the "ghettoization" of women's history (it is "a separate but not equal enclave within the historical profession"), Randi R. Warne, a religion scholar, complains that "a two-tiered system has been created which is particularly visible in the academic study of religion: male/mainstream scholarship and the feminist scholarship of the margins."[11] When women's studies programs and courses were created, many hoped that they would act as a wedge for integrating women into the rest of the curriculum. Instead, however, they have often led to the segregation of women as a special, separate topic of inquiry. Only "women's historians" consistently write and teach about women, while other historians often ignore them.

Unfortunately, this troubling division between "women's history" and (for lack of a better term) "mainstream" history is a striking feature of scholarship on American religion. While "women's" or "gender" historians have often tried to make significant contributions to traditional areas of study such as theology, revivalism, politics, or immigration, the reverse has less frequently been true. For example, Ann Douglas's book, *The Feminization of American Culture*, which argues that nineteenth-century Protestant female writers helped give rise to theological liberalism, is clearly addressed to both women's historians and intellectual historians. Douglas claims that nineteenth-century American theology was profoundly shaped (in negative ways) by women's embrace of sentimentality. In contrast, E. Brooks Holifield's groundbreaking book about American theology, *Theology in America*, barely mentions women at all. For reasons he does not explain, Holifield left the task of exploring women's theological views to those who specialize in women's history.[12] Similarly, Nancy Hardesty's book about nineteenth-century revivalism, *Your Daughters Shall Prophecy: Revivalism and Feminism in the Age of Finney*, is addressed to historians of both the Second Great Awakening and women's religious leadership. Besides explaining the rise of female evangelism, Hardesty offers a new interpretation of Charles Finney's theological commitment to perfectionism (the belief that humans could become perfect in this life). In contrast, Nathan Hatch's monumental study of the Second Great Awakening, *The Democratization of American Christianity*, which is one of the finest studies of revivalism ever published, devotes only two pages to women. While Hardesty obviously wanted her book to be read by historians of revivalism, Hatch does not seem to have imagined women's historians as part of his audience.[13]

This pattern of exclusion is repeated in American religious history textbooks, which rarely include sustained discussions of women's religious ideas, beliefs, experiences, or leadership. Of course, one would not expect textbooks written before the 1970s to include much material on women. Because historians who write survey texts are crucially dependent on the work of others, their books usually reflect the strengths and weaknesses of their scholarly moment. It is no surprise, then, that such influential books as Martin Marty's *Righteous Empire: The Protestant Experience in America*, which was published in 1970, or Sydney Ahlstrom's *A Religious History of the American People*, published two years later, mention women only briefly. (To his credit, when Marty published a revised edition of his book in 1986, he added a new chapter on women, "The Protestant Majority," which made his book one of the most inclusive surveys available at the time and, unfortunately, still more inclusive than some of the books currently being published twenty years later.)[14] More troubling is the pattern of careless exclusion—or at best, nominal inclusion— that has emerged since the 1980s. For example, George Marsden's textbook, *Religion in American Culture*, which was published in a second edition in 2001, mentions only 29 women by name (as compared to 246 men), and if one excludes queens (Elizabeth I, Mary I, Mary II, and Catherine of Aragon), celebrities (Clara Bow, Jane Russell, Monica Lewinsky, and Shirley Mac-Laine), and the Virgin Mary, the number of female religious characters is even smaller. In an attempt to be comprehensive, Marsden includes several brief, separate sections on women's history: "The Age of the Spirit and the Woman's Place" (two pages), "New Public Roles" (two pages), "Women and Reform" (two pages), and "Feminism" (three pages). But the first two of these sections appear, oddly, under the larger heading of "Nonevangelical America," next to Native American, Catholic, and Protestant "outsiders." Marsden's implication, which he never explains, is that even though women represented the majority of church members, they were still somehow re-ligious "outsiders." (His structural organization is especially confusing be-cause many of the women he discusses under the rubric of "nonevangelical America" were in fact evangelicals.) In his third section on female reform, he runs into a different kind of conceptual problem by discussing "women" as an undifferentiated group. For example, he tells his readers that "most women" before the Civil War "continued to operate in the home sphere and the neighborhood," but he never mentions that enslaved women, factory girls, and immigrant women rarely had the luxury of devoting themselves to the home. Only two of the women who appear in Marsden's book are Catho-lic (Maria Monk, who is best described as a nativist and an ex-Catholic, and Dorothy Day) and only three are African American (Phillis Wheatley, Jarena Lee, and Barbara Harris). While some of Marsden's exclusions can be ex-plained by the explicitly Protestant focus of his book—he argues in the in-troduction that American religious history, "if it is to hang together as a narrative, must focus on the role played by certain groups of mainstream Protestants"—he pays very little attention to even white Protestant women. Overall, his book treats women's history as a diversion from the more impor-tant history of men.[15]

Other textbooks are marked by similar omissions. Catherine L. Albanese's book, *America: Religion and Religions*, which is widely used in undergraduate classrooms, ignores much of the recent research on women's history. Albanese never mentions women's numerical predominance in churches, and although she describes several female religious leaders, she does not discuss women in many sections where it would have seemed natural—for example, in her discussion of Salem witchcraft, where she could have tried to answer the question of why most "witches" were women, or in her description of black theology, where she could have discussed womanist theology.[16] (Like Marsden, Albanese says very little about the religious lives of black women, mentioning only Barbara Harris, Rosa Parks, and Joan Campbell by name. Campbell was elected moderator of the Presbyterian Church in 1989.) Although these examples are minor, they are only a few of many, and they add up to a disappointing series of narrative exclusions. In *The Religious History of America*, Edwin Gaustad and Leigh Schmidt have obviously tried to be more comprehensive, and they have admirably listed some of the most important scholarship on women in each chapter's "suggested readings." Yet despite the strengths of their book, they still do not give adequate space to such important topics as female reform and the role of religion in the suffrage movement.[17]

John Corrigan's book, *Religion in America*, offers a much larger cast of female characters, as well as a deeper analysis of women's religious activism. Although numbers are only a crude index to a book's contents, it is worth noting that Marsden mentions twenty-nine women by name in his text; Albanese, twenty-nine; Gaustad and Schmidt, thirty-one; and Corrigan, ninety-six. Corrigan's decision to discuss so many women not only reflects his fascination with personal experience—he clearly savors individual life stories—but also a disciplined effort to broaden the traditional narrative beyond its focus on men. Particularly impressive is his attempt to integrate the stories of women outside of the white, Protestant mainstream. For example, in a discussion of African American churches after the Civil War, he emphasizes that "women performed the crucial work of organizing the 'mutual benefit societies,' the voluntary associations that oversaw the welfare of black communities on the local and everyday level."[18] Yet perhaps because this book is a revision of one that was originally published by Winthrop Hudson in 1965, most of the sections on women are separated from the rest of the text. The unintended result is that women often appear marginal to the main story. For example, readers learn that an ex-slave named Elizabeth became a preacher during the Second Great Awakening, but instead of reading about her in the chapter on the revivals, they encounter her in a separate chapter on women's religious leadership that appears 150 pages later.[19] While

Corrigan has made a valiant effort to revise Hudson's book, it still bears the marks of its 1965 origins.

Only a few American religious historians have managed to integrate women more seamlessly into traditional survey texts. In the preface to their collaborative book, *Religion in American Life*, Jon Butler, Grant Wacker, and Randall Balmer assert that American religious history is "the story of women—Anne Hutchinson, Phoebe Palmer, and Dorothy Day—as well as the story of men—Teskwatawa, George Whitefield, Isaac Mayer Wise, and Billy Graham," and in the pages that follow, they discuss women side by side with men instead of segregating them into separate sections. Although they could have made their book even stronger by asking how religion shaped women's (and men's) understanding of gender, they offer a valuable example of how to begin incorporating women as historical agents into traditional, chronological narratives.[20] Other scholars have been so eager to move the field of American religious history beyond its conventional focus on white, male Protestants that they have experimented with thematic rather than chronological approaches. Philip Goff and Paul Harvey's edited collection, *Themes in Religion and American Culture*, offers an introduction to American religion that is organized thematically and that deliberately highlights both gender and race.[21]

If these two books, both published recently, are widely adopted in college classrooms, they may begin to change the way American religious history is typically taught. At the present time, however, women's history seems to play only a small role in most introductory courses. Based on the syllabuses available on the websites of the American Academy of Religion, the Young Scholars of American Religion, and H-AMREL (the American religious history group affiliated with H-NET), a surprising number of historians either never mention women as a topic or relegate them to one or two reading assignments—and those assignments almost always focus exclusively on white, Protestant women, not women of color. Perhaps some try to discuss women in depth without assigning special reading or crafting special lectures, but it seems unlikely. One historian who taught a course titled Religion in the South posted both his syllabus and the full texts of his lectures on the American Academy of Religion website, and in twenty lectures, he mentioned women only four times—each time in only one sentence.[22]

Given the extraordinary levels of female participation in churches and synagogues throughout American history, the choice to ignore women's history is perplexing. Inspired by the invention of computers, historians in the 1970s began analyzing enormous amounts of historical data about church membership, and over the past thirty-five years they have repeatedly found that women have almost always outnumbered men in the pews. In the First

Congregational Church of New Haven, Connecticut, for example, women made up the majority of new members from the 1680s to the 1980s.[23] Although historians are still collecting evidence, this pattern of female dominance seems to characterize many non-Christian religions in the United States as well, including Reform and Conservative Judaism. Sociologists have found that when world religions such as Hinduism, Buddhism, Sikhism, and Islam are transplanted to the United States, immigrant women often become particularly active in their religious communities. As Ann Braude has noted, "The numerical dominance of women in all but a few religious groups constitutes one of the most consistent features of American religion, and one of the least explained."[24]

Is Women's History Methodologically Distinctive?

Explaining women's absence in narratives of American religious history is difficult. Why has women's history remained on the margins of the field? After thirty years of scholarship on women, why haven't more historians integrated women into their books and courses? One possible answer, which seems to be an underlying assumption among "mainstream" historians, is that women's history is methodologically distinctive from other kinds of history and therefore difficult to integrate into our current narratives of America's religious past. Indeed, I have often encountered sympathetic scholars who have confided their desire to include more women in their books but also their uncertainty about how "to do" women's history. Since I tend to view most women's historians as fairly conservative in terms of method, the comment always takes me by surprise. Is there anything unique about the way that women's historians approach the past? Do they "do history" in a distinctive way?

The answer is both yes and no. "Yes," women's historians have brought different kinds of questions to their study of the past. As historian Linda Gordon has commented, they have redefined "what counts as evidence," broadening our understanding of what's important to know and understand.[25] Instead of focusing solely on the ideas and actions of great men, they have treated information about women's lives as worthy of serious study. For example, the historians in this volume pose questions about women's images of God, female friendships, and women's power within religious institutions that were rarely asked before the 1970s. The answers to these questions have sometimes challenged standard historical periodization. For example, in her study of early American evangelical women, *Disorderly Women: Sexual Politics and Evangelicalism in Revolutionary New England*, Susan Juster has suggested that the American Revolution was not as "revolutionary" for white women as it was for white men.[26]

Women's historians have also approached their research with a distinctive epistemology, by which I mean "a theory of knowledge" that explains who can know and what can be known. While few historians today would claim that they can be truly "scientific" in their research, women's historians tend to be particularly skeptical of the claim to unbiased neutrality. To be clear, they certainly want to write histories that are factually accurate, and they strive to be fair in their depiction of people and events. (A claim to be "fair" is less sweeping than a claim to be "scientific" or "neutral.") But because they have devoted their careers to rectifying women's exclusion from standard narratives of the past, they are painfully aware that history is always written from a particular standpoint. Like historians of other overlooked groups, including African Americans, Asian Americans, Native Americans, and Latinos, they have argued that researchers inevitably approach the past through the lens of their own experiences and assumptions. In the words of Randi R. Warne, "*Knowledge production is not a neutral process. Who* is asking the question determines in large measure what questions are asked, particularly when intellectual inquiry is proceeding in fresh new directions."[27]

This does not mean, however, that women's historians believe that "anything goes" or that their work is "political" in a way that other history is not. While women's history certainly has political implications—as theologian Anne Carr notes, "There is politics involved in taking the growing body of knowledge about women seriously, in overcoming or continuing the devaluation, trivialization, and indifference that attaches to the question"—it is not political in the sense of being distorted.[28] Unfortunately, women's historians have often been accused of being "biased" or misrepresenting historical evidence in order to promote a feminist agenda.[29] Perhaps because of these kinds of criticisms, they have tended to be especially attentive to issues of factual accuracy and interpretive fairness. Their critique of the historical profession is not simply destructive, but constructive: they argue that because perfect neutrality is impossible, historians must be particularly careful to think about the way their own biases might shape their interpretations.

Most historians of women and American religion can best be described as "moderate historicists" who believe, in Thomas Haskell's words, that "objectivity is not neutrality." As Haskell argues, it would be absurd to claim that historians can examine the past with utter neutrality, but they can still strive to be objective—that is, they can practice a kind of "ascetic self-discipline" that requires them "to achieve some distance from one's own spontaneous perceptions and convictions, to imagine how the world appears in another's eyes, to experimentally adopt perspectives that do not come naturally."[30] To be clear, many women's historians (like historians more generally) avoid the term "objectivity" because it has become such a contested word in the profession. No historian truly believes in the possibility of being objective if this means virtually stepping outside of one's historical moment and examining the past with detached indifference. But according to Haskell's definition, "objective" historians are not those who write about the past without moral convictions or political commitments, but instead those who cultivate their imaginations to try to overcome their preconceptions and self-centeredness. This is precisely the goal of most women's historians. Rather than concluding that scholarly detachment is nothing more than an illusion, they have insisted that fairness and honesty are possible. As Joyce Appleby, Lynn Hunt, and Margaret Jacobs have affirmed in their book, *Telling the Truth about History*, "Truths about the past are possible, even if they are not absolute, and hence are worth struggling for."[31] To argue the opposite, as some postmodernists have done, is to suggest that history is so tainted by self-interest that it is a form of fiction.[32]

Given the strong commitment of women's historians to "telling the truth," what is most striking about their work is not its novelty but its traditionalism. To return to the question of whether women's history is methodologically distinctive, the answer is mostly "no." While their critical edge might seem to link them to deconstructionists or poststructuralists, most have paid little attention to theoretical debates about such foundational concepts as agency, freedom, experience, selfhood, and truth.[33] Literary scholars have been deeply influenced by Jacques Derrida, who emphasized the unstable meanings of texts, and Michel Foucault, who asked us to rethink our understanding of how power functions and agency is constituted, but many women's historians (and historians more generally) have looked askance at "theory," which they have tended to lump together in a single category.[34] Of course, there are exceptions. For example, in her book about a Catholic women's basketball team, Julie Byrne considers whether the Catholic Church should be understood in Foucauldian terms as an institution that produced disciplined bodies. (Echoing a common criticism of Foucault, she argues that this interpretation negates women's agency.)[35] In most cases, however, women's historians seem to assume that "theory" is too abstract or philosophical to shape their research.[36] (I use the word "seem" here because so few American religious historians have explicitly reflected on their choice to ignore theoretical studies.)

Most women's historians of American religion have also ignored some of the most innovative theoretical work on gender. To be sure, most have incorporated gender analysis into their work, and many describe themselves as historians of gender, not women. (In some cases, though not all, this choice of language unfortunately seems to be a strategic one. As many have noted, studying "gender" sounds more "objective" and "neutral" than studying "women.")[37] Influenced by Joan Scott's groundbreaking article, "Gender as a Useful Category for Historical Analysis," which was first published in 1986, they have explored how American religion has both shaped and reflected understandings of "gender," which they define as the cultural construction of both "masculinity" and "femininity." In order to challenge the assumption that men are the "norm," they have carefully examined how *both* men and women have been shaped by ideals of gender. Rather than assuming that the categories of male and female have been stable throughout history, they have shown how gender has been redefined in response to religious, economic, and political forces. For example, Nancy Cott has shown that the rise of evangelical religion between the 1790s and the 1830s led to a new conception of white women's "passionlessness," a striking departure from the Puritans' view of women as naturally licentious.[38] (Black women, however, continued to be viewed as sexually voracious—a view that legitimated their sexual exploitation in slavery.) Gender historians have been particularly interested in how gender has functioned as "a primary way of signifying relationships of power."[39] Religious, political, and economic institutions have not only used gendered rhetoric to enforce women's subordination, but also to legitimate their power over other groups or individuals who seem to pose a threat to their hegemony. Historically, enemies have often been "feminized." As Marilyn Westerkamp argues in her chapter for this volume, Puritans discredited religious dissenters by labeling them as "feminine" and therefore deviant.

Yet despite their careful attention to the historical instability of the categories of "masculinity" and "femininity" over time, few historians of women and American religion have wrestled with more radical challenges to the very category of "women." While these scholars are sensitive to women's racial, ethnic, religious, and economic diversity, most continue to assume that "woman" is a coherent category of analysis, whether because of biological difference or shared experiences. (It is important to emphasize that women's historians occupy a wide range of positions on this issue, with disagreement about whether gender is partially or entirely a cultural construction.) While some have borrowed Judith Butler's performative theory of gender in order to emphasize the fluidity of gender categories, few have echoed Butler's more radical assertion that the gendered body is entirely the product of discourse. ("Discourse" is a slippery word, but in Butler's work, it not only encompasses language, but also institutions and practices.) Most historians assume that gender, which they usually link to bodily difference, produces particular kinds of religious discourses, not that religious discourses produce gender.[40]

While there are good reasons for women's historians to be suspicious of some of the most skeptical strains of poststructuralism, their methodological conservatism has not always been good for the field. Some have not been reflective enough about their most important categories, including "women," agency, selfhood, and experience. To give one example, women's historians have written hundreds of books and articles about women's "experience," but they have rarely examined their assumptions about this term. They tend to treat experience as something irreducible, but experience does not stand outside of history. It is at least partially constructed by it. As Joan Scott has argued, if historians believe that their goal is simply to describe or recover women's historical experiences without asking difficult questions about *why* women had these experiences, they may inadvertently end up presenting "women" as a static, unchanging category. In other words, their work might be read as suggesting that women had certain experiences simply because they were biologically female, not because of larger historical forces. As Scott explains:

> When experience is taken as the origin of knowledge, the vision of the individual subject (the person who had the experience or the historian who recounts it) becomes the bedrock of evidence on which explanation is built. Questions about the constructed nature of experience, about how subjects are constituted as different in the first place, about how one's vision is structured—about language (or discourse) and history—are left aside. The evidence of experience then becomes evidence for the act of difference, rather than a way of exploring how difference is established, how it operates, how and in what ways it constitutes subjects who see and act in the world.

The challenge for women's historians is to pay attention to both women's distinctive experiences *and* the discourses that shaped their experiences. In Scott's words, "experience" should not be "the origin of our explanation, but that which we want to explain."[41]

Given the tendency of women's historians of religion to sidestep theoretical debates in feminist philosophy, it makes little sense to describe them as "radicals." Like "mainstream" scholars, most have remained deeply committed to empiricism. At a time when many literary scholars have emphasized the fragmentary, contested nature of texts, women's historians continue to assume that language bears a close correspondence to reality. Ironically, women's historians are among the most vocal critics of traditional American

Catherine A. Brekus

religious history, but they are also among the most vocal supporters of the empirical method underlying it. Instead of criticizing the social scientific method, they argue that previous historians have not been rigorous enough in adhering to it. The problem, they argue, is not the profession's foundational assumptions, but historians who write biased history.

If women's historians of American religion were methodologically radical, the continuing marginalization of their work might be easier to understand. In fact, however, their radicalism lies almost entirely in their questions. They do not "do history" any differently than other American religious historians.

Explaining Women's Absence

Why, then, hasn't women's history had a greater impact on the way historians teach and write about American religion? Why haven't the questions posed by women's historians been asked more widely or taken more seriously? Here I would like to offer five suggestions. First, despite the commitment of feminist scholars in the 1970s and 1980s to exposing androcentrism, both men and women in the historical profession have found it difficult to move beyond the singular category of "man." Second, historians have often overlooked women because of inherited assumptions about what is "important" and what counts as serious history. Third, they have feared that women's history will contribute to the fragmentation of older narratives, making it difficult to tell coherent stories about the past. Fourth, they have had difficulty developing models of historical change that take seriously both structural constraints and individual agency. Finally, women's historians have sometimes failed to draw explicit connections between their work and central themes in the field.

The first obstacle to consider is androcentrism. Androcentrism, to borrow Darlene Juschka's definition, "refers to a perspective that proposes to be gazing from 'human' eyes at 'human' subjects but the 'human' in both instances is always male and masculine. Within an androcentric frame the term 'man' is said to be inclusive of both men and women, but if we use such a term we erase women as subjects." Although androcentrism is not the same as misogyny, "an active negative attitude toward women as *female*," it is perhaps even more entrenched.[42] Influenced by centuries of Western thought, we tend to see "man" as the universal standard and "woman" as derivative. (Christianity has contributed to this norm by emphasizing the hierarchical creation account in Genesis 2:21—in which Eve was created from Adam's rib—over the simultaneous creation account in Genesis 5:2—"male and female he created them.") Although most historians no longer use the word "he" or "man" when speaking of humanity in general, they still sometimes assume that speaking about "women" is superfluous because they are "covered" by men.[43] For example, Paul Johnson's classic study of the Second Great Awakening, *A Shopkeeper's Millennium*, offers an interpretation of the revivals that focuses on men alone—this despite the fact that his painstaking statistical analysis of church membership records suggests that "women were converting their men."[44] He unintentionally presents men as the natural subjects of history and women as particular or "other." Even though he clearly recognizes the crucial role of women in spreading the revivals, he does not treat women as central characters in his book.

My point here is not to condemn particular scholars for their blindness. Nor do I want to suggest that those who are most guilty of androcentrism are men. There are many examples of male scholars—one thinks immediately of Robert Orsi and David Hackett—who have written first-rate studies of women and gender.[45] As Pamela Nadell explains in her chapter in this volume, *all* historians, including those of us who identify ourselves as feminists, have been so shaped by traditional canons of knowledge that we find it difficult not to replicate past mistakes. Nadell's first book, which she published in 1988, included only a single woman. Rather than scolding her or other historians for not being more inclusive, it makes more sense to acknowledge that all of us—both men and women—must struggle to widen our perspective. In the words of Elizabeth Kamarck Minnich, who specializes in broadening the curriculum, "*The principles that require and justify the exclusion of women, and the results of those principles appearing throughout the complex artifices of knowledge and culture, are so locked into the dominant meaning system that it has for a very long time been utterly irrelevant whether or not any particular person intended to exclude women.* The exclusion was and is effected by the forms and structures within which we *all* try to live, work, and find meaning."[46] Even the most self-conscious historians find that "it involves tremendous intellectual effort, and a good deal of practice, to decentre maleness as the human norm and ideal which informs our imaginations."[47]

Connected to androcentrism is another crucial issue: namely, historians' assumptions about what questions are most important to ask. Until the 1970s, most American religious historians were confident that they knew what the field was "about." Beginning with Robert Baird's survey of American religious history in 1844, and extending until Sydney Ahlstrom's comprehensive *A Religious History of the American People*, which was published in 1972, American religious historians assumed that their main task was to explain how religion (usually Protestantism) had influenced American political and civic culture. Organizing their narratives around political turning points such as the American Revolution and the Civil War, they examined how the dominant Protestant tradition had shaped public life in the United States. For example, they explored how Protestant pluralism in early America had led to the First Amendment's guarantee of religious freedom; how Protestant revivalism had fueled reform movements such as temperance and antislavery; and how Puritan ideas of America as a "city on a hill" or a redeemer nation influenced American nationalism. The *specific* goals of these books differed: for example, Daniel Dorchester, writing in 1888, hoped that his narrative would convince readers that America was a "Christian nation," while Winthrop Hudson, writing in 1965, wanted to emphasize America's religious pluralism.[48] More generally, however, all of these historians assumed that their work should contribute, first and foremost, to a greater understanding of the American nation-state.

Women's historians have also been interested in these questions, and they have written scores of books and articles exploring women's public activism. In the 1970s and early 1980s, most of this scholarship focused on white Protestant women. Following the example of prominent historians such as Sydney Ahlstrom, who assumed that white Protestants had been the most powerful shapers of American culture, women's historians looked for examples of white Protestant women who had influenced civic life, and they found them in such remarkable figures as Catharine Beecher, Harriet Beecher Stowe, and Elizabeth Cady Stanton.[49] By the mid-1980s, as historians began to realize the limitations of their exclusive focus on white Protestant women, they also began to examine influential female leaders outside of the mainstream, whether Catholic nuns, women rabbis, or African American female preachers. More recently, sociologists have begun asking questions about women's leadership within immigrant communities of Buddhists, Muslims, and Hindus. Scholars of women and American religion have published more books and articles about female leadership than on any other topic.

Yet besides asking fairly traditional questions about how women, like men, shaped American civic culture, women's historians have also asked a different set of questions about women's lives—and these are the questions that have proven most controversial. Indeed, they have challenged assumptions about which historical information is important and why. (As I argued earlier, the distinctive contribution of women's history has come more from its questions than its methods.) Although most women's historians continue to view older questions about the relationship between religion and American democracy as significant ones, they do not see them as the *only* questions, or, depending on the scholar, even the most crucial ones. So, for example, they have explored the relationship between religion and ideas about female subordination. They have also asked questions about how religion has shaped women's understanding of their lives, whether their images of God, their understandings of family life, or their interpretations of suffering.

Critics have complained that these kinds of questions are trivial. The real stuff of history, they argue, has to do with politics and public life. In an essay criticizing the "new history" for its lack of attention to high politics, Gertrude Himmelfarb complains, "If no subject is more important than any other, how can any question be more significant than any other? Who is to say, the new historian may object, that the question of what it means to be a citizen of the United States is more central to the historical enterprise than what it means to be a woman in the United States—or, perhaps, a homosexual or a homeless person? Who is to say that 'national identity' is more important than race, gender, or class—or, for that matter, that class is more important than gender?"[50] According to her, historians should be primarily concerned with answering questions about citizenship. They should write in service to the state: their duty is to help people understand what it means to be citizens of a free society, not what it means to be a particular kind of self—whether female, homosexual, or homeless. (It's hard not to smell the whiff of elitism in Himmelfarb's words. In order to make "new" historians look ridiculous, she juxtaposes the serious study of citizenship to supposedly trifling subjects such as women.)

While it is true that some questions are more important than others, few historians would accept Himmelfarb's scale for determining what qualifies as "important." Rather than making the sweeping claim that questions about citizenship should always be paramount, most historians argue that the most crucial, valuable questions are those that help us explain our modern situation. On that scale, questions about women's history are indeed significant— even central. Without an understanding of women's history, it would be difficult to explain some of the most dramatic transformations taking place in our culture today—not only changes in politics, but in employment, family life, and religious activism.

Besides criticizing Himmelfarb for her narrow definition of historical importance, women's historians have also argued that the "private" and the "public" cannot be so neatly separated. Despite an ideology of feminine domesticity, the reality is that women have never been entirely confined to the home, and they have participated in public debates about everything from slavery to immigration. The question of what it means to be a woman in the United States is, in fact, closely related to the question of what it means to be a citizen. Women were not given the full rights of citizenship until the Nineteenth Amendment was passed in 1920, and the struggles over equal treatment have continued until our own day. Indeed, many of the women's history books that Himmelfarb would probably find irrelevant to questions about citizenship are in fact deeply concerned with political issues, though not specifically with statecraft. For example, one can imagine Himmelfarb criticizing R. Marie Griffith's fascinating new book about evangelicalism and dieting in modern America because of its focus on popular culture. But, in fact, Griffith's book offers us valuable insights into American politics: the hidden politics of coding some bodies as more deserving of respect, wealth, power—and citizenship—than others.[51]

Women's historians have also asked why history is important only when it contributes to an understanding of the nation-state. Must all American history ultimately take the nation as its reference point? Or should American historians also help us to think critically about other features of the American experience—for example, our modern assumptions about what it means to be female or male? These questions lead to others that are equally pressing: For whom do historians write their books, and why? What do historians want to explain? My own conviction is that American historians have a crucial role to play in educating American citizens about the state, but they should also try to help people think critically about other features of American life. For example, Griffith's book offers us something that is deeply valuable in today's culture: a critical understanding of the Christian roots of our contemporary obsession with fitness and slimness.[52] By insisting that many different kinds of stories are worth telling (stories about *both* American nationalism and ordinary people's lives), women's historians have challenged the old consensus on what American religious history should be "about." The response, unfortunately, has often been resistance.

Two of the ingredients of this resistance, as we have seen, are androcentrism and long-standing assumptions about what questions are important. The third relates to historical models of change. To state the point bluntly, many historians have written as if only male leaders—and a small number of elite female leaders, usually white Protestants—have had the political, economic, or religious power to bring about change. Because American women could not attend colleges until the middle of the nineteenth century, few became leading intellectuals. Because they could not vote or hold political office until the Nineteenth Amendment in 1920, they did not have access to formal political power. Even in churches, where they often outnumbered men in the pews, they were rarely given formal positions of authority. Given their oppression throughout American history, some historians have hesitated to treat them as historical agents. In a section titled "Agents and Agency" in his book *The Rise of Evangelicalism*, Mark Noll argues that "the shaping of early evangelicalism was very much a male affair." Women "might provide exemplary narratives of conversion," and they regularly provided both "critical personal or financial support" and "a major proportion . . . of participants," but the "public movement was driven by men." Because there were no female leaders equal to George Whitefield or Jonathan Edwards in the eighteenth century, Noll concludes that the main "agents" of the revivals were male.[53] While Noll admirably included many women's stories in his textbook, *The History of Christianity in the United States and Canada,* he clearly has questions about whether women should be treated as "agents" if they were not famous leaders.[54] Did women in the past "make" history in the same way as men?

Asking such a question might sound surprising at a time when social historians and cultural historians have tried to complicate our understanding of who makes history. "Social history" emerged in the 1960s and 1970s as a reaction against the perceived elitism of earlier historical scholarship, and over the past thirty years, social historians have published thousands of articles and books exploring the lives of those who were once ignored, whether immigrants, slaves, or women. While social historians do not share a single methodology or even a common set of questions, they are linked together by their common belief that historical change does not only come from the top down, but also from the bottom up. They also share an understanding of agency that moves beyond its older definition as self-conscious choice. (An "agent," in older historical narratives, is usually a visionary leader who deliberately decides to change the world, not an ordinary person who might not be fully aware of how his or her individual decisions create historical change.) Emphasizing the collective power of groups, social historians claim that when large numbers of people make similar decisions about their lives, they set events in motion that have far-reaching consequences—sometimes unwittingly. Social historians' goal, in the words of Olivier Zunz, is "to connect everyday experience to the large structures of historical analyses and major changes of the past."[55]

Since the 1980s, "cultural" historians have also tried to broaden historical study beyond a focus on elites. Many "cultural" historians began their careers as "social" historians, but when they found that quantitative data and sociological theory failed to answer some of their most pressing questions about how individuals had made sense of their lives, they began borrowing methods from anthropologists, particularly Clifford Geertz. Although cultural historians often differ in their implicit definitions of "culture," with some treating it as something distinct from concrete social forces (such as demography and technology), and others treating it as the totality of human relations, all are interested in exploring the "webs of significance" or "the system of symbols and meanings" that have framed people's lives.[56]

Because of their interest in everyday life, both social historians and cultural historians have been particularly sensitive to women's history. For example, when David Hall and Anne S. Brown amassed a large body of quantitative data about early American church membership, they chose to ask questions about women's as well as men's religious lives. Motivated by their desire to understand everyday religious experience, they made the fascinating discovery that women often disregarded official church teachings about baptism because of their anxieties about their children's salvation. Similarly, Robert Orsi's cultural history of an Italian Catholic street festival, *The Madonna of 115th Street*, asks provocative questions about Catholic women's devotion to the Virgin Mary. As Orsi tried to understand the underlying meanings of an annual festa in honor of the Madonna, he concluded that women were at its center. According to his interpretation, the festa subverted but ultimately reinforced Catholic women's roles as suffering mothers.[57]

Despite this imaginative research on women, both social and cultural historians have been more successful at recovering ordinary people's lives than in showing the relationship between individual experience and structural transformations. As Olivier Zunz noted twenty years ago (and his criticism is still valid today), social historians have failed to develop "a coherent explanation of social change."[58] Marxism, with its focus on class tensions as the driving force in history, has largely lost its appeal, but no other compelling theories have arisen to take its place. Instead, social historians focus narrowly on processes of change among particular groups or communities (for example, churches, towns, or ethnic groups). The result, as Thomas Bender has complained, is that social historians have built "a large number of separate but highly cultivated boxes" without considering how and whether they fit together. Without a model of causation, it is difficult to determine whether all these "parts" make a "whole."[59]

Cultural historians have offered little help in sorting out these conceptual difficulties. Inspired by Clifford Geertz, who argues that cultural analysis is "not an experimental science in search of law but an interpretive one in search of meaning," they have focused more on "thick description" of rituals, practices, or symbols than change over time. Their most important question tends to be "how"—how did Catholic immigrants understand suffering? or how did Pentecostals "interpret their religious experiences?"—rather than "why."[60] Because of their emphasis on the coherence and power of culture, they have found it especially difficult to explain individual agency or large-scale historical transformations. If culture is hegemonic, how do people re-sist and create new cultural expectations? While historians such as William Sewell have become increasingly interested in trying to answer these kinds of questions, their work has not yet had a major impact on American religious history.[61]

Gender theorists have also failed to offer compelling models of how indi-viduals create change. Influenced by Michel Foucault, they have argued that power is not centralized in the state but is dispersed throughout the social body. As Foucault explained, "The state is superstructural in relation to a whole series of power networks that invest the body, sexuality, the family, kinship, knowledge, technology, etc."[62] Even the self, or, in his language, the "subject," is a site of power. Rejecting the humanist view that there is a stable, inviolable "self" that transcends history, Foucault argued that the "subject" is created by language and cultural practices. Given Foucault's emphasis on the "tentacles" and "webs" of power in which all humans are entangled, many feminists have used his ideas to explain the persistence of domination. (His books have been especially influential because they speak to our current anxieties about the fragility of human freedom.) Yet feminists have also found it difficult to explain how women can create historical change if they are always imprisoned by structures of power. Joan Scott, for example, sug-gests that women have agency, but only in a limited sense: "Subjects are constituted discursively, but there are conflicts among discursive systems, contradictions within any one of them, multiple meanings possible for the concepts they deploy. And subjects do have agency. They are not unified, au-tonomous individuals exercising free will, but rather subjects whose agency is created through situations and statuses conferred on them." In response to this limited vision of human freedom as the product of conflicting dis-courses, many feminists have struggled to create new theoretical models for understanding how women have resisted domination and created change.[63]

Without compelling models of either individual historical agency or large-scale historical causation, many American religious historians have fallen back on older models that privilege the actions and ideas of a few "great men"—or, in the work of historians who struggle to be more inclusive, great women. Historians have found it easier to show that leaders left a visible mark on the historical landscape than to argue the same about ordinary people, whether women or men. (The astonishing popularity of recent books on the "Founding Fathers" illustrates the enduring appeal of this focus on elites. Despite magnificent studies of the popular roots of the American Revolution, these books tend to portray the creation of the new nation as the accomplishment of a small number of male leaders.)[64] In sum, even though many American religious historians want to include ordinary women in their books, they do not know how to make them integral to their story, so they either ignore them or relegate them to separate chapters that do not tackle questions about agency or causation. The problem, in this case, goes far beyond androcentrism and involves deep theoretical issues that are difficult to resolve.

This leads to the fourth issue: namely, historians' fears about the fragmentation of the field. As many women's historians have argued, it is impossible to simply "add women and stir." When historians have tried to include women in their narratives, they have sometimes found that their old story lines do not make sense anymore, leaving them with nothing more than the shards of older narratives. When several prominent American religious historians were asked to respond to the question, "Is there a center to American religious history?" most said no. Although none wanted to return to a history centered solely on white, male Protestants, they all expressed concern about a loss of coherence. Given contemporary debates over church-state relationships and personal religious freedom, they believe that both students and the American public need a comprehensive understanding of American religious history. As Stephen Stein commented, "We have much to lose by completely abandoning the goal of constructing meaningful large narratives or centered accounts of American religious history."[65]

Women's historians have intensified this sense of crisis by sharply criticizing landmark books (such as Sydney Ahlstrom's *A Religious History of the American People*) and by insisting that coherence has been overvalued. As historian Isabel Hull has commented, women's historians have been particularly skilled at the work of destruction, demolishing interpretations that "mainstream" historians thought were settled.[66] Rather than creating new narratives, they have eagerly dismantled the old ones in order to expose the field's androcentrism. "The coherences that are falling are no longer useful," Hull argues. "We should not rush to erect new ones in their stead, for these, too, are liable to be constructed at the cost of ideas that cannot be thought, research that cannot be conceived, and relations that cannot be apprehended."[67] She and many other women's historians have viewed fragmentation as a small price to pay for deeper knowledge about the past.

In addition, a few women's historians (like historians more generally) have questioned the wisdom of writing narratives at all. They especially object to what they call "master narratives" or "grand narratives" that claim to tell the story of an entire nation or all of humanity. (Jean Francois Lyotard defined the term "postmodern" as "incredulity toward metanarratives.")[68] Since such narratives often celebrate progress—the triumphant ascent of democracy, for example, or the growing mastery of technology—some historians fear that they erase the reality of conflict and injustice. Most important, they argue that grand narratives obscure the messy reality of the past by forcing contradictory pieces of evidence into a unitary story with a beginning, a middle, and an end. Grand narrative, they claim, is a form of domination. To avoid creating a false sense of unity out of the multiplicity of the past, they urge historians not to tell stories, but to write as social scientists analyzing specific, narrow problems.[69]

Given how zealously critics have challenged traditional narratives, it is no surprise that many historians have expressed anxiety about the future of the field. Their concerns are well-founded. While historians should certainly be suspicious of narratives that claim to be nothing less than "total history," it is hard to imagine teaching classes or writing books without any narrative frameworks at all. Either implicitly or explicitly, all historians make use of them. For example, American Catholic history is often narrated as the story of the church's growing acceptance of religious freedom and American Jewish history as an escape from religious persecution. Those who try to write about the entire span of American religious history tend to narrate it as either the story of how Protestants have shaped American culture or the story of how various faiths have competed for converts in America's pluralistic religious marketplace. To be sure, all of these narratives fail to capture the full complexity of the past, but they help satisfy Americans' deep desire to understand their world. They also reflect the reality of how most people actually experience their lives. None of us are able to experience the totality of the historical moment in which we live, nor would we want to. (As Thomas Haskell has noted, the bombardment of sensory data would overwhelm us.[70] Like Pip in *Moby Dick*, who gazed at the immense totality of the universe while floating alone in the sea, we might even lose our sanity.) What most people seem to desire, instead, is guidance in creating coherence out of the buzzing confusion of the present and the past. "Mainstream" historians rightly fear that if women's historians (and historians of other marginalized groups) abandon the quest for coherence out of the conviction that all coherence is inevitably discriminatory and arbitrary, history will become a specialized, narrow discipline. If historians stop writing narratives, preferring to solve narrow analytical problems instead, they may seem irrelevant to a public that is hungry for meaning.

These fears about fragmentation have been exacerbated by a fifth and final issue, which is that women's historians have been so eager to recover women's stories that they have sometimes failed to answer the "so what" question. As

Louise Tilly has explained, "In the understandable urgency of retrieving women's lives and achievements, many women's historians have conceived these as sufficient unto themselves." Instead of showing how their research contributes to "the explanation of other, more general problems either already on the historical agenda or readily understandable in terms of central historical concepts," they have focused more narrowly on description.[71] For instance, Carol Coburn and Martha Smith's impressively researched book, *Spirited Lives: How Nuns Shaped Catholic Culture and American Life,* contains a wealth of fascinating information about Catholic sisters' work in hospitals and schools, but it does not explicitly answer the question of historiographical significance. While Coburn and Smith clearly believe that their research should change dominant interpretations of American Catholicism, they do not explain how, leaving this crucial analytical task to others. As Tilly has argued, however, if women's historians "want to address historians at large," then "analysis that makes explicit 'what difference it makes' is vital."[72] Recovering women's stories is certainly crucial, but it is not enough. Especially at this point in the evolution of women's history, when so much has been discovered about women's lives in the past, historians must try to answer difficult questions about historical significance.

Encouraging women's historians to seek greater connections between their research and "mainstream" history does not mean that all of their work should be guided by traditional historical questions. On the contrary, their bold refusal to accept "history as usual" has helped to broaden the field beyond high politics, and if they suddenly stopped asking their own distinctive questions, the entire study of history would be impoverished. "Most history is male-centered and male-defined," Judith Bennett argues. "If we uncritically accept its questions as our main questions, we will be ignoring Mary Beard's wise caution against taking 'man as the measure' of historical significance." (Mary Beard was a pioneering women's historian who published *Woman as Force in History* in 1946.) Nevertheless, the best historians strive to write not only for specialists in their field but for a broader audience. Despite her reservations about trying to fit women's history into traditional paradigms, Bennett concludes that "women's history, like other historical fields, must both contribute to general historical discourses (about say, class formation or the French Revolution) and develop discourses internal to its own endeavors."[73] If women's historians try to make all of their work fit neatly into "mainstream" categories, they may lose their critical edge, but if they fail to engage in conversations with other historians, they run the risk of perpetuating their marginalization.

Religion's Absence from Women's History

Women's historians of religion have been especially daunted by the task of reimagining the past because they not only lack support from "mainstream" historians, but from most other women's historians as well. At the same time as American religious historians have failed to write about *women*, many American women's historians have failed to consider *religion*. As Merry Wiesner-Hanks, a Reformation scholar, has commented, many women's historians of religion feel like "missionaries" to two separate disciplines. Besides trying to convince mainstream historians to be more attentive to women, they have also been busy "proclaiming the significance of religious history to our feminist friends and colleagues."[74]

Like all missionaries, historians of women and American religion have known the frustration of "preaching" to the resistant or indifferent. Although it is clear that religion has always been a meaningful part of many women's lives, women's historians rarely discuss religion in their textbooks or documentary collections. For example, in their book, *Major Problems in American Women's History*, which is widely used in undergraduate classrooms, Mary Beth Norton and Ruth M. Alexander have collected an impressive variety of primary documents and essays about women's lives, but they virtually ignore religion. While there are separate sections on such important topics as "The Economic Roles of Women in the Northern Colonies," "White Women and Politics in the Antebellum Years," "White Women and the Civil War Crisis," "Women in the Trans-Mississippi Frontier West," and "Work and Work Cultures in the Era of the 'New Woman,' 1880–1920s," there is no section on religion, and it is the main subject of only two essays and one document. Of course, many of the primary documents contain material that would interest religious historians. For example, a letter by Mary Still, a black abolitionist, contains poignant evidence of her belief that the abolitionist movement was inspired by God. "Humanity in general calls upon us," she wrote. "And He who holds the destiny of nations in his hand, is calling upon us." Yet despite this religious rhetoric, the editors did not identify religion as one of the "major problems" that women's historians must address.[75]

Other collections look the same. Otherwise excellent books, such as Linda K. Kerber and Jane Sherron De Hart's *Women's America: Refocusing the Past*, Glenda Riley's two-volume textbook, *Inventing the American Woman*, and Sara Evans's *Born for Liberty*, all contain very little discussion of religion.[76] In the first edition of Ellen Carol DuBois and Vicki L. Ruiz's much-lauded book, *Unequal Sisters: A Multicultural Reader in U.S. Women's History*, only one of the thirty essays focused on religion. In the second, expanded edition (with thirty-six essays) and the third edition (with thirty-nine essays), none of them do. Because many Latina, African American, Chinese, and other minority women have been profoundly influenced by their religious beliefs, several of the authors in the volume mention religion. But for whatever reason—inability to find excellent essays? indifference?—the editors did not choose to publish any essays specifically focusing on women's religious beliefs or activism.[77]

This kind of neglect has not always been the case. In fact, many of the leading women's historians of the 1970s and early 1980s were particularly interested in religion, especially nineteenth-century white Protestantism. To mention just a few examples, Kathryn Kish Sklar wrote a groundbreaking biography of Catharine Beecher, whose religious beliefs deeply shaped her understanding of female domesticity; Barbara Welter, Joan Jacobs Brumberg, and Jane Hunter examined women's home and foreign missionary work; and Nancy Cott argued that religion offered women a means of "defining self and finding community."[78] Many other historians, including Gerda Lerner, Nancy Hewitt, Ruth Bordin, and Barbara Leslie Epstein, connected women's involvement in social reform, whether temperance or antislavery, to their religious convictions.[79]

After the mid-1980s, however, most women's historians seem to have lost their interest in religion, leaving the field to those who identified themselves explicitly as religious historians. Perhaps this shift was simply the result of the fashions of academia: women's historians may have thought their work would make a bigger "splash" (and earn them more job offers) if it addressed politics, economics, labor, or the law. But it is worth noting that their turn away from religious topics came at the same time as the Religious Right rose to political power. In the early 1980s, conservative Christian groups such as James Dobson's Focus on the Family, Jerry Falwell's Moral Majority, and Beverly LaHaye's Concerned Women of America waged a strenuous campaign against "secular" feminism, homosexuality, and "godlessness" that captured the public imagination.[80] When Ronald Reagan won the 1980 presidential election by combining a conservative political agenda with a defense of school prayer and traditional "family values," liberal feminists were surprised and dismayed. Troubled by Reagan's mixing of political and religious rhetoric as well as intense media coverage of fundamentalism and evangelicalism, many feminist scholars became convinced that religious belief was closely associated with political conservatism. Like Elizabeth Cady Stanton almost a hundred years earlier, they seem to have concluded that religion was not a potentially liberating force for women, but an oppressive one.[81]

If women's historians had simply wanted to recapture the diversity of female experience in America, they could have turned the popularity of conservative groups such as the Concerned Women of America into a research problem. Who were the historical foremothers of women such as Phyllis Schlafly and Beverly LaHaye? When and why had their ideas originated? But the field of women's history had bloomed alongside the women's rights movement in the late 1960s and early 1970s, and even in the 1980s and 1990s, women's historians tended to be more interested in studying feminist women than conservative ones. As "religion" was increasingly equated with "conservatism," many women's historians turned their attention to topics that seemed more useful for nurturing a feminist consciousness, such as women's heroic struggles against labor discrimination and racism.[82]

As women's historians drifted away from religious topics in the 1980s, the resulting division between historical studies and religious studies weakened both. On one hand, women's historians of religion have sometimes exaggerated the liberating potential of religion in order to combat assumptions about its essentially patriarchal character.[83] Some hold strong personal religious beliefs, and they resent the notion that religious women cannot be true feminists. Others are more secular-minded, but because of their education in religion departments, they have taken exception to simplistic views of religion as "the opiate of the people." Either way, they have responded to negative stereotypes of religion with defensiveness, publishing scores of articles and books demonstrating that, historically, religious women have been empowered by their faith. (Many feminist sociologists of religion have echoed this scholarship. For example, Carolyn Chen has argued that contemporary Taiwanese women who have converted to Buddhism or Christianity have carved out "spaces of independence and authority for themselves, albeit never at the cost of threatening the nuclear family.")[84] Although this kind of work is certainly important, it has largely precluded serious studies of less appealing aspects of women's religious history, such as white women's embrace of the Christian Identity movement today, a violent white supremacist movement that targets Jews, homosexuals, and blacks. Most troubling, many scholars have been so focused on the question of empowerment that they have tended to lump religion into one of two categories—liberating or oppressive—instead of moving beyond such "outworn dichotomies."[85]

On the other hand, by deciding to steer clear of religious topics, women's historians have presented distorted interpretations of women's lives in both the past and the present. Ironically, women's historians have prided themselves on recovering the stories of forgotten women, yet whether intentionally or not, they have engaged in their own kind of forgetting. Many have virtually erased women's religious identities. For example, in her textbook,

Born for Liberty, Sara Evans includes a brief biographical sketch of Fannie Lou Hamer, the African American founder of the Mississippi Freedom Democratic Party, but she never explains that Hamer was motivated by a profound sense of religious calling. (The only clue is a brief mention of Hamer's inspirational gospel singing.)[86] Similarly, Deborah Gray White's immensely influential book about enslaved women, *Ar'n't I a Woman*, never discusses the popularity of Christianity in the slave quarters. One would never know from reading her book that large numbers of enslaved women used the Christian language of sin, grace, and exodus to make sense of their suffering.[87]

Women's historians have been especially blind to the continuing power of religion in modern America. Susan Ware's book, *Modern American Women: A Documentary History*, includes fascinating documents about education, work, sexuality, and the feminist movement, but none about religion, as if modern women never went to churches, synagogues, or mosques.[88] Oddly, most women's historians would affirm that nineteenth-century women's rights activists were inspired by liberal Protestantism, but they seem to assume that women no longer needed religion after winning the suffrage in 1920. (Their implicit assumption is that religious belief is the product of political, economic, or social deprivation.) When they have written about the feminist movement of the 1960s and 1970s, they have simply assumed that it was secular in nature. Yet as Ann Braude shows in her chapter for this volume, a closer examination of the evidence reveals that Catholic, Protestant, and Jewish women were prominent members of the movement.

The women's historians who have been most sensitive to questions about religion have tended to be those who study African American women. Perhaps because of the prominent role of black churches in African American culture, historians of black women have published many books and articles exploring how religion shaped both public and private life. For example, Nell Painter's biography of Sojourner Truth explores Truth's religious convictions as well as her abolitionism and her feminist activism, and Darlene Clark Hine's influential, three-volume *Encyclopedia of Black Women in America* contains a wealth of articles about religion.[89]

Partially because of the excellent model set by this research on African American women, and partially because religious debates have become such a visible and inescapable part of the American landscape in recent years, many women's historians have begun to reconsider their neglect of religion. As it has become clear that the upsurge of conservative religious activism that began in the late 1970s is not simply an aberration but an entrenched feature of modern life, scholars from many different fields—including political science, English, sociology, history, anthropology, and women's studies—have rushed to study religion with a new sense of seriousness. To give just two examples, Kathi Lynn Kern has written a marvelous study of Elizabeth Cady Stanton, who condemned the Bible as patriarchal; and Beryl Satter has written a groundbreaking book about women's attraction to New Thought, a late nineteenth-century movement that laid many of the foundations for the contemporary "New Age" movement.[90] Neither of these scholars would identify themselves first and foremost as American religious historians, but rather as women's historians or American historians. Yet their work is crucial reading for anyone interested in American religion.

Encouraged by this new interest in religion, many of the contributors to this volume have not only tried to show what difference it makes to add women to religious history but also what difference it makes to add religion to women's history. While Ann Braude examines the religious dimensions of "second-wave" feminism, Kristy Nabhan-Warren urges women's historians to reconsider their assumption that Catholic women's devotion to the Virgin Mary necessarily makes them passive or submissive. Estela Ruiz, the subject of her chapter, would never identify herself as a feminist, and yet her religious defense of women's rights links her to feminists in surprising ways. Similarly, in a chapter about Catholic sisters in the 1960s, Amy Koehlinger shows that women's historians must broaden their cast of characters if they want to explain women's activism in the civil rights movement. Taken together, these chapters are meant as an invitation to women's historians to explore religion in greater depth.

Women's Religious Diversity

Any book about women in American religious history must wrestle with the issue of women's diversity. The singular category of "women" hides important differences of race, education, class, region, ethnicity, sexual orientation, and political affiliation, and even the popular use of the term "women" has changed over time: seventeenth-century Americans had a different understanding of "womanhood" than we do today.[91]

The category of "religion," too, imposes a false unity on a staggering variety of religious expressions throughout American history. On one hand, the American religious landscape has been dominated by Christians since the first European settlements in Plymouth, Santa Fe, and Jamestown, and, as a result, Christianity has usually occupied the center of American religious historical narratives. Even as recently as 2004, according to the National Opinion Research Center, 79.4 percent of the American public identified themselves as Christian.[92] Yet on the other hand, Christianity itself is a pluralistic category, and Christians in both the past and the present have often argued with one another over both theology and practice. In the seventeenth and eighteenth centuries, for example, Puritans branded Anglicans and Quakers as "heretics," and in the nineteenth century, Congregationalists disdained Methodists as "enthusiasts." Today, American Christianity encompasses hundreds of groups, including (to name just a few) Korean Presbyterians, Latino Pentecostals, Mormons, Roman Catholics, African Methodists, and Episcopalians. In turn, this varied assortment of Christians has rubbed elbows with Jews, Native Americans, and increasingly since the 1965 Immigration Act, Muslims, Sikhs, Hindus, and Buddhists.

In recognition of this pluralism, the contributors to this volume have written chapters on a wide range of American women and American religious traditions. Perhaps most notably, while this volume recognizes the profound role of Protestants in shaping American civic culture, it also tries to move beyond the Protestant focus of previous scholarship by including chapters on women in other religious groups. Out of twelve case studies, seven depart from the Protestant paradigm: four are about Catholics, one focuses on Mormons, one focuses on Jews, and one examines Protestant, Catholic, and Jewish responses to the women's rights movement. (It is also worth noting that one of the chapters on Protestants focuses on African American women, which certainly separates it from the traditional focus on the white Protestant mainstream.) The chapters self-consciously highlight the multiplicity of women's racial, ethnic, and regional identities, with chapters that discuss black Catholic women in Louisiana, Mormon women in Utah, Mexican American women in Arizona, Baptist women in New Jersey, Quaker women in Philadelphia, white Catholic sisters in Chicago, South Carolina, and Washington, D.C., African American Holiness and Pentecostal women in the South, and white Puritan women in New England. The chapters also strive for chronological breadth, with four chapters on the seventeenth and eighteenth centuries, four on the nineteenth century, and four on the twentieth century.

Yet despite our attempt to consider the past from different vantage points, there are still many historical women missing in these pages. Some of the absences are simply due to difficulties in finding American religious historians who could participate in the collective conversation that gave rise to this volume—the reason there are no chapters about Native American women. Since it is clear that research on native women has the potential to transform our understanding of traditional native religions, native conversions to Christianity, and cross-cultural encounters, this omission is particularly regrettable. Susan Sleeper-Smith, for example, has argued that seventeenth- and eighteenth-century native women from the western Great Lakes served as "cultural mediators" between native societies and French settlers. Through their conversions to Catholicism, their marriages to French fur traders, and their extensive kin networks, they helped to create a "middle ground" that preserved natives' power. According to Sleeper-Smith, they were also crucial to the spread of Christianity among native peoples, especially after the suppression of the Jesuits in 1773.[93]

Other absences are the unintended consequence of the analytical approach taken in this volume. Unlike historians such as Susan Hill Lindley, Rosemary Skinner Keller, and Rosemary Radford Ruether, who have published encyclopedic overviews of all American women's religious experiences, the contributors to this volume have focused on creating in-depth case studies that challenge the reigning narratives in both women's history and religious history.[94] They have particularly concentrated on "reimagining" the intensively researched topics that loom large in each field: for example, Puritanism, the Enlightenment, the women's rights movement, the rise of the "black church," and social reform. What is missing, as a result, is sustained attention to women in religious groups that are either understudied (like the Amish) or relatively new to the American scene, like Hindus.

Nevertheless, the contributors to this volume hope that their case studies will serve as models for historians pursuing new avenues of research. For example, although there are some excellent sociological studies of women in American Buddhism, few historians have tried to place these women's experiences in longer historical perspective. (One exception is Thomas Tweed's groundbreaking book, *The American Encounter with Buddhism*, which suggests that American women in the late nineteenth century were attracted to Buddhism because of its egalitarianism.)[95] American Buddhist women have been almost invisible in the fields of both women's history and American religious history. Yet one can imagine a historian asking the same questions about emerging narratives of American Buddhism as the contributors to this volume have asked about the more established narratives of Puritanism, Catholicism, Judaism, African American religion, and Mormonism. For example, Paul Numrich, in the first scholarly study of Theravada Buddhism in the United States, has argued that immigrant temples have become increasingly "American," transforming their worship to conform more closely to American Protestant models. In his most striking finding, Numrich claims that the process of "Americanization" has been both accelerated and complicated by the presence of separate, "parallel congregations" of American-born converts and immigrants worshipping at the same temples. Because of converts' influence, Numrich predicts that Theravada Buddhism in the United

States will increasingly focus on meditation and will blur the boundaries between lay people and monastics.[96] After reading Kristy Nabhan-Warren's chapter in this volume, however, a historian might also ask questions about the large numbers of women who practice Theravada Buddhism, especially since they seem to make up the majority of members. Numrich's narrative might have looked different if he had examined how women (both immigrant and American-born) have understood the tradition and how they hope to either preserve or transform it. (Nabhan-Warren shows how lay Catholic women's grassroots organizations have redefined Mexican American Catholicism, making it more evangelical.) In addition, after reading Susanna Morrill's chapter about Mormon women's theology, a historian might ask questions about whether women who practice Theravada Buddhism have begun to create distinctive, popular theologies to make sense of their place within a tradition whose major leadership roles have been reserved for men. As Wendy Cadge, a sociologist, has shown in a recent book, the practice of Theravada Buddhism in the United States remains visibly gendered—this despite the fact that American-born, female converts insist on its egalitarianism.[97] It is clear that future narratives of American Buddhism will have to reckon with women's efforts to develop it into a more explicitly feminist faith.[98] Finally, after reading both Kristy Nabhan-Warren's and Ann Braude's chapters, a historian of American Buddhist women might ask questions about how to narrate the modern feminist movement. Do Buddhist women, both immigrants and American-born converts, belong in histories of the movement? And, if so, how might their stories change our understanding of what it means to be a feminist in the twenty-first century?

Both American religious history and women's history are composed of hundreds of interlocking narratives. Although the contributors to this volume have tried to reimagine a small number of them, much work remains to be done. Indeed, as the United States becomes increasingly pluralistic, with immigrants continuing to arrive from around the globe, historians will have to rewrite their narratives again and again, asking new questions about the diversity of both women and religion.

Toward New Narratives

Through detailed case studies, the contributors to this volume have tried to accomplish several goals. Besides offering models for how to write histories that are not androcentric, they have demonstrated some of the many ways in which women have "made" American religious history. Without solving the theoretical problem of how to link individual agency to structural change (a daunting task that social and cultural historians must continue to confront), they have still tried to show "mainstream" historians why they should treat women seriously as historical agents. Most important, they have tried to "reimagine" American religious history and women's history, bridging the divides between them.

Rather than simply discarding traditional narrative frameworks in favor of multiplicity, fragmentation, and diversity (the typical stance of postmodernists), the twelve scholars whose chapters are collected here have tried to show how these frameworks should be reimagined. While a few have aimed their chapters at the "master narratives" that tend to structure American religious history textbooks, such as Puritanism or the Enlightenment, others have challenged dominant narrative frameworks in Catholic history, Mormon history, the history of theology, African American history, or Jewish history. To give an example of each approach, my chapter on Sarah Osborn, an eighteenth-century evangelical woman, argues that women as well as men were responsible for spreading the ideas of the "Enlightenment"; and Kathleen Cummings argues that historians have missed the influence of Progressive ideals on Catholicism because of their failure to study the lives of Catholic sisters.

Since many women's historians also identify themselves as historians of gender, the contributors to this volume could have taken a different approach to answering the question of "what difference does it make?" Rather than focusing explicitly on women, they could have argued that both institutional and personal expressions of religion have been gendered. Such an approach would offer surprising new angles of vision on familiar stories. For example, as Marilyn Westerkamp shows in this volume, the history of Puritanism could be retold as the story of how Puritan leaders used discourses of gender difference to reinforce their power; and, as Amy Koehlinger illustrates, the history of Catholic sisters could be narrated as a story about unstable gender boundaries. More generally, building on Gail Bederman's superb work on the early twentieth-century Men and Religion Forward movement that insisted that Jesus had been a "manly man" rather than a "sissy," historians could explore how American Christianity has both shaped and reflected understandings of what it means to be male or female.[99]

The contributors to this volume, however, have chosen to approach gender history as a supplement to women's history rather than as a substitute or replacement for it. To be clear, all the historians in this book believe that women's history and gender history are virtually inseparable (it would be difficult to study women without knowing how they imagined femininity and masculinity). But instead of exploring the many ways in which American religion has been shaped by discourses of gender, a question that would naturally lead to research on men and "masculinity," they have tried to demonstrate women's agency in creating historical change. Since the field of women's history began with the assumption that women have indeed been historical agents, this may seem like a backward-looking project, but given the skepticism about women's agency that seems to mark both "mainstream" history and feminist theory today, a focus on women remains essential. In recent years, scholars from many different disciplines have found it difficult to explain how women—or more generally, members of subordinate groups —have created historical change. Influenced by Michel Foucault's dark view of the totalizing power of discourse, they have questioned older humanistic assumptions about human freedom and self-determination. "Can the subaltern speak?" Gayatri Spivak famously asked in 1988. Her answer was no. In response, theorists such as Michel de Certeau, Judith Butler, and Saba Mahmood have tried to develop new models for understanding human agency, especially by focusing on everyday practices.[100]

Although most of the contributors to this volume have not brought explicitly theoretical questions to their research, these chapters can be read as a collective attempt to reaffirm women as subjects of history, though not fully autonomous ones. On one hand, it is clear that women's inequality has powerfully constrained their ability to create change, and historians cannot speak of women's agency—or for that matter, men's agency—in simplistic terms. Historically, women have been deeply shaped by the dominant discursive formulations of their culture. On the other hand, it is also clear that women have managed to transform those discourses in order to create meaningful change. *How* they have done this is an ongoing subject of theoretical debate, but this book illustrates that women, like men, have indeed remade their religious worlds.

The aim of this volume is not to replace the traditional "master narrative" centered around white male Protestants with a new one solely focused on women. Such a project would simply turn the old stories upside down, creating new kinds of exclusions and problems. Women's history is not the master key to understanding *all* of American religious history, and the contributors to this volume are not interested in making such a hegemonic claim. There are many important historical topics, such as Jonathan Edwards's understanding of free will, that have little to do with real women. (As historians have shown, however, these kind of topics may naturally lend themselves to gender analysis.)[101] Instead of trying to craft a single narrative with women at the center, the contributors hope to chart the way toward *multiple* narratives that are more inclusive and more representative of the real lives of people in the past. Whether these narratives are centered around the relationship between American religion and the nation-state or alternatively, personal religious experience, they must not ignore women's historical agency.

What would more inclusive histories look like? Although I have partially demonstrated women's absence in American religious history textbooks by counting their names, there are significant problems with an approach that privileges numbers. Part of the reason that historians have ignored women is that so few women took part in national political events such as the Constitutional Convention. When historians have counted names of major political or religious leaders, they have found relatively few women, and rather than treating women's absence as a problem to be explained, they have focused on men. Counting, by itself, is not an effective method for judging importance.

Rather than urging historians to always include exactly the same number of male and female characters, which would almost certainly lead to cursory attempts at inclusion, my vision is far less rigid. My hope is that historians will always ask themselves whether their research could be transformed or enriched if they asked questions about women's lives as well as men's. In some cases, the answer will be no. But in the many cases when the answer is yes, my hope is that historians will follow their evidence wherever it naturally leads.

Not all the authors in this volume are convinced (as I am) of the ultimate usefulness of narrative approaches to history. Yet even those who are skeptical have a pragmatic reason for contributing to this book. They recognize that if they are not able to construct new stories that capture the imaginations of students and the general public, the old stories will remain dominant. Books such as Winthrop Hudson's *Religion in America* (1965), now in its seventh edition, and Sydney Ahlstrom's *A Religious History of the American People* (1972), recently published in a second edition, have remained the touchstones of the field because they offer a comprehensive vision missing in newer work.[102] To borrow a favorite word in the profession today, "complicating" classic books isn't enough. They must be fundamentally rewritten.

What is at stake in revising American religious history is not only how we imagine the past, but the future as well. If historians do not become more self-conscious about who is included in their stories and who is not, they will perpetuate the fiction that male leaders alone have made history. When my undergraduate students are willing to be blunt, they tell me that women are not in history books "because they didn't do anything important." Unless American religious historians think more deeply about how women's history changes our understanding of the past, future students will continue to assume that "women" should be a "search term" not easily "found."

Notes

1. Ann Braude, "Women's History *Is* American Religious History," in *Retelling U.S. Religious History*, ed. Thomas A. Tweed (Berkeley: University of California Press, 1997), 87–107. On narratives of "declension," see also Harry S. Stout and Catherine A. Brekus, "Gender, Declension, and the 'New Religious History,'" in *Belief and Behavior: Essays in the New Religious History*, ed. Philip R. VanderMeer and Robert P. Swierenga (New Brunswick, N.J.: Rutgers University Press, 1991), 15–37.

2. For a sampling of this work, see William L. Andrews, ed., *Sisters of the Spirit: Three Black Women's Autobiographies of the Nineteenth Century* (Bloomington: Indiana University Press, 1986); Edith Waldvogel Blumhofer, *Her Heart Can See: The Life and Hymns of Fanny J. Crosby* (Grand Rapids, Mich.: Eerdmans, 2005); Ruth Birgitta Anderson Bordin, *Frances Willard: A Biography* (Chapel Hill: University of North Carolina Press, 1986); Carolyn De Swarte Gifford, ed., *Writing Out My Heart: Selections from the Journal of Frances E. Willard, 1855–96* (Urbana: University of Illinois Press, 1995); Allan Greer, *Mohawk Saint: Catherine Tekakwitha and the Jesuits* (New York: Oxford University Press, 2005); Jean M. Humez, "'Ye Are My Epistles': The Construction of Ann Lee Imagery in Early Shaker Sacred Literature," *Journal of Feminist Studies in Religion* 8, no. 1 (1992): 83–104; Carla L. Peterson, *Doers of the Word: African-American Women Speakers and Writers in the North (1830–1880)* (New York: Oxford University Press, 1995); Marjorie Procter-Smith, "'Who Do You Say That I Am?' Mother Ann as Christ," in *Locating the Shakers: Cultural Origins and Legacies of an American Religious Movement*, ed. Mick Gidley with Kate Bowles (Exeter: University of Exeter Press, 1990), 83–95.

3. Lori D. Ginzberg, *Women and the Work of Benevolence: Morality, Politics, and Class in the Nineteenth-Century United States* (New Haven: Yale University Press, 1990); Barbara Leslie Epstein, *The Politics of Domesticity: Women, Evangelism, and Temperance in Nineteenth-Century America* (Middletown, Conn.: Wesleyan University Press, 1981); Julie Roy Jeffrey, *The Great Silent Army of Abolitionism: Ordinary Women in the Antislavery Movement* (Chapel Hill: University of North Carolina Press, 1998); Gerda Lerner, *The Grimké Sisters from South Carolina: Pioneers for Woman's Rights and Abolition* (New York: Oxford University Press, 1998); Dana Lee Robert, *Gospel Bearers, Gender Barriers: Missionary Women in the Twentieth Century* (Maryknoll, N.Y.: Orbis Books, 2002).

4. Marla Faye Frederick, *Between Sundays: Black Women and Everyday Struggles of Faith* (Berkeley: University of California Press, 2003); Maureen Ursenbach Beecher and Lavina Fielding Anderson, ed., *Sisters in Spirit: Mormon Women in Historical and Cultural Perspective* (Urbana: University of Illinois Press, 1987); Claudia L. Bushman, *Mormon Sisters: Women in Early Utah*, rev. ed. (Logan: Utah State University Press, 1997); Yvonne Patricia Chireau, *Black Magic: Religion and the African American Conjuring Tradition* (Berkeley: University of California Press, 2003); Jill M. Derr, Janath R. Cannon, and Maureen Ursenbach Beecher,

Women of Covenant: The Story of Relief Society (Salt Lake City: Deseret Book Company, 2000); R. Marie Griffith, *God's Daughters: Evangelical Women and the Power of Submission* (Berkeley: University of California Press, 1997); Suellen M. Hoy, *Good Hearts: Catholic Sisters in Chicago's Past* (Urbana: University of Illinois Press, 2006); E. Paula Hyman and Deborah Dash Moore, *Jewish Women in America: An Historical Encyclopedia* (New York: Routledge, 1998); Paula M. Kane, James Joseph Kenneally, and Karen Kennelly, eds., *Gender Identities in American Catholicism* (Maryknoll, N.Y.: Orbis Books, 2001); James Joseph Kenneally, *The History of American Catholic Women* (New York: Crossroad, 1990); Karen Kennelly, *American Catholic Women: A Historical Exploration* (New York: Macmillan, 1989); Robert A. Orsi, *The Madonna of 115th Street: Faith and Community in Italian Harlem, 1880–1950* (New Haven: Yale University Press, 1985); Robert A. Orsi, *Thank You, St. Jude: Women's Devotion to the Patron Saint of Hopeless Causes* (New Haven: Yale University Press, 1996); Nell Irvin Painter, *Sojourner Truth: A Life, a Symbol* (New York: W. W. Norton, 1996); Judith Weisenfeld and Richard Newman, *This Far by Faith: Readings in African-American Women's Religious Biography* (New York: Routledge, 1996).

5. Griffith, *God's Daughters*; Laurel Ulrich, *Good Wives: Image and Reality in the Lives of Women in Northern New England, 1650–1750*, 1st ed. (New York: Knopf, 1982); Marilyn J. Westerkamp, *Women and Religion in Early America, 1600–1850: The Puritan and Evangelical Traditions*, Christianity and Society in the Modern World (New York: Routledge, 1999); Karin E. Gedge, *Without Benefit of Clergy: Women and the Pastoral Relationship in Nineteenth-Century American Culture* (New York: Oxford University Press, 2003).

6. Ann Braude, *Radical Spirits: Spiritualism and Women's Rights in Nineteenth-Century America*, 2d ed. (Bloomington: Indiana University Press, 2001); Catherine A. Brekus, *Strangers and Pilgrims: Female Preaching in America, 1740–1845* (Chapel Hill: University of North Carolina Press, 1998); Carol Coburn and Martha Smith, *Spirited Lives: How Nuns Shaped Catholic Culture and American Life, 1836–1920* (Chapel Hill: University of North Carolina Press, 1999); Hasia R. Diner and Beryl Benderly, *Her Works Praise Her: A History of Jewish Women in America from Colonial Times to the Present* (New York: Basic Books, 2002); Elizabeth Elkin Grammer, *Some Wild Visions: Autobiographies by Female Itinerant Preachers in Nineteenth-Century America* (New York: Oxford University Press, 2003); Evelyn Brooks Higginbotham, *Righteous Discontent: The Women's Movement in the Black Baptist Church, 1880–1920* (Cambridge: Harvard University Press, 1993); Rebecca Larson, *Daughters of Light: Quaker Women Preaching and Prophesying in the Colonies and Abroad, 1700–1775*, 1st ed. (New York: Knopf, 1999); Diane Batts Morrow, *Persons of Color and Religious at the Same Time: The Oblate Sisters of Providence, 1828–1860* (Chapel Hill: University of North Carolina Press, 2002); Pamela Susan Nadell, *American Jewish Women's History: A Reader* (New York: New York University Press, 2003); Michelene E. Pesantubbee, *Choctaw Women in a Chaotic World: The Clash of Cultures in the Colonial Southeast* (Albuquerque:

University of New Mexico Press, 2005); Susie Cunningham Stanley, *Holy Boldness: Women Preachers' Autobiographies and the Sanctified Self* (Knoxville: University of Tennessee Press, 2002); Carolyn Moxley Rouse, *Engaged Surrender: African American Women and Islam* (Berkeley: University of California Press, 2004).

7. On Hindu women, see Sheba George, "Caroling with the Keralites: The Negotiation of Gendered Space in an Indian Immigrant Church," in *Gatherings in Diaspora: Religious Communities and the New Immigration*, ed. R. Stephen Warner and Judith G. Wittner (Philadelphia: Temple University Press, 1998); Prema Kurien, "Gendered Ethnicity: Creating a Hindu Indian Identity in the United States," *American Behavioral Scientist* 42, no. 4 (1999): 648–70; and Aparna Rayaprol, *Negotiating Identities: Women in the Indian Diaspora* (New York: Oxford University Press, 1997). On Muslim women, see Barbara C. Aswad and Barbara Bilgâe, *Family and Gender among American Muslims: Issues Facing Middle Eastern Immigrants and Their Descendants* (Philadelphia: Temple University Press, 1996); Yvonne Yazbeck Haddad, Jane I. Smith, and Kathleen M. Moore, *Muslim Women in America: The Challenge of Islamic Identity Today* (New York: Oxford University Press, 2006); and Jane I. Smith, *Islam in America*, Columbia Contemporary American Religion Series (New York: Columbia University Press, 1999), 104–25.

8. Susan Hill Lindley, *You Have Stept Out of Your Place: A History of Women and Religion in America*, 1st ed. (Louisville, Ky.: Westminster John Knox Press, 1996).

9. For more on the Haddash-Brandeis Institute, see <http://www.brandeis.edu/hirjw/>. On Harvard's Women's Studies in Religion Program, see <http://www.hds.harvard.edu/wsrp/>.

10. For more information on the Dempsey Prize, see the American Society of Church History website: <http://www.churchhistory.org/>.

11. Judith M. Bennett, "Feminism and History," *Gender and History* 1, no. 2 (1989): 252; Randi R. Warne, "Making the Gender-Critical Turn," in *Secular Theories on Religion: Current Perspectives*, ed. Tim Jensen and Mikael Rothstein (Copenhagen: Museum Tusculanum Press, 2000), 250. See also Rita M. Gross, "Where Have We Been? Where Do We Need to Go: Women's Studies and Gender in Religion and Feminist Theology," in *Gender, Religion, and Diversity: Cross Cultural Perspectives*, ed. Ursula King and Tina Beattie (New York: Continuum, 2004), 17–27. Laura Lee Downs is one of the few scholars to offer a more optimistic assessment: "Over the past 10–15 years, historians outside the field of women's and gender history have overwhelmingly integrated gender into their analyses, often as a prime category of analysis. All this suggests that in a relatively short period of time, scholars have come to agree that it is no longer possible to write history—whether of the military, political, economic, social or intellectual varieties—without taking gender into account." See Laura Lee Downs, *Writing Gender History* (London: Hodder Arnold, 2004), 185. As I discuss below, I disagree with her contention that women's history and gender history have achieved this level of integration.

12. E. Brooks Holifield, *Theology in America: Christian Thought from the Age of the*

Puritans to the Civil War (New Haven: Yale University Press, 2003); Ann Douglas, *The Feminization of American Culture*, 1st ed. (New York: Knopf, 1977).

13. Nathan O. Hatch, *The Democratization of American Christianity* (New Haven: Yale University Press, 1989); Nancy A. Hardesty, *Your Daughters Shall Prophesy: Revivalism and Feminism in the Age of Finney* (Brooklyn, N.Y.: Carlson, 1991). Since Hatch's book was published two years before Hardesty's, my point is not that Hatch should have paid more attention to Hardesty's work. My argument is simply that "mainstream" historians have often failed to view women as a natural research topic. Hatch briefly discusses female preachers (pp. 78–79), but only a few scattered female names appear elsewhere in his book.

14. Sydney E. Ahlstrom, *A Religious History of the American People* (New Haven: Yale University Press, 1972); Martin E. Marty, *Righteous Empire: The Protestant Experience in America* (New York: Dial Press, 1970). For the revised version, see Martin E. Marty, *Protestantism in the United States: Righteous Empire*, 2nd ed. (New York: Scribner's, 1986), 97–106.

15. George M. Marsden, *Religion and American Culture*, 2d ed. (Belmont, Calif.: Wadsworth, 2001). I have arrived at these numbers by using Marsden's index in conjunction with a close reading of his book. For example, Pocahontas is not mentioned in the index but makes a brief appearance on p. 20. For the quotations, see pp. 123, 5.

16. Albanese published the first edition of her book in 1986, but she extensively revised it in 1999. Catherine L. Albanese, *America: Religion and Religions*, 3rd ed. (Belmont, Calif.: Wadsworth, 1999). Her revisions did not include significant new material on women. For her discussion of Salem witchcraft, see pp. 259–60. On black theology, see pp. 213–14. A new, 4th edition of *America: Religion and Religions* was published in 2006 as this volume was going to press and may include deeper revisions.

17. Edwin Gaustad and Leigh Schmidt, *The Religious History of America: The Heart of the American Story from Colonial Times to Today*, rev. ed. (San Francisco: Harper-Collins, 2002), 220–22.

18. Winthrop Still Hudson and John Corrigan, *Religion in America: An Historical Account of the Development of American Religious Life*, 7th ed. (Upper Saddle River, N.J.: Pearson/Prentice Hall, 2004), 181.

19. Ibid. Corrigan discusses the Second Great Awakening in chapter 6 (pp. 150–58). Elizabeth appears on p. 305. Corrigan obviously struggled with the question of how to include women in a textbook that was originally published before the outpouring of women's history. While he carefully integrates a discussion of female antislavery activism into his discussion of antislavery (p. 219), he also creates a separate section on women and social reform (pp. 306–9) that seems chronologically out of place.

20. Jon Butler, Grant Wacker, and Randall Herbert Balmer, *Religion in American Life: A Short History* (New York: Oxford University Press, 2003), x. Their index includes 65 women's names and 335 men's names.

21. Philip Goff and Paul Harvey, *Themes in Religion and American Culture* (Chapel Hill: University of North Carolina Press, 2004). For another thematic introduction to American religion that highlights women, though not gender, see Julia Corbett Hemeyer, *Religion in America*, 5th ed. (Upper Saddle River, N.J.: Prentice Hall, 2006).

22. See the syllabus posted by Terry Matthews, "Religion in the South." This course was taught at Wake Forest in 1995. See <http://www.aarweb.org/syllabus/>. Matthews posted another syllabus as well for "Religion in America," which he also taught at Wake Forest in 1995. Out of thirty-three listed topics, he devoted only one to women's history: namely, feminist theology. Otherwise he discussed women only in the following contexts: a brief mention of Anne Hutchinson in a lecture on Puritanism; another mention of women in the Second Great Awakening, which purportedly "helped advance the liberation of women"; a joke about Joseph Smith's practice of polygamy, a "feat" that Smith "pulled off" by "claiming that there would be no salvation for women unless they were married"; a remark about mixed seating in Reform Jewish synagogues; a reference to the prominence of women in the temperance movement; and an allusion to the Community Church movement's support of "women facing unwanted pregnancies." In a lecture on contemporary America, Matthews argued that mainstream Protestantism was declining: "Unfortunately Things Aren't Likely to Get Easier." His seventh reason for pessimism is that "the male dominated world is disappearing. 'A new set of women's values will dominate all areas of life. Day care, maternity/ paternity leave, and full and part-time jobs both at home and away will become common.'" It is not clear whom he is quoting in this sentence. For this lecture, see Lecture 29, "Main-Line or Old-Line," in his course, "Religion in America," available at <http://www.aarweb.org/syllabus/>.

23. Harry S. Stout and Catherine Brekus, "A New England Congregation: Center Church, New Haven, 1638–1989," in *Portraits of Twelve Religious Communities*, vol. 1 of *American Congregations*, ed. James P. and James W. Lewis Wind (Chicago: University of Chicago Press, 1994), 41. See also Richard Shiels, "The Feminization of American Congregationalism, 1730–1835," *American Quarterly* 33 (1981): 46–62; Stephen Grossbart, "Seeking the Divine Favor: Conversion and Church Admission in Eastern Connecticut, 1711–1832," *William and Mary Quarterly* 46, no. 4 (October 1989): 696–740; and Mary P. Ryan, "A Women's Awakening: Evangelical Religion and the Families of Utica, New York, 1800–1840," *American Quarterly* 30 (Winter 1978): 602–23.

24. Raymond Williams has argued that "in the United States, religion is the social category with clearest meaning and acceptance in the host society, so the emphasis on religious affiliation and identity is one of the strategies that allows the immigrant to maintain self-identity while simultaneously acquiring community acceptance." See Raymond Brady Williams, *Religions of Immigrants from India and Pakistan: New Threads in the American Tapestry* (New York: Cambridge University Press, 1988). Many scholars have argued that world religions have

become more egalitarian because of the American environment. See, for example, Gurinder Singh Mann, Paul David Numrich, and Raymond Brady Williams, *Buddhists, Hindus, and Sikhs in America*, Religion in American Life (New York: Oxford University Press, 2001), 143; Rayaprol, *Negotiating Identities: Women in the Indian Diaspora*; and Smith, *Islam in America*, 104–12. For more critical assessments, see Wendy Cadge, "Gendered Religious Organizations: The Case of Theravada Buddhism in America," *Gender and Society* 18, no. 6 (2004): 777–93; Kurien, "Gendered Ethnicity: Creating a Hindu Indian Identity in the United States"; and Braude, "Women's History *Is* American Religious History," 88.

25. Linda Gordon, "What's New in Women's History," in *Feminist Studies/Critical Studies*, ed. Teresa de Lauretis (Bloomington: Indiana University Press, 1986), 29. See also Gisela Bock, "Women's History and Gender History: Aspects of an International Debate," *Gender and History* 1, no. 1 (Spring 1989): 7–30. Bok argues that women's history is not original because of its method but because of the questions it brings to the past (p. 8).

26. See Susan Juster, *Disorderly Women: Sexual Politics and Evangelicalism in Revolutionary New England* (Ithaca, N.Y.: Cornell University Press, 1994). See also Susan Juster, *Doomsayers: Anglo-American Prophecy in the Age of Revolution* (Philadelphia: University of Pennsylvania Press, 2003). Juster's work was built on an outpouring of impressive scholarship on women in the American Revolution. See Linda K. Kerber, *Women of the Republic: Intellect and Ideology in Revolutionary America* (New York: Norton, 1986); and Mary Beth Norton, *Liberty's Daughters: The Revolutionary Experience of American Women, 1750–1800*, 1st ed. (Boston: Little, Brown, 1980).

27. Randi R. Warne, "(En)gendering Religious Studies," in *Feminism in the Study of Religion: A Reader*, ed. Darlene M. Juschka (New York: Continuum, 2001), 154. The italics are in the original. On this point, see also Ursula King, "Introduction: Gender and the Study of Religion," in her edited collection, *Religion and Gender* (Malden, Mass.: Blackwell, 1995), 19.

28. Anne E. Carr, "The Scholarship of Gender: Women's Studies and Religious Studies," chapter 4 of her *Transforming Grace: Christian Tradition and Women's Experience* (San Francisco: Harper and Row, 1988), 75.

29. Gertrude Himmelfarb, "Some Reflections on the New History," *American Historical Review* 94, no. 3 (1989): 668.

30. Thomas L. Haskell, *Objectivity Is Not Neutrality: Explanatory Schemes in History* (Baltimore: Johns Hopkins University Press, 1998), 148–49.

31. Joyce Oldham Appleby, Lynn Avery Hunt, and Margaret C. Jacob, *Telling the Truth about History* (New York: Norton, 1994), 7.

32. Robert F. Berkhofer, *Beyond the Great Story: History as Text and Discourse* (Cambridge: Belknap Press of Harvard University Press, 1995); David Harlan, *The Degradation of American History* (Chicago: University of Chicago Press, 1997); Hayden V. White, *Tropics of Discourse: Essays in Cultural Criticism* (Baltimore: Johns Hopkins University Press, 1978).

33. Poststructuralists reject the "structuralist" theory that language is a closed system of meaning, arguing instead that it is always multiple and in flux. As a result, some question whether there is any reality outside of language. Are there unchanging, stable foundations for knowledge? (Not all poststructuralists, particularly Jacques Derrida, deny the existence of a reality outside of language.) Deconstructionists argue that texts always hold multiple meanings, and they try to "deconstruct" the binary oppositions that have structured Western knowledge: for example, male and female. For introductions to deconstruction and poststructuralism, see Kevin Passmore, "Poststructuralism and History," in *Writing History: Theory and Practice*, ed. Stefan Berger, Heiko Feldner, and Kevin Passmore (New York: Oxford University Press, 2003), 118–40; and Jane Caplan, "Postmodernism, Poststructuralism, and Deconstruction: Notes for Historians," *Central European History* 22, no. 3/4 (1989): 260–78.

34. For a sampling of Foucault's work, see Michel Foucault, *Discipline and Punish: The Birth of the Prison*, 1st U.S. ed. (New York: Pantheon Books, 1977); Michel Foucault, *The History of Sexuality*, 1st U.S. ed. (New York: Pantheon Books, 1978); Michel Foucault, *The Archaeology of Knowledge*, 1st U.S. ed. (New York: Pantheon Books, 1972); Michel Foucault and Colin Gordon, *Power/Knowledge: Selected Interviews and Other Writings, 1972–1977*, 1st U.S. ed. (New York: Pantheon Books, 1980); and Paul Rabinow, ed., *The Foucault Reader* (New York: Pantheon Books, 1984). On Derrida, see Jacques Derrida, *Of Grammatology*, 1st U.S. ed. (Baltimore: Johns Hopkins University Press, 1976); and Jacques Derrida, *Writing and Difference* (Chicago: University of Chicago Press, 1978).

35. Julie Byrne, *O God of Players: The Story of the Immaculata Mighty Macs* (New York: Columbia University Press, 1993), 13.

36. On this point, see Ann-Louise Shapiro, "History and Feminist Theory, or Talking Back to the Beadle," *History and Theory* 31, no. 4 (1992): 1–14.

37. In an essay originally published in 1986, Joan Scott noted that some scholars were attracted to the term "gender" because of their desire to distance themselves "from the (supposedly strident) politics of feminism." Joan Wallach Scott, *Gender and the Politics of History*, Gender and Culture (New York: Columbia University Press, 1988), 31. Ten years later, Jane Purvis suggested that the term "gender" had become so popular in British women's history because it "is less threatening to the male establishment in higher education in Britain." Jane Purvis, "From 'Women Worthies' to Poststructuralism? Debate and Controversy in Women's History in Britain," in *Women's History: Britain: 1850–1945*, ed. Jane Purvis (New York: St. Martin's Press, 1995), 13.

38. Nancy F. Cott, "Passionlessness: An Interpretation of Victorian Sexual Ideology, 1790–1850," in *A Heritage of Her Own: Toward a New Social History of American Women*, ed. Nancy F. Cott and Elizabeth H. Pleck (New York: Simon and Schuster, 1979), 162–81.

39. Joan Wallach Scott, "Gender: A Useful Category of Analysis," in *Gender and the*

Politics of History (New York: Columbia University Press, 1988), 44. This essay was originally published in *American Historical Review* in 1986.

40. Judith Butler, *Gender Trouble: Feminism and the Subversion of Identity* (New York: Routledge, 1999). For a model of what this kind of history would look like, see Saba Mahmood, *Politics of Piety: The Islamic Revival and the Feminist Subject* (Princeton, N.J.: Princeton University Press, 2005). In her study of the women's mosque movement in Egypt, Mahmood argues that the "feminine" qualities of modesty and piety are created through disciplined religious practice. For a critique of Butler's view of gender as performance, see Susan Bordo, *Unbearable Weight: Feminism, Western Culture, and the Body* (Berkeley: University of California Press, 1993), 289–95. R. Marie Griffith has made a few interesting moves in Butler's theoretical direction. See R. Marie Griffith, "Female Suffering and Religious Devotion in American Pentecostalism," in *Women and Twentieth-Century Protestantism*, ed. Margaret Lamberts Bendroth and Virginia Lieson Brereton (Urbana: University of Illinois Press, 2002), 184–208.

41. Joan W. Scott, "The Evidence of Experience," *Critical Inquiry* 17 (Summer 1991): 777, 797. She was responding to John E. Toews, "Intellectual History after the Linguistic Turn: The Autonomy of Meaning and the Irreducibility of Experience," *American Historical Review* 92, no. 4 (1987): 879–907. For critical responses to Scott's article, see Mariana Valverde, "Comment," *Journal of Women's History* 5, no. 1 (Spring 1993): 121–25; Kathleen Canning, "Comment: German Particularities in Women's History/Gender History," *Journal of Women's History* 5, no. 1 (Spring 1993): 102–14; and especially Paula M. L. Moya and Michael Roy Hames-Garcia, *Reclaiming Identity: Realist Theory and the Predicament of Postmodernism* (Berkeley: University of California Press, 2000). Sheila Davaney raises questions about the ahistorical category of "experience" in feminist theology, and, like Scott, she emphasizes that we must examine women's experience, like men's, as a "social product." Sheila Greeve Davaney, "The Limits of the Appeal to Women's Experience," in *Shaping New Vision: Gender and Values in American Culture*, ed. Clarissa W. Atkinson, Constance H. Buchanan, and Margaret R. Miles (Ann Arbor: UMI Press, 1987), 47. Interestingly, even feminist scholars who are hostile to gender studies admit that the category of "experience" is problematic. Even though Joanna de Groot and Mary Maynard criticize the kind of work that Joan Scott does, they explain that "to simply let women speak for themselves, and then repeat and describe this, is to celebrate, rather than necessarily to make sense of, their circumstances." We must recognize that people's accounts of themselves are "culturally embedded." Joanna de Groot and Mary Maynard, "Facing the 1990s: Problems and Possibilities for Women's Studies," in *Women's Studies in the 1990s: Doing Things Differently?* ed. Joanna de Groot and Mary Maynard (New York: St. Martin's Press, 1993), 162. Nevertheless, Scott's critique of the category of "experience," unlike her call for greater attention to "gender," has not gained a wide hearing among women's historians of American religion. In contrast, historians who work on women and religion in other periods have paid more attention to

her critique. See especially Elizabeth A. Clark, "Women, Gender, and the Study of Christian History," *Church History* 70, no. 3 (September 2001): 395–426; and Elizabeth A. Clark, "The Lady Vanishes: Dilemmas of a Feminist Historian after the Linguistic Turn," *Church History* 67, no. 1 (March 1998): 1–31.

42. Darlene M. Juschka, "General Introduction," *Feminism in the Study of Religion: A Reader* (New York: Continuum, 2001), 2–3. For another useful discussion of androcentrism, see Rita M. Gross, *Buddhism after Patriarchy: A Feminist History, Analysis, and Reconstruction of Buddhism* (Albany: State University of New York Press, 1993), 295–96.

43. On this point, see Nancy Auer Falk and Rita M. Gross, "Introduction," *Unspoken Worlds: Women's Religious Lives*, 3rd ed., ed. Nancy Auer Falk and Rita M. Gross (Belmont, Calif.: Wadsworth, 2001), xv.

44. Paul E. Johnson, *A Shopkeeper's Millennium: Society and Revivals in Rochester, New York, 1815–1837*, 1st ed. (New York: Hill and Wang, 1978), 108.

45. Orsi, *Thank You, St. Jude*; Orsi, *The Madonna of 115th Street*. David Hackett has published a reader that is distinguished by its inclusiveness. See David G. Hackett, *Religion and American Culture: A Reader* (New York: Routledge, 1995); and David G. Hackett, "Gender and Religion in American Culture, 1870–1930," *Religion and American Culture* 5, no. 2 (1995): 127–57.

46. Elizabeth Kamarck Minnich, *Transforming Knowledge* (Philadelphia: Temple University Press, 1990), 32. The italics are in the original.

47. Warne, "Making the Gender-Critical Turn," 251.

48. Robert Baird, *Religion in America* (New York: Harper and Brothers, 1844); Ahlstrom, *A Religious History of the American People*; Daniel Dorchester, *Christianity in the United States from the First Settlement Down to the Present Time* (New York: Phillips and Hunt, 1888); Winthrop Still Hudson, *Religion in America* (New York: Scribner, 1965).

49. Lois W. Banner, *Elizabeth Cady Stanton, a Radical for Woman's Rights* (Boston: Little, Brown, 1980); Jeanne Boydston, Mary Kelley, and Anne Throne Margolis, *The Limits of Sisterhood: The Beecher Sisters on Women's Rights and Woman's Sphere* (Chapel Hill: University of North Carolina Press, 1988); Elizabeth Battelle Clark, "The Politics of God and the Woman's Vote: Religion in the American Suffrage Movement, 1848–1895" (Ph.D. diss., Princeton University, 1989); Kathryn Kish Sklar, *Catharine Beecher: A Study in American Domesticity* (New Haven: Yale University Press, 1973).

50. Himmelfarb, "Some Reflections on the New History," 664.

51. R. Marie Griffith, *Born Again Bodies: Flesh and Spirit in American Christianity* (Berkeley: University of California Press, 2004).

52. Ibid.

53. Mark A. Noll, *The Rise of Evangelicalism: The Age of Edwards, Whitefield and the Wesleys* (Leicester, England: Inter-Varsity, 2004), 132.

54. Mark A. Noll, *A History of Christianity in the United States and Canada* (Grand Rapids, Mich.: Eerdmans, 1992).

55. Olivier Zunz, "Introduction," in *Reliving the Past: The Worlds of Social History*, ed. Olivier Zunz (Chapel Hill: University of North Carolina Press, 1985), 5. Zunz based his succinct definition on Charles Tilly's comments in "Retrieving European Lives," in Zunz, *Reliving the Past*, 12.

56. Clifford Geertz, "Thick Description: Toward an Interpretive Theory of Culture," in *The Interpretation of Cultures: Selected Essays* (New York: Basic Books, 1973), 5; William H. Sewell, Jr., "The Concept(s) of Culture," in *Beyond the Cultural Turn: New Directions in the Study of Society and Culture*, ed. Victoria E. Bonnell and Lynn Hunt (Berkeley: University of California Press, 1999), 46.

57. Anne S. Brown and David D. Hall, "Family Strategies and Religious Practice: Baptism and the Lord's Supper in Early New England," in *Lived Religion in America: Toward a History of Practice*, ed. David D. Hall (Princeton: Princeton University Press, 1997), 41–68; Orsi, *The Madonna of 115th Street*. See also Grant Wacker, *Heaven Below: Early Pentecostals and American Culture* (Cambridge: Harvard University Press, 2001), which includes an insightful chapter on women.

58. Zunz, *Reliving the Past*, 101. For a case study that considers the relationship between individual agency and structural change, see Thomas W. Gallant, "Agency, Structure, and Explanation in Social History: The Case of the Foundling Home on Kephallenia, Greece, during the 1830s," *Social Science History* 15, no. 4 (1991): 479–508.

59. Thomas Bender, "Wholes and Parts: The Need for Synthesis in American History," *Journal of American History* 73, no. 1 (1986): 128. Thomas Haskell points out that historians have largely abandoned their interest in causation. They tend to focus on "understanding" rather than "explanation." See Haskell, *Objectivity Is Not Neutrality: Explanatory Schemes in History*, 13–14.

60. Orsi, *The Madonna of 115th Street*; Wacker, *Heaven Below*, 9. Of course, some cultural historians have tried to combine "thick" description with an explanation of change over time. For one example, see Leigh Eric Schmidt, *Holy Fairs: Scottish Communions and American Revivals in the Early Modern Period* (Princeton, N.J.: Princeton University Press, 1989).

61. Sewell, "The Concept(s) of Culture," 35–61.

62. Rabinow, *The Foucault Reader*, 64.

63. Scott, "The Evidence of Experience," 793. For examples of feminist historians who have criticized Scott's view of agency, see Louise Tilly, "Gender, Women's History, and Social History," *Social Science History* 13, no. 4 (1989): 452; Linda Gordon, "Review of Joan Wallach Scott, *Gender and the Politics of History*," *Signs* 15, no. 4 (Summer 1990): 853–58; Catherine Hall, "Politics, Post-structuralism and Feminist History," *Gender and History* 3, no. 2 (Summer 1991): 210; and Christine Stansell, "A Response to Joan Scott," *International Labor and Working-Class History* 31 (Spring 1987): 24–29. For feminist critiques of poststructuralism more generally, see Joan Hoff, "Gender as a Postmodern Category of Paralysis," *Women's History Review* 3, no. 2 (1994): 149–68; and Purvis, "From 'Women Worthies' to Poststructuralism? Debate and Controversy in Women's History in

Britain," 1–22. For excellent overviews of recent debates over women's agency, see Amy Hollywood, "Agency and Evidence in Feminist Studies of Religion," in *The Future of the Study of Religion: Proceedings of Congress 2000*, ed. Slavica Jakelic and Lori Pearson (Leiden: Brill, 2004), 243–49; Amy Hollywood, "Gender, Agency, and the Divine in Religious Historiography," *Journal of Religion* 84 (October 2004): 514–28; Saba Mahmood, "Women's Agency within Feminist Historiography," *Journal of Religion* 84 (October 2004): 573–79; and Susanna Heschel, "Gender and Agency in the Feminist Historiography of Jewish Identity," *Journal of Religion* 84 (October 2004): 580–91.

64. See Joseph J. Ellis, *Founding Brothers: The Revolutionary Generation*, 1st ed. (New York: Alfred A. Knopf, 2000); and David G. McCullough, *John Adams* (New York: Simon and Schuster, 2001). Gary Nash has objected to this focus on elites. See Gary B. Nash, *The Unknown American Revolution: The Unruly Birth of Democracy and the Struggle to Create America* (New York: Viking, 2005).

65. Stephen J. Stein, "American Religious History—Decentered with Many Centers," *Church History* 71, no. 2 (2002): 376.

66. Isabel V. Hull, "Feminist and Gender History through the Literary Looking Glass: German Historiography in Postmodern Times," *Central European History* 22, no. 3, 4 (1989): 280. To give one example, because of scholarship on women, African Americans, and Native Americans, American historians rarely describe the American Revolution in purely celebratory terms. Instead, they argue that the American Revolution was an unfinished revolution that failed to offer true equality to all people.

67. Hull, "Feminist and Gender History through the Literary Looking Glass," 300. For another critique of the quest for "coherence," see Allan Megill, "Coherence and Incoherence in Historical Studies: From the *Annales* School to the New Cultural History," *New Literary History* 35, no. 2 (2004): 207–31. Megill argues that "it is a considerable mistake to regard history as an enterprise that ought to be fixated on a search for coherence. On the contrary, part of the function of historical study is surely to shuffle the cards, showing the various ways in which the past is actually incoherent with itself and our expectations of it, and in which the study of the past relies on conflicting modes of understanding and engagement" (p. 226). See also Allan Megill, "Fragmentation and the Future of Historiography," *American Historical Review* 96, no. 3 (1991): 693–98.

68. Jean Francois Lyotard, *The Postmodern Condition: A Report on Knowledge* (Minneapolis: University of Minnesota Press, 1984), xxiv. Quoted in Martin Kreiswirth, "Trusting the Tale: The Narrativist Turn in the Human Sciences," *New Literary History* 23, no. 3 (1992): 640.

69. There are several good articles that discuss controversies over narrative. See Dorothy Ross, "Grand Narrative in American Historical Writing: From Romance to Uncertainty," *American Historical Review* 100, no. 3 (1995): 651–77; Kreiswirth, "Trusting the Tale: The Narrativist Turn in the Human Sciences," 629–57; Allan Megill, " 'Grand Narrative' and the Discipline of History," in *A New Philosophy of*

History, ed. Frank Ankersmit and Hans Kellner (Chicago: University of Chicago Press, 1995), 151–73; and Thomas A. Tweed, "Introduction: Narrating U.S. Religious History," in *Retelling U.S. Religious History* (Berkeley: University of California Press, 1997), 1–23.

70. Haskell, *Objectivity Is Not Neutrality*, 3.

71. Louise A. Tilly, "Gender, Women's History, and Social History," *Social Science History* 13, no. 4 (Winter 1989): 447.

72. Coburn and Smith, *Spirited Lives*; Tilly, "Gender, Women's History, and Social History," 458.

73. Judith M. Bennett, "Feminism and History," *Gender and History* 1, no. 2 (Autumn 1989): 259. Sandra Harding argues that feminist scholars should not simply study women's "contributions to activities in the public world." "This leads us to ignore such crucial issues as how changes in the social practices of reproduction, sexuality, and mothering have shaped the state, the economy, and the other public institutions." It also fails to ask what "the *meanings* of women's contributions to public life *for women*" have been. Sandra Harding, "Introduction: Is There a Feminist Method?" in her *Feminism and Methodology: Social Science Issues* (Bloomington: Indiana University Press, 1987), 4–5.

74. Merry E. Wiesner-Hanks, "Women, Gender, and Church History," *Church History* 71, no. 3 (September 2002): 600–620. Ursula King has noted that feminist scholars of religion have to combat a "double blindness": gender studies are religion blind, while religion is gender blind. See Ursula King, "General Introduction: Gender-Critical Turns in the Study of Religion," in *Gender, Religion, and Diversity: Cross-Cultural Perspectives*, ed. Ursula King and Tina Beattie (New York: Continuum, 2004), 1–2. Ann Braude has criticized women's historians for their "squeamishness" toward religion. See Braude, *Radical Spirits*, xxii. For other historians who make the same critique, see Bendroth and Brereton, *Women and Twentieth-Century Protestantism*; and Griffith, *God's Daughters*.

75. The two essays are about religion in the antebellum women's rights movement and about modern Muslim women. The document concerns Muslim women. See Nancy Isenberg, "Women's Rights and the Politics of Church and State in Antebellum America," 124–30; Kathleen Moore, "Muslim Women, the Hijab, and Religious Liberty in Late-Twentieth-Century America," 505–10; and the primary document, "Asma Gull Hasan Comments on American Muslim Women Who Live 'Between Two Worlds,'" 492–93; all in *Major Problems in American Women's History*, ed. Mary Beth Norton and Ruth M. Alexander (Boston: Houghton Mifflin, 2003). On Mary Still, see ibid., 137.

76. Linda Kerber and Jane Sherron De Hart, eds., *Women's America: Refocusing the Past*, 5th ed. (New York: Oxford University Press, 2000); Glenda Riley, *Inventing the American Woman: An Inclusive History*, 3rd ed. (Wheeling, Ill.: Harlan Davidson, 2001); Sara M. Evans, *Born for Liberty: A History of Women in America* (New York: Free Press, 1989).

77. Virginia Sánchez Korrol, "In Search of Unconventional Women: Histories of Puerto Rican Women in Religious Vocations before Mid-Century," in *Unequal Sisters: A Multicultural Reader in U.S. Women's History*, ed. Ellen Carol DuBois and Vicki L. Ruiz (New York: Routledge, 1990), 322–32. In comparison, see Vicki Ruíz and Ellen Carol DuBois, eds., *Unequal Sisters: A Multicultural Reader in U.S. Women's History*, 2nd ed. (New York: Routledge, 1994); and Vicki Ruíz and Ellen Carol DuBois, eds., *Unequal Sisters: A Multicultural Reader in U.S. Women's History*, 3rd ed. (New York: Routledge, 2000).

78. Sklar, *Catharine Beecher: A Study in American Domesticity*; Barbara Welter, *Dimity Convictions: The American Woman in the Nineteenth Century* (Athens: Ohio University Press, 1976); Joan Jacobs Brumberg, *Mission for Life* (New York: Free Press, 1980); Jane Hunter, *The Gospel of Gentility: American Women Missionaries in Turn-of-the-Century China* (New Haven: Yale University Press, 1984); Nancy F. Cott, *The Bonds of Womanhood: "Woman's Sphere" in New England, 1780–1835*, 2nd ed. (New Haven: Yale University Press, 1997), 138.

79. Lerner, *The Grimké Sisters*; Nancy A. Hewitt, *Women's Activism and Social Change: Rochester, New York, 1822–1872* (Ithaca, N.Y.: Cornell University Press, 1984); Ruth Birgitta Anderson Bordin, *Woman and Temperance: The Quest for Power and Liberty, 1873–1900*, American Civilization (Philadelphia: Temple University Press, 1981); Bordin, *Frances Willard: A Biography*; Barbara Leslie Epstein, *The Politics of Domesticity: Women, Evangelism, and Temperance in Nineteenth-Century America* (Middletown, Conn.: Wesleyan University Press, 1981).

80. Focus on the Family was founded in 1977, the Moral Majority in 1979, and the Concerned Women of America in 1979.

81. Kathi Kern, *Mrs. Stanton's Bible* (Ithaca, N.Y.: Cornell University Press, 2001).

82. Jacqueline Jones, *Labor of Love, Labor of Sorrow: Black Women, Work, and the Family from Slavery to the Present* (New York: Basic Books, 1985); Ruth Milkman, *Women, Work, and Protest: A Century of U.S. Women's Labor History* (Boston: Routledge and Kegan Paul, 1985).

83. For one example, see Leslie J. Lindenauer, *Piety and Power: Gender and Religious Culture in the American Colonies, 1630–1700* (New York: Routledge, 2002). Troubled by stereotypes of early American Protestant women as "victims of a deeply ingrained patriarchy," Lindenauer presents an inflated argument about their religious power (p. xii).

84. Carolyn Chen, "A Self of One's Own: Taiwanese Immigrant Women and Religious Conversion," *Gender and Society* 19, no. 3 (2005): 336.

85. The phrase is R. Marie Griffith's. See R. Marie Griffith, "American Religious History and Women's Divides and Recent Developments," *Reviews in American History* 25, no. 2 (1997): 224.

86. Evans, *Born for Liberty*, 271.

87. Deborah Gray White, *Ar'n't I a Woman?: Female Slaves in the Plantation South*, 1st ed. (New York: Norton, 1985).

88. Susan Ware, *Modern American Women: A Documentary History*, 2nd ed. (New York: McGraw-Hill, 1997). Ware includes a document written by Frances Willard, the founder of the Woman's Christian Temperance Union, but the document is not about her religious convictions (pp. 15–18). For an excellent collection of essays that explores the persistence of religiosity among twentieth-century women, see Bendroth and Brereton, *Women and Twentieth-Century Protestantism.*

89. Darlene Clark Hine, *Black Women in America*, 2nd ed., 3 vols. (New York: Oxford University Press, 2005); Painter, *Sojourner Truth: A Life, a Symbol.*

90. Kern, *Mrs. Stanton's Bible*; Beryl Satter, *Each Mind a Kingdom: American Women, Sexual Purity, and the New Thought Movement, 1875–1920* (Berkeley: University of California Press, 1999).

91. For a critical approach to the category of "women," see Denise Riley, *"Am I That Name?" Feminism and the Category Of "Women" in History* (Minneapolis: University of Minnesota Press, 1988).

92. See the results of the 2004 General Social Survey, available on the National Opinion Research Center website: <http://www.norc.uchicago.edu>.

93. Susan Sleeper-Smith, "Women, Kin, and Catholicism: New Perspectives on the Fur Trade," *Ethnohistory* 47, no. 2 (2000): 423–52. Sleeper-Smith was responding to Richard White's influential book. See Richard White, *The Middle Ground: Indians, Empires, and Republics in the Great Lakes Region, 1650–1815* (New York: Cambridge University Press, 1991). In contrast to Sleeper-Smith, other historians have argued that native women who converted to Christianity lost their autonomy. See Karen L. Anderson, *Chain Her by One Foot: The Subjugation of Native Women in Seventeenth-Century New France* (New York: Routledge, 1993); Carol Devens, *Countering Colonization: Native American Women and Great Lakes Missions, 1630–1900* (Berkeley: University of California Press, 1992).

94. Rosemary Skinner Keller and Rosemary Radford Ruether, *In Our Own Voices: Four Centuries of American Women's Religious Writing*, 1st ed. (San Francisco: HarperSanFrancisco, 1995); Lindley, *You Have Stept Out of Your Place: A History of Women and Religion in America*; Rosemary Radford Ruether and Rosemary Skinner Keller, *Women and Religion in America: The Nineteenth Century*, 1st ed. (San Francisco: Harper and Row, 1981); Rosemary Radford Ruether and Rosemary Skinner Keller, *Women and Religion in America: The Colonial and Revolutionary Periods*, 1st ed. (San Francisco: Harper and Row, 1983); Rosemary Radford Ruether and Rosemary Skinner Keller, *Women and Religion in America: 1900–1968*, 1st ed. (San Francisco: Harper and Row, 1986).

95. Thomas A. Tweed, *The American Encounter with Buddhism, 1844–1912: Victorian Culture and the Limits of Dissent*, Religion in North America (Bloomington: Indiana University Press, 1992), 86. See also Thomas A. Tweed, "Inclusivism and the Spiritual Journey of Marie de Souza Canavarro (1849–1933)," *Religion* 24 (January 1994): 43–58.

96. Paul David Numrich, *Old Wisdom in the New World: Americanization in Two Immigrant Theravada Buddhist Temples*, 1st ed. (Knoxville: University of Tennessee Press, 1996), 146–47.

97. Wendy Cadge, *Heartwood: The First Generation of Theravada Buddhism in America* (Chicago: University of Chicago Press, 2005). For other studies of Buddhist women in the United States, see Sandy Boucher, *Turning the Wheel: American Women Creating the New Buddhism* (Boston: Beacon Press, 1993); Chen, "A Self of One's Own: Taiwanese Immigrant Women and Religious Conversion"; Richard Hughes Seager, *Buddhism in America*, Columbia Contemporary American Religion Series (New York: Columbia University Press, 1999), 185–200; Sharon A. Suh, *Being Buddhist in a Christian World: Gender and Community in a Korean American Temple* (Seattle: University of Washington Press, 2004); and Karma Lekshe Tsomo, *Buddhism through American Women's Eyes* (Ithaca, N.Y.: Snow Lion Publications, 1994).

98. For one example of an American-born convert who has been committed to transforming Buddhist practice in the United States, see Rita M. Gross, *Buddhism after Patriarchy: A Feminist History, Analysis, and Reconstruction of Buddhism* (Albany: State University of New York Press, 1993).

99. Gail Bederman, "'The Women Have Had Charge of the Church Work Long Enough': The Men and Religion Forward Movement of 1911–1912 and the Masculinization of Middle-Class Protestantism," in *A Mighty Baptism: Race, Gender, and the Creation of American Protestantism*, ed. Susan Juster and Lisa MacFarlane (Ithaca, N.Y.: Cornell University Press, 1996). *A Mighty Baptism* offers many excellent examples of how to use gender studies to approach American religious history.

100. Gayatri Chakrovorty Spivak, "Can the Subaltern Speak?" in *Marxism and the Interpretation of Culture*, ed. Cary Nelson and Larry Grossberg (Chicago: University of Illinois Press, 1988), 271–313. Michel de Certeau's focus on practices as the locus of resistance has been extraordinarily influential. See Michel de Certeau, *The Practice of Everyday Life* (Berkeley: University of California Press, 1984). In debates over women's agency, Judith Butler's concept of "citationality" has been especially important. In *Gender Trouble*, Butler argues that gender is an essentially unstable category that has to be constantly reproduced through performance. In her later book, *Bodies That Matter*, she uses the term "citationality" to emphasize the way that gender norms have to be constantly reiterated. The need for reiteration opens up the possibility—though not the guarantee—of subversion. See Judith Butler, *Bodies That Matter: On the Discursive Limits Of "Sex"* (New York: Routledge, 1993); and Butler, *Gender Trouble: Feminism and the Subversion of Identity*. Saba Mahmood has objected to Butler's understanding of agency as primarily resistance. See Mahmood, *Politics of Piety: The Islamic Revival and the Feminist Subject*. For a useful introduction to feminist understandings of power, see Amy Allen, *The Power of Feminist Theory: Domination, Resistance, Solidarity* (Boulder, Colo.: Westview Press, 1999).

101. Sandra M. Gustafson, *Eloquence Is Power: Oratory and Performance in Early America* (Chapel Hill: University of North Carolina Press, 2000).

102. Ahlstrom, *A Religious History of the American People*; Sydney E. Ahlstrom, *A Religious History of the American People*, 2nd ed. (New Haven: Yale University Press, 2004); Hudson, *Religion in America*; Hudson and Corrigan, *Religion in America: An Historical Account of the Development of American Religious Life*.

1

Puritan Women, Spiritual Power, and the Question of Sexuality

Marilyn J.
Westerkamp

In this chapter, Marilyn Westerkamp draws on the insights of both women's history and gender history to enrich our understanding of Puritanism, one of the most researched topics in American religious history. Since hundreds of books have been published about Puritan theology, politics, and piety, it may be hard to imagine that women's history can offer any new perspectives. But as Westerkamp shows, women's history adds new individuals and episodes to the history of Puritanism; it raises new questions about how Puritan theology shaped everyday life, including childrearing, family responsibilities, and death; it reveals that male clergy tried to establish orthodoxy by labeling witchcraft, heresy, and dissent as "feminine" deviance; and it leads scholars to central questions about religion, gender, and power.

When Perry Miller published *Orthodoxy in Massachusetts* (1936), followed by the breathtaking two-volume *New England Mind* (1939, 1956), he charted the course for Puritan studies and, in the process, transformed historical understanding of Puritan New England.[1] Before Miller, New England had been seen as an exceptional, unpleasant place characterized by intolerance, theocracy, and hypocrisy—the New England of Nathaniel Hawthorne's *Scarlet Letter.* Miller redeemed the Puritans and their colonies, reconstructing their worldview and their theology while recognizing their complexity, dedication, and focus upon the divine. Encountering anxious men seemingly plagued with ideological contradictions, Miller untangled the contradictions and argued that the Puritans' intellectual system was a logically constructed network of scientific, theological, and philosophical views. Miller's Puritans were men of high principle and commitment who strove to create a godly community in the New World.

Yes, Miller's Puritans were men. Very few women appeared in his narrative, his analysis, or his notes. In fact, when reading Miller's *New England Mind*, one gets the impression that women were singularly unimportant, even in crises that lesser scholars might argue revolved around women. In

Miller's productive years, when high school students read the literary canon, the best-known Puritan woman may indeed have been Hester Prynne. Of course, Anne Hutchinson ran a close second and Mary Dyer a distant third, followed by Anne Bradstreet, first published poet in British America, but judged sadly derivative and unimaginative. And, of course, there were Abigail Williams, Elizabeth Proctor, and Rebecca Nurse, all of whom, though actual persons, probably owed their fame to Arthur Miller's *The Crucible.*

Let me note, for the record, that in dealing with the Antinomian crisis of 1636–37, Miller preferred to focus upon four Johns and two Thomases,[2] rendering Hutchinson peripheral to an orthodoxy debate about salvation, free grace, and human endeavor. In his consideration of the 1650s and 1660s, when the Quakers, women and men, were undermining the strength of the magistracy, Miller devoted far greater attention to the Half-Way Covenant, a debate among the clergy about the terms of membership in the church. (To this day, many professors plague students with the esoterica surrounding the Half-Way Covenant while failing to notice that the Puritans actually tortured and executed Quakers during these same years.) Finally, Miller more or less ignored the shake-up of the 1690s, when several young women, with the assistance of their elders, managed to ignite a witch scare across Massachusetts during which 185 people were accused of witchcraft—26 were convicted, 19 were executed (most of them women), and 1 was pressed to death.

In this fashion Perry Miller set the agenda for understanding what was and was not significant to Puritan studies. With two possible exceptions, historians did not incorporate women into the story until the mid-1980s, when women's history finally reached back into the early centuries.[3] Thus at its most basic level, women's history has provided inclusivity. Anne Hutchinson, whose trials before the colonial assembly and the Church of Boston ended a major social, political, and theological conflict during the first decade of settlement, has returned to a central role in the story of the Antinomian crisis.[4] And Anne Bradstreet has been rediscovered and found to be more than a derivative and second-class poet. However, inclusion should take historians beyond some "great women" counterpoint. Consider, for example, the case of Marmaduke Mathews.

In May 1649, Marmaduke Mathews, minister at Hull, was called before the General Court of Massachusetts to answer for "severall erroneous expressions, others weake, inconvenient, and unsafe." Although admonished and officially separated from his congregation, Mathews continued preaching, using "other unsafe, offensive expressions." The government warned the congregation at Malden "not to proceed to the ordination of Mr. Mathewes . . . yett, contrary to all advice, and the rule of Gods word, as also the peace of the churches, the church of Malden hath proceeded to the ordination of Mr Mathewes." Two years later, the General Court, finding all parties recalcitrant, fined Mathews £10 and the town of Malden £50. In the end, Mathews did deliver some form of confession, not as complete as had been hoped, but accepted nonetheless. Neither fine, however, was remitted, for the court considered it had experienced a great amount of trouble clearing up this incident.[5] Compared with the magnitude of previous conflicts, this seems a minor incident. It is interesting that the town appears to have been in collusion with its heterodox minister—Malden, as well Mathews, was chastised. Also significant, however, is a petition from the women of Malden, who explained that "god in great mercie to our souls as we Trust hath after many prayers Indeavors & long wayting brought Mr. Mathews Among us & putt him into the worke of the Ministrie." Through his "pious life & labour the Lord hath Afforded [the town] Many Saving convictions . . . and Consolations."[6] The town had been spiritually bereft, the women shared the longing, and they claimed benefit from this minister, implicitly asserting their participation in the life of the congregation and the colony.

In all of its unimportance—just another tale of Massachusetts government trouncing upon a town of upstarts and asserting the right of the state to determine orthodoxy—this little story reveals a central feature of Puritanism, namely, the explicit involvement of women. While historians have found that from at least the seventeenth century onward women provided the core membership in most Christian organizations, the institutions themselves expected women to sit quietly in pews, to be guided by male ministers or priests and leading laymen. Women's beliefs and activities have been teased out of official minutes, texts, and reactions recorded by men. Among Puritans, however, women as individuals pursued their own spiritual journeys and participated in the life of their congregations. Although Puritan leaders certainly preferred that women sit quietly in the pews, and although Puritan women may have frequently spoken through husbands, fathers, or male church elders, they did sometimes speak for themselves, and their voices were heard and heeded.

This extension of spiritual power to women was a key aspect of Puritan culture. Mary Oliver, for example, was imprisoned, fined, put in stocks, and threatened with the whip before she was permitted to leave the colony forever. Initially cited for her complaints about church membership, later accusations included "contemning the ordinance of God" and proclaiming that the governor was unjust, corrupt, and a wretch. Rather than brush her off as an insignificant, middling-class woman, the magistrates issued increasingly harsh sentences as they failed to silence her criticisms or extricate themselves from her argument.[7] Anne Hutchinson caused a problem not because she spoke out and criticized the ministers, but because her spiritual gifts were recognized and admired, leading people, women and men, to grant her speech authority. Historians of women are becoming wary of what might be called the system's trap. Before reconstructing and analyzing the systematic efforts and strategies used by Puritan leaders to silence women like Hutchinson, historians must recognize that Hutchinson was making a lot of noise and attracting a significant following of men and women. Leaders did not simply excommunicate and ignore her; they acknowledged her power and demonstrated their own fear when they threw her out of the colony.

From this perspective, the inclusion of individual women in the historical reconstruction of Puritanism is essential if historians hope to comprehend the complexities of this spiritual movement. And historians might go further and investigate the nature of women's experiences as Puritans in more general terms. Turning to women in this way pushes scholars to envision Puritanism as multivalent at the popular level. Of course, for the past twenty years, historians have granted that Puritanism per se, even New England Puritanism, was not a monovocal system, but one comprising multiple theologies and practices that were debated and processed.[8] Women's religious history travels farther along this pathway. While scholars have found a gender dichotomization of spirituality to be increasingly simplistic, explorations of the experiences of women *as women* may provide alternative pieces of Puritan spirituality.

To explore such possibilities, what would happen if Anne Dudley Bradstreet displaced John Winthrop or Thomas Shepard as the quintessential Puritan? She, too, arrived on board the *Arbella* with Winthrop; she was the daughter of one governor and wife of another. She lived to be sixty and bore eight children; seven survived her. In Ipswich and, later, Andover, Massachusetts, she had responsibility for a large household of children and servants, often as the primary authority figure, since her husband was frequently absent from home serving in the colony assembly. Amid her ordinary duties, Bradstreet also composed an interesting sort of personal journal through poetry. One set of verses engaged conventional themes with conventional rhythms and language and was judged worthy of publication by contemporary standards. However, a second group, not intended for publication, contemplated the crises and blessings of her own life. Of a radically different quality and nature, these verses reflected a depth of emotion and personal engagement that made for intimate, touching, and, undoubtedly, better poetry. While it is unclear who the intended audience was—perhaps no one aside from herself—the verses read like spiritual self-reflection, not unlike the diaries of Michael Wigglesworth or Thomas Shepard. The texts enable historians to explore the particular anxieties and experiences of a Puritan woman through the prism of her religious world.

Bradstreet experienced complex, contradictory feelings over childbearing. While she undoubtedly participated in the gracious female community of birthing, she, like other women, grimly accepted the possibility of death. A woman might die giving birth to her first child, or a woman who had lived through eight pregnancies might not survive the ninth. Any woman facing childbirth was likely to have known more than one woman who had died giving birth.[9] Moreover, in the seventeenth century, most women had suffered the death of at least one infant, and some lost half their children at birth.[10] Healthy Puritans frequently spoke in general terms about death looming over everyone, but no healthy Puritan was more aware of mortality than an expectant woman. As she neared the end of one pregnancy, Bradstreet wrote a farewell poem to her husband.[11] In later poems she memorialized a daughter-in-law who died in childbirth as well as three grandchildren who died before reaching the age of four.

Within Bradstreet's mourning for her three-year-old grandchild, Anne, her grief is joined to guilt and self-recrimination at her own selfish sorrow.

> I knew she was but a withering flower,
> That's here today, perhaps gone in an hour; . . .
> More fool then I to look on that was lent
> As if mine own, when thus impermanent.

And again, she counters her own pain at the loss of her grandchild Elizabeth, aged eighteen months, with her ultimate Puritan faith.

> Blest babe, why should I once bewail thy fate,
> Or sigh thy days so soon were terminate,
> Sith thou art settled in an everlasting state.[12]

Among the most revealing of these poems on death is her memorial to her daughter-in-law, who died in childbirth. According to the poem, Mercy Bradstreet was twenty-eight; she had previously had four children, three of whom died. This fifth child died within a week of the mother's death. Bradstreet expressed grief for herself and her son, who "hath lost both tree and fruit." Yet the verses also reveal a cosmology that enabled her to process these losses. Mercy was at peace, "All freed from grief (I trust) among the blest;" and one child remained to bring joy and comfort. Bradstreet finished the poem with a faithful encouragement to her son to trust in God.

Cheer up, dear son, thy fainting bleeding heart,
In Him alone that caused all this smart;
What though thy strokes full sad and grievous be,
He knows it is the best for thee and me.[13]

Bradstreet's strong connection to her family was revealed in these private poems, more than half of which explicitly focused upon children, grandchildren, and her husband. Like Margaret Winthrop, whose letters always expressed acceptance of divine providence, Bradstreet tempered her love for spouse Simon with resignation to his magisterial duties and to God's will. But also like Winthrop, anxiety and longing came through: "If two be one, as surely thou and I, / How stayest thou there, whilst I at Ipswich lie?"[14] For as concerned as she was with her family, Bradstreet's writings did not neglect herself. Ten poems responded to her own illnesses, providing opportunities to explore not fears as much as the expectation of death and salvation. She lamented the pain and tedium of illness and regretted her husband's absence, "but my God, who never failed me, was not absent but helped me and graciously manifested his love to me."[15] Such trust in God is prevalent throughout these writings where complaints about sickness and hardship were balanced with an understanding of God's purpose in this providence: "[God] hath never suffered me long to sit loose from Him. . . . I have no sooner felt my heart out of order, but I have expected correction for it, which most commonly hath been upon my own person in sickness . . . sometimes on my soul, in doubts and fears of God's displeasure. . . . Sometimes He hath smote a child with a sickness, sometimes by losses in estate. . . . I have found them the times when the Lord hath manifested the most love to me."[16]

Bradstreet's theology explained hardships as trials, punishments, and gifts of grace that God sent even as he provided the strength and comfort to endure them. Here her relationship with God was that of a wayward and troubled child corrected and consoled by a nurturing parent. This paternal framework appeared more frequently than others did, perhaps because it was the one that best responded to afflictions. Still, there was an alternative image of God standing side by side with the other. Within the second construction, God moved as husband and lover, and the relationship was described as one of communion. "Thou art my Creator, I Thy creature, Thou my master, I Thy servant. But hence arises not my comfort, Thou art my Father, I Thy child . . . but lest this should not be enough, thy maker is thy husband. Nay more, I am a member of His body, He my head."[17] Bradstreet spoke not only of grace, faith, and assurance, but also of a personal relationship with God. She noted her confusion that she had not experienced the waves of assurance that conversion brought to many believers. She had "not found that constant joy in my pilgrimage and refreshing which I supposed most of the servants of God [had]," although she had, nonetheless, "some-times tasted of that hidden manna that the world knows not." Her love for God was such that she would endure hell itself in order to find it: "Were I in hell itself and could there find the love of God toward me, it would be a heaven."[18] She found comfort in her trust in God, looking toward the end of her life and her final union with God.

> Then soul and body shall unite
>   And of their Maker have the sight.
> Such lasting joys shall there behold
>   As ear ne'er heard nor tongue e'er told.
> Lord make me ready for that day,
>   Then come, dear Bridegroom, come away.[19]

Initially, Bradstreet's writings could be used to drop her into a simple place of separate spheres, where her acceptance of her fate as wife and mother and the importance of childbearing and childrearing could be said to mark her as a model woman. However, the understanding and acceptance of divine providence was a critical component in Puritan ideals, and while childbearing may have brought women into closer, more frequent touch with their own mortality, engaging suffering and death were central to Puritan theology. Furthermore, Bradstreet's dual understanding of God as Father and God as husband/lover was not unique to women. As Amanda Porterfield and I have argued elsewhere, this Puritan spirituality cuts across gender.[20] What Bradstreet provides for the historian is her incorporation of family life into her theology along with the spiritual significance of the hardships, irritations, and small blessings of daily life. The point is not that only women had homes and families, but that men, who shared those experiences, generally did not reconstruct their own spiritual journeys in such terms. Diarists such as Cotton Mather and Samuel Sewall wrote about their children; John Winthrop enjoyed intimately spiritual correspondence with his wife, Margaret; yet men's personal spiritual sagas seemed apart from such details. Placing Bradstreet at the center pushes historians to explore how Puritan religious culture affected the daily lives of all Puritans. The end result is not so much the identification of another branch of Puritanism—Separatists, Baptists, women —as the discovery of additional complexities within Puritan culture.

In asking questions about women's religious experience and participation in their congregational communities, historians are approaching larger questions of how lived experience vis-à-vis identity affected contemporary understandings of the natural and supernatural worlds. In the past twenty years, women's historians have elaborated upon their empirical findings about specific women as they incorporate gender into the analytical paradigm.[21] After all, women were more than men who bore children and tended the hearth; that is, women were more than the socioeconomic roles and legal restrictions that bound their lives. Was there some commonality in women's experiences that set them apart, as a group, from men? More important, when women and men shared common theologies and experiences, did their culture and ideology cause them to comprehend and respond to similar stimuli in different ways?

The incorporation of women pushes students of religion to explore different sets of questions that grow out of the intersection of theologies and praxes with the paradigms that constructed gender identity in those societies in which historically specific religious systems developed. Consider, for example, the problem of religious deviance, or heresy, within the Puritan community. When many intellectual historians have examined the problem of heresy, they focus upon the heretical idea itself, probing with greater or lesser finesse the complex nuances of the particular theological tenet at risk in relation to an established orthodoxy. More recently, some have challenged assumptions about a priori orthodoxy as a foundation against which a heresy could be defined, seeing instead a dialectical relationship between heresy and orthodoxy.[22]

When women's historians confront the problem of female heretics, their analysis incorporates a range of social and cultural factors that extends beyond the intricacies of a history of ideas. The very definition of orthodoxy takes on a gendered emphasis, since a female heretic would be defined as a woman who dissents not from a politically neutral orthodoxy but from an orthodoxy established by male leaders. Occasionally, the appropriate fit of this definition was explicitly demonstrated by the reaction of Puritan leaders, ministers, and magistrates, who connected these women's ideological sins with gender transgressions. From what historians can garner from the documents in the Hutchinsonian controversy, Anne Hutchinson's "blasphemous" beliefs were not much different from those of John Cotton, something that deeply disturbed clergy and magistrates. (The clerics devoted much energy to convincing Cotton of their arguments or, alternatively, to accommodating their beliefs to Cotton.) It was Hutchinson's daring to lead private prayer/study groups in her home and her criticizing of most of the colony ministers that ignited the fury of colony leaders. These were the charges brought against her at her trial before the General Court. She herself, before the court, did proclaim her revelation, opening a theological debate that could not be settled since John Cotton would not issue a simplistic denunciation of her claims. In the end, she was banished for sedition, a charge proved only through the sworn testimony of her clerical accusers turned witnesses. Theological charges concerning her beliefs were left to a trial before the Boston Church held four months later, after she had been banished by the state. Yet even in the midst of this examination about Hutchinson's questionable theology, Hugh Peters concluded that she had "rather bine a Husband than a Wife and a preacher than a Hearer; and a Magistrate than a Subject."[23]

Yet the issue was more complicated than a woman's failure to subject herself to male authority. Puritan authors also connected heresy with sexual transgressions and sexual transgressions with women. In lamenting women's proclivity to "take up errors," one Puritan writer noted that "women are more easily seduced than men, and have their judgments first, and soonest poysoned."[24] Once seduced into error, women became leaders of factions, promoting heresy; women proved unreachable by the calm voice of reason because they were governed by their overwhelming emotions. "Passion and Affection in [women] either in love or hatred, is much more extream and violent then in Men."[25] While women were frequently portrayed as pitiable and weak, the language of passion moved the discussion in a malevolent direction. Seduction followed seduction naturally, and the seduced became the seducer, reproducing wickedness and heresy across the landscape. For example, in response to Hutchinson's questioning a doctrine about the resurrection of the body, John Cotton expostulated with Hutchinson about "that filthie Sinne of the Comunitie of Woemen and all promiscuus and filthie cominge togeather of men and Woemen without Distinction or Relation of Marriage, will necessarily follow." He continued his admonishment, with absolutely no evidence: "And though I have not herd, nayther do I thinke, you have bine unfaythfull to your Husband in his Marriage Covenant, *yet that will follow upon it*."[26]

This same language of illicit sexuality and sexual metaphor was employed in describing witches, the ultimate blasphemers and heretics. Witches were said to have been seduced by the devil, and contemporary engravings from the continent portray witches copulating with Satan. Witches had special teats that were sucked by demons or familiars, providing nourishment for the familiar and/or sexual pleasure for the witch. These excrescences were often found near the breasts and genitals, as in the case of Margaret Jones, who was discovered to have a "teat in her secret parts as fresh as if it had been newly sucked"; a later search revealed that it had withered, and "another began on the opposite side." Further, while she was in prison, she had been seen sitting on the floor, "her clothes up."[27] The confluence in people's minds between deviant sexuality and witchcraft appears in the fact that many women who were accused of witchcraft in New England had been previously convicted of sexual crimes.[28]

This linguistic and cultural turn, and its full implications, can only be understood in terms of the ideological construction of gender. Within seventeenth-century old and New England, medical and theological writers found a link between womanhood and sexuality. Sexuality was attached to femaleness, so that woman, as a category, was sexualized, and women were perceived as highly charged, sexually unstable persons requiring strict control.[29] Just as witchcraft was, in one sense, illicit relations with the devil, heresy became an uncontrolled intellectual whoring. The English congregation leader Susanna Parr, for example, was excommunicated from her church, a community that she and seven others founded, because she began to attend sermons at a nearby church. Her transgression, in simple terms, involved dissenting from her minister. She explained that "*I* did delight in the image of God where ever *I* found it." Her minister's response was that she "might as well delight in another man that was not my husband, because the Image of God shined more in him then in my husband."[30] The perhaps unconscious implication that a believer's relationship with her pastor included sexual elements is illuminating. Just as husbands must guide and restrict their wives' physical passions, pastors had the responsibility of maintaining women's spiritual purity.[31] In other words, not only were women spiritually at risk because they were intellectually weak, petty, and vain, but also because they were afflicted with the moral weakness and depravity that went with being oversexed. Such illicit passion and lack of control led women into sexual and theological sin, so that women were more likely than men to be heretics. With Puritan authors complaining of women "gadding about" after false preachers, heresy became a feminine crime.

The gendering of witchcraft and heresy, and the idea that such ideological deviance was directly related to sexual excess, enables historians to perceive the embodiment of religion. Seventeenth-century culture worked to establish a kind of dualistic, analogical relationship between female/male, human/divine, body/soul—a series that might be extended to evil/good, diabolical/divine. In the cross-pollination of language employed by establishment clerics concerning female dissenters, believers' relationships with the supernatural were inscribed upon the body. Women's inclination toward blasphemy was matched biologically by the production of "monster births." A common and extremely popular subject for the penny press, such accounts, whether broadsides or octavo booklets, generally included a picture and always a lurid, detailed description.[32] When Mary Dyer and Anne Hutchinson both suffered childbirth tragedies, New England leaders had no difficulty interpreting these as the products of their heresies.[33] While Cotton saw the still-birth of Dyer's malformed child as a private rebuke for the parents, John Winthrop discovered public evidence of divine displeasure of both parents, "the highest forme of our refined Familists," and midwife, "notorious for her familiarity with the devill, and now a prime Familist."[34] After Hutchinson had been banished to Rhode Island, she was reported to have given birth to some thirty monsters, for "as she had vented mishapen opinions, so she must bring forth deformed monsters." These were judgments, to be sure, but they were punishments growing out of their corrupted femaleness. Both women produced, "out of their wombs, as before they had out of their braines, such monstrous births as no Chronicle (I thinke) hardly every recorded."[35] Yet it should be added that even without much effort, a woman's body represented the pollution of evil. Minister Peter Bulkeley once asserted that the damned "are to [God] as the filthiness of a menstruous woman."[36]

The simplest reading of these vituperative texts about two women's trage-dies reveals that gendering religious deviance worked to disempower dissent-ing women. Dissent was a central facet of Puritan identity. During the fifty years that preceded the migration to New England, Puritans developed pride in their differences with the established Anglican Church. Tolerated during Elizabeth's reign, Puritans had seen an increase in strictures and penalties following the accession of James I. They came to shun government inter-ference in religion and to despise the state church and its bishops. Puritan resistance included private prayer and Bible study meetings led, in the ab-sence of acceptable clergymen, by laymen and laywomen who came to be recognized for their wisdom and piety. John Winthrop, it will be recalled, was a layman, and yet he delivered a sermon on board the *Arbella* before the pas-sengers disembarked. Nevertheless, in Massachusetts, most clergymen would have been sympathetic to Puritan polity, theology, and piety. The need for lay leadership to support and maintain the community lost some of its urgency, and Puritan leaders found themselves with the unenviable task of enforcing a uniform political and religious system in a society populated by deeply re-ligious individuals accustomed to following their own ways. In pursuit of the work of establishing orthodoxy, magistrates and ministers found the tools of gender politics extremely helpful. While Puritan religiosity may have opened pathways for charismatic women to assume spiritual leadership, traditional, biblically grounded patriarchal structures provided the means by which male leaders could restrict or even discount female dissenters. Moreover, when confronted with male dissenters, leaders might, as they did with male Quak-ers in the 1650s, ascribe to them effeminate characteristics and thus weaken any Quaker claim to religious authority.

Pursuing the question of gender beyond the issue of dissent and control opens interesting insights into Puritan spirituality. The writings of Bradstreet portray a God who is gendered male. Sometimes he was the father; sometimes the bridegroom. When believers interacted with God the father, they retained their gender identities as sons or daughters, and the perception of self might have been affected by perceived likeness to God. A man could be seen to have more of the image of God, to be more godlike, in the same way that sons identified with fathers, reinforcing the dualistic cosmology that placed divine/human against male/female. However, when God was the bridegroom, the believer, whether a man or a woman, was gendered female in relation to the male God, and rather than striving to uncover the image of God in the soul, a believer sought union with God.

Puritan theologians had argued that women were weak, passionate, sexual; women were first seduced, and then they seduced others. The construction of the witch as one who had carnal relations with Satan, producing imps and familiars that sucked nourishment from the witches' teats, represented only the extreme end of a cosmology that conflated sexuality with evil. Yet Anne Bradstreet's longing for her Bridegroom revealed the sexualized character of the believer's relationship with God—heterosexual, even marital sexuality—but unarguably sexual. Puritans often invoked the erotic language of the *Song of Solomon,* the Old Testament love poem that described the "love of Jesus Christ, the true Salomon and King of peace, and the faithful soule." John Cotton had delivered (and published) a series of sermons upon these canticles, using the sensuous language as a means of enticing his listeners toward God. Thomas Hooker assured believers that they were spouses of Christ, while Thomas Shepard longed to accept Christ as "Lord and Savior and Husband."[37] Similarly, Anne Hutchinson heard the "voice of my beloved," while other women wrote that they took "delight in the Image of God," and that "his Spirit . . . has stirred me up. My heavenly bridegroom is come."[38] The most graphic, illuminating example of such emotional outpourings remains the poetry of Edward Taylor who, in his meditations upon Canticles, recorded his experience of the excitement and joys of spirituality as the thrills and pleasures of marital sexuality.

> Thy Saving Grace my Wedden Garment make:
> Thy Spouses Frame into my Soul Convay.
> I then shall be thy Bride Espousd by thee
> And thou my Bridesgroom Deare Espousde shalt bee.[39]

The language of father/child gives a sense of the comfort and security that believers experienced in their relationship with God. The language of bridegroom and beloved suggests the excitement and personal power that Puritans found there.

In the end, the incorporation of women and their experiences leads historians to central questions about religion and power, not only the power of religion in a society but also the workings of power within religious systems. Until the last twenty-five years, religious history generally addressed church institutions, heroic clerics, and elite theology. However, with the onset of the new social history, historians of religion have devoted serious attention to the people in the pews. While social historians frequently argued that religion exercised a hegemonic control over its adherents, some historians of religion became unbelievably romantic. Religion became the force empowering individuals, enabling believers to come into their own identity and express their own voices, revealing to historians the ways that people determined their own destinies. Puritanists have been assisted in this task by the scholarship of exemplary social historian Christopher Hill, whose extensive incorporation of sectarian religion as a primary tool of the common people has transformed the historiography of the English Civil War. Historians have granted that Puritanism, as a religious system that emphasized the individual's relationship with God, united and energized the rising mercantile and gentry classes. Hill and his colleagues have demonstrated that radical religion reached below the new bourgeoisie to the middling and lower sorts.[40] Most recently, women's historians have extended these same expectations to women and have searched the archives for connections between Puritan radicalism and women's voices and agency.[41]

The examination of Puritan women requires that questions about power be attacked at multiple levels. Some explicitly involved sexual politics, although it does not follow that other inequalities fell outside a gender paradigm. The consideration of class separately from gender, for example, is a mistake. Not only do both groups fall within the broad political language of disfranchised populations, but also sexualized language was a key rhetoric used to discount the lower classes. Pamphlets decrying radical sects often expressed outrage at the presence of "women and mechanick" preachers, lumping together two groups that appear to historians so manifestly different. Moreover, such pamphlets often described the lower classes as vulgar, uncontrolled, irrational, and oversexed or sexually deviant—in essence portraying them as women.

If power is first understood as the endowment of personhood, or, in current parlance, subjectivity, then the historian must ask: did a woman have the ability to control her own ideas and make decisions based upon her own knowledge, beliefs, and desires? Did she find within herself the strength and authority to think and to speak? This is difficult to consider since individuals were trained to accept and enjoy roles prescribed by the literature and enforced by law and custom. To some extent, the ability of an individual to choose a pathway different from the prescription reveals the possibilities for selfhood. In crafting and publishing her poetry, Anne Bradstreet, who in other ways demonstrates the ideal characteristics of a Puritan woman, challenges expectations and thus provides evidence of some ownership of her ideas and voice. Her decision to articulate publicly her thoughts, feelings, and insights stands out in a society in which many women appeared unable, even though asked, to testify to their experience of the spirit.[42] Anne Hutchinson, Mary Oliver, and Lady Deborah Moody, a Baptist who voluntarily left the colony rather than submit to its orthodoxy, all reflected Puritan women's capacity to develop and follow their own theological visions.

Mary Dyer stands out as an example of independent self-fashioning: one who found in herself and her relationship with the Holy Spirit the authority to find her own truth and proclaim it. At a fairly young age she arrived in Massachusetts with her husband, William, and joined the many Bostonians who attended Hutchinson's meetings. In the winter following Hutchinson's banishment, Dyer's pregnancy ended in the stillbirth of a severely deformed child. Although John Cotton interpreted this special providence to the parents as a divine rebuke, Dyer remained loyal to her wayward dissent, accompanying Hutchinson as she left the Boston congregation following her excommunication. Like many Hutchinsonians, the Dyers left Massachusetts for Rhode Island, and Mary Dyer disappeared from the public sphere for twenty years. In 1657, she returned from a five-year sojourn in England, where she discovered and joined the Quakers. Upon her return to New England, her ship landed in Boston, and, although she had intended to go directly to Rhode Island, she was arrested and imprisoned along with other Quakers on board. She was later released to join her husband in Newport, only to return to Massachusetts to support Quaker efforts there and, eventually, suffer imprisonment and death.

A second conception of power involves the exercise of influence or authority within a community. The source of such power is external to the self, ascribed to the individual by the group, but it does not include the capacity to act through official or institutional channels. In particular it does not grant the individual authority over those who are not members of the group. Here is the phenomenon of charisma, identifiable usually because of the numbers of people attracted by it. Since Puritan spirituality privileged the connection of the Holy Spirit to individual souls, the space for charisma was enormous. During the 1630s, Roger Williams is known to have had a pied piperish ethos surrounding him, with any community he entered immediately surrendering itself to him.[43] Anne Hutchinson held some of that same power, with significant numbers of neighbors, friends, and acquaintances following her lead. Dyer's experiences did not reflect this same level of positive influence, although other New England Quakers, women as well as men, were quite successful in attracting followers and building a Quaker community despite the hostility of the colonial governments.[44]

Yet another aspect of power is that of the individual in relation to the state and, by extension among Puritans, the institutional church. Within this arena, the voices of women are carefully restricted and their authority explicitly contained if not denied. The women in Marmaduke Mathews's congregation judged themselves authorized and able to express their approbation of Mathews, and the congregation included the women's petition in their testimonies before the General Court. Yet the court discounted this petition, as they rejected all the pleas of the town in their review of Mathews and the town of Malden. Anne Hutchinson's activities undermined the work of the clergy, and for that reason she was called into theological discussions with them, a tacit acknowledgment of her influence among Bostonians. However, the clergy were outraged that she, a layperson and a woman, dared to challenge their effectiveness and their theological expertise. When John Winthrop brought her before the General Court, she was charged with dishonoring her parents, vis-à-vis the governors. While intriguing layers of spiritual authority, sexual politics, and Puritan theology intersected in a display of unbounded opportunities for charismatic women, the end result was the clear denial of a woman's right to follow such opportunities in opposition to institutionalized leadership.

Mary Dyer's confrontations with the Massachusetts government ended in the same demonstration. For fifteen years after she and Hutchinson had left Massachusetts, Dyer remained quietly in Rhode Island or England. Following her return to Newport by way of Boston and her imprisonment for Quakerism, Dyer took on an activist career. In 1658 she traveled as an itinerant to the New Haven colony, only to be expelled. In September 1659 she returned to Boston to visit Quakers in prison; she was banished again, upon threat of execution. She returned in October, was sentenced to hang, and was reprieved from the scaffold. Unwilling to accept a reprieve while her colleagues suffered, she returned to Boston, and in May 1660 she was executed. Growing out of her own sense of spiritual power, Dyer challenged with her voice and her presence the right of the state to torture, banish, and execute Quakers. Yet, in a supreme exercise of its power, the state denied Dyer's right to speak and act, first through words and decisions of banishment, then through violence. Like Hutchinson's banishment, Dyer's death seems a final demonstration of ultimate power.

What about the power to disrupt, to force the state to pay attention, to thoroughly undermine the state's ability to control the community, to cause laws to be changed? This last power is deeply important to historians of all disfranchised groups, and historians of women have especially pursued these themes. At a basic level, one might say that Mary Dyer demonstrated, at the end of her life, the ability and power to choose death. However, in exercising that choice, she upset the carefully balanced authority exercised by colonial magistrates. When Hutchinson was banished, she departed and stayed away from Massachusetts, thus acknowledging the government's power over her life and liberty. In returning to the colony despite whippings and banishment, Dyer and other Quakers declared that the state had no right to control their travel, their activities, or their persons. In denying the rightful authority of the state, in challenging the government to mete out the physical brutality that had been threatened by returning after banishment, the Quakers demonstrated the inability of the magistrates to control the colony through consensus, intimidation, or force. In fact, when Quakers brought the four executions of Quakers to the attention of King Charles II in 1662, the king ordered Massachusetts to stop its brutalities. In her death, Dyer and three fellow sufferers became the means by which the king was convinced to interfere with Massachusetts's treatment of Quakers and, by extension, dissenters.

How does the inclusion of Mary Dyer's story change the history of Puritanism in New England? At its most basic, I believe that the fact of Mary Dyer's execution brought the Quaker crisis into the history of New England Puritanism. Williams, Hutchinson, and the Quakers were not the only dissenters in seventeenth-century New England. Yet very few students know about the behavior of Samuel Gorton, disturber of the peace of Rhode Island and Plymouth as well as Massachusetts, or about the Baptists. The presence of Mary Dyer, through her connection with the original female heretic Hutchinson, has brought notoriety to the Quakers. In fact, the presence of charismatic women within the Quaker movement has created a narrative of Quaker exceptionalism in which Quaker men disappear from the story. Dyer's death has masked the fact that three men were executed, and that two of these men were grievously tortured before they were killed. Ironically, the study of Mary Dyer has also made known the sufferings of her male compatriots.

The application of gender analysis to the Quaker crisis also provides an illuminating example of the employment of feminization to disfranchise an effective group of leaders. As an unacceptable, deviant community, Quakers were gendered feminine, and many of the strategies employed by Puritan leaders used the dismissive language of gender. The Quakers were a disreputable sect because a significant number of members were women, because women were permitted to speak in meetings, even preach, and because Quaker men refused to discipline, to denounce, to dominate those women. At their core, Quakers rejected what they called the artificial hierarchies of rank, class, education, and gender that established lines of authority. When Quaker women assumed the male role of preaching, the fact that they were permitted, even encouraged to leave their husbands and children to missionize demonstrated to Puritans that Quakers had rejected the sanctity of marriage and the family. As with Hutchinson, who was warned that it was only a matter of time before she committed adultery, and with many accused witches who were known to be women of questionable character, Puritans argued that Quaker beliefs and practices led naturally to sexual licentiousness.[45] The first two Quakers who disembarked in Boston in 1656 were women, and they were immediately imprisoned and searched for witch's marks.

Perhaps more significantly, feminization did not solve the magistrates' problems. Quakers continued to come into the colony, and residents continued to join the movement. The increasingly harsh response of the colonial government (it continued to make up more laws and add more severe penalties until stopped by the intervention of the king) reflected the frustration of leaders at their own ineffectiveness. Magistrates expected obedience and respect for authority and found themselves caught in an escalating battle of mental toughness with a religious group of men and women who denied the basic structures of the social order. In the end, communities of Quakers remained in Massachusetts, virtually ignored by a government unable to oust or control them.

Indeed, women's history has changed the history of Puritanism by adding not only individuals but also significant episodes to the narrative. While historians have generally seen the Antinomian controversy as a central moment in New England's religious and political history, women's historians have reclaimed the importance of Anne Hutchinson. Moreover, with the recovery of the religious witness of Mary Dyer, Puritanists have incorporated the Quaker persecutions into the narrative. Anne Bradstreet supplies a portrait of Puritan piety that points historians toward the family and interpersonal relationships as formative systems in the creation of a believer's spirituality. The very presence of women among the spiritual leaders in New England alters the overall characterization of Puritanism itself, since it underscores the egalitarian thrust of its radical religiosity.

This reconfiguration of Puritan studies to include all believers opens other ways of envisioning the dynamics of religious groups. Women's history demands that historians ask questions about the construction of gender and the political and social realities of women's lives and in relation to the religious community. Because the nature of gender as conceived in the seventeenth century is so strongly connected to sexuality, historians have turned to an analysis of religious culture, sexuality, and the body. This is perhaps not an unexpected development, since historians of religion, in their explorations of asceticism, were among the earliest scholars to engage the history of the body.[46] In exploring the ideological categories of gender and the body in relation to Puritan cosmology and theology, historians have been able to elaborate the nature of the believer's spiritual journey in relation to a God that was gendered male.

Finally, by incorporating groups that are almost guaranteed to be unequal, women's history forces historians away from any inclination to sentimental-ize religion and to consider instead the multiple relationships of power inher-ent in any religious system. The ability of a Hutchinson to garner a massive following must be balanced against her ultimate inability to act out her leadership in the face of the church and the state. Nevertheless, the examples of women's participation and achievements also offer historians a new appre-ciation for that power to disrupt, challenge, and transform through resis-tance. Puritanism was, after all, a culture of dissent. The incredible power of that piety has been revealed through the women.

Notes

1. Perry Miller, *Orthodoxy in Massachusetts, 1630–1650: A Genetic Study* (Cam-bridge: Harvard University Press, 1933); Perry Miller, *The New England Mind*, 2 vols. (Cambridge: Harvard University Press, 1939, 1956).
2. John Winthrop, John Cotton, John Wilson, John Wheelwright, Thomas Shepard, and Thomas Hooker.
3. The two exceptions are Edmund S. Morgan, *The Puritan Family: Essays on Reli-gion and Domestic Relations in Seventeenth-Century New England* (1944; New York: Harper and Row, 1966); and Emery Battis, *Saints and Sectaries: Anne Hutch-inson and the Antinomian Controversy in the Massachusetts Bay Colony* (Chapel Hill: University of North Carolina Press, 1962).
4. Incidentally, the old paradigm still flourishes. The most recent scholarly treatment of the Antinomian crisis returns, in its emphasis upon theology, to a primary engagement with male leaders and thinkers. See Michael Winship, *Making Here-tics: Militant Protestantism and Free Grace in Massachusetts, 1636–1641* (Princeton, N.J.: Princeton University Press, 2002).
5. Nathaniel G. Shurtleff, ed., *Records of the Governor and Company of the Mas-sachusetts Bay in New England*, 5 vols. (Boston: William White, 1853), 3:158–59;

4:21; 4:42–43; 4:71; 4:90. Marmaduke Mathews response to accusations, May 26, 1651; letter from Mathews to General Court, June 13, 1651, Massachusetts State Archives.

6. Petition from the women of Malden to the General Court, October 28, 1651, Massachusetts State Archives.

7. John Winthrop, *Winthrop's Journal, "History of New England," 1630–1649*, ed. James Kendall Hosmer, 2 vols. (New York, 1908), 1:281–82.

8. See, for example, Philip F. Gura, *A Glimpse of Sion's Glory: Puritan Radicalism in New England, 1620–1660* (Middletown, Conn.: Wesleyan University Press, 1984).

9. See Laurel Thatcher Ulrich, *Good Wives: Image and Reality of the Lives of Women in Northern New England, 1650–1750* (New York: Oxford University Press, 1980), 126–45, for a good discussion of pregnancy, labor, and women's rituals surrounding birthing during the late seventeenth and early eighteenth centuries. John Demos, *A Little Commonwealth: Family Life in Plymouth Colony* (New York: Oxford University Press, 1970), and Philip Greven, *Four Generations: Population, Land, and Family in Colonial Andover* (Ithaca, N.Y.: Cornell University Press, 1970), 27, 100, both suggest that the number of women who died in childbirth in Plymouth and Andover, respectively, was as high as 20 percent.

10. For example, Hannah Sewall bore fourteen children and lost seven in infancy. Bradstreet was fortunate, with all children surviving infancy and only one predeceasing her.

11. Anne Bradstreet, "Before the Birth of One of Her Children," in *The Works of Anne Bradstreet*, ed. Jeannine Hensley (Cambridge: Harvard University Press, 1967), 224.

12. Bradstreet, "In Memory of My Dear Grandchild Anne Bradstreet," *Works*, 236; "In Memory of My Dear Grandchild Elizabeth Bradstreet," *Works*, 235.

13. Ibid., "In Memory of My Dear Daughter-in-Law, Mrs. Mercy Bradstreet . . . ," 238–39.

14. Ibid., "A Letter to Her Husband, Absent upon Public Employment," 226.

15. Ibid., "Meditations When My Soul Hath Been Refreshed," 251.

16. Ibid., "To My Dear Children," 241–42.

17. Ibid., "Meditations," 250.

18. Ibid., "To My Dear Children," 243.

19. Ibid., "As Weary Pilgrim," 295.

20. Amanda Porterfield, *Female Piety in Puritan New England: The Emergence of Religious Humanism* (New York: Oxford University Press, 1992); Marilyn J. Westerkamp, "Engendering Puritan Religious Culture in Old and New England," *Pennsylvania History* 64 (1997): 105–22.

21. An early articulation of the possibilities of such analysis is Joan Wallach Scott, "Gender: A Useful Category of Historical Analysis," in her *Feminism and History* (New York: Oxford University Press, 1996), 152–80. The essay was first published in 1986. Some excellent examples of the application of gender analysis to religious history of early America include Porterfield, *Female Piety in Puritan New En-*

gland; Elizabeth Reis, *Damned Women: Sinners and Witches in Early New England* (Ithaca, N.Y.: Cornell University Press, 1997); Susan Juster, *Disorderly Women: Sexual Politics and Evangelicalism in Revolutionary New England* (Ithaca, N.Y.: Cornell University Press, 1994); and Jane Kamensky, *Governing the Tongue: The Politics of Speech in Early New England* (New York: Oxford University Press, 1997).

22. Analysts of Puritan heresy owe a debt to Kai T. Erikson, *Wayward Puritans: A Study in the Sociology of Deviancy* (New York: John Wiley, 1966). Historians who have questioned the assumption of a single, accepted orthodoxy include Gura, *Glimpse of Sion's Glory*, and Stephen Foster, *The Long Argument: English Puritanism and the Shaping of New England Culture, 1570–1700* (Chapel Hill: University of North Carolina Press, 1991), both of whom argue for a range of Puritan theologies growing out of the variation among English Puritans. Janice Knight, *Orthodoxies in Massachusetts: Rereading American Puritanism* (Cambridge: Harvard University Press, 1994), challenges the concept of a single orthodoxy in her outline of two separate, parallel systems.

23. "A Report of the Trial of Mrs. Anne Hutchinson before the Church of Boston," March 1638, in *The Antinomian Controversy: A Documentary History, 1636–1638*, ed. David D. Hall (Middletown, Conn.: Wesleyan University Press, 1968), 383.

24. John Elborow, *Evodias and Syntyche: or, the Female Zealots of the Church of Philippi* (London, 1637), 4.

25. William Hill, *A New-Years Gift for Women Being a True Looking-Glass* (London, 1660), 41.

26. "A Report of the Trial of Mrs. Anne Hutchinson before the Church of Boston," 372. The nature and implications of the mortalist heresy, i.e., the denial of the resurrection of the body after death, is fully explored in James Fulton Maclear, "Anne Hutchinson and the Mortalist Heresy," *New England Quarterly* 54 (1981): 74–103. The documents that we have, accounts of the trial before the General Court as well as clerical correspondence and records of synods at which clergy and Hutchinson discussed theology in 1636, do not indicate that this heresy, or other errors noted at the church trial, had been an issue. These questions appear to have been raised with Hutchinson while she was held under virtual house arrest in the home of a clergyman until winter's end, so that she would not need to travel in unseasonable weather.

27. Winthrop, *Winthrop's Journal*, June 4, 1649, 2:344.

28. Carol Karlsen, *The Devil in the Shape of a Woman: Witchcraft in Colonial New England* (New York: Norton, 1987), 134–41.

29. One of the best discussions of the scientific construction of gender in the seventeenth century is Thomas Laqueur, *Making Sex: The Body and Gender from the Greeks to Freud* (Cambridge: Harvard University Press, 1990), 114–92. See also Phyllis Mack, *Visionary Women: Ecstatic Prophecy in Seventeenth-Century England* (Berkeley: University of California Press, 1992), 15–86.

30. Susanna Parr, *Susanna's Apology against the Elders* (1659), 25. Parr continued in her text with her outrage at such "grosse" discussion.

31. The sexual overtones of the pastor/congregant relationship are beyond the scope of this chapter. Karin Gedge's work explores some of the implications of this dynamic in the nineteenth century. Karin E. Gedge, *Without Benefit of Clergy: Women and the Pastoral Relationship in Nineteenth-Century American Culture* (New York: Oxford University Press, 2003).

32. Katharine Park and Lorraine J. Daston, "Unnatural Conceptions: The Study of Monsters in Sixteenth- and Seventeenth-Century England and France," *Past and Present* 92 (1981): 20–54; David D. Hall, *Worlds of Wonder, Days of Judgment: Popular Religious Belief in Early New England* (Cambridge: Harvard University Press, 1990), 71–116. See Tessa Watt, *Cheap Print and Popular Piety, 1550–1640* (New York: Cambridge University Press, 1991), 124, 143, 165, 288, on the popularity of this subject in the popular press in England.

33. Anne Jacobson Schutte, "'Such Monstrous Births': A Neglected Aspect of the Antinomian Controversy," *Renaissance Quarterly* 38 (1985): 85–106. A detailed discussion of Dyer's and Hutchinson's births can be found on pp. 90–91 nn. 13, 14.

34. John Winthrop, "A Short Story of the Rise, Reign, and Ruine of the Antinomians, Familists & Libertines," in Hall, *The Antinomian Controversy*, 281. Medical historians have judged the graphic description to be consistent with severe spina bifida. See Battis, *Saints and Sectaries*, 346–48.

35. Thomas Weld, "Preface" to Winthrop, "A Short Story of the Rise, Reign, and Ruine of the Antinomians, Familists & Libertines," in Hall, *The Antinomian Controversy*, 214. Hutchinson's tragedy is thought to have been the expulsion of a tumor rather than a birth.

36. Peter Bulkeley, *The Gospel Covenant or the Covenant of Grace Opened* (London, 1651).

37. Introduction to "An Excellent Song Which Was Salomons," *Geneva Bible*, facsimile edition, ed. Lloyd E. Berry (Madison: University of Wisconsin Press, 1969); John Cotton, *A Brief Exposition with Practical Observations upon the Whole Book of Canticles* (London, 1655); Thomas Hooker, *The Unbelievers Preparation for Christ* (London, 1638), 72; Thomas Shepard, *God's Plot: The Paradoxes of Puritan Piety, Being the Autobiography & Journal of Thomas Shepard*, ed. Michael McGiffert (Amherst: University of Massachusetts Press, 1972), 45. Porterfield, *Female Piety in Puritan New England*, has identified a superfluity of these sexual allusions in the writings of Cotton, Hooker, and Shepard.

38. Winthrop, "A Short Story of the Rise, Reign, and Ruine of the Antinomians, Familists & Libertines," in Hall, *The Antinomian Controversy*, 273; also quoted in "Examination of Hutchinson," in ibid., 337; Parr, *Susanna's Apology against the Elders*, 21; and Anne Wentworth, *A Vindication of Anne Wentworth* (London, 1677), 9, similar reference on 4.

39. Edward Taylor, "Meditation. Cant. 4.8. My Spouse," in *The Poems of Edward Taylor* (New Haven: Yale University Press, 1960), 39.

40. See, for example, Christopher Hill, *The World Turned Upside-Down: Radical Ideas during the English Revolution* (New York: Viking, 1972). Historians pursuing the

connection between radical religion and class unrest include Arthur L. Morton, *The World of the Ranters: Religious Radicalism in the English Revolution* (London: Lawrence and Wishart, 1970); B. S. Capp, *The Fifth Monarchy Men* (London: Faber, 1972); J. F. McGregor and Barry Reay, eds., *Radical Religion in the English Revolution* (New York: Oxford University Press, 1984); Barry Reay, *The Quakers and the English Revolution* (London: Temple Smith, 1985); and Jerome Friedman, *Blasphemy, Immorality, and Anarchy: The Ranters and the English Revolution* (Athens: Ohio University Press, 1987).

41. Although most of the work is still in essays, book-length studies include Patricia Crawford, *Women and Religion in England, 1500–1720* (London: Routledge, 1993); Mack, *Visionary Women*; and Hilary Hinds, *God's Englishwomen: Seventeenth-Century Radical Sectarian Writing and Feminist Criticism* (Manchester: Manchester University Press, 1996).

42. Puritans were required to attest to their conversion experiences in order to become members of their congregations. In some congregations women were not permitted to speak before the congregation; instead, their stories were recorded and then read. However, in others, women were given the option to speak, and many chose to remain silent and have their words read by an elder or the pastor.

43. A clear overview of the Williams's episode can be found in Edmund S. Morgan, *The Puritan Dilemma: The Story of John Winthrop* (Boston: Little, Brown, 1958), 115–33.

44. For an excellent discussion of the work of Quakers in New England, see Carla Gardina Pestana, "The City upon a Hill under Siege: The Puritan Perception of the Quaker Threat to Massachusetts Bay, 1656–1661," *New England Quarterly* 56 (1983): 323–53; Carla Gardina Pestana, *Quakers and Baptists in Colonial Massachusetts* (New York: Cambridge University Press, 1991).

45. See Pestana, "The City upon a Hill under Siege," 348–53, for a discussion of Puritan perception of Quakers' threat to the family.

46. See, for example, Caroline Walker Bynum, *Holy Feast and Holy Fast: The Religious Significance of Food to Medieval Women* (Berkeley: University of California Press, 1987); Caroline Walker Bynum, *Fragmentation and Redemption: Essays on Gender and the Human Body in Medieval Religion* (New York: Zone Books, 1991); and Peter Brown, *The Body and Society: Men, Women, and Sexual Renunciation in Early Christianity* (New York: Columbia University Press, 1988).

2

Revelation, Witchcraft, and the Danger of Knowing God's Secrets

Elizabeth Reis

This chapter, like the previous one by Marilyn Westerkamp, asks what difference it makes to include women in narrative histories of Puritanism. Does our historical understanding of Puritanism change when we examine women's experiences as well as men's?

Like Westerkamp, Reis answers yes, but she offers a darker portrait of women's relationship to Puritanism. Focusing on attitudes toward divine revelation and witchcraft, Reis argues that Puritans were deeply suspicious of women's claims to religious authority. When women dared to claim that they had received revelations from God, they were accused of being witches. According to Reis, Puritanism was a deeply gendered faith—a faith that offered women spiritual equality in theory but denied it in practice.

The differences between Westerkamp's and Reis's chapters remind us that written history is always an act of interpretation, not simply a factual record of people and events. Adding women to American religious historical narratives does not yield a single interpretation of the past, but multiple and often conflicting ones.

By ignoring the gendered dynamic of witchcraft accusations at Salem and elsewhere, historians of American religion have missed not only a compelling part of the witch-hunting saga, but also the broader relationship between Puritanism and womanhood. Scholars of American religion have taken for granted the simple fact that although witches could be male or female, in New England they tended to be women. In fact, so many of the accused witches at Salem were women (approximately 78 percent) that it is worth exploring Puritan attitudes towards women, sin, and the devil. While it would be easy to characterize the Puritans simply as misogynists, Puritan New Englanders considered themselves to be rather more enlightened than others when it came to women's place in society and in their cosmology. They did not subscribe to the prevailing European view that women were inherently more evil than men. And yet womanhood and witchcraft were inextricably linked both to each other and to Puritan interpretations of evil and sin.[1]

American religious history textbooks have slighted the gendered dimension of the witch trials. Scholars have highlighted the political, economic, and social tensions that led to the Salem crisis rather than focusing on the dynamics of the trials themselves, which involved primarily women as both the accused and the accusers. For example, Mark Noll mentions women's involvement, but his brief reference to lonely elderly women, hysterical teenagers, and the slave Tituba marginalizes the complexity of female participation. He writes:

> A number of factors fueled the alarm: political strife between Salem Village and the larger town of Salem, voodoo practices associated with a West Indian slave, the recent publication of an ancient book presenting ways to combat witchcraft, tension with marauding Native Americans and their French allies, judges and ministers nervous about the colony's spiritual decline and eager to find new ways of checking it, simmering community hostility against a few lonely old women and a few new families, a wide range of occult practices, and adolescent hysteria in a few teenage girls along with judicial hysteria in a few old men.

Similarly, Edwin Gaustad and Leigh Schmidt leave gender out of their explanation for the crisis, although they do connect witchcraft belief with Puritan religious ideology: "Amid . . . fears of religious decline and socioeconomic change, Puritans often resorted to a more insidious side of their theology, namely, confronting the dangers of Satan and his minions. Witchcraft, demonic possession, curses, and necromancy were theological no less than biblical realities, and they were regularly inserted into one social conflict after another, sometimes with terrifying results. This became especially evident in the notorious witchcraft episode at Salem, Massachusetts in the 1690s."[2] Historians who have ignored women have failed to adequately explain the reasons for witchcraft accusations and confessions. They have also failed to appreciate the deeply gendered character of Puritanism as it was actually lived by the women and men of New England.

Until recently, few early American historians were interested in asking what the witchcraft trials could tell us about either Puritanism or women. While Perry Miller treated witchcraft as an aberration from Puritanism, claiming that it had "no effect on the ecclesiastical or political situation" or "institutional and ideological development," Paul Boyer, Stephen Nissenbaum and Kai Erikson saw it as the product of socioeconomic tensions. Erikson viewed the Salem crisis as an attempt to redefine acceptable boundaries at a time of social change, and Boyer and Nissenbaum argued that the witchcraft crisis grew out of deep anxieties about the growth of a market-based economy. Building on their insights, John Demos moved beyond sociological analysis to ask deeper questions about why witches were almost always women, but his answer focused on the psychological characteristics of both victims and accusers, not Puritanism as a religious system. It was not until 1987, when Carol Karlsen's groundbreaking book, *The Devil in the Shape of a Woman*, appeared that historians finally began to concentrate on the question of why women tended to be the majority of accused witches—a question whose answer no longer seemed self-evident. But, like Boyer and Nissenbaum, Karlsen was more interested in the economic tensions underlying witchcraft accusations than religious ones. (She made the fascinating discovery that many of the accused witches seemed particularly threatening because they stood to inherit property independently of men.) Five years later, in his book *The Devil's Dominion: Magic and Religion in Early New England*, Richard Godbeer argued that the Salem trials were the product of religious as well as socioeconomic tensions, but despite the strengths of his book, he made little reference to gender.[3]

In contrast, my book, *Damned Women: Sinners and Witches in Puritan New England* (1997), interprets the witchcraft episodes through the lens of *both* religious belief and gender. I argue that while Puritan theologians taught that male and female were equal in the sight of God, the sexes were far from equal in the hearts and minds of both women and men. Women were physically weaker than men, their natures ideally quiescent, submissive, and passive; their souls, therefore, must be easier prey for Satan than the stouter souls of men. During the trials, accused women were damned if they did and damned if they didn't: if they confessed to witchcraft charges, their admissions would prove the cases against them; if they denied the charges, their very intractability, construed as the refusal to admit to sin more generally, might mark them as sinners and hence allies of the devil. Theology thus conspired with mundane practice, making it easier for Puritans (women as well as men) to imagine that women were more likely than men to submit to Satan and become witches. Other accounts—sociological, psychological, or economic—of what took place at Salem retain their explanatory power, but by ignoring the relationship between New Englanders, particularly women, and the devil, these interpretations obscure what the Puritans saw as the primary focus of the crises that ruptured their lives.

This chapter advances my earlier work in *Damned Women* by examining Puritanism from the vantage point both of women who claimed to have received divine revelations and of women who were accused of being witches. It explores the gendered aspects of Puritanism in New England, particularly the ways that women and men were expected to express their spirituality.[4] By focusing on women's access to the supernatural (including all phenomena thought to be inspired by God, devils, or angels), I will argue that Puritanism denigrated women's religious experiences. Gender often created a double standard about knowing God's secrets: even such spiritual knowledge as revelations or angel sightings, both of which could have been interpreted as godly, were often thought to come from Satan when claimed by women rather than men. This chapter considers the complicated knot of divine secrecy, human knowledge, and gender difference. It examines issues of Puritan salvation, Puritans' interpretations of wonders and revelations, their exposure of the nefarious deeds of witches, and, lastly, their ambiguous recognition of angels—demonstrating, in each case, how gender shaped Puritan perception and judgment.

To Puritans, both revelation and witchcraft were polar extremes of communication with a supernatural intelligence. Believers were anxious to know God's will and to have foreknowledge of his design for their lives and especially for their afterlives, yet they recognized that such surety was impossible. Indeed, claiming celestial certainty was considered a damnable offense. Puritans examined puzzling phenomena for knowledge and guidance, but they differentiated between those events that they considered evidence of God's grace and those they considered "miracles." The former were signs and wonders meant to be interpreted and understood by mortals. The latter, popular within the Roman Catholic tradition, were interpreted by Puritans as human or diabolical manipulations, not the work of God's revelation.[5] Skilled medical practitioners might use what seemed like magic to discern God's intentions when illness and death threatened, but their efforts were designed to reveal, not to alter, God's plans for the sick.[6]

Attempts to influence or change God's providence were thought even more heretical than assertions of heavenly certainty, and the predilection for this depravity seemed characteristic of the weaker sex. "Witches" were threatening, in part, because they seemed to be guilty of manipulating God's providence.[7] Using infernal means, they obtained forbidden knowledge and caused spectacular occurrences that exhibited signs of devilish maleficium. These occurrences would have been seen as inexplicable wonders had no sinful involvement been suspected. In addition, the felt reality of witches forced people to confront the question of what could and should be known of God's plans for Judgment Day. Ironically, even as the community suspected witches of knowing what "normal" people would not ordinarily know, it acted with confidence in its own knowledge of the unknowable when it convicted and executed an alleged witch. Presumed intelligence of a witch's damnation—a secret technically known only to God—justified her execution.

In spite, or perhaps because, of the proscription against assuming understanding of the mind of God, Puritans looked to providences to ascertain God's judgments and wishes, particularly on the issue of salvation. Seeking assurance of their salvation, they searched themselves and others for signs that they would be among the chosen. Such signs had two interpretations: they could indicate the likelihood of one's salvation, but more often they were seen as warnings that Judgment Day was imminent—and thus that conversion was an immediate necessity. The more unusual the event, the stronger the warning. Michael Winship has ably detailed the kinds of manifestations through which Puritans found portents in a world that was at once "unpredictable and communicative."[8] Sometimes God sent signs to caution individual souls. More spectacular occurrences, like ships lost at sea, comets, or weather disasters, were meant to chasten the entire population.

Rarely in the seventeenth century did God show his divine pleasure toward the colonists. It was not unheard of—one's personal good fortune or the good fortune of the community as a whole, could certainly be interpreted as God's beneficence—but it was more common for Puritans to perceive God's hand in the world through negative presentiments. In fact, David D. Hall contends that "portents never seemed to hint at progress or improvement but at degeneration."[9]

Of course, there were exceptions. When Matthew Cradock's house in Marblehead burned down in 1634, for example, John Winthrop, the first governor of Massachusetts, glossed over the loss of property and interpreted the rescue of its occupants and contents as "a speciall providence of God."[10] And more significantly, the English saw deific design in their expropriation of Native American land, especially that land which fell to them as Indians succumbed to epidemic disease while Europeans providentially survived. Analyzing a smallpox epidemic in 1634 that destroyed scores of Indians but left colonists relatively unscathed, William Bradford wrote, "The cheefe Sachem him selfe now dyed, & allmost all his freinds & kinred. But by the marvelous goodnes & providens of God not one of the English was so much as sicke, or in the least measure tainted with the disease."[11]

If God's beneficence was most apparent in the Puritan understanding of health and recovery, his chastisement explained everything from catastrophic weather to what we might think of as plain bad luck. Why should the supernatural hand manifest most clearly and conventionally through adverse events? Such was not the case after the beginning of the eighteenth century, when otherworldly messages were largely accepted by ordinary believers across denominations as positive and credible, albeit unusual, communications. Yet in early New England, extraordinary communications were suspect as the devil's work and potentially as grounds for banishment from the godly commonwealth.

Of all communications from the beyond, revelations specifically were not tolerated in the Puritan world. What made revelations dangerous? Although Puritans were constantly searching for such signs from God, they presumed that they would be few and far between. The clergy might rarely be vouchsafed mystical insight, but ordinary people, particularly women, would not likely be direct beneficiaries of God's disclosure. When women reported extraordinary experiences that seemed like revelations from God, authorities often considered them delusions of the devil.

Revelations were risky. They came perilously close to challenging the Puritan theology of predestination. Believers sought to surmise God's will but ultimately contented themselves with the knowledge that they would learn of their fates on Judgment Day. Ordinary churchgoers who claimed to have revelations from God were asserting, in effect, privileged understanding of the greatest mystery in the Puritan world: God's determination of their spiritual futures. According to Edward Taylor, "Extraordinary discoveries of the minde of God, ordinarily, are made to Persons of more than an ordinary, or Common concern. . . . Hence it is from Satan that any should assert that Extraordinary discoveries are with ordinary and common people."[12]

Anne Hutchinson was expelled from the Massachusetts Bay Colony for expounding the subjective doctrine of "grace in the heart." Testing the limits of autonomous female faith, Hutchinson encouraged her followers to seek the same "immediate revelation" that she believed she received. When pressed, her minister, John Cotton, admitted that certain revelations might be acceptable, that is, if Hutchinson had looked "for deliverance from the hand of God by his providence," or if "the revelation be in a word or according to a word." But Winthrop persisted in his conviction that her revelations were not, in fact, of that nature. Hers sprang from the "immediate revelation of the spirit and not by the ministry of the word." This was how she "abused the country"; this was the cause of "all these tumults and troubles."[13] Her revelations were too immediate. God spoke not through her minister, as ministers presumed he would, but directly to her. "This runs to enthusiasm," Hugh Peters declared. "It overthrows all," agreed the governor.[14] Finally, all were persuaded that Anne Hutchinson must have been deluded by the devil. There was no other plausible explanation for her stubborn belief.

No one doubted that God sent signals. Puritan theologians agreed on the doctrine of providence; assuming that God ordered the universe, every un-usual event had moral significance.[15] Sometimes God sent subtle signs; other times, depending presumably on the severity of the offense, his messages were more obvious. Mary Dyer's unfortunate malformed baby was one such blatant expression. Dyer had been a follower of Anne Hutchinson and later became a Quaker. In 1637 she gave birth to a terribly malformed baby that Winthrop describes this way:

> It was a woman child, stillborn, about two months before the just time, having life a few hours before; it came hiplings till she turned it; it was of ordinary bigness; it had a face, but no head, and the ears stood upon the shoulders and were like an ape's; it had no forehead, but over the eyes four horns, hard and sharp; two of them were above one inch long, the other two shorter; the eyes standing out, and the mouth also; the nose hooked upward; all over the breast and back full of sharp pricks and scales, like a thornback; the navel and all the belly, with the distinction of sex, were where the back should be, and the back and hips before, where the belly should have been; behind, between the shoulders, it had two mouths, and in each of them a piece of red flesh sticking out; it had arms and legs as other children; but, instead of toes, It had on each foot three claws, like a young fowl, with sharp talons.[16]

The Reverend John Cotton suggested that Dyer conceal the birth. He saw "a providence of God in it . . . and had known other monstrous births, which had been concealed, and that he thought God might intend only the instruc-tion of the parents and such other to whom it was known, etc." But God apparently wanted all to know, for even during labor, about two hours prior to the birth, the bed shook violently, and Dyer's body emitted a "noisome savor"; the shaking and that foul-smelling aroma indicated that Satan lurked nearby.[17] Most of the women attending Dyer "were taken with extreme vom-iting and purging" and were forced to leave.

What were Dyer's specific sins? She was a woman, according to Winthrop, "of a very proud spirit, and much addicted to revelations."[18] Many scholars have commented on the gendered nature of Puritan notions of sin and evil. That Dyer was a woman in Hutchinson's circle and considered a proud spirit was justification for her severe trial, but here I would like to turn atten-tion to Winthrop's accusation that Dyer was "much addicted to revelations." Though Winthrop had the licit revelation that Dyer's "monstrous birth" had the "providence of God in it," he saw her revelations as dangerous, not divine communication.[19] Dyer's revelations, though never specified in Winthrop's journal, implied some divine knowledge to which, as a woman, she was not entitled. For Winthrop, Dyer was either a liar or a woman deluded by Satan. The birth of Dyer's misshapen child, it seems, confirmed God's disapproval; this was a negative providence, one designed to teach Dyer and others a lesson about the dangers of claiming supernatural cognition.[20]

Though Winthrop assigned blame to Dyer only tentatively (he never explicitly tied her behavior to the stillborn baby), other Puritan theologians saw a more direct correlation between monstrous births and dangerous opinions. In a sixteenth-century English text dealing with such births, the conclusion was unequivocal. These births, it explained, "signifie the monstrous and deformed myndes of the people mysshapened with phantastical opinions, dissolute lyvynge, licentious talke, and such other vicious behavoures which mounstrously deformed the myndes of men in the syght of god who by suche signes dooth certifie us in what similitude we appere before hym, and thereby gyveth us admonition to amende before the day of his wrath and vengeance."[21] Through divine providences, God gave his children warnings so that they might reform their behavior. Dyer no doubt participated in all four sins specified: fantastic opinions, dissolute living, licentious talk, and other miscellaneous vicious behaviors such as her addiction to revelations. As a result, she received God's explicit physical warning in the figure of the deformed child. Thomas Weld's account of Dyer's daughter's birth concurred: "Then God himselfe was pleased to step in with his casting voice . . . by testifying his displeasure against their [Dyer's and Hutchinson's] opinions and practices, as clearly as if he had pointed with his finger."[22]

God sent an unambiguous warning to Mary Dyer, according to Weld, but even though the baby's deformity revealed the mother to be an egregious sinner, Dyer's ultimate fate remained uncertain. According to Puritan theology, God allowed for the possibility that sinners might repent, and if they did so and were among the chosen, they might yet be admitted to heaven on Judgment Day. God's providence was thus but a warning, not a settled truth about one's salvation.[23] Revelations, on the other hand, unlike admonitory portents or signs, were one step closer to God's truth. Revelations implied that their recipients were honored by godly and definitive knowledge. Claims of revelation, especially when made by obvious sinners, struck authorities as incredible and were dismissed as inauthentic.

Concealment and disclosure coexisted uneasily in Winthrop's world. Secrets were at the heart of Puritan theology. Sinners tried to learn God's hidden judgments concerning their fates, while they worried that God might expose their own personal secrets, uncovering sins they had tried to obscure. Secret sins, hidden from public view, would be found out, according to Puritan ministers. In an unequal relationship, mortals could never know God until Judgment Day, but an all-knowing God was privy to whatever secrets people tried to hide.

I have argued elsewhere that individuals' hidden sins were considered the most dangerous evils of all, both to the sinner and to the wider community.[24] Sins that remained covert produced in the transgressor a sense of self-division, the outward appearance of righteousness masking inward and essential corruption. The undiscovered sinner, though a reprobate, could pretend innocence—not ultimately before God, of course, but before the community. Only abjuring secrecy through public disclosure, confession, and repentance restored the possibility of grace. These public acts might realign the divided Puritan self, conforming outward presentation to a more honest representation of the inner nature or soul.

Eventual public knowledge of a reprobate's sins was inevitable, according to Puritan thought. People's inner selves could (and would) be known; it was impossible for anyone to keep sin secret from God, and God would visibly demonstrate his displeasure. Drawing a parallel between the inevitable disclosure of sin and the birth of a baby, Obadiah Sedgwick subtly denigrated female interiority: "secret sins will become publike sins if they be not cleansed. [T]he Child in the wombe hath not stronger throwes to get out of its private lodging, then sin secretly wrought to fly into open and manifest action."[25] Withheld sins were characterized in terms of gender; they would be forced from hiding just as a baby is forced from the womb.

Witchcraft was related to secrecy and revelation. In a society in which believers watched the skies, themselves, and their neighbors closely for signs of election or damnation, secrecy, threats of witchcraft, and rumors of revelation took on special significance. Though only God on the Day of Judgment would reveal who had truly covenanted with him and who with Satan, during the witchcraft episodes it became obvious that some of the accused were not truly the godly people they represented themselves to be. The court chastised Rebecca Nurse: "It is very awfull to all to see these agonies & you an old Professor thus charged with contracting with the Devil."[26] The court tried to pressure her into admitting guilt, in part by stressing the contrast between what they thought she had been—a godly woman who had professed her faith—and what they now believed she was—a witch. In the witchcraft case against her, the court thought, Nurse's true self had been revealed. Similarly, during Martha Corey's examination, Edward Putnam and Ezekiel Cheever mentioned that they had no reason to suspect Corey of witchcraft initially, "for shee had made a profession of christ and had rejoyced to go and hear the world of god and the like." Even though the two warned her that duplicity would not clear her, as everyone knew that "witches had crept into the churches," they believed that she continued in her charade to "ma[k]e her profession a cloake to cover all."[27] Corey's previous piety did not stand in her favor; indeed it testified against her, for it was considered but a villainous disguise of her true nature.

Testimony brought to the court against accused witches must have seemed particularly appealing when it purported to bare long-held secrets. Exposure engendered both relief and anxiety; on the one hand, deeply hidden secrets were finally revealed, but on the other hand, this unmasking suggested that sins of other dangerous sinners remained undiscovered. Sarah Andrews's father initially had warned his daughter against impugning a pious woman's character when she testified against Elizabeth How. Andrews's testimony was all the more powerful, then, when she insisted that How was not the person everyone believed her to be. The charges—that How had tried to throw Andrews's sister into fire and water—proved, according to Andrews, that How served Satan rather than God. Andrews declared that, despite her father's warning, she had to tell what "she was sure twas true," and that she "should stand to it to her death."[28] The supposition that denunciation required extraordinary honesty and courage on the part of accusers (at least that was how some represented their testimony) made witnesses more believable. A kind of circular logic prevailed: accusations leveled against an upstanding person strained the court's credulity. Once the accusations achieved a certain threshold of plausibility through persistence or dramatic content, the witnesses gained enhanced credibility. Their accusations were legitimated by their readiness to challenge apparent goodness and persevere against anguished denials, and thus the accusers were considered to be particularly sincere and brave.

Several of the accused, especially the women, believed that the accusations against them, even though untrue, were in some measure justified by their commission of previous, unacknowledged secret sins. Recognizing the fine line between sins that did not involve supernatural commerce, but which nevertheless bonded sinners to the devil, and the more egregious sin of explicitly signing the devil's book, many accused women confessed unwittingly to the latter in the course of their examinations. This failure to distinguish between the human propensity toward sinfulness and active participation in witchcraft was influenced by the centrality of covenant in Puritan theology. Just as an individual or a community could covenant with God, so too could an individual covenant with the devil. The sinners themselves were unable to make a firm distinction between "normal" sins that, since they were transgressions, were surely instigated and supported by the devil and sins that unequivocally signified a conscious pact with Satan.

The confession of accused witch Rebecca Eames typifies this blend of earthly sins and other-worldly transgressions. She admitted adultery and then went on to say that by this black mark she had sealed the devil's covenant: "She was then in such horror of Conscienc that she tooke a Rope to hang herselfe and a Razer to cutt her throate by Reason of her great sin in Committing adultery & by that the Divell Gained her he promiseing she should not be brought out or ever discovered."[29] Did she believe that the adultery itself signified a pact with the devil? Had she also become the devil's partner when she took an illicit sexual partner? One sees in her confession an admission of both actual sin and a terrified attempt at cover up. She could not depend on God to keep her secret, for her ministers had assured her that all sins were eventually exposed. She may have thought that, by keeping her sin covert, she had relied on the devil. Her hazy dependence on the devil's discretion may, to her Calvinist mind, have been an indication of her consent to witchcraft.

Although Puritans believed that all sins would eventually be exposed, civil and religious leaders were most assiduous about gaining confessions to the damning sin of entering the devil's covenant. It was crucial that the heinous private ceremony of signing the devil's book in blood be made public in order to root out Satan's influence in the community, as a warning and example to others and, most important, as a necessary first step toward the repentance and redemption of the sinner. Confession not only established guilt but also affected the sinner's relinquishment of further unholy secrecy— a relinquishment that some confessing women experienced as a relief. Elizabeth Knapp, a servant who was supposedly in the devil's possession, confessed in 1671 that the devil "took a little sharpened sticke, & dipt in the blood, & put it into her hand, & guided it, & shee wrote her name with his help." Knapp knew that signing the devil's pact would surely be exposed. During her ordeal, she expressed concern that "if shee were a witch, shee should bee discovered, & brought to a shamefull end; which was many times a trouble on her spirits."[30]

Confession was the surest way of knowing for certain who had bonded with the devil and would go to hell, but it was also the crucial step toward potential salvation. Ministers fostering the spiritual regeneration of sinners stressed that salvation was possible only if transgressors repented. Strict adherence to the framework of the covenant demanded confession and repentance as the only means for the guilty to be readmitted into God's graces, just as a conversion narrative, which acknowledged one's sinfulness and attested to one's regeneration, preceded initial church membership. Within the terms of the covenant, those guilty of witchcraft—as well as other more mundane sins—theoretically were able to confess, repent, and return to God's embrace.

It must have seemed fairly certain to most, however, that witches were unredeemable. Indeed, Deodat Lawson preached during the Salem outbreak, "Therefore KNOW YE, that are guilty of such Monstrous Iniquity . . . to enter into Covenant with Satan; He that made you will not save you, and he that formed you will shew you no favour."[31] Puritan ministers, generally, seemed to delight in detailing the horrors of hell. An eternity of torment, lingeringly described, was the deserved fate of those who had chosen Satan and sin over God and virtue. Sermons were replete with images of fire and God's eternal anger against the unrepentant. For example, Samuel Willard's congregation was warned: "If you are resolved in your way . . . know and be assured that you are going to a bottomless pit. . . . [Y]ou are going to dwell with the devils and damned spirits, and to be tormented with the flames of the bottomless pit, where you shall be filled brim full in soul and body with the wrath of God."[32]

As I argued in *Damned Women,* the Calvinist theology of predestination offered no certain salvation for the godly, but damnation for sinners was assured. "It is true," warned Thomas Hooker, "though thy good workes are not perfectly good and cannot save thee, yet thy bad workes are perfectly naught and will condemne thee."[33] Though opposed to strict Calvinism, the Arminian teaching that all were capable of determining their destiny was embraced by scrupulous Puritans—but only in reference to hell. That is, individuals could not merit salvation, for only God could grant the joys of heaven to his elect. But the torments of hell were freely available to every sinner.[34] And who was a more deserving candidate for hell's gate than a witch? A witch had unambiguously chosen the devil's path by signing his book, and thus she willingly decided her fate. Left unrepentant, a witch would surely be damned.

Perhaps the certitude of damnation helps explain the court's seemingly contrary treatment of confessors and deniers during the Salem witchcraft trials. As many scholars have pointed out, none of the confessed witches in 1692—those who admitted collusion with Satan—was executed. All of the deniers—those who insisted on their innocence—were hanged. Common wisdom has it that the confessors were spared because the magistrates hoped they would name more names in the devil's conspiracy to overthrow the godly kingdom. We might come to a different understanding of the court's decision to spare the confessors and kill the deniers if we look instead to the thorny issues of certainty and secrecy.

It can be argued that a confession of witchcraft, the most grievous of sins, reintroduced an element of ambiguity into the question of a witch's salvation. If she confessed and repented, then was she not entitled to the same measure of redemption afforded any other sinner? A witch's fate became uncertain after a confession, and the community left the judgment to God. Deniers, on the other hand, were not believed to be innocent. An accused witch who denied her involvement with the devil, despite evidence to the contrary, placed herself even more firmly in the devil's camp in the eyes of contemporaries. Her guilt as both a sinner and a liar proved that she was indeed the devil's accomplice and thus confirmed that she should be hanged. Her indisputable consignment to perdition justified her execution.

Public knowledge decided public action. Communal certainty of witches' destinies in the next world determined witches' earthly fates, including hanging. Private knowledge too was powerful. Witches' supposed knowledge of others' lives could warrant suspicion or even conviction of the crime of witchcraft. What witches knew and how they acquired that intelligence took on enormous significance precisely because of the tension within Puritan society surrounding divine omniscience, secrecy, and disclosure. If a woman knew something that no one would "naturally" know, she was under suspicion. How had she gained information, known only to God, if not with the devil's assistance? On the other hand, the community also felt certain of information known only to God: the witch's damnation. Officials were so assured of their possession of this unknowable insight into the mind of God that they were willing to execute women on the strength of their certainty. That they espoused a double standard escaped their notice: if they could guiltlessly, and even self-righteously, possess secret knowledge—a certainty about the future—why could not the accused?

In 1669, the accused witch, Katherine Harrison, was indicted in Connecticut for "not haueing the fear of God before thine eyes [and because she] hast had familiaritie with Sathan the grand enemie of god and mankind and by his help hast acted things beyond and beside the ordinary course of nature."[35] Katherine Harrison knew things about her neighbors "that did come to pass." She "foretold many matters that in future times were to be accomplished."[36] In addition to her primary offense of siding with Satan against God, Katherine Harrison committed the offense of possessing knowledge unavailable to mere mortals.

As historian Walter Woodward has suggested, fortune-telling was an especially troublesome offense in the eyes of many clergy and magistrates because it came perilously close to the mysterious art and science of intellectual magic. Woodward argues convincingly that church officials fiercely guarded magical knowledge precisely because they assumed this information was divinely inspired. Whether certain forms of magic came from God or from the devil became a matter of debate. Elites assumed that their forms of knowledge came from God; witches displaying unusual magical skill, on the other hand, must be aided by Satan.[37]

A line was drawn, Woodward argues, between natural and diabolical magic; the former constituted a sanctioned endeavor if performed by the right people. The elite who studied astrology, alchemy, and alchemical medicine, led by hermeticist John Winthrop Jr. and Gershom Bulkeley, for example, believed that their researches fell within the acceptable category of natural magic. Convinced that their knowledge had spiritual origins, they doubted that ordinary lay folk would be privy to it, and they worried that their own occult practices might come under suspicion if improperly associated with the diabolic magic allegedly practiced by witches.[38]

Because of their own alchemical experiments, ministers had an investment in dissociating the devil from most magical activity, lest they themselves come under suspicion of being in his camp. At the same time, the ministers' condemnation of divination—defined as attainment of "certain knowledge" —reflects broader Puritan concerns about secrecy and assurance. Having "certain knowledge" was dangerous, whether it be in the form of divination by alleged witches or revelation by women like Anne Hutchinson.

Although some ministers and lay practitioners successfully protected their alchemy, numerology, and natural astrology from public condemnation and repression, insisting that the devil had nothing to do with their magical enterprises, Katherine Harrison could not avoid public censure. Her divination fell outside of safeguarded categories. As a fortune-teller, a healer, and a woman, Harrison lacked the necessary authority or education to justify her activities. Though ministers believed their own magical practice was inspired by God rather than the devil, they admitted Satan's role in some magical activity, especially in matters of divination. This was the charge many of the accusers laid on Harrison. Gershom Bulkeley wrote, "Hence the communication of such things, in way of Divination (the person pretending the certain knowledge of them) seems to us, to argue familiarity with ye Devil."[39]

In Calvinist New England, "certain knowledge" was gained from familiarity with the devil, and so those who purported to have attained divine information were necessarily suspect. But what if such knowledge emanated from a positive supernatural source: an angel, for example? Puritans believed in angels, and they also believed, hesitatingly, that angels could come to earth bearing heavenly messages. Yet they could not wholeheartedly embrace angels because their celestial visitations could be dangerous; one could never be sure if an angel came from God, or, more likely, from Satan.

Though saints and angels were celebrated and revered in medieval Europe, in John Calvin's revolutionary religious teachings their significance was de-emphasized in favor of God's centrality and supremacy. For this reason and perhaps also because Puritans were far more likely to perceive the dark clouds of God's anger than the silver linings of angelic goodwill, reports of angel sightings scarcely appeared in the written records of both clergy and lay-people in the seventeenth century. Angels appeared in the Bible but seemed rarely to venture abroad. Especially if reported by women, angel manifesta-tions were regarded with skepticism.[40] Fallen angels were the only angels seventeenth-century New England ministers thought women likely to en-counter, and therefore any reported beneficent visitations were thought to be delusions—not angels at all but the devil in disguise.

At the heart of the Puritan understanding of both revelation and witch-craft were complex and unresolved tensions between certainty and doubt, knowledge and deception, disclosure and secrecy, all further vexed with the dichotomies of gender. Even the most central question in Puritanism—the yearning to know God's will—was gendered in the asking and in the answers that might be supplied. Believers assumed God's omniscience and the human mind's limitations, yet they tried to wrest meaning from the observation of providence. Was illness a sign of God's displeasure or a blessed trial sent to refine the soul of the elect? If a woman confessed to ordinary sin, was she guilty of compacting with the devil or of less demonic crimes? This chapter has argued that knowledge of, and access to, the supernatural were contested, as New England Puritans created, defined, and clarified their convictions regarding God's ultimate *mysterium* in a gendered world.

Notes

1. Carol F. Karlsen, *The Devil in the Shape of a Woman: Witchcraft in Colonial New England* (New York: Norton, 1987), 47. See Richard Godbeer, *The Devil's Domin-ion: Magic and Religion in Early New England* (New York: Cambridge University Press, 1992), 235–42, for useful appendixes of names and outcomes of cases before and during the Salem crisis. For other cases that never came to trial, see John Demos, *Entertaining Satan: Witchcraft and the Culture of Early New England* (New York: Oxford University Press, 1982), 402–9.
2. Mark Noll, *A History of Christianity in the United States and Canada* (Grand Rapids, Mich.: Eerdmans, 1992), 49–50; Edwin Gaustad and Leigh Schmidt, *The Religious History of America: The Heart of the American Story from Colonial Times to Today* (New York: HarperSanFrancisco, 2002), 57.
3. Perry Miller, *The New England Mind: From Colony to Province* (Cambridge: Harvard University Press, 1953), 191; Kai T. Erikson, *Wayward Puritans: A Study in the Sociology of Deviance* (New York: J. Wiley, 1966); Paul Boyer and Stephen Nissenbaum, *Salem Possessed: The Social Origins of Witchcraft* (Cambridge: Har-

vard University Press, 1974); Demos, *Entertaining Satan*; Karlsen, *Devil in the Shape of a Woman*; Godbeer, *Devil's Dominion*.

4. My exploration of the meaning of revelation for women builds on that of Marilyn Westerkamp, "Puritan Patriarchy and the Problem of Revelation," *Journal of Interdisciplinary History* 23, no. 3 (Winter 1993): 571–95.

5. Robert Bruce Mullin, *Miracles and the Modern Religious Imagination* (New Haven: Yale University Press, 1996), 9–25.

6. See Walter W. Woodward, "The Magic in Colonization: Religion, Science, and the Occult in the Colonization of New England" (Ph.D. diss., University of Connecticut, 2000). See also Patricia A. Watson, *The Angelical Conjunction: The Preacher-Physicians of Colonial New England* (Knoxville: University of Tennessee Press, 1991).

7. I hope it is clear from the context that when I use the words "witch" and "witchcraft" I am referring to Puritan constructions of those concepts. For simplicity's sake, I do not place these words in quotation marks each time they are used; readers must understand that I report, but do not share, the Puritan point of view.

8. Michael P. Winship, *Seers of God: Puritan Providentialism in the Restoration and Early Enlightenment* (Baltimore: Johns Hopkins University Press, 1996), 2.

9. David D. Hall, *Worlds of Wonder, Days of Judgment: Popular Religious Belief in New England* (New York: Alfred A. Knopf, 1989), 80.

10. Richard S. Dunn, James Savage, and Laetitia Yeandle, eds., *The Journal of John Winthrop, 1630–1649* (Cambridge: Harvard University Press, 1996), 109.

11. William Bradford, *Of Plymouth Plantation: The Pilgrims in America* (New York: Alfred A. Knopf, 1952), 177. Just as frequently, Indians could be used by God, Puritans believed, almost as natural forces, to punish New England for its sins. See, for example, Increase Mather's explanation of King Philip's War of 1675–76 in which, he claims, Indians were God's rod, used to chastise Puritans. See Increase Mather, *A Brief History of the Warr with Indians in New England* (Boston, 1676); and Increase Mather, *A Relation of the Trouble Which have Hapned in New England, by Reason of the Indians There* (Boston, 1677).

12. Edward Taylor, *Harmony of the Gospels*, ed. Thomas M. and Virginia L. Davis with Betty L. Parks, 3 vols. (Delmar, N.Y.: Scholars' Facsimiles and Reprints, 1983), 1:67, cited in Winship, *Seers of God*, 20.

13. David D. Hall, ed., *The Antinomian Controversy, 1636–1638*, 2nd ed. (Durham, N.C.: Duke University Press, 1990), 341–42. For a compelling discussion of Anne Hutchinson and the threat of enthusiasm, see David S. Lovejoy, *Religious Enthusiasm in the New World* (Cambridge: Harvard University Press, 1985), 62–86. See also Edmund S. Morgan, "The Case against Anne Hutchinson," *New England Quarterly* 10 (December 1937): 635–49; and Lyle Koehler, "The Case of the American Jezebels: Anne Hutchinson and Female Agitation during the Years of Antinomian Turmoil, 1636–1640," *William and Mary Quarterly*, 3rd ser., 31 (1974): 55–78. For a brilliant discussion of the gendered implications of Hutchinson's revela-

tions, see Jane Kamensky, *Governing the Tongue: The Politics of Speech in Early New England* (New York: Cambridge University Press, 1997), 71–81.

14. Hall, *The Antinomian Controversy*, 343.

15. Keith Thomas, *Religion and the Decline of Magic* (New York: Scribner, 1971), 91, 110–11. According to Thomas, events related to providence were often explained using "scientific" interpretations rather than an appeal to "folklore" or "fortune."

16. Dunn, Savage, and Yeandle, *The Journal of John Winthrop*, 254.

17. Ibid., 254–55. On the signs that indicated the devil's presence, see Karlsen, *The Devil in the Shape of a Woman*, 16–17.

18. Dunn, Savage, and Yeandle, *The Journal of John Winthrop*, emphasis added, 253.

19. Ibid., 254.

20. According to Anne Jacobson Schutte, " 'Such Monstrous Births': A Neglected Aspect of the Antinomian Controversy," *Renaissance Quarterly* 38 (Spring 1985): 85–106, Winthrop avoided making a direct correlation between Dyer's birth and God's punishment for her sins (p. 97). My reading of Winthrop's comments suggests that he implied a relationship between Dyer's addiction to revelations and the negative, harsh message from God embodied in a malformed baby.

21. Quoted in Robert Blair St. George, *Conversing by Signs: Poetics of Implication in Colonial New England Culture* (Chapel Hill: University of North Carolina, 1998), 172.

22. *The Antinomian Controversy*, 214.

23. Anne Jacobson Schutte asks this provocative question: "Could the two monsters, then, be not only warnings to the elect but also evidences of Dyer's and Hutchinson's damnation?" See Schutte, "Such Monstrous Births," 99. I agree with Schutte that Puritan theologians would not have seen providences as an explicit sign of damnation.

24. Elizabeth Reis, *Damned Women: Sinners and Witches in Puritan New England* (Ithaca, N.Y.: Cornell University Press, 1997), 126–28.

25. Obadiah Sedgwick, *The Anatomy of Secret Sins* (London, 1660), 11. Thomas Shepard and members of his congregation mentioned secret sins as the root of various punishments they received from God. Shepard believed his wife's travail during the birth of their son, Thomas, to be the direct result of his secret sins, a well-deserved lesson for his violations. He was fortunate in that though the sins were his, the pains were hers. See Michael McGiffert, ed., *God's Plot: The Paradoxes of Puritan Piety, Being the Autobiography and Journal of Thomas Shepard* (1640; Amherst: University of Massachusetts Press, 1972), 55. See also Mary Rhinelander McCarl, ed., "Thomas Shepard's Record of Relations of Religious Experience, 1648–1649," *William and Mary Quarterly*, 3rd ser., 48 (July 1991): 443, 445.

26. Paul Boyer and Stephen Nissenbaum, eds., *The Salem Witchcraft Papers: Verbatim Transcripts of the Legal Documents of the Salem Witchcraft Outbreak of 1692*, 3 vols. (New York: Da Capo Press, 1977), 2:585.

27. Ibid., 1:261–62.

28. Ibid., 2:454.

29. Ibid., 1:128.

30. Samuel Willard, *A Briefe Accounte of a Strange & Unusuall Providence of God Befallen to Elizabeth Knap[p] of Groton,* in *Groton in the Witchcraft Times,* ed. Samuel Green (Groton, Mass., 1883), 14–15.

31. Deodat Lawson, *Christ's Fidelity, the Only Shield against Satan's Malignity* (Boston, 1704), 68.

32. Samuel Willard, *The Christians Exercise by Satans Temptations* (Boston, 1701), 148.

33. Samuel Willard, *The Compleat Body of Christian Divinity* (Boston, 1726), 241.

34. Reis, *Damned Women,* 18–19.

35. John M. Taylor, *The Witchcraft Delusion in Colonial Connecticut* (1908; Williamstown, Mass.: Corner House Publishers, 1984), 48.

36. David D. Hall, *Witch-Hunting in Seventeenth-Century New England: A Documentary History, 1638–1692* (Boston: Northeastern University Press, 1991), 177–78.

37. Woodward, "The Magic in Colonization: Religion, Science, and the Occult in the Colonization of New England." On the ministers' understanding of magic, see Godbeer, *Devil's Dominion,* 5. See also Watson, *The Angelical Conjunction.*

38. Walter W. Woodward, "The Magus as Mediator: Witchcraft, Alchemical Knowledge and Authority in the Connecticut Witch Hunt of the 1660s," unpublished paper, 33.

39. Ibid., 35.

40. See Elizabeth Reis, "Immortal Messengers: Angels, Gender, and Power in Early America," in *Mortal Remains: Death in Early America,* ed. Andrew Burstein and Nancy Isenberg (Philadelphia: University of Pennsylvania Press, 2002), 163–75.

3

Hail Mary Down by the Riverside

Emily Clark

Black and White Catholic Women in Early America

The rise of the immigrant Catholic Church in the cities of nineteenth-century America has long been accepted as Catholicism's representative strand in the larger narrative of American religious history. In the following chapter, Emily Clark shows how an exploration of a convent of teaching nuns leads to a revision not only of that narrative, but of the history of religion among enslaved Africans. The largest Catholic congregation in a European colony that would later become part of the United States was not in Maryland, but in Louisiana. Its pews were not dominated by English recusants, but by Africans and their descendants. Records preserved by a missionary community of Ursuline nuns who arrived in New Orleans in 1727 reveal an evangelization campaign that they began among the enslaved. They were joined in this project by laywomen catechists and, by the middle of the eighteenth century, by women of African descent. The result was a thriving black Catholic Church. It was an immigrant church, to be sure, but its African congregation and origins in a female missionary campaign provide an alternative origin story for American Catholicism to challenge the long-standing narrative peopled by European immigrants and ambitious bishops.

Jay Dolan's description of the Catholic Church in nineteenth-century America presents us with its most familiar historical face: "In 1810, one Catholic parish served a community of ten thousand people in New York; fifty years later, Catholics numbered about four hundred thousand and the city had thirty-two Catholic churches. Of these churches, 70 percent could be described as Irish, and the clergy was said to be 'almost entirely Irish.' The next largest group was the Germans, who occupied one out of every four churches in the city."[1]

Here is the immigrant church in full flower, eclipsing the colonial Maryland seedling onto which it was grafted. Maryland's small community of persecuted colonial Catholics was succeeded by the burgeoning nineteenth-century immigrant European church—the American-born Anglophones succeeded by the polyglot infusion.[2] These are the two episodes that make up the standard narrative of how American Catholicism developed. What then do we make of the observations of John Watson, a Philadelphia journalist who traveled to New Orleans shortly after the Louisiana Purchase and reported that no matter when you visited its teeming Catholic churches, "the chief audience is formed of mulatresses and negresses"?[3] Where do these women fit into the story?

Revisionism often preoccupies itself with what has been left out, and it usually rests on one of two strategies: examining a subject from the perspective of actors and evidence not considered in prior scholarship, or from the vantage point of a longer temporal perspective that uncovers developmental themes previously overlooked. This chapter employs both approaches as it traces the origins and development of the Catholic community Watson described in early national New Orleans and makes a place for its story in the grand narrative of nineteenth-century American Catholicism. It is a story that reveals itself only by looking beyond the priests and parishes that planted the administrative apparatus of Tridentine Catholicism in colonial Louisiana to women, black and white, religious and lay. Without them, the orderly structure of the colonial church would have been an empty husk of unrealized organizational ambition, not a living church. Without them, the history of Catholicism in America is a story only partially told. And without them we lose part of yet another story: the development of Christianity among enslaved Africans in America.

The historiography of American Catholicism has long been dominated by the ethnic immigrant paradigm. In the three decades before the outbreak of the Civil War, thousands of Irish and German immigrants poured into America and its Catholic Church, swamping the small community anchored by Maryland Catholics that preceded it. The church that took shape in the nineteenth century was large, fast growing, urban, and largely constituted by working men and women of European ancestry. The parish became a vehicle both for the preservation of ethnic identity and for assimilation into American society. The pattern held after the Civil War, with the addition of cohorts of Italian and Polish immigrants, and in the twentieth century, Spanish-speaking countries contributed their thousands to the immigrant American church. The scholarship that has presented this history, most of it produced by descendants of those who lived it, has shaped the identity of American Catholics and the prevailing historical image of American Catholicism.[4]

There is an interesting resonance between this historiographical path and another, which will be familiar to anyone who has waded into the vast scholarship on American slavery. The seminal early historical studies of slavery were penned by Ulrich Bonnell Phillips, a Southerner born in 1877 who became a historian at Yale in the early twentieth century. His best-known work, *Life and Labor in the Old South*, portrayed the Old South at the height of the cotton slave regime. His portrayals of planter patriarchs and slaves and the economy and society they made together were the foundation of a historiographical paradigm that endured for more than half a century, as one study after another ploughed its furrows in the field of Old South slavery.[5] Phillips's generally benign appraisal of slavery reflected his nineteenth-century Southern roots; by the end of the 1960s, slave history gave no quarter in its condemnation of the institution. But while the new scholarship pilloried the slaveholder and fixed its gaze firmly on the agency and achievement of the enslaved, it remained grounded in its original chronological niche. Slavery was acknowledged to have existed in colonial America, but its historiography presented the peculiar institution as a sort of atemporal monolith, a fixed target of study whose complexity could be captured in the snapshot provided by its antebellum example.[6]

Old South slave scholarship described how slavery operated in all of its horror, but it did not explain to a generation educated by the civil rights movement how and why such an aberrant institution came into being. Historians began to look for answers to those questions in the colonial period, and what they found set in motion a revision of the historiography of slavery that continues to unfold. A succession of studies, beginning with Peter Wood's *Black Majority* and Edmund Morgan's *American Slavery, American Freedom*, revealed a complex developmental history for American slavery and a variety in slave experience shaped by geography, demographics, and crop-dictated labor patterns that cracked the Old South monolith. Among the most provocative and still-controversial assertions of this body of work is the notion that in the earliest stages of its establishment in a colonial setting, slavery was a less restrictive institution than its antebellum counterpart and boundaries between the races were less firmly drawn. The frontier settings of early Virginia, South Carolina, Georgia, and Louisiana, it was suggested, did not permit strict racial hierarchies and rigid slave regimes to operate, and a kind of "saw horse equality" operated for a time.[7]

The recovery of this history not only explained to Americans how they were drawn by degrees down the road to perdition, but revealed to them the existence of an alternative to the absolute segregation that had seemed an eternal, essential feature of American race relations. And it revealed a nation whose foundation owes as much to the intelligence, culture, and energy of enslaved Africans as it does to the contributions of Euro-Americans. For a society habituated to looking to its origins for inspiration in meeting contemporary social and political challenges, this bit of recovered national memory had redemptive potential. In showing us the diversity of our origins, it challenged us to revise our national identity to reflect a newly known past.

In its own small way, the work on Catholic women in early Louisiana that has engaged me now for nearly a decade attempts a similar restoration of historical complexity to two standard historical narratives. Taking these women into account complicates the history of American Catholicism by revealing an earlier stratum of the institution in which people of African descent constituted the largest and most active segment of one of the church's most sizable colonial congregations. The first of the laboring immigrants to lay the foundations of the American Catholic Church were forced immigrants from Africa, not Europe. The agents of their introduction to Catholicism were missionary nuns and converted women among them whose story limns an episode in church building quite different from the male-dominated muscular parochialism that marked American Catholicism in the nineteenth century. Finally, the path of Catholicism in Louisiana argues for an expansion of the historiography of American slave religion. Evangelical Protestantism marked neither the only nor the first success for Christianity among the enslaved in the territory that would become the United States. The *Hail Mary* and the spiritual both issued from the mouths of the enslaved in the decades before the Civil War.

This chapter offers an overview of Catholic women in early Louisiana. It is divided into four interlocking sections that briefly describe actors who figure prominently in the development of Catholicism in and near the colonial capital of New Orleans. I begin with the Ursuline nuns. Studying them led me to the richer history that subsequently unfolded before me. I move next to Afro-Catholics as a group, focusing particularly on the role of laywomen of African descent in the creation and growth of an Afro-Catholic community. From among this larger group, I next home in on two extraordinary women who played particularly important roles in building the Catholic Church in the Lower Mississippi Valley, Felicité Girodeau and Henriette Delille, two free women of color who advanced Catholicism generally, and Afro-Catholicism in particular, in the antebellum period.

The Ursulines were the first major order of teaching nuns. Originating as a religious congregation in Italy in the middle of the sixteenth century, the Ursulines only became a recognized order of nuns in early seventeenth-century France, where they grew rapidly to prominence. In 1639 a missionary community of Ursulines was established in Quebec, where it hoped to advance the project of Indian conversion begun by the Society of Jesus.[8] Nearly a century later, in 1727, twelve Ursulines made their way to New

Orleans, the capital of the French colony of Louisiana, ostensibly to undertake a similar mission.[9] In the Lower Mississippi Valley, however, they encountered a different missionary field. Less than a year after their arrival, a young novice reported to her father that the Ursulines had "seven slave boarders to instruct for baptism and first communion" and that "a large number" of African girls came to the convent enclosure each day for two hours of religious instruction.[10]

In 1730, the nuns extended their missionary reach to Africans when they provided sponsorship to a confraternity for laywomen that embraced the cause of slave catechesis. The constitution of the organization, called the Children of Mary, required the eighty-five women who joined to have "special zeal" for the religious instruction of their slaves.[11] The sacramental records of New Orleans show that the confresses did as their constitution dictated: they and their close family members are disproportionately represented as godparents of enslaved people who received the sacrament of baptism during the 1730s and 1740s, the decades when the confraternity was active. The Capuchin missionaries charged with the parochial care of the Louisiana colony, meanwhile, showed no interest in the project of African conversion beyond delivering the sacrament of baptism.[12] They made a halfhearted and ultimately unsuccessful attempt to organize a mission school for Indians in the 1720s, but never contemplated a similar project for enslaved Africans. The work of proselytization among the enslaved was left to the women of New Orleans, vowed and lay.

A quick comparison with what was occurring at the same time in the British mainland colonies gives us the first complicating divergence from the standard history of slave religion in America. In the plantation colonies of Virginia, South Carolina, and Georgia, efforts to convert the enslaved to Christianity and baptize them into the established church of the colonizing power were limited and unsuccessful during this period. A handful of missionary Anglican clergymen carried out a small-scale campaign of evangelization among the enslaved under the auspices of the Society for the Propagation of the Gospel in Foreign Parts (SPG). Their efforts essentially met with failure. Planters were, for the most part, resistant to the project and the enslaved found little in Anglicanism to attract them. But the Anglican effort was also hampered by a shortage of missionary personnel. The small cadre of priests was scattered among a huge population of ungathered souls. As a Protestant church, Anglicanism lacked the female army of catechists furnished to the Catholic Church by female religious orders and confraternities. The Louisiana church was equally poor in clergymen, but nuns and the laywomen's confraternity extended its reach in the matter of catechesis. There was a nun or confreress for every thirty-seven enslaved persons in Louisiana in 1731, a degree of saturation that the spg could not hope to approach with its limited troops in South Carolina.[13]

The paucity of clerical personnel is only one of the factors to which the failure of Anglicanism among enslaved people has been attributed. A worship style uncongenial to African tradition, the enslaved's aversion to adopting the religion of the slaveholder, and planter resistance to conversion are also frequently cited explanations. The role of gender in the failure remains unexplored, even though the attractions of evangelicalism for enslaved women have long been recognized.[14] Might not the exclusion of women from organized religious leadership in Anglicanism have been a significant factor in its failure among the enslaved? The example of Louisiana suggests that it was. Catholicism—the religion of the slaveholder—did take root among the enslaved population there, particularly among its women.

Of 221 people baptized in New Orleans in 1733, 165, or 75 percent, were enslaved people. Even though enslaved females represented only 44 percent of the total slave population, they made up 54 percent of those who approached the baptismal font during those years.[15] We cannot know why so many of the city's enslaved women and girls became Catholics. Perhaps the sacrament was simply imposed, and women resisted less successfully or insistently than men. But subsequent patterns in baptism and godparenting suggest that something else was at work. In the 1750s and 1760s, more adult men than adult women among the enslaved were baptized, in numbers disproportionate to the population. The implication is that the baptized daughters of the adult women baptized in the 1730s conducted an intimate campaign of conversion when they began to choose life partners in the 1750s and 1760s.[16]

More telling than the baptismal record, however, is the trajectory of godparenting by people of African descent. In the early 1730s, the godparents of the enslaved were almost always free people of European descent. Only 2 percent of the enslaved people baptized in 1733, for example, were sponsored by people of African descent. That figure rose to 21 percent by 1750, and by 1765 it stood at 68 percent. In 1775, 89 percent of the enslaved people baptized were sponsored by people of African descent. Women, enslaved and free, were particularly active as godparents, especially during periods when there were large influxes of new Africans in the late eighteenth century and again as a steady stream of enslaved people from the Anglophone, Protestant, upper South began arriving in the early 1800s.[17]

In the earliest generation, it is likely that enslaved women accepted the sacrament of baptism for themselves and their children for a mixture of reasons that had little, if anything, to do with belief in Catholic doctrine. The pressure exerted by the Ursuline nuns and the women of the confraternity would have been inescapable. Some two-thirds of the city's free females of marriageable age belonged to the Children of Mary, so eluding their attentions would have been difficult. Acceding to the ritual might also have won the kind of approval from slaveholders that made life more bearable than it might otherwise have been. But there may have been other, less coercive, factors at play. The gendered division of religious labor in Catholicism—the recognition of a special class of female religious specialists, delineation of a sacred female space closed to men, and the practice of reposing in the hands of women the responsibility for preparing girls for the rite of religious initiation—was also a feature of the traditional religion practiced in Senegambia, the locale from which most of the first generation of Louisiana's enslaved people came. Rather than the content of Catholicism, it was its form in New Orleans—female religious specialists (nuns), female sacred space (convent enclosure), and a female association to oversee religious initiation (confraternity)—that was familiar to enslaved Senegambian women. Within this form, they could continue to enact a traditional religious function. Whatever the admixture of coercion and attraction may have been, gender was the feature upon which formal conversion turned.[18]

Gender then, was at the center of the development of a large Afro-Catholic community in colonial New Orleans. People of African descent dominate the baptismal register throughout the period. They constituted between 64 percent and 74 percent of those baptized in four sample years between 1763 and 1795.[19] Enslaved and free people of African descent demanded much of the clergy's time. In 1790, for example, the week of a parochial clergyman was filled with sacramental attention to this community. In May of that year, Father Olot of St. Louis Cathedral baptized a free woman of color and a young enslaved boy on Sunday. On Tuesday, Julia Bonne, a free quadroon, and the enslaved Honorario were presented to him at the font. Wednesday brought two free blacks to the sanctuary for baptism, and Friday he baptized an enslaved boy.[20]

The sacramental records offer the only indication of the congregation's makeup during the colonial period. After the Louisiana Purchase, Anglophone visitors wrote narrative descriptions of the city's religious life that confirm the dominance not only of people of African descent, but of Afro-Creole women in the New Orleans church. John Watson described a congregation in 1805 that was black, female, and pious. "Some," he reported of the Afro-Creole women who filled the pews, "are seen counting their beads with much attention and remain long on their knees." Some fourteen years later, Benjamin Latrobe captured another scene of striking female piety. A temporary altar had been built in the cathedral for the "Adoration of the Cross" that traditionally took place on Good Friday. In addition to the crucifixion, an image of the Virgin was prominently placed. Latrobe reported that the worshippers, "of whom 3/4 at least were colored, & of those a very large majority were women, in their best dresses," surged toward the altar where, "after crossing themselves they kneeled down & kissed the hands, feet, and body of the crucifix which lay upon the carpet, & at the same time put a piece of money into the waiters." Latrobe was struck by the intensity of the pious emotion he witnessed among the women: "Several of the young women appeared to mix a kind of devotional passion with their kisses, & one woman, after getting near the door, turned back & kissed the image again most passionately, while tears were running down her face."[21]

If one stood on the edge of Benjamin Latrobe's time horizon and gazed back at the history of Catholicism in the Lower Mississippi Valley around New Orleans, the church would appear as a black, female-dominated institution. Two groups of women of European descent waged a campaign of conversion that laid its human foundations, and successive generations of women of African descent constituted it and sustained it. This colonial and early national past offers its portrait grudgingly. Its features had to be teased from statistics distilled from sacramental records and a smattering of other sources, almost none of them narrative. What emerges is a group portrait, rich in its implications but a little bloodless. When we look ahead, we begin to see distinct faces, two of them belonging to extraordinary women who extended the colonial legacy of Catholic women of color into the antebellum period.

Henriette Delille was born to a free woman of color in New Orleans in 1812, the year that Louisiana became a state. She was descended from a long line of women who had played a part in building the New Orleans church. Her great-great-grandmother was a Senegambian woman named Nanette, whose conversion to Catholicism was almost certainly related to the Children of Mary Confraternity: Nanette was an enslaved domestic in the household of Marie Payen Dubreuil, a founding member of the association. Nanette and her daughters, Marianne and Cecile, established a family tradition of active piety by becoming godmothers as young women and serving frequently as baptismal sponsors for the rest of their lives.[22] Cecile, who was Henriette Delille's great-grandmother, set an example for her daughter, Henriette LeBeau, and granddaughter, Maria Josefa Diaz, who were also virtuoso godmothers. From the early 1770s on, all of Henriette Delille's maternal ancestors were free women of color, a factor that informs our understanding of the degree to which they chose to become active Catholics.[23]

Like other women of African descent who became frequent godmothers, the Delille ancestors especially concerned themselves with bringing those not born into Catholicism into the embrace of the church. In the late eighteenth century, women of African descent frequently stood beside newly enslaved Africans who waited to receive the sacrament of baptism at large group inductions celebrated at Eastertide and Pentecost. When the internal slave trade began to bring significant numbers of Anglophones from the upper South to New Orleans at the turn of the nineteenth century, these women took a special interest in sponsoring them and their children. Their efforts were crucial to maintaining a black Catholic Church in the city as evangelical Protestant congregations sprang up in the decades following the Louisiana Purchase.[24]

Henriette Delille's maternal ancestors exemplify the laywomen of African descent who constituted the vital and self-sustaining core of the New Orleans Catholic community. Delille took her familial tradition of piety a step further when she founded a religious order for women of color in antebellum New Orleans. In the context of her family history and education, her vocation was not particularly remarkable. Nuns often come from intensely religious families and frequently are educated by nuns themselves.[25] Delille was descended from four generations of devout Catholic women, and she was educated at a school for free girls of color sponsored by the Ursulines. When she became an adult, it probably felt natural to her to pursue a deeper religious commitment.[26]

As a young woman in the 1820s, Henriette Delille apparently joined a lay confraternity of free women of color sponsored by a French missionary priest. He marveled at the young women who managed lives of exemplary devotion and righteousness despite the "Babylonian scandals" that permeated New Orleans and especially threatened the virtue of free women of mixed race. The confreresses were "like angels; they teach the Blacks to pray, they catechize, they instruct." In the 1830s, Henriette and a small group of women who had belonged to this association organized themselves into a formal religious community of a type that lay between the confraternity and the religious order. The Sisters of the Congregation of the Presentation of the Blessed Virgin Mary pledged, in 1836, to serve "the sick, the infirm, and the poor" and to "teach the principal mysteries of religion and the most important points of Christian morality."[27]

Delille and two companions began to live communally around 1840, and some twelve years later they adopted modified religious dress and took private vows. The community continued its broad apostolate of catechesis and ministry to the poor and the infirm among the enslaved and free black population and added an orphanage to their portfolio. They were recognized as a religious order of nuns in 1872 under the name Soeurs de Sainte Famille (Sisters of the Holy Family). Henriette Delille died in 1862, but the Sisters of the Holy Family survived the Civil War and Reconstruction and continued their ambitious apostolate to a thriving Afro-Catholic community in New Orleans. An English missionary priest who arrived in the city in 1875 keen to minister to the city's freed blacks commented of the city's Afro-Catholics that "the French clergy would not like to have them withdrawn from their churches because they are their chief support."[28]

The Sisters of the Holy Family and Henriette Delille remain a major presence in New Orleans, and the sisters also minister to Catholics in Texas, Washington, D.C., Belize, and Nigeria. The cause for Delille's canonization was opened several years ago. If it is successful, she will be the first native-born African American to be recognized as a saint by the Catholic Church.[29]

Henriette Delille has recently achieved a degree of international celebrity, but Felicité Girodeau remains almost unknown outside her hometown of Natchez, Mississippi. Yet she, like Delille, played a key role in sustaining Catholicism in the Lower Mississippi Valley in the decades following the Louisiana Purchase, when the immigration of Anglophone Protestants, black and white, challenged it. The story of Felicité Girodeau's full restoration to the history of American Catholicism is almost as fascinating as the narrative of her achievement. It is a striking example of the capacity of popular memory, shaped by what is comfortable and simple, to obscure the complicated, sometimes disturbing, past that rises from the archives.

In the twentieth century, white Southerners latched onto a distinctive art form to commemorate and celebrate their antebellum past: the pageant. The Southern pageant, like the Christmas pageant that is a staple of the American church calendar, is a reenactment that blends dramatization with narration to recount an actual historical era or event. The Southern pageant features men in gray, ladies in hoop skirts, moonlight, and magnolias. In Natchez, the pageant has played a starring role in an annual festival dubbed the Natchez Pilgrimage, a tour of dozens of lovingly maintained plantation houses that culminates in a nightly dramatization of Natchez life during the reign of King Cotton. When St. Mary's Church prepared to celebrate its 175th anniversary in 1991, the congregation naturally chose to mount a pageant as the centerpiece of commemoration.

St. Mary's parishioners commissioned the archivist of the Archdiocese of New Orleans, a historian, to research and write a history of the parish to serve, among other things, as the basis for the pageant. They also told him that they wanted to build the pageant around four individuals who had been critical to the life of St. Mary's over its long history. They were unanimous about who the first of these should be, a woman known to the parish as Grandma, the matriarch of the parish in its first decades. Her name was Felicité Girodeau. According to yet another Natchez matriarch, Laura Edwards Monteith, Felicité Girodeau was a "woman of culture." This label was not lightly given by Laura Monteith. As the head of the local chapter of the Daughters of the Confederacy and the Confederate Memorial Association, she was the keeper of the Old South identity that early twentieth-century Natchez held in memorial trust. The parishioners of St. Mary's assumed that Girodeau was, like Monteith, a member of the Natchez elite: a white woman.[30]

When archivist Charles Nolan began his search for traces of Girodeau in the historical record, he began at the beginning, with baptismal registers. She was not to be found in those of Natchez, so he checked the New Orleans sacramental registers at his own archive and found her. In 1817, Felicité Pomet married Gabriel Girodeau at St. Louis Cathedral before three witnesses. She and her groom were, the priest noted, both free people of color.[31]

By the 1990s, Natchez, like the rest of Mississippi, was fully engaged in recovering and claiming all of its past. The enslaved and free people of color who helped build the cotton boomtown made their way into the narratives that accompanied the Natchez Pilgrimage. When Nolan reported what he had learned about Felicité Girodeau to the committee in charge of the St. Mary's celebration, "they didn't bat an eye." The first figure on stage in the St. Mary's pageant, "Bless this House," was Felicité Girodeau, who faced the audience and announced, "I am a free woman of color."[32]

Girodeau earned the honorific "Grandma" because she nearly single-handedly ensured the survival of the Catholic Church in Natchez during decades of clerical neglect and aggressive Protestant proselytization. During the 1820s and 1830s, Natchez was served only intermittently by priests. Some came through as itinerants, sent out by the diocese to administer communion to people who had not received the sacrament for years. When they came to town, Girodeau's house became the rectory and the sanctuary. The priests slept on her sofa, heard confession in her closet, and said Mass in her parlor. Offering a place for the celebration of the sacraments and shelter for those who administered them gave the struggling Natchez congregation essential physical and ritual anchors. But Girodeau's greatest contribution was to build the congregation. She was a virtuoso godmother, sponsoring thirty-two infants, children, and adults, black and white, for baptism between 1836 and 1860.[33]

Ironically, Felicité Girodeau had a hand in obscuring her contribution to Catholicism in the Lower Mississippi Valley. When William Henry Elder was appointed bishop of Natchez on the eve of the Civil War, he sought her out and asked her to provide him with a chronicle of the church over which he had come to preside. Felicité gave him a vivid account of every priest who had passed through, detailed the trials of finding a physical home for the parish, and celebrated the occasions when visiting priests administered the sacraments to parishioners who had gone without communion for years. On her own work she was silent. She offered a history of the church in Natchez, not the story of its congregation, the community of the faithful to which she provided sustaining leadership.[34]

The recovered stories of the Catholic women of the Lower Mississippi Valley are only now making their way into print. The revision of the standard histories of American Catholicism and African American religion happens now only in the minds of those who come into contact with this limited body of work. When it comes to a consideration of the colonial French contribution to American Catholicism, even the most recent works focus on missionary work among the Indians in New France. When Louisiana appears, it is as a footnote, and the people of African descent who largely constituted the church in the Lower Mississippi Valley are invisible.[35] An eminent scholar of American religion wrote in 1995 that "most of the story of Catholic New France belongs to Canadian, not United States history. . . . [The French] were the Catholics who paid attention to the personalities and practices of Native Americans." The monument to early French Catholic influence, he continues, "is much of Canada and a special coloring in selective areas of Catholicism in the United States."[36] I am sure that he would include Louisiana among those "selective areas," but I suspect that he might not have chosen to speak of a "special coloring" had he known more about Louisiana Catholicism's particular past.

I encountered the story of Felicité Girodeau toward the end of my investigation of the Catholic women of New Orleans. Neither her race nor her achievements surprised me. She had relatives in New Orleans and was clearly part of the tradition of Afro-Catholic female leadership that developed in the Lower Mississippi Valley over more than a century. I suspect that a little digging in other long-lived Catholic congregations on the Gulf Coast would turn up more women like Felicité Girodeau and the Delille ancestors. Someday, I hope that we will find Jarena Lee and Henriette Delille sharing space in the same book about African American religion. And I look forward to finding the church built by the women of African descent in the Lower Mississippi Valley written into the next survey of American Catholicism. In the meantime, I am thankful for small changes. The most recent major study of Christianity among the enslaved was Sylvia Frey and Betty Wood's *Come Shouting to Zion: African American Protestantism in the American South and British Caribbean to 1830*. Its subtitle makes clear the limitations of its scope, and for this I am grateful. From my perspective, I view the advent of titles that acknowledge what has been left out as welcome first steps toward the more richly textured, inclusive history that belongs to us all.

Notes

1. Jay P. Dolan, *The American Catholic Experience: A History from Colonial Times to the Present* (Notre Dame, Ind.: University of Notre Dame Press, 1992), 161.
2. Early American Catholicism gained some ground under the administration of John Carroll, the first bishop in the United States, and gained an important membership boost when some 10,000 refugees of the Haitian Revolution arrived in Baltimore, Norfolk, and other cities of the young republic's eastern seaboard. But this episode, like that of colonial Louisiana, has failed to alter the prevailing narrative arc of American Catholicism. Paul F. Lachance, "The Foreign French," in *Creole New Orleans: Race and Americanization*, ed. Arnold R. Hirsch and Joseph Logsdon (Baton Rouge: Louisiana State University Press, 1992), 103.
3. John Watson, "Notia of Incidents at New Orleans in 1804 and 1805," *American Pioneer* 2 (May 1843): 230.
4. The literature is vast. For some of the most recent examples, see Dolan, *The American Catholic Experience*, 127–383; Chester Gillis, *Roman Catholicism in America* (New York: Columbia University Press, 1999), 48–81; and Martin E. Marty, *A Short History of American Catholicism* (Allen, Tex.: Thomas More, 1995), 111–42.
5. Ulrich Bonnell Phillips, *Life and Labor in the Old South* (Boston: Little, Brown, 1929). See also his *American Negro Slavery: A Survey of the Supply, Employment and Control of Negro Labor as Determined by the Plantation Regime* (New York: D. Appleton, 1918); and his *Racial Problems, Adjustments and Disturbances in the Antebellum South* (Richmond, Va.: Southern Publication Society, 1909).
6. Among the major contributions to this historiography are Kenneth M. Stampp, *The Peculiar Institution: Slavery in the Ante-Bellum South* (New York: Vintage, 1956); Eugene Genovese, *Roll Jordan, Roll: The World the Slaves Made* (New York: Pantheon Books, 1974); Eugene Genovese, *The Political Economy of Slavery: Studies in the Economy and Society of the Slave South* (New York: Pantheon, 1965); Stanley Elkins, *Slavery: A Problem in American Institutional and Intellectual Life*

(Chicago: University of Chicago Press, 1959); James Oakes, *The Ruling Race: A History of American Slaveholders* (New York: Knopf, 1982); and Robert W. Fogel and Stanley L. Engerman, *Time on the Cross: The Economics of American Negro Slavery* (Boston: Little, 1974). Peter J. Parish, *Slavery: History and Historians* (New York: Harper and Row, 1989), provides an excellent and comprehensive historiographical study of the scholarship of slavery.

7. On colonial slavery, see especially Ira Berlin, *Many Thousands Gone: The First Two Centuries of Slavery in North America* (Cambridge: Harvard University Press, 1998); Gwendolyn Midlo Hall, *Africans in Colonial Louisiana: The Development of Afro-Creole Culture in the Eighteenth Century* (Baton Rouge: Louisiana State University Press, 1992); Edmund S. Morgan, *American Slavery, American Freedom: The Ordeal of Colonial Virginia* (New York: Norton, 1975); Philip D. Morgan, *Slave Counterpoint: Black Culture in the Eighteenth-Century Chesapeake and Lowcountry* (Chapel Hill: University of North Carolina Press, 1998); Daniel H. Usner Jr., *Indians, Settlers & Slaves in a Frontier Exchange Economy: The Lower Mississippi Valley before 1783* (Chapel Hill: University of North Carolina Press, 1992); Betty Wood, *Slavery in Colonial Georgia, 1730–1775* (Athens: University of Georgia Press, 1984); and Peter H. Wood, *Black Majority: Negroes in Colonial South Carolina from 1670 through the Stono Rebellion* (New York: Knopf, 1974).

8. Leslie Choquette, " 'Ces Amazones du Grand Dieu': Women and Mission in Seventeenth-Century Canada," *French Historical Studies* 17, no. 3 (Spring 1992): 627–54; Marie de l'Incarnation, *Word from New France: The Selected Letters of Marie de l'Incarnation*, ed. and trans. Joyce Marshall (Toronto: Oxford, 1967); Teresa Ledochowska, *Angela Merici and the Company of St. Ursula According to the Historical Documents*, trans. Mary Teresa Neylan (Rome: Ancora, 1967); Linda Lierheimer, "Female Eloquence and Maternal Ministry: The Apostolate of Ursuline Nuns in Seventeenth-Century France" (Ph.D. diss., Princeton University, 1994); Elizabeth Rapley, *The Dévotes: Women and Church in Seventeenth-Century France* (Montreal: McGill-Queen's University Press, 1990).

9. "Déliberations du Conseil" and "Private Archives III," Ursuline Convent Archives, New Orleans (hereafter UCANO).

10. Marie Madeleine Hachard, *Letters of Marie Madeleine Hachard, 1727–28*, trans. Myldred Masson Costa (New Orleans: n.p., 1974), 59.

11. "Premiere Régistre de la Congrégation des Dames Enfants de Marie," UCANO, 7.

12. Emily Clark, " 'By All the Conduct of Their Lives': A Laywomen's Confraternity in New Orleans, 1730–1744," *William and Mary Quarterly*, 3d ser., 54 (October 1997): 769–94. The chief Capuchin cleric in New Orleans, Raphael de Luxembourg, wrote at length in 1726 of the school he was trying to establish for French children and asked as an afterthought for financial support so that he could add a little school for Indians. There is no mention of Africans. Archives des Colonies, Correspondance Général, Louisiane, Archives Nationales de France, Series C13A, Paris, France, 10:43–46v, May 18, 1726. A report by Raphael de Luxembourg on

the state of the church in Louisiana in 1728 dwells on French immorality and ignores the issue of Indian and African conversion. Archives des Colonies, Correspondance Général, Louisiane, Archives Nationales de France, Series C13A, Paris, France, 11:217–19.

13. On the failure of Anglicanism, see Sylvia R. Frey and Betty Wood, *Come Shouting to Zion: African American Protestantism in the American South and British Caribbean to 1830* (Chapel Hill: University of North Carolina Press, 1998), 63–79. The ratio of nuns and confreresses to the enslaved population is calculated from "Premiere Régistre," Charles R. Maduell, *Census Tables for the French Colony of Louisiana from 1699 through 1732* (Baltimore: Genealogical Publishing Company, 1972); and Emily J. Clark, "A New World Community: The New Orleans Ursulines and Colonial Society, 1727–1803" (Ph.D. diss., Tulane University, 1998), Appendix One.

14. Frey and Wood, *Come Shouting to Zion*, 94–95, 104–6, 108–10, 121–22, 124, 126–28, 139, 169–72, 187–89, 210–12.

15. Baptismal statistics based on St. Louis Cathedral Baptisms, 1731–1733, Archives of the Archdiocese of New Orleans; population figures nearest in date to this year are drawn from Paul Lachance, "Summary of Louisiana Census of 1737" (unpublished manuscript), based on "Recapitulation du recensement general de la Louisiane en 1737," Archives des Colonies, Archives Nationales, Series C, C13, Paris, France, C4:197.

16. Emily Clark and Virginia Meacham Gould, "The Feminine Face of Afro-Catholicism in New Orleans, 1727–1852," *William and Mary Quarterly*, 3d ser., 59, no. 2 (April 2002): 423.

17. Ibid., 425.

18. Ibid., 421.

19. Statistics based on Jacqueline K. Voorhies, trans. and comp., *Some Late Eighteenth-Century Louisianians: Census Records, 1758–1796* (Lafayette: University of Southwestern Louisiana, 1973); and also on St. Louis Cathedral Baptisms and Marriages, 1763–1766; St. Louis Cathedral Baptisms, 1772–1776; St. Louis Cathedral Baptisms, 1786–1796; and "Libro quinto de bautizados negros y mulatos de la parroquia de San Luis de esta ciudad de la Nueva Orleans: contiene doscientos treinta y sieta folios utiles, y de principia en primero de octubre de mil setecientos noventa y dos, y acaba [en 1798]," Archives of the Archdiocese of New Orleans.

20. "Libro quinto de bautizados negros y mulatos."

21. Watson, "Notia of Incidents at New Orleans," 234; Benjamin Henry Boneval Latrobe, *Impressions Respecting New Orleans, Diary & Sketches, 1818–1820*, ed. Samuel Wilson Jr. (New York: Columbia University Press, 1951), 121–22.

22. See, for example, May 28, 1746, June 29, 1746, February 7, 1747, March 5, 1747, June 11, 1748, St. Louis Cathedral Baptisms and Marriages, 1744–1753; March 23, 1760, May 25, 1760, September 7, 1760, St. Louis Cathedral Baptisms, 1759–1762; Octo-

ber 27, 1765, St. Louis Cathedral Baptisms and Marriages, 1763–1766; May 13, 1775, St. Louis Cathedral Baptisms, 1772–1776; and March 4, 1775, July 23, 1775, in "Libro 1781 que es el corrente . . . ," Archives of the Archdiocese of New Orleans.

23. Marie Ann, Delille's great-aunt, was first freed privately before the French colonial governor, Louis de Kerelec, and was later publicly emancipated by notarial act under the Spanish regime. Emancipation of Marie Ann, Acts of Andrés Almonester y Roxas, January 10, 1770, Notarial Archives of New Orleans. Marianne and her children were freed in 1772. Cecile, Delille's mother, was freed two years later. Emancipation of Cecile, Acts of Fernando Rodriguez, 1772, Notarial Archives of New Orleans. Marianne's emancipation is recorded in Acts of Juan Garic, February 11, 1772, September 23, 1772, Notarial Archives of New Orleans. For examples of these women's baptismal sponsorship, see August 9, 1781, in "Libro donde se asientan las partidas de baptismos . . . 1777 que empezó hasta el año de 1781 que es el corrente"; February 19, 1784, "Libro quinto de bautizados negros y mulattos"; St. Louis Cathedral Baptisms of Slaves and Free People of Color, March 1825–December 1826; and St. Louis Cathedral Baptisms of Slaves and Free People of Color, September 1827–June 1829, Archives of the Archdiocese of New Orleans.

24. Clark and Gould, "Feminine Face of Afro-Catholicism," 436.

25. For examples of this phenomenon in French convents, see Elizabeth Rapley, *A Social History of the Cloister: Daily Life in the Teaching Monasteries of the Old Regime* (Montreal: McGill-Queen's University Press, 2001), 154–58. Numerous examples of New Orleans Ursulines who entered religious life after attending the convent school appear in "Lettres circulaires," UCANO.

26. Clark and Gould, "Feminine Face of Afro-Catholicism," 442.

27. Portier to Cholleton, September [n.d.] 1820, in Records of La Propagation de la Foi, Oeuvres Missionaires Pontificale, Lyon; "Rules and Regulations of the Sisters of the Congregation of the Presentation of the Blessed Virgin Mary," Archives of the Sisters of the Holy Family, New Orleans; manuscript notes of Sr. Mary Borgia Hart, Archives of the Sisters of the Holy Family, New Orleans.

28. Virginia Meacham Gould and Charles E. Nolan, *No Cross, No Crown: Black Nuns in Nineteenth-Century New Orleans* (Bloomington: University of Indiana Press, 2001), 3; Peter L. Benoit, diary entry, April 9, 1875, in Mill Hill Fathers' Archives, quoted in Clark and Gould, *Feminine Face of Afro-Catholicism*, 448.

29. For photographs of Henriette Delille and modern-day Sisters of the Holy Family, go to the following websites: <http://www.cmswr.org/membercommunities/SHF.htm> and <http://www.nutrias.org/~nopl/exhibits/fmc/fmc.htm>.

30. Charles E. Nolan, interview by author, August 21, 2001; Laura Edwards Monteith, interview by Richard O. Gerow, September 18, 1832, photocopy, Archives of the Archdiocese of New Orleans; "Grand Old Lady of Natchez Given Honor by Friends," *Natchez Democrat*, September 19, 1933.

31. St. Louis Cathedral Marriages, 1806–1821, entry #675, July 3, 1817, Archives of the Archdiocese of New Orleans.

32. Nolan interview; *Bless This House*, produced and directed by Tommy Jackson, November 24, 1991, Archives of the Archdiocese of New Orleans.

33. Henry Elder, "Copy of Notes Written Sept. 2d 1859 from the Account Given by Mad. Felicité Girodeau. Written Originally in Her Presence by Me," photocopy of original, Archives of the Archdiocese of New Orleans.

34. Ibid.

35. See, for example, Dolan, *The American Catholic Experience*; Gillis, *Roman Catholicism in America*; and Marty, *A Short History of American Catholicism*.

36. Marty, *A Short History of American Catholicism*, 63.

4

Sarah Osborn's Enlightenment

Reimagining Eighteenth-Century Intellectual History

Catherine A. Brekus

American religious historians have typically treated the Enlightenment as an elite move-ment that had little to do with women. When writing about intellectual or theological history, they have almost always assumed that the great intellectual movements of the past were shaped by men alone.

Did eighteenth-century women have an Enlightenment? The answer, according to Catherine Brekus, partially depends on how one defines the term. Drawing on recent scholarship connecting the birth of evangelicalism in the eighteenth century to enlightened thought, Brekus argues that women, like men, belong in narrative histories of the Enlight-enment in America. Her case study of Sarah Osborn, an eighteenth-century teacher from Newport, Rhode Island, reveals that evangelical women were deeply attracted to the Enlightenment's emphasis on experience. Through their personal testimonies of faith, they helped to popularize this experiential language among other evangelical Christians.

In 1743, Sarah Osborn, a schoolteacher in Newport, Rhode Island, began writing a spiritual memoir. Influenced by the excitement of the Great Awak-ening, the religious revivals that brought thousands of converts into New England's churches, she decided to reflect on the spiritual meaning of her life. How had God ordered her experiences? What could her life story tell her about both herself and God? Filling more than 130 pages with her bittersweet memories of God's "dealings" with her, she wrote about her childhood sin-fulness, her conversion, and her painful battles against despair—what we would call depression. The lesson she had learned along her religious pil-grimage could be summarized in just a few words. "Trust in the Lord," she advised, "and never dispair of his mercy."[1]

After finishing her memoir, Sarah Osborn continued to write, reflecting on her life in hundreds of letters to friends, a short theological tract that she published anonymously in 1755, and an astonishing number of diaries, more than fifty volumes in all. As she explained in 1754, writing helped her "get near or wrestle with God." "I seem to Lie u[nder] necessity to improve my

Pen if [I w]ill be at all Lively in religion," she wrote. According to Samuel Hopkins, her minister in Newport, she wrote 5,000 to 15,000 pages, more than 1,500 of which still survive.[2]

Osborn seems to have written for many reasons: to examine her heart for signs of corruption, to strengthen her relationship to God, and to help make sense of events that stretched the limits of her understanding, such as the death of loved ones. Most of all, she seems to have wanted to transform her life into a "text" that could be "read" during times of trouble or despair. Because her life was filled with poverty and illness, she sometimes found it difficult to keep her faith, but writing helped her to remember God's goodness. Obsessively recording her religious experiences in thousands of pages of entries, she repeatedly examined them for rational "evidence" of divine providence. As she wrote on the cover of her memoir twenty years after composing it, "this Book I Have reread again and again."[3]

Her rich devotional manuscripts offer a fascinating glimpse of popular Christianity in eighteenth-century America. They also offer a unique perspective on the intellectual movement that historians describe as the Enlightenment. Like John Locke, who claimed that "all our knowledge is founded" on "EXPERIENCE," Osborn believed that if she examined her life with scientific detachment, she could make discoveries about both herself and God. "*How do I know this God is mine; and that I myself am not deceived?*" she asked. "By the *Evidences* of a *Work of Grace* wrought in my Soul."[4] She believed that Christians could be virtually certain of their salvation if they objectively examined their lives for "evidence" of divine grace.

It may seem surprising to discuss Sarah Osborn, a little-known evangelical woman, in the same breath as John Locke, one of the most renowned philosophers in the modern world. But Sarah Osborn wrestled with many of the same questions that Enlightenment thinkers raised in their work—questions about original sin, the possibilities of human knowledge, and the nature of God—and her diaries are saturated with an "enlightened" language of evidence, experience, and certainty. Her writings raise two provocative questions for historians: First, did evangelicals—who are often portrayed as backward looking—embrace the Enlightenment? And second, did women play a role in constructing Enlightenment ideas? Or to state the question more baldly, did women have an Enlightenment?

The most common answer to both questions has been no. Although intellectual historians have increasingly recognized that the Enlightenment was not a monolith, most have tended to depict it as an elite, masculine movement that had little to do with women's lives. Indeed, when Adrienne Koch published *The American Enlightenment* in 1965, she included extracts from the writings of just five male leaders: Benjamin Franklin, John Adams, Thomas Jefferson, James Madison, and Alexander Hamilton.[5] Historians have also portrayed the Enlightenment as aggressively secular in its outlook. According to Peter Gay, for example, the Enlightenment involved a small number of French philosophers, all men, whose rallying cry was Voltaire's "ecrasez l'infame." Similarly, Henry May, whose 1976 book, *The Enlightenment in America*, remains the only one-volume survey of the movement in America, focuses almost entirely on learned men such as Thomas Jefferson and Benjamin Franklin who were hostile to organized religion. Although May recognizes that nineteenth-century Protestants embraced elements of Enlightenment thought (particularly Thomas Reid's Common Sense tradition), he suggests that eighteenth-century evangelicals were engaged in a battle against the "Age of Reason." Given May's interpretation, one would never imagine that an evangelical woman like Sarah Osborn might belong in a book about the Enlightenment in America.[6]

This chapter, in contrast, argues that Sarah Osborn's story—the story of an evangelical woman who had little in common with Franklin or Jefferson—should also be read as a story about the Enlightenment. More broadly, this chapter suggests that women's history forces us to rethink many of our assumptions about the Enlightenment in America. Contrary to what many historians have implied, the Enlightenment was not an elite, male movement but a broader transformation that affected the way ordinary converts, including women, made sense of their lives. Nor was the Enlightenment entirely a secularizing force. Building on the work of recent historians, especially David Bebbington, I will argue that evangelicalism, despite its hostility to the most skeptical strains of Enlightenment thought, should be understood as an Enlightenment form of Protestantism.[7] Finally, I will argue that even though Sarah Osborn and other evangelical women were troubled by many strands of the Enlightenment, they embraced the new emphasis on experience and certainty because it gave them greater religious authority.

Reimagining the Enlightenment

How should we define the Enlightenment? Writing in 1784, Immanuel Kant suggested that its "motto" was "dare to know!" Rather than offering blind obedience to the state or the church, "enlightened" men defended the "freedom to use reason publicly in all matters."[8] Echoing Kant's words, historians traditionally have portrayed the Enlightenment as a seventeenth- and eighteenth-century intellectual movement that enshrined reason and free inquiry as the ultimate human values. Paul Hazard explained that the Enlightenment should be understood as a "revolution" against authority, dogma, and Christianity, and Lester G. Crocker described it as "a group of writers, working self-consciously for over a hundred years," who "sought to enlighten men, using critical reason to free minds from prejudices and unexamined authority, and—somewhat later within that period—using the same weapon to explore the ills of society and devise remedies."[9] Peter Gay, one of the most distinguished historians of the Enlightenment, underlined its commitment to *freedom.* "The men of the Enlightenment," he explained, "united on a vastly ambitious program, a program of secularism, humanity, cosmopolitanism, and freedom, above all, freedom in its many forms—freedom from arbitrary power, freedom of speech, freedom of trade, freedom to realize one's talents, freedom of aesthetic response, freedom, in a word, of moral man to make his own way in the world." Despite differing in the details of their interpretations, all these historians claimed that the Enlightenment had rejected the "mythical thinking" of Christianity in favor of "critical thinking" based on reason. They also portrayed the Enlightenment as a singular movement that had crossed international boundaries. As Gay argued, the "little flock of *philosophes*" often quarreled over how to understand human nature and society, but they remained unified by "their tension with Christianity, and their pursuit of modernity."[10]

Although this portrait of the Enlightenment continues to exert a powerful hold on the public imagination, recent historians have challenged it on several grounds. First, historians such as Roger Chartier, Robert Darnton, and Roy Porter have argued that the Enlightenment should be understood as a popular as well as an elite movement that involved "a vastly larger number of relatively obscure thinkers, writers, readers, and contact loops."[11] Because of the expansion of print culture and rising levels of literacy, many educated people participated in debates over "enlightened" ideas. Historians used to assume that the Enlightenment had not affected ordinary people's lives, but most now make the opposite claim. For example, John McManners has shown that the Enlightenment decisively reshaped attitudes toward death and dying in eighteenth-century France, and Norman Fiering has argued that most eighteenth-century Americans assumed that humans beings were instinctively compassionate—a startling reversal of the Puritan past that suggests the growing acceptance of humanitarian ideas.[12]

Second, many social and cultural historians have argued that the Enlightenment cannot be studied in isolation from larger seventeenth- and eighteenth-century transformations. Without claiming that the Enlightenment was nothing more than the by-product of material conditions, they argue that it must be placed in a larger context of political, economic, social, and religious change. For example, British historians have connected the Enlightenment in England to the Glorious Revolution, the growth of religious toleration, the expansion of print culture, and the rise of capitalism.[13]

Third, historians have questioned older assumptions about the singularity of the Enlightenment, often preferring to discuss multiple "enlightenments" that differed according to national circumstance. The Enlightenment "occurred in too many forms to be comprised within a single definition and history," J. G. A. Pocock has written. Historians must imagine "a family of Enlightenments, displaying both family resemblances and family quarrels (some of them bitter and even bloody)."[14]

Fourth, historians have objected to simplistic definitions of the Enlightenment as the "Age of Reason." To be fair, earlier scholars such as Peter Gay also objected to such pat slogans, but because of their fascination with enlightened debates over human rationality, they paid less attention to other aspects of the Enlightenment, especially its privileging of experience. As a result, when other historians have tried to offer concise overviews of this research in textbooks or popular histories, they have often reduced the Enlightenment to a single-minded quest for rationality. But as Roy Porter has argued, enlightened thinkers were less focused on "*a priori* reason" as the key to knowledge than "experience and experiment." Instead of making judgments based on clerical authority or inherited tradition, they insisted on the value of "firsthand experience." Influenced by the scientific method, they insisted that every hypothesis about human nature and society had to be empirically tested.[15]

Fifth, historians have argued that the portrait of a rigorously rational Enlightenment doing battle with religious "superstition" is incomplete. On one hand, there is good reason to describe much of enlightened thought as hostile to religion. Many enlightened intellectuals condemned the "priestcraft" of Christianity and portrayed the church as an enemy of human progress. "All national institutions of churches—whether Jewish, Christian, or Turkish—appear to me no other than human inventions set up to terrify and enslave mankind and monopolize power and profit," wrote Thomas Paine in 1794.[16] But, on the other hand, historians have increasingly recognized that the Enlightenment was a diverse movement, not a singular one, and they have presented a far more complicated picture of the relationship between enlightened thought and Christianity. Some, for example, have wondered whether the Enlightenment may have grown out of the Protestant Reformation: for example, John Locke was raised in a Puritan family, and he may have been shaped by Reformed thought, despite rejecting it later.[17] Historians have also suggested that the Enlightenment contributed to the growth of "more optimistic and tolerant types of Protestantism" such as Latitudinarianism, Deism, and in New England, "Catholick" Congregationalism.[18] In addition, American historians have shown that Protestant thinkers eventually assimilated aspects of enlightened thought in order to buttress their faith against skepticism. As Henry May argued in his 1976 survey, *The Enlightenment in America*, nineteenth-century Protestants defended their faith by appealing to Frances Hutcheson's Common Sense tradition and claiming that all humans have an innate moral sense given by God.[19]

Although all of these studies have found crucial links between enlightened thought and Protestantism, David Bebbington's analysis of eighteenth-century transatlantic evangelicalism offers the most intriguing analysis of the Enlightenment's profound influence on religion. According to Bebbington, the roots of modern evangelicalism can be traced back to the eighteenth century, when the older faith of the Puritans was replaced by a new kind of confident, optimistic Protestantism. Rejecting stereotypes of eighteenth-century evangelicals as reactionary, Bebbington has made the provocative claim that "the Evangelical version of Protestantism was created by the Enlightenment." Unlike earlier Protestants, evangelicals tended to be more optimistic, pragmatic, and humanitarian, and most important, they expressed much greater assurance about their salvation. Influenced by John Locke's emphasis on the authority of personal experience, they insisted that converts could "feel" and "know" whether they had been saved. Jonathan Edwards, for example, insisted that converts gained a "new sense" of grace that fundamentally changed their perception of reality. (Edwards was influenced by Anthony Ashley Cooper, earl of Shaftesbury, and Francis Hutcheson, who argued that all humans have an innate "moral sense" that helps them to distinguish good from evil. Although Edwards, unlike later Protestants, rejected this positive view of human nature, he still agreed that knowledge comes from sense perception.)[20] Rather than arguing that the Enlightenment was constructed against Protestantism, Bebbington has insisted that it also took place *within* Protestantism. What made evangelicals unique—what separated them from the seventeenth-century Puritans—was their embrace of the Enlightenment language of assurance, certainty, experience, and proof.[21]

To be clear, the rise of evangelicalism did not mark a complete break with the Protestant past, and the roots of evangelical experientialism can be traced back to seventeenth-century Puritanism. In both England and America, Puritan ministers urged Christians to examine their experiences in order to make judgments about their relationships to God. Yet Puritans also insisted that humans were too tainted by original sin to attain full knowledge of either the self or God, and they condemned assertions of religious certainty as arrogance. In contrast, ministers in the early eighteenth century, eager to defend Christianity from rationalism, gradually began to expand their trust in firsthand experience. In his tract, *Reason Satisfied and Faith Established* (1712), Cotton Mather defended Christian orthodoxy against "rational" religion by emphasizing the genuine truth contained in personal religious experience, and in *A Treatise Concerning Conversion* (1719), Solomon Stoddard argued that people could know they had experienced conversion by listening to the voice of their consciences. Rejecting the earlier Puritan belief that the moment of conversion was often imperceptible and unknowable, he insisted, "Men may have the knowledge of their own conversion." During the revivals that took place in New England during the 1740s, this "experimental religion," as Cotton Mather called it, flowered into a distinctive kind of evangelical "enlightened" faith that particularly valued experience, sensation, and evidence.[22]

Influenced by David Bebbington's argument, historians have found surprising traces of Enlightenment thought throughout the new transatlantic evangelical movement. Mark Noll has argued that British, American, and Scottish evangelicals, like Locke, believed that "the self's personal experience was foundational for obtaining reliable knowledge," and both Frederick Dyer and David Hempton have noticed close parallels between Enlightenment ideas and Methodist religious practice. As Hempton explains, "The characteristic features of Methodist spirituality—its tendency to morbid introspection, its ruthless self-examination, and its compulsion to share and tell—are all products of its Lockean emphasis on sensible experience." (Describing the Methodists as "enlightened" would have surprised many eighteenth-century intellectuals, who criticized Methodists for their "enthusiasm.") In addition, Bruce Hindmarsh has suggested that Protestants not only absorbed the Enlightenment's empiricist strands, but its individualistic ones as well.[23]

Because of this wide-ranging new research, the term "Enlightenment" has become much more difficult to define and also much more sweeping. Roy Porter's book, *The Creation of the Modern World: The Untold Story of the British Enlightenment*, which was published in 2000, not only discusses thinkers such as John Locke but also changes in everyday life. Although admitting that it would be silly to attribute all the changes that took place in the eighteenth century to enlightened ideas, Porter also insisted that "it would be equally silly to deny that notions of human nature and the ideas of the good life developed by the *philosophes* found wide expression in art and letters, in print culture, and in practical life."[24] When Alan Kors published his massive, four-volume *Encyclopedia of the Enlightenment* in 2003, he included almost 700 entries on topics as diverse as "reason," "hospitals," "law," "poverty," "pornography," "sociability," and "sentimentalism." Reflecting the new interest in the relationship between the Enlightenment and religion, he also included several entries on religious topics, including a biographical sketch of the influential evangelical theologian, Jonathan Edwards.[25]

Besides debating over how to define the Enlightenment, historians have also argued, often heatedly, over its essential meaning. Because scholars tend to view the Enlightenment as a historical watershed—the moment when our "modern" values of individualism, capitalism, and liberalism took shape—they have been sharply divided over how to assess its legacy. Some echo Kant's rhetoric of progress and liberation; others have taken a darker view. As early as 1944, Max Horkheimer and Theodor W. Adorno argued in their influential book *Dialectic of Enlightenment* that the Enlightenment emphasis on reason had led to fascism, not liberation, and in recent years, it has become fashionable to criticize the "Enlightenment project" for laying the groundwork for Western totalitarianism, sexism, imperialism, and racism.[26] Michel Foucault's critical studies of the Enlightenment have been particularly influential. In several books published during the 1960s and 1970s, Foucault contended that the Enlightenment had not represented progress but rather new and more sinister forms of subjection. For example, in *Discipline and Punish: The Birth of the Prison*, he challenged the assumption that the decline of public torture in the eighteenth century had represented a humanitarian triumph. Instead, he argued that prison reformers had created a "disciplinary society" in which people were controlled through constant surveillance rather than brute force. Monarchs had demonstrated their power sporadically through the public spectacle of torture, but enlightened "reformers" aimed for nothing less than "total power"—most ominously, the internal regulation of the "soul."[27] Far from being a harbinger of freedom, the Enlightenment had led to new kinds of repression. In the acerbic words of Eric Hobsbawm, the Enlightenment now appears as nothing more than a "conspiracy of dead white men in periwigs to provide the intellectual foundation for Western imperialism."[28]

Feminist scholars have been particularly suspicious of the Enlightenment's legacy. Influenced by Foucault, they have condemned the Enlightenment for creating "a single truth and a single rationality" that legitimated women's political, economic, and religious subordination.[29] Rather than simply arguing that the Enlightenment was constructed without women, they have made the more radical claim that it was constructed *against* them. According to historian Joan B. Landes, for example, the Enlightenment led to the creation of a bourgeois public sphere that implicitly excluded women on the grounds of their irrationality and "effeminate" vice. Although a few female intellectuals such as Mary Wollstonecraft participated in public debates, their writings echoed "masculinist values." Instead of overturning the social and political order, these women inadvertently reinforced its masculine bias by accepting "male" definitions of humanity. In another study of the gendering of the public sphere, the political theorist Carole Pateman has argued that liberal political theory, one of the greatest "accomplishments" of enlightened thought, is premised on men's sexual control over women.[30]

Like other feminist scholars, women's historians of religion have criticized the Enlightenment for its privileging of "masculine" norms of rationality. For example, Phyllis Mack suggests that the Enlightenment marked a decline in women's spiritual authority. Unlike seventeenth-century women, who had often used ecstatic language to describe their personal relationship to God, eighteenth-century women felt compelled "to cultivate the traits of restraint and rationality at the expense of the more 'feminine' qualities of enthusiasm and spiritual ardor." Rather than expanding women's opportunities for religious expression, the Enlightenment limited them. Similarly, Susan Juster has argued that one of the results of the Enlightenment commitment to rationality and middle-class respectability was the marginalization of female visionaries. Although infamous female prophets such as Jemima Wilkinson and Joanna Southcott certainly made their voices heard in the Anglo-American public sphere, they were ridiculed for eschewing the "enlightened" qualities of civility, gentility, and rationality. Their notorious reputations "exemplify the intractable hostility of Anglo-American men of letters toward women in public."[31]

Although these bleak interpretations of the Enlightenment's effect on women reveal that the Enlightenment cannot be understood in simplistic terms as "progress," they also obscure the many ways in which women were inspired by enlightened ideas. Indeed, many women's historians have objected to viewing female intellectuals such as Mary Wollstonecraft or Mary Astell as "colluding with the oppressor" because of their defense of enlightened ideas.[32] British and French historians have studied women's participation in freemasonry, salons, and the public world of print, but American historians (who have generally written less about the Enlightenment) have also pointed to evidence of eighteenth-century women's growing activism in the public sphere. Rejecting the argument that the Enlightenment led to inherently "masculine" definitions of liberalism, Rosemarie Zagarri has argued that women's exclusion from American citizenship was "contingent, not essential."[33]

Yet despite these contentious debates over how to understand women's relationship to the Enlightenment, few historians have questioned the argument that the Enlightenment undercut women's religious authority. The reason for this is simple. Despite Susan Juster's warning that historians should not treat "the enlightenment and religious enthusiasm as distinct and antagonistic forces," most have echoed traditional interpretations of the Enlightenment as a profoundly skeptical movement that shook the foundations of traditional Christianity.[34] Pointing to the examples of thinkers such as John Locke, who insisted that Christianity must be "reasonable," and the radical David Hume, who insisted that miracles were impossible, they have assumed that most Christians, both male and female, were marginalized in an increasingly secular, rationalist world.[35]

Yet if women's historians take seriously the argument that one of the many "enlightenments" took place within Protestantism as well as against it, a more complicated picture emerges. Perhaps evangelical women such as Sarah Osborn were marginalized by enlightened thought, but perhaps they found ways to adopt it as their own.

Sarah Osborn's "Enlightenment"

If Sarah Osborn could speak to us across the generations, she would not choose to frame her remarkable story around the "Enlightenment," but around divine grace. She could not imagine any other way to explain how a "feeble worthless worm," as she called herself, had overcome poverty and tragedy to become one of the most respected female religious leaders of her time.[36] Her life story, as she confessed in her memoir, was as dramatic as a novel. Raised by parents whom she later described as "severe," she seems to have had a difficult childhood. As a teenager (the dates aren't clear, she was probably fourteen or fifteen) she struggled with temptations to commit suicide. The rest of her life was marked by recurring tragedy. She eloped at the age of seventeen with a sailor, Samuel Wheaten, who died two years later, leaving her with an infant son to support; remarried a successful tailor, Henry Osborn, a widower with three children, who suffered a breakdown that left him unable to work; and toiled long hours as a schoolteacher and a seamstress in order to pay her family's bills. Soon after her second marriage in 1742, she and her husband were forced to sell all their possessions in order to repay their creditors. Despite her constant battle to achieve economic security, she remained indigent throughout her life and her name never appeared on Newport's tax lists. Her beloved son, her only child, died at the age of eleven. Through everything, she suffered chronic bouts of illness. She spent the last twenty years of her life almost entirely confined to her house, unable to walk and almost entirely blind.[37]

Yet despite all these tragedies, Osborn was so charismatic that many people in Newport sought her spiritual counsel. Like the followers of medieval women saints, they seemed to interpret her afflictions as a mark of her sanctity, a symbol of her closeness to a suffering Christ. Reputed to be gifted in prayer, she became more popular than any of the ordained ministers in her town. During the winter of 1766–67, she emerged as the leader of a remarkable religious revival that brought as many as five hundred people—including more than one hundred slaves—to her house each week for prayer meetings. Although she remained poor, strangers from as far away as Canada and the West Indies sent money to help defray her expenses, eager to help a woman who had become virtually a Protestant saint. After her death in 1796, the Reverend Samuel Hopkins heightened her fame by publishing extracts from her writings in two books, *Memoirs of the Life of Mrs. Sarah Osborn* and *Familiar Letters, Written by Mrs. Sarah Osborn and Miss Susanna Anthony, Late of Newport, Rhode Island.*[38]

Osborn seems to have been especially admired by religious conservatives who were ambivalent about the dramatic economic, social, and religious changes that were reshaping their world. As Timothy Breen and Timothy Hall have argued, nothing seemed certain in mid-eighteenth-century America: the expansion of the market, the breakdown of social hierarchy, and increasing religious pluralism meant that individuals were able to exercise greater personal choice than ever before.[39] In Newport, a thriving seaport that was the fourth-largest city in colonial America, people could buy a stunning variety of goods, whether books, furniture, or clothing. "Just imported," announced an ad in the *Newport Mercury* in 1759. "A Variety of European and India Goods, at the most reasonable Rate, for Cash or short credit."[40] People in Newport could also choose among a bewildering plurality of religious traditions. Sarah was a Congregationalist, but Newport was also home to Roman Catholics, Quakers, Anglicans, Moravians, Baptists, and even a small group of Jews.[41] (Touro Synagogue, the oldest synagogue in the United States, was built in Newport in 1762.) Many people must have been intoxicated by this new religious and economic freedom, but others seem to have found it overwhelming. With so many choices, how could one be sure of making the right decision? After Osborn had a conversation with "some serious good sort of people" who were Seventh-Day Baptists, she wrote a letter to a trusted minister asking him to help her defend the custom of keeping Sunday as the Sabbath. "I seem much more confused than usual," she admitted.[42]

Eighteenth-century Protestantism was not only transformed by capitalism and growing religious pluralism, but also by new currents of ideas. Although few American ministers were as radical as England's Samuel Clarke, who challenged the doctrine of eternal punishment, or Daniel Whitby, who complained that the entire idea of original sin was "exceeding cruel, and plainly inconsistent with the Justice, Wisdom, and goodness of our gracious God," growing numbers of clergy began to challenge traditional Calvinist doctrines during the 1740s and 1750s.[43] Indeed, the change may have come even earlier. Reflecting on religion in New England, for example, Jonathan Edwards claimed that "the great noise that was in this part of the country, about Arminianism" began in 1734.[44] (The term "Arminianism" refers to the belief that humans could earn God's favor through good works. In contrast, Calvinists like Sarah Osborn insisted that humans were utterly sinful and could be saved only be divine grace, not by good behavior.) Edwards may have been exaggerating, but it is clear that by the 1740s and 1750s, many ministers had begun to challenge traditional Calvinist beliefs. For example, in 1757, Samuel Webster published a tract condemning the doctrine of original sin as cruel, especially because it logically led to the conclusion that infants as well as adults could be damned. He found it difficult to reconcile a belief in infant damnation with "the *goodness, holiness* or *justice* of God."[45] According to the Reverend Samuel Niles, the doctrine of original sin was the "most eagerly struck at, and virulently opposed by many, in the present age."[46]

Evidence suggests that these theological controversies were not only the product of disputes among learned clergy but also of popular discontent. In other words, changes in religious life happened from the top down and from the bottom up. For example, at the same time as Webster condemned the doctrine of infant damnation as cruel, ordinary Christians began drifting away from older ideas of innate depravity. As Jonathan Edwards complained, many of his congregants mistakenly described their children as "innocent." By the early nineteenth century, Protestantism had been subtly transformed by a growing faith in human goodness and compassion.[47]

Because Sarah Osborn lived in one of the most religiously diverse and tolerant cities in America, she was no stranger to theological controversy, and she seems to have feared that her Calvinist faith was under attack. In the 1740s and 1750s, the ministers whom she most admired—men like Gilbert Tennent, Jonathan Edwards, and Samuel Buell—all offered stern warnings about the insidious "spread of Arminianism, Socinianism, Arianism, and Deism," and when Samuel Hopkins became her minister in 1770, taking tea at her house every Saturday afternoon, she joined him in condemning the alarming spread of infidelity.[48] As a member of the First Congregational Church in Newport, a church that had a reputation for theological rigor, she was especially critical of the more liberal Congregationalists who worshipped nearby in Newport's Second Congregational Church. In 1755, the members of that church happily appointed Ezra Stiles as their pastor even though, as historian Edmund Morgan wryly notes, he had "preached to them on 'the Excellency of the Christian Religion' without once mentioning Christ."[49] Although Stiles became more conservative during his time in Newport, Osborn still found him far too optimistic about human nature for her taste. After hearing him preach on a reassuring text from Psalms, "the Lord is good to all," she asked God to "rouse this servant, alarm Him with a sence of the awful danger there is of His rocking His People more and more to sleep in the cradle of security instead of Exciting them to fly from the wrath to come." Despite admiring his "Lovely Engaging benevolent temper," she thought he focused too much on good works rather than grace, failing "to make clear distinctions between the secure sinner, the Hypocrite, and the real Christian."[50]

Despite her poverty and her lack of formal schooling (she attended a girls' academy for only a few months as a child), Sarah Osborn was well educated for her time. Her parents struggled throughout their lives to make ends meet, but they seem to have emphasized the importance of education. Her family, in some ways, was a distinguished one in Protestant circles: her maternal uncle, John Guyse, was a British minister who published several theological treatises. (Perhaps his most lasting claim to fame is that he, along with Isaac Watts, wrote the preface to the first edition of Jonathan Edwards's *A Faithful Narrative of the Surprising Work of God*, the book that helped inspire the revivals of the Great Awakening.) Although it would be a mistake to identify Osborn as an intellectual, she was a voracious reader who was deeply interested in Protestant theology.[51]

Some of the books that she read heightened her fears of the "awful danger" of straying from Calvinism. On at least one occasion, she seems to have unwittingly chosen a book to share with her female prayer group that was critical of Calvinist teachings. Osborn believed that only a small number of "elect" had been chosen for salvation, and since God had chosen who would be saved and who would be damned even before birth, humans could not earn salvation by performing good works. But when she and her friends read this book together (unfortunately, she did not record its title), they were troubled by its challenge to their belief in predestination. "Defeat satan in his attempt to break us," she implored God, "and prevent His taking advantage and discouraging any by what was read on predestination and reprobation. Lord, thou art infinitely Just in choosing whom thou wilt, and infinitely Just in withholding that Grace thou art no ways bound to Give."[52] More commonly, she learned about liberal or Deist tracts secondhand. For example, she admired David Hamilton's book, *The Private Christian's Witness for*

Christianity, which condemned "the notional and erroneous apprehensions of the Arminian, Socinian, and Deist of the Age."[53]

Osborn responded to the theological controversies of her day by strongly affirming her own orthodoxy. Unlike ministers who questioned the doctrine of original sin, she insisted that humans were essentially corrupt. Reflecting on her childhood, she did not remember herself as an innocent child of nature, but as "a monster in sin," a "lyar," and "the most ignorant and vile of all creatures." Her "bace ingratitude," her "deep-rooted enmity" against God, her "angry ungratefull temper," and her dreadful "corruptions" made her entirely unworthy of God's love.[54] As she confessed over and over again in her diaries, she was "guilty," "peevish," "wretched," "filthy and Poluted," "churlish," and "worthless."[55] (Although judgments about style are hard to quantify, she sounds more harsh than either seventeenth-century Puritans or later generations of evangelicals. As we have seen in our own day, people tend to express their beliefs in especially extreme terms when they feel threatened.) In her opinion, her childhood proved the dark wisdom of the Psalms: "The wicked are estranged from the womb: they go astray as soon as they are born, speaking lies."[56]

Given Sarah Osborn's pessimism about human nature, it is not surprising that she also objected to enlightened thinkers' positive view of self-interest. Newport's wealthy merchants seem to have eagerly embraced Adam Smith's capitalist ethic, but she refused to believe that selfishness could have a silver lining. In contrast to Benjamin Franklin, who assured his readers that self-interest could foster the virtues of hard work and thrift, Osborn insisted that true Christians had to crucify the self. "Strip me intirely of self," she begged God in 1757. "Wean me wholly from the world and all things therein." Four years later, after reading a sermon, "The Evil of Self Seeking," published by her uncle, the Reverend John Guyse, she "bitterly bemoan'd" her selfishness. "The soul that is full of self in any consideration of it, hath no room for CHRIST," Guyse warned. "It is self-sufficient, and becomes a GOD to itself." Nothing but evil could come from the unbridled pursuit of individual desire.[57]

Finally, Osborn also rejected the strain of Enlightenment thought that historians have described as "humanitarianism." As Protestants began to rethink their assumptions about human nature, they also began to shift their understanding of God. Unlike earlier Christians, who had described God as both loving and angry, merciful and vengeful, liberals insisted that God was too compassionate to ever deliberately inflict suffering on his creation. As the Reverend Jonathan Mayhew protested, "If I were to form my conception of God's moral character, by such discourses as I have sometimes heard and read, and such as were, by many, thought to be truly evangelical; instead of thinking Him . . . essentially good, and infinitely the best of Beings, I could not but conclude Him to be infinitely more unjust and cruel, than any other being in the universe!" First and foremost, God was *benevolent*, and he had created the world to make humans happy.[58]

Although Osborn portrayed God as a "tender, indulgent father" and Jesus as a "sympathizing savior" who was "sensibly touched" by her sufferings, she was too much of a Calvinist to question the reality of divine punishment.[59] Because of her faith that God had created the universe to demonstrate his glory, not to promote human happiness, she insisted that suffering and evil were ultimately part of his plan. Consider, for example, one of the most horrifying passages in her memoir, in which she claimed that when she was nine years old God had brutally punished her for the crime of playing on the Sabbath. As she and her mother sailed across the Atlantic to join her father in New England, she became so sinful that God sentenced her to an excruciating ordeal: "On board the ship I Lost my good impressions and grew vile so that I could play upon the sabbath then. But I was convinced of that sin by an accident that befel me, or rather what was orderd by infinite wisdom to that end. For as I was busey a boyling some thing for my babee [a doll], I fell into the fire with my right hand and burnt it all over, which I presently thought was just upon me for playing [on] a sabath day. And I was ashaimd and sorry I had done so." Even though she had been only a child, Osborn believed she had been so "vile" that God had chastised her for her sins, intentionally sending her into the flames.[60] Her God was not serenely "benevolent," but sovereign, majestic, uncontrollable, and sometimes violent. (Given how many eighteenth-century ministers imagined God as benevolent, it is significant that she never seems to have used this word to describe God in a single one of her diaries.)

As these examples illustrate, Sarah Osborn had little in common with enlightened thinkers who wanted to create a more liberal view of humanity and God. Given her hostility to new ideas about the goodness of humanity, the benefits of self-love, and the benevolence of God, it would be easy to portray her as a reactionary who wanted to defend Calvinism against the acids of modernity. According to Charles Hambrick-Stowe, for example, Osborn was a Puritan at heart: she shared more in common with Thomas Shepard, the famous Puritan minister, than with eighteenth-century provincials who prided themselves on their refinement and cosmopolitanism.[61]

Yet despite Osborn's theological conservatism, she looked forward as well as backward, and she was not a Puritan but an evangelical. (She described herself simply as a "Protestant," but she seemed to realize that she stood on the brink of something new, and like many other converts, she settled on the word "evangelical" to describe it. For example, after a night of prayer, she wrote about her experience of "true evangelical repentance.")[62] Inspired by the revivals of the "Great Awakening," she helped to construct a new kind of individualistic faith that drew much of its inspiration from the Lockean emphasis on experiential knowledge. In 1755, for example, she published an anonymous tract with a title that sounded curiously "enlightened": *The Nature, Certainty, and Evidence of True Christianity*. Originally written as a letter to a female friend who was anxious about the state of her soul, the tract explained that conversion could be objectively verified by "*Evidences* of a *Work of Grace*." As Osborn admitted, her "Evidences" were sometimes "clouded" by anxiety or despair, but in times of doubt, she reflected on her past experiences. "Having treasur'd up the Experiences of many Years," she wrote, "I repair to them in a dark and cloudy Day. . . . this as an Anchor holds me sure." At a time when liberal Christians demanded that faith be more rational, Osborn responded by appropriating the Lockean language of experience. "Religion is no imaginary Thing," she testified, "but a substantial Reality."[63] She insisted that true Christian faith was "experimental": it was not only based on received wisdom but also on firsthand experience of divine grace.[64]

It is likely that Sarah Osborn absorbed this experiential language from listening to her ministers, talking with like-minded Christians, and reading religious books. Although there is no evidence that she ever read Locke, she did read the works of Cotton Mather, Jonathan Edwards, and many other ministers who advocated an "experimental" religion. For example, in 1767, when she read Samuel Buell's narrative of the revivals in his congregation, she not only learned that converts were "taught" their faith through "Experience," but that they "exhibit Evidence" of "a change of Nature."[65] Since her church required converts to share their stories of conversion before being admitted to full membership, she also heard many lay Christians describing their religious "experiences."

Today the word "experience" has become such a common part of our language that we may find it difficult to hear its revolutionary cadences. We tend to use the word "experience" as a synonym for individual subjectivity, and we describe our experiences in the same way as our "feelings"—as interior and private. Indeed, modern-day scholars of religion have criticized an emphasis on "the experiential dimension of religion" because personal experience is "inaccessible to strictly objective modes of inquiry."[66] But in the eighteenth century, the word "experience" had a much more scientific connotation, and philosophers as diverse as Adam Smith, John Locke, and

Frances Hutcheson argued that it was the foundation of true knowledge. Rejecting the view of Descartes, who had claimed that ideas were innate, they insisted that all knowledge is the product of sense impressions. This idea may sound like common sense to us today, but it had radical implications in the seventeenth and eighteenth centuries. Intoxicated by scientific and technological advances, Enlightenment thinkers insisted that ideas had to be subjected to the test of experiment and observation. Empiricism would liberate people from blind devotion to the past.

Osborn did not want to be "liberated" from tradition, particularly not Christian tradition, but she, too, believed that firsthand experience could offer rational evidence about the universe. On one hand, she was suspicious of the "enlightened" exaltation of reason. In 1757, for example, when she was vexed with financial problems and found it difficult to place her complete trust in God, she equated "carnal reason" with satanic temptation: "O, what a confederacy do Satan, unbelief, and carnal reason, keep, to drive me out of my strong tower, my hiding place, my rest in God."[67] Yet even though she denied her ability to understand God through "shallow" reason alone, she still described her religious views as "rational," and she viewed her personal experiences of divine grace as rational proof of God's existence.[68] Out of all the books that she read, one of her favorites was John Johnson's *A Mathematical Question, Propounded by the Viceregent of the World; Answered by the King of Glory*, a book that argued that true Christians were the only ones capable of solving the greatest "mathematical" problems in the universe. Johnson, a British Baptist, crafted an elaborate allegory featuring a "grand Geometrician" (God) whose secrets were ultimately too mysterious for mere humans to understand. But those who became part of his "country" (the saved) were able to gain a partial understanding of the universe with the help of the "king's secretary" (the Holy Spirit), who "opens, interprets, and guides our understandings into these mysteries." They became "true mathematicians" whose "solutions" to problems were "grounded upon facts." In contrast, all others who claimed the mantle of learning were simply "parrots" or "monkeys" who tried to "mimick the king's subjects," but whose knowledge amounted to nothing more than "chaff or dung." Eagerly copying long passages of this book into her diary (her extracts stretched to twelve pages), Osborn described it as "one of the Grandest Pieces I think yt I Ever met with and yet as clear as Grand."[69] This book confirmed one of her strongest beliefs: reason without revelation was virtually worthless, but with the help of the Holy Spirit, Christians could draw "factual" and rational conclusions about the universe.

Searching for "evidences of grace," Osborn combined rapturous descriptions of her religious "affections" with an almost clinical scrutiny of her everyday life. Like a scientist making notations in a lab notebook, she carefully recorded her experiences in order to make discoveries about God. (In yet another echo of the scientific, empirical language of the Enlightenment, she particularly liked the word "discovery." "Let me have some more discoveries of Eternal things Lord," she wrote in 1753.)[70] At a time when British Deists depicted God as a clock maker who stood apart from his creation, Osborn took special care to record instances when he had directly answered her prayers. In 1757, when food supplies were low because of the French and Indian War, she rejoiced that "Our God sent us dainties from day to day, squab, pigeon, sparrograss [asparagus]—pudding, gingerbread—tarts."[71] (Presumably her friends and neighbors had delivered the food, but Osborn did not mention them by name. She knew that they were simply doing God's will.) In 1759, after rereading a desperate prayer for food that she had written a year earlier, she once again thanked God for not allowing her family to go hungry. All her fears had been for naught.[72]

Osborn's diaries are filled with accounts of her experiences. "Blessed be God for the experience of His Mercy truth and faithfulness recorded in this Book," she wrote on the cover of her 1757 diary. As she struggled to understand God's will, she not only examined scripture but also the record of her own life. How did she feel about God? Did she passionately long for his presence? Did she feel as if she stood at a distance from him? More important, how did God seem to feel about her? How had he intervened to direct her life? Nothing escaped her providential imagination. For example, after awaking one morning to "the most terrible wind that i ever knew" and praying "earnest[ly] with god to abate the violence of the storm and to have compation on the poor souls in distress," she marveled that the storm ceased almost immediately. Although others complained that "it was a peice of pride and presumption" for her to conclude that God had answered her prayer, she disagreed. If she had used academic, theological language, she would have responded that God could work through "second causes": in other words, she was not claiming that God had performed a miracle for her, but only that he had answered her prayer through ordinary natural laws that could be rationally apprehended. "This i know," she testified. "God is both the hearer and answerer of prayer for jesus sake."[73]

Whenever Osborn wrestled with doubts—whenever she feared that her troubles meant that God had abandoned her—she comforted herself by reading her experiences. Sometimes, as she admitted to her friend, the Reverend Joseph Fish, she felt overwhelmed by her responsibilities. In 1759, exhausted by the pressures of teaching school, caring for the boarding students who

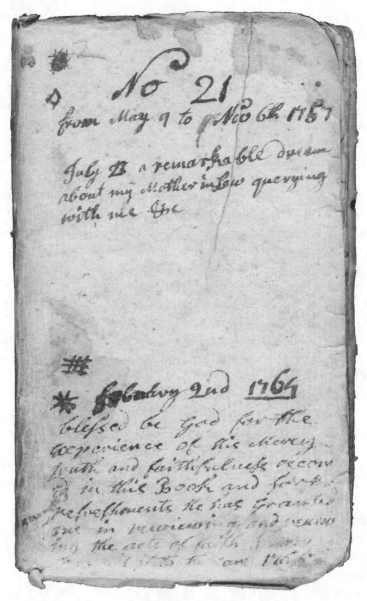

Cover of Sarah Osborn's diary, where she wrote: "February 2nd 1764 blessed be God for the Experience of His Mercy truth and faithfulness recorded in this Book and for the refreshments He has Granted me in reviewing and remembering the acts of faith." (Courtesy of Beinecke Rare Book and Manuscript Library, Yale University)

lived with her, and managing her family's finances, she plaintively described herself as "a poor over-Loaded weak animal crouching under its burden."[74] But rereading her diaries always brought her consolation. "I have been reviewing former writings," she wrote, "and find, notwithstanding many, many deficiencies in every thing, yet God has kept me reaching after greater degrees of grace, and *heart* holiness."[75] In a revealing moment, she described her writings as a "witness" for God and for herself "to the confusion of hell." "These Experiences are Mine," she wrote after rereading one of her diaries. "Let Satan say what He will. Thus God Has begun to deliver and He will Go on to deliver. God has deliverd me out of the Paw of the Lion and the bear."[76] Because she believed that a sovereign, majestic God controlled every detail of her life, she never used the phrase "religious experience," but only "experience." *All* experience was inherently religious.

Although seventeenth-century Puritans had also kept diaries as a means of self-examination, they had hesitated to make definitive judgments about their experiences because of their deep sense of sinfulness.[77] What if they were deceived? In contrast, even though Osborn admitted that God sometimes "hid his face," she was much more confident about her ability to determine his will. Although she was deeply aware of her own spiritual corruption, she also believed, like Jonathan Edwards, that converts gained a new spiritual "sense" during conversion that enabled them to gain a clearer view of reality. Even more than Edwards, she seems to have trusted her "sensations" as tangible evidence of her encounters with God. Echoing Locke's belief that knowledge came through sense impressions, she insisted that God had given her a "sense" of his "excellence, glory and truth."[78] On one occasion, she rejoiced that she had felt "sencible communion" with him, while on another, she marveled that "Grace was for a few minutes drawn forth into sensible, lively exercise." "Grant I may indeed sensibly grow in grace," she prayed.[79]

Osborn was especially attracted to the Enlightenment language of certainty. In 1742, during the height of the New England revivals, when ministers argued over how sure converts could be of their salvation, she seems to have expressed herself with so much confidence that she caused offense. Seventeenth-century Puritans had tended to see declarations of certainty as evidence of pride, and Osborn may have sounded dangerously radical to those who criticized the revivals' "enthusiasm." In an angry moment, she admitted that she "was accountd a bold pretender for saying i was sure of heaven as if i was there." In response, she quoted Romans 8: "Whom he did predestinate, them he also called, and whom he called, them he also justified, and whom he justified, them he also glorified." Scripture, like personal experience, offered concrete proof of her faith. "*I was enabled here to prove my calling*," she affirmed.[80]

By the 1750s, as moderate evangelical ministers like Jonathan Edwards discouraged this kind of "enthusiastic," radical language, Osborn seems to have grown more cautious in her public speech. She probably wanted to distinguish herself from the Strict Congregationalists, or "Separates," as they were more popularly known, who were the most radical wing of the American evangelical movement. They were infamous for claiming, in Ebenezer Frothingham's words, that "doubting is sinful." "True Evangelical Humility is forever accompanied with Faith and love," Frothingham wrote, "and doubting is as contrary to Faith, as Water is to Fire."[81] In *The Nature, Certainty, and Evidence of True Christianity*, Osborn explicitly set herself apart from the Separates by denying any desire to "establish Assurance as the Essence of saving Faith."[82] Yet in her private writings, she still sounded remarkably confident about God's love for her. In a particularly poignant diary entry that she wrote at a time when she had little money or food, she reminded herself that her past experiences offered convincing proof of God's goodness. Addressing God directly, she wrote: "My own experience has ever Provd to me, that thou art the God that has fed me all my Life Long—the God that didst never Leave me upon the mount of difficulty, but always appeard and wrought deliverance."[83] Based on her past experiences, she could be certain that God would not allow her to sink into utter poverty.

Like other evangelicals, Osborn seems to have been attracted to the Enlightenment language of experience, evidence, and proof for several reasons. First, it offered her a sense of security at a time when the old world seemed to be disappearing and a new world—one marked by scientific discovery, political controversy, transatlantic commerce, and upward mobility—had begun to take shape. Second, evangelicals embraced the scientific language of the Enlightenment because it helped them to defend Christianity against attack. Ironically, they fought against the skeptical strains of the Enlightenment with the weapons of the Enlightenment. At the same time as wealthy, liberal merchants in Newport argued that Christian doctrines should be supported by rational evidence, Osborn claimed that her faith was based on both the living voice of scripture and sensory experience.

Finally, evangelical women seem to have been particularly drawn to Enlightenment language because of the growing restrictions on their participation in public life. Unfortunately, Enlightenment philosophers were rarely "enlightened" when it came to the subject of women, and instead of trying to dismantle sexual inequality, they sought to strengthen it. According to Jean-Jacques Rousseau, for example, women belonged at home, where they should devote themselves to pleasing their husbands and raising their children. As he explained in *Émile* (1768), "To oblige us, to do us service, to gain our love and esteem . . . these are the duties of the sex at all times, and what they ought to learn from their infancy."[84] In contrast, evangelical women claimed to have "evidence" and "proof" of their calls to religious service.

Given the long history of Christian women who justified their religious authority on the grounds of divine inspiration, this strategy hardly seems new. Although Osborn probably knew little about the female religious leaders who had fought the same battles before her, she stood in a long line of remarkable women who claimed to have been transformed by their personal experience of God's grace. Hildegard of Bingen, a medieval visionary; Anne Hutchinson, the "American Jezebel" who claimed to have received revelations from God; Sarah Osborn—all of them insisted that they knew, without a doubt, that God had chosen them.

Yet despite these continuities with the past, the eighteenth century seems to have marked a watershed in understandings of "experience." Because Enlightenment philosophers elevated firsthand experience as the only reliable source of knowledge, even more reliable than the Bible, empirical language sounded particularly potent. Experience was no longer imagined as an alternative to formal knowledge, but as the very foundation of it.

Osborn's life bears witness to the extraordinary power of this language when put into practice. In 1764, at the age of fifty, she began holding religious meetings in her home for Newport's large population of slaves. (Newport was an important slave-trading port, and almost 30 percent of families there owned slaves.)[85] Although it is not clear exactly how or why the meetings began, they probably grew out of her long friendship with a slave woman named Phyllis, who had been a member of her women's prayer group for many years. By 1766, her meetings had generated so much excitement that other people began flocking to her house as well—hundreds of them. Although she hosted different groups each evening (Africans on Sundays, white girls on Mondays, white boys on Tuesdays, white women on Thursdays, and white men on Saturdays), her small house could barely hold the throngs. "We were so crouded there was scarce room to stir Hand or foot," she marveled in 1767.[86] If her numbers can be trusted—and they were echoed by Newport's ministers—at the height of the revivals as many as 525 people came to her meetings each week, including more than 100 slaves. (This means that about one out of every ten members of Newport's black population passed through her doors every Sunday evening.)[87]

Osborn's meetings were controversial. Not only did some of Newport's leading matrons accuse her of "keeping a Negro House," but her minister, the

Reverend William Vinal, who had once been a close friend, turned against her. (Vinal was suffering from alcoholism at the time, which was probably part of the reason that so many of his congregation sought Osborn's spiritual guidance.)[88] Even one of her warmest supporters, the Reverend Joseph Fish, questioned whether she had "moved beyond her line." Yet Osborn insisted that she had undeniable evidence of her special call to leadership. Besides describing her strong inward sense of calling, she pointed to the positive effects of the revival. In her diary, which she wrote in nearly every day, she took detailed notes about how many people had attended her meetings, how they had behaved, and how many had been "born again." According to her careful accounting, all the evidence pointed in her favor. "Tho I was born as the wild asses Colt and fit for nothing till brot too by soverign grace," she wrote, "yet He can Serve Himself of me and Glorifie Himself in me and in His own way too, However Misterious to me and all around me—he Has chosen the weak things of this world."[89]

Osborn was unusually well educated and articulate, but scores of other evangelical women also borrowed the Enlightenment language of experience, evidence, and certainty. Some, like Sarah, claimed that their personal conversion experiences gave them the authority to exhort others to repent; more radical women insisted that their "experiences" included revelations from God. According to Hannah Heaton, who belonged to a Separate church in Connecticut, she was so swallowed up by God's love during her conversion that she seemed to actually see Christ. "Me thot i see jesus with the eyes of my soul stand up in heaven," she wrote. "A lovely god man with his arms open ready to receive me his face was full of smiles he lookt white and ruddy and was just such a saviour as my soul wanted."[90] Empowered by her belief that she had directly experienced God's presence, she became a crusader for the Separates' cause.

By the nineteenth century, the evangelical absorption of the Enlightenment was complete.[91] Words such as experience, experimental, certainty, proof, and evidence were a common part of the evangelical vocabulary: Methodists held "experience" meetings, Baptists preached "experimental" religion, and clergy from many denominations confidently proclaimed that true Christians could be virtually sure of their salvation. (Given the Protestant belief in original sin, few were willing to say that assurance could ever be absolute.) Given the widespread popularity of this language among men as well as women, it would be an exaggeration to suggest that it was gendered, but it strongly appealed to those who were excluded from formal positions of power, whether white women, lower-class men, or male and female slaves.

Osborn's story raises crucial questions about the effects of the Enlightenment on women. On the one hand, it is clear that Enlightenment philosophers failed to challenge negative stereotypes of women's frailty and passivity, and even the most radical found it difficult to imagine a world where men and women would be completely equal. Significantly, Osborn repeatedly described herself in her diaries and letters as a "weak" woman, and even though she probably knew more about Reformed Protestant theology than most of the men in her church, she never defended herself on the grounds of her intelligence, but only of her experience.

Yet, on the other hand, Osborn's story suggests that historians may have exaggerated the conservatism of enlightened thought. By claiming that women's voices were silenced by the new emphasis on rationality, they have underestimated the equally powerful language of experience and certainty. Most important, they have underestimated women's ability to devise new theological strategies to overcome the limitations placed upon them. As Judith Butler has explained, gender is an unstable category, and it has to be continually reproduced through both speech and practice. Because of Osborn's desire to be a good Christian, she reminded herself, again and again, that she was not supposed to step beyond her "line." Yet the very fact that she had to repeatedly subject herself to this discipline suggests that the gendered discourse of the Enlightenment was never a completely hegemonic one.[92] (She would not have felt the need to reiterate this language if not for her difficulty in maintaining a subordinate posture.) Each time that evangelical women reminded themselves of their feminine weakness, they left open a space for the possibility that they were not actually weak at all. Although they often echoed Enlightenment thinkers by portraying the female sex as inferior, they also claimed to have been transformed by their experience of God's grace. They were *certain* of it.

This chapter has used Sarah Osborn's story to argue that women helped to construct a new religious movement, evangelicalism, that drew much of its inspiration from the Enlightenment. To be sure, most intellectual historians would express surprise at the claim that an eighteenth-century woman's devotional writings can tell us something new about the Enlightenment. But scholars who have defined the Enlightenment narrowly around a small group of elite male thinkers have obscured the dramatic religious transformation that took place in eighteenth-century America. Not only did the Enlightenment have a much stronger impact on Protestantism than we have realized, but it gave women a powerful vocabulary to justify their leadership.

Like many other conservative Protestants of her time, Sarah Osborn was deeply ambivalent about Enlightenment "progress." Yet at the same time as she rejected its theological liberalism, she echoed its faith in experiential knowledge. When she died in 1796 at the age of eighty-two, frail and nearly blind, she left few possessions: a gold locket, a silver spoon inscribed with her husband's initials, a cloak.[93] But more valuable, in her opinion, were the thousands of pages of devotional writings she had sewn together into neat booklets, each marked with a number and date. For more than thirty years, until her eyesight failed, she had carefully written down her experiences, reading them over and over again as a defense against despair. Inspired by her evangelical faith, a faith that had grown in the soil of the Enlightenment, she had searched every page of her life for "evidence" of God. What she found, despite her many sorrows, was the unmistakable gift of grace. "*Surely,*" as she testified in her diaries, "I have had experience of the goodness of the Lord, all my life long."[94]

Notes

1. Sarah Osborn, Memoir, Beinecke Rare Book and Manuscript Library, Yale University, New Haven, Connecticut (hereafter Beinecke Library).
2. Sarah Osborn, Diary #15 (1754), undated entry at end of diary, 129, Connecticut Historical Society, Hartford, Conn. According to Hopkins, Osborn wrote more than fifty volumes of diaries, "the least containing near 100 pages, the bigger part above 200, and a number 300, and more, besides letters to her friends, and other occasional writing." See Samuel Hopkins, *Memoirs of the Life of Mrs. Sarah Osborn* (Worcester, Mass.: Leonard Worcester, 1799), 358. Although the majority of Sarah's diaries and letters have been lost, more than 1,500 pages have been preserved in the following collections: Sarah Osborn, Diaries, 1753–1772, Newport Historical Society, Newport, R.I.; Sarah Osborn, Diaries and Memoir, 1757–1769, Beinecke Library; Sarah Osborn, Letters, 1743–1770, 1779, American Antiquarian Society, Worcester, Mass.; Sarah Osborn, Diaries, 1754, 1760–1761, Connecticut Historical Society, Hartford, Conn.; Sarah Osborn, Letter to Samuel Hopkins, August 26, 1769, Simon Gratz Manuscript Collection, Historical Society of Pennsylvania, Philadelphia; and Sarah Osborn, Five Letters, 1769–1770, Simon Gratz Manuscript Collection, Historical Society of Pennsylvania, Philadelphia. See also Sarah Osborn, *The Nature, Certainty, and Evidence of True Christianity* (Boston: S. Kneeland, 1755); and Samuel Hopkins, ed., *Familiar Letters, Written by Mrs. Sarah Osborn and Miss Susanna Anthony, Late of Newport, Rhode Island* (Newport, R.I.: Newport Mercury, 1807). Several of Hopkins's letters to Osborn are preserved in the Samuel Hopkins Papers, Andover Library, Andover Newton Theological School, Newton, Mass. Since Osborn did not include punctuation in any of her manuscripts, I have added it when needed for clarity.
3. Sarah Osborn, Memoir, Beinecke Library.

4. John Locke, *An Essay Concerning Human Understanding* (1690), reprinted in *The Portable Enlightenment Reader*, ed. Isaac Kramnick (New York: Penguin, 1995), 186; Osborn, *Nature, Certainty, and Evidence*, 3.

5. Adrienne Koch, *The American Enlightenment: The Shaping of the American Experiment and a Free Society* (New York: G. Braziller, 1965).

6. Peter Gay, *The Enlightenment: An Interpretation*, 2 vols. (New York: Knopf, 1966, 1969); Henry Farnham May, *The Enlightenment in America* (New York: Oxford University Press, 1976). For other studies of the Enlightenment in America, see Norman Fiering, *Moral Philosophy at Seventeenth-Century Harvard: A Discipline in Transition* (Chapel Hill: University of North Carolina Press, 1981); John Corrigan, *The Prism of Piety: Catholick Congregational Clergy at the Beginning of the Enlightenment* (New York: Oxford University Press, 1991); Donald H. Meyer, *The Democratic Enlightenment* (New York: G. P. Putnam's Sons, 1976); Christopher Grasso, *A Speaking Aristocracy: Transforming Public Discourse in Eighteenth-Century Connecticut* (Chapel Hill: University of North Carolina Press, 1999); and Ned C. Landsman, *From Colonials to Provincials: American Thought and Culture, 1680–1760* (New York: Twayne Publishers, 1997).

7. See D. W. Bebbington, *Evangelicalism in Modern Britain: A History from the 1730s to the 1980s* (Boston: Unwin Hyman, 1989), 1–74.

8. Immanuel Kant, "What Is Enlightenment," in Kramnick, *Portable Enlightenment Reader*, 1–6.

9. Paul Hazard, *The European Mind, the Critical Years, 1680–1715* (New Haven: Yale University Press, 1953); Lester G. Crocker, *The Age of Enlightenment* (New York: Walker, 1969), 1. See also Robert A. Ferguson, *The American Enlightenment, 1750–1820* (Cambridge: Harvard University Press, 1997), 22.

10. Peter Gay, *The Enlightenment: An Interpretation*, vol. 1 (New York: Knopf, 1966), 3, 423, 8. On the unity of the Enlightenment, see also Ernst Cassirer, *The Philosophy of the Enlightenment* (Princeton: Princeton University Press, 1951). On the "secularization of European thought," see Roy Porter, *The Enlightenment*, 2nd ed. (New York: Palgrave, 2001), 66. See also Jonathan Irvine Israel, *Radical Enlightenment: Philosophy and the Making of Modernity, 1650–1750* (New York: Oxford University Press, 2001).

11. Roger Chartier, *The Cultural Origins of the French Revolution*, Bicentennial Reflections on the French Revolution (Durham, N.C.: Duke University Press, 1991); Robert Darnton, *The Forbidden Bestsellers of Pre-Revolutionary France* (New York: W. W. Norton, 1995). The quote is from Porter, *The Enlightenment*, 40.

12. John McManners, *Death and the Enlightenment: Changing Attitudes to Death among Christians and Unbelievers in Eighteenth-Century France* (New York: Oxford University Press, 1981). Norman Fiering, "Irresistible Compassion: An Aspect of Eighteenth-Century Sympathy and Humanitarianism," *Journal of the History of Ideas* 37 (April–June 1976): 195–218.

13. Roy Porter, *The Creation of the Modern World: The Untold Story of the British*

Enlightenment, 1st U.S. ed. (New York: Norton, 2000); Margaret C. Jacob, *The Newtonians and the English Revolution, 1689–1720* (Ithaca, N.Y.: Cornell University Press, 1976).

14. Roy Porter and Mikulás Teich, *The Enlightenment in National Context* (New York: Cambridge University Press, 1981); J. G. A. Pocock, *The Enlightenments of Edward Gibbon, 1737–1764*, vol. 1 of *Barbarism and Religion* (Cambridge: Cambridge University Press, 19991), 9. For another discussion of the difficulty of defining the Enlightenment, see James Schmidt, "The Legacy of the Enlightenment," *Philosophy and Literature* 26 (2002): 432–42.

15. Porter, *The Enlightenment*, 2, 15.

16. Thomas Paine, *Common Sense* (1794), in Kramnick, *Portable Enlightenment Reader*, 175.

17. On the relationship between Calvinism and the Enlightenment, see Helena Rosenblatt, "Calvinism," in *Encyclopedia of the Enlightenment*, ed. Alan Charles Kors (New York: Oxford University Press, 2003), accessed at the University of Chicago, September 7, 2006, <http://www.oxfordreference.com>.

18. The quote comes from ibid. "Latitudinarians" were British Anglicans who prized tolerance and rationality. See John Gascoigne, "Latitudinarianism," in ibid. Deists were skeptics who rejected traditional Christian doctrine, including the divinity of Christ, but who still believed in a God who created a mechanistic universe. See Kerry S. Walters, *The American Deists: Voices of Reason and Dissent in the Early Republic* (Lawrence: University Press of Kansas, 1992); Kerry S. Walters, *Rational Infidels: The American Deists* (Durango, Colo.: Longwood Academic, 1992); and Peter Byrne, *Natural Religion and the Nature of Religion: The Legacy of Deism* (New York: Routledge, 1989). "Catholicks" were New England Congregationalists who incorporated enlightened ideas about the "rational order of the universe, and human capability to detect that order," in the early eighteenth century. See Corrigan, *The Prism of Piety*, vii.

19. May, *Enlightenment in America*. See also Mark A. Noll, "The Rise and Long Life of the Protestant Enlightenment in America," in *Knowledge and Belief in America: Enlightenment Traditions and Modern Religious Thought*, ed. William M. Shea and Peter A. Huff (Cambridge: Cambridge University Press, 1995), 88–124; and E. Brooks Holifield, *Theology in America: Christian Thought from the Age of the Puritans to the Civil War* (New Haven: Yale University Press, 2003).

20. Jonathan Edwards, "A Treatise Concerning Religious Affections," in *Religious Affections*, vol. 2 of *The Works of Jonathan Edwards*, ed. John E. Smith (New Haven: Yale University Press, 1959), 93–461.

21. Bebbington, *Evangelicalism in Modern Britain*, 74.

22. Cotton Mather, *Reason Satisfied and Faith Established* (Boston: J. Allen, 1712); Solomon Stoddard, *A Treatise Concerning Conversion* (Boston: Franklin, 1719), cited in James Spencer Lamborn, "Blessed Assurance? Depraved Saints, Philosophers, and the Problem of Knowledge for Self and State in New England, 1630–1820" (Ph.D. diss., Miami University, 2002), 212. I am indebted to this disserta-

tion for its clear explanation of changing attitudes toward religious knowledge in New England. On Mather's "experimental religion," see Robert Middlekauff, *The Mathers: Three Generations of Puritan Intellectuals, 1596–1728* (New York: Oxford University Press, 1971), 305–19.

23. See Mark A. Noll, *The Rise of Evangelicalism: The Age of Edwards, Whitefield and the Wesleys* (Leicester: Inter-Varsity, 2004), 140; David Hempton, *Methodism: Empire of the Spirit* (New Haven: Yale University Press, 2005), 52; Frederick A. Dreyer, *The Genesis of Methodism* (Bethlehem, Pa.: Lehigh University Press, 1999); Bruce Hindmarsh, "Reshaping Individualism: The Private Christian, Eighteenth-Century Religion, and the Enlightenment," in *The Rise of the Laity in Evangelical Protestantism* (New York: Routledge, 2002), chap. 5; and D. Bruce Hindmarsh, *The Evangelical Conversion Narrative: Spiritual Autobiography in Early Modern England* (New York: Oxford University Press, 2005). See also Brian Stanley, "Christian Missions and the Enlightenment: A Reevaluation," in *Christian Missions and the Enlightenment*, ed. Brian Stanley (Grand Rapids, Mich.: Eerdmans, 2001). Gertrude Himmelfarb has argued that the Methodists should also be included in histories of the Enlightenment because of their "democratic" faith in free will and universal salvation. Gertrude Himmelfarb, *The Roads to Modernity: The British, French, and American Enlightenments* (New York: Knopf, 2004), 129.

24. Porter, *Creation of the Modern World*, 59.

25. Allen C. Guelzo, "Edwards, Jonathan," in Kors, *Encyclopedia of the Enlightenment*.

26. Max Horkheimer and Theodor W. Adorno, *Dialectic of Enlightenment* (New York: Continuum, 1993). Keith Michael Baker and Peter Hanss Reill criticize a postmodernist, caricatured view of the Enlightenment that makes it responsible for "rationalism, instrumentalism, scientism, logocentrism, universalism, abstract rights, eurocentrism, individualism, humanism, masculinism, etc." See Keith Michael Baker and Peter Hanns Reill, *What's Left of Enlightenment? A Postmodern Question* (Stanford, Calif.: Stanford University Press, 2001), 1.

27. Michel Foucault, *Discipline and Punish: The Birth of the Prison*, 1st U.S. ed. (New York: Pantheon Books, 1977), 209, 16, 129.

28. Eric Hobsbawm, *On History* (1997; London: Abacus Books, 1998), 336, quoted in *Women, Gender, and Enlightenment*, ed. Sarah Knott and Barbara Taylor (New York: Palgrave Macmillan, 2005), xvi.

29. The quote is from Caroline Belsey, "Afterword: A Future for Materialist-Feminist Criticism," in *The Matter of Difference: Materialist-Feminist Criticism of Shakespeare*, ed. Valerie Wayne (Ithaca, N.Y.: Cornell University Press, 1991), 262, quoted in Porter, *Creation of the Modern World*, 338.

30. Joan B. Landes, *Women and the Public Sphere in the Age of the French Revolution* (Ithaca, N.Y.: Cornell University Press, 1988), 135; Carole Pateman, *The Sexual Contract* (Stanford, Calif.: Stanford University Press, 1988).

31. Phyllis Mack, "Women and the Enlightenment: An Introduction," in Hunt et al., *Women and the Enlightenment*, 9–10; Susan Juster, "Mystical Pregnancy and

Holy Bleeding: Visionary Experience in Early Modern Britain and America," *William and Mary Quarterly* 57, no. 2 (April 2000): 249–88; Susan Juster, *Doomsayers: Anglo-American Prophecy in the Age of Revolution* (Philadelphia: University of Pennsylvania Press, 2003), 218. For another perspective, see Elizabeth Fox-Genovese, "Women and the Enlightenment," in *Becoming Visible: Women in European History*, ed. Renate Bridenthal, Claudia Koontz, and Susan Stuard, 2nd ed. (Boston: Houghton Mifflin, 1987).

32. See the introduction to Knott and Taylor, *Women, Gender, and Enlightenment*, xvi. For historians who have argued that "enlightened" thought had sexually egalitarian possibilities, see Margaret C. Jacob, "Freemasonry, Women, and the Paradox of the Enlightenment," in *Women and the Enlightenment*, ed. Margaret Hunt, Margaret Jacob, Phyllis Mack, and Ruth Perry (New York: Haworth Press, 1984); Margaret Jacob, *The Enlightenment: A Brief History with Documents* (Boston: Bedford/St. Martin's, 2001); Porter, *Creation of the Modern World*, 320–38; and Israel, *Radical Enlightenment*, 82–96.

33. On freemasonry, see Janet M. Burke and Margaret C. Jacob, "French Freemasonry, Women, and Feminist Scholarship," *Journal of Modern History* 68, no. 3 (September 1996): 513–49. On women authors, see Carla Hesse, *The Other Enlightenment: How French Women Became Modern* (Princeton: Princeton University Press, 2001); and Rosemary Zagarri, "The Rights of Man and Woman in Post-Revolutionary America," *William and Mary Quarterly* 55, no. 2 (1998): 229.

34. Juster, *Doomsayers*, viii.

35. For one example, see Paula McDowell, "Enlightenment Enthusiasms and the Spectacular Failure of the Philadelphia Society," *Eighteenth-Century Studies* 35, no. 4 (2002): 515–33. McDowell not only argues that "enthusiasm" was discredited in the eighteenth century but also that modern literary studies continue to disdain "enthusiastic" forms of speech and writing.

36. Sarah Osborn, Letter to Joseph Fish, May 29, 1753, Folder 2, in Sarah Osborn, Letters, American Antiquarian Society, Worcester, Mass.

37. On Osborn's early life, see her Memoir, Beinecke Library. Scholarship on Osborn includes Charles E. Hambrick-Stowe, "The Spiritual Pilgrimage of Sarah Osborn (1714–1796)," *Church History* 61, no. 4 (December 1992): 408–21; Sheryl Anne Kujawa, "'A Precious Season at the Throne of Grace': Sarah Haggar Wheaten Osborn, 1714–1796" (Ph.D. diss., Boston College, 1993); Sheryl Anne Kujawa, "Religion, Education, and Gender in Eighteenth Century Rhode Island: Sarah Haggar Wheaten Osborn, 1714–1796" (Ph.D. diss., Columbia University Teacher's College, 1993); and Mary Beth Norton, ed., "'My Resting Reaping Times': Sarah Osborn's Defense of Her 'Unfeminine Activities,'" *Signs* 2 (1976): 515–29.

38. Hopkins, *Memoirs of the Life of Mrs. Sarah Osborn*; and Hopkins, *Familiar Letters*.

39. T. H. Breen and Timothy Hall, "Structuring Provincial Imagination: The Rhetoric and Experience of Social Change in Eighteenth-Century New England," *American Historical Review* 103, no. 5 (December 1998): 1411–39.

40. *Newport Mercury* (Newport, R.I.), August 14, 1759.

41. For statistics on church membership in Newport, see Elaine Forman Crane, "Uneasy Coexistence: Religious Tensions in Eighteenth-Century Newport," *Newport History* 53, no. 5 (Summer 1980): 101–11.

42. Sarah Osborn, Letter to Joseph Fish, September 17, 1750, in Sarah Osborn, Letters, American Antiquarian Society, Worcester, Mass.

43. Samuel Clarke, *Discourse Concerning the Unchangeable Obligations of Natural Religion* (London: W. Botham, 1706); Daniel Whitby, *A Discourse* (London: John Wyat, 1710), quoted in H. Shelton Smith, *Changing Conceptions of Original Sin: A Study in American Theology since 1750* (New York: Charles Scribner's, 1955), 12–13.

44. Jonathan Edwards, *A Faithful Narrative of the Surprising Work of God* (London: John Oswald, 1737), cited in Holifield, *Theology in America*, 83. Holifield offers a helpful overview of theological controversies over rationalism, nature, and the supernatural, pp. 56–101.

45. Samuel Webster, *A Winter Evening's Conversation upon the Doctrine of Original Sin* (New Haven: James Parker, 1757), 5.

46. Samuel Niles, *The True Scripture-Doctrine of Original Sin Stated and Defended* (Boston: S. Kneeland, 1757), 40.

47. Jonathan Edwards, "Some Thoughts Concerning the Present Revival" (1742), in *The Great Awakening*, vol. 4 of *The Works of Jonathan Edwards*, ed. C. C. Goen (New Haven: Yale University Press, 1972), 394. On changing attitudes toward original sin, see Merle Curti, *Human Nature in American Thought: A History* (Madison: University of Wisconsin Press, 1980); Conrad Wright, *The Beginnings of Unitarianism in America* (Starr King Press, 1955), 59–90; Clyde A. Holbrook, "Original Sin and the Enlightenment," in *The Heritage of Christian Thought: Essays in Honor of Robert Lowry Calhoun*, ed. Robert E. Cushman and Egil Grislis (New York: Harper and Row, 1965); and Smith, *Changing Conceptions of Original Sin.*

48. The quote is from Gilbert Tennent, *The Danger of an Unconverted Ministry*, cited in Holifield, *Theology in America*, 95. Samuel Buell expressed his fear of "a Decay of the Life and Power of Godliness among us, and the Prevalency of Arminian Principles in some Places," in Samuel Buell, *The Excellence and Importance of the Saving Knowledge of the Lord Jesus Christ in the Gospel Preacher* (New York: James Parker, 1761), ii.

49. Edmund Sears Morgan, *The Gentle Puritan: A Life of Ezra Stiles, 1727–1795* (New Haven: Yale University Press, 1962), 111–12.

50. Sarah Osborn, Diary (no number on cover, March 1759–April 1760), entry for November 25, 1759, Newport Historical Society, Newport, R.I. Osborn doesn't explicitly identify this minister as Stiles, but it is clear from the context that she was describing his preaching. See also Sarah Osborn, Diary (no number on cover, February 19, 1758–April 2, 1758), entry for March 12, 1758, Newport Historical Society, Newport, R.I.; and Sarah Osborn, Diary #27 (June 22, 1760–January 18, 1761), entry for November 21, 1760, Connecticut Historical Society, Hartford, Conn.

51. On Guyse, see "Guyse, John," in *The Dictionary of National Biography* (Oxford: Oxford University Press, 1964), 8:837.

52. Sarah Osborn, Diary (no number on cover, 1767), entry for March 28, 1767, Newport Historical Society, Newport, R.I.

53. David Hamilton, *The Private Christian's Witness for Christianity* (London: Thomas Cockerill, 1697). Osborn recorded reading this book in Diary #30 (February 21, 1762–April 29, 1762), entry for March 17, 1762, Beinecke Library.

54. Sarah Osborn, Memoir, Beinecke Library, 1–3.

55. Sarah Osborn, Diary #14 (July 8, 1753–March 1, 1754), entries for the following dates: July 9, 1753, September 8, 1753, September 19, 1753, October 30, 1753, Newport Historical Society, Newport, R.I.

56. Sarah Osborn, Memoir, Beinecke Library, 17. She was quoting from Psalm 58:3.

57. Sarah Osborn, Diary #20 (January 1, 1757–May 7, 1757), entry for January 16, 1757, Newport Historical Society, Newport, R.I. John Guyse, *A Collection of Seventeen Practical Sermons on Various and Important Subjects* (London: Edward Dilley, 1761), 19. Osborn records reading this sermon in Sarah Osborn, Diary #29 (April 28, 1761–February 18, 1762), entry for November 8, 1761, Beinecke Library. On the new positive idea of selfhood, see Daniel Walker Howe, *Making the American Self: Jonathan Edwards to Abraham Lincoln* (Cambridge: Harvard University Press, 1997).

58. Jonathan Mayhew, *Two Sermons on the Nature, Extent and Perfection of the Divine Benevolence* (Boston: Kneeland, 1763), quoted in Ava Chamberlain, "The Theology of Cruelty: A New Look at the Rise of Arminianism in Eighteenth-Century New England," *Harvard Theological Review* 85, no. 3 (1992): 348. Elizabeth Clark has argued that Protestants "shifted their focus from the drama of God, the sovereign judge, sentencing the depraved human to an afterlife of unremitting suffering, to that of God, the benevolent father, working for his children's physical and spiritual well-being. The purpose of worship shifted from the glorification of God to the salvation and celebration of man." See Elizabeth B. Clark, "The Sacred Rights of the Weak: Pain, Sympathy, and the Culture of Individual Rights in Antebellum America," *Journal of American History* 82, no. 2 (September 1995): 471.

59. Sarah Osborn, Diary #20, September 1, 1757, Newport Historical Society, Newport, R.I.; Hopkins, *Memoirs of the Life of Mrs. Sarah Osborn*, 70.

60. Sarah Osborn, Memoir, Beinecke Library, 6–7.

61. Hambrick-Stowe, "The Spiritual Pilgrimage of Sarah Osborn."

62. Sarah Osborn, Diary #21 (May 9, 1757–November 6, 1757), entry for July 20, 1757, Beinecke Library.

63. Osborn, *Nature, Certainty, and Evidence*, 3, 8, 10.

64. Sarah Osborn, Memoir, Beinecke Library.

65. Osborn recorded reading this narrative in Sarah Osborn, Diary (no number, 1767), entry for March 17, 1767, Newport Historical Society, Newport, R.I. See

Samuel Buell, *A Faithful Narrative of the Remarkable Revival of Religion* (New York: Samuel Brown, 1766), 34, 40.

66. Robert H. Sharf, "Experience," in *Critical Terms for Religious Studies*, ed. Mark C. Taylor (Chicago: University of Chicago Press, 1998), 95; Wayne Proudfoot, *Religious Experience* (Berkeley: University of California Press, 1985). For an overview of historical controversies over "religious experience" in America, see Ann Taves, *Fits, Trances, and Visions: Experiencing Religion and Explaining Experience from Wesley to James* (Princeton: Princeton University Press, 1999).

67. Hopkins, *Memoirs of the Life of Mrs. Sarah Osborn*, 215. She also linked "the devil and carnal reasoning" in her memoir. See ibid., 42.

68. For Osborn's descriptions of her faith as "rational," see Sarah Osborn, Diary (no number on cover, March 1759–April 1760), entry for April 24, 1760 ("my views were rational and solid"), Newport Historical Society, Newport, R.I., and Diary #27, entry for November 11, 1760 ("I would only act the rational Part and Leave all my cares with thee. Leave thee to work in thy own way"), Connecticut Historical Society, Hartford, Conn. For her use of the phrase "shallow reason," see Hopkins, *Memoirs of the Life of Mrs. Sarah Osborn*, 215.

69. John Johnson, *A Mathematical Question, Propounded by the Viceregent of the World; Answered by the King of Glory*, 3rd ed. (Boston: Green and Russell, 1762), 2, 43, 45–47. Osborn referred to reading this in Sarah Osborn, Diary (no number on cover, March 1759–April 1760), entry for March 17, 1760, Newport Historical Society, Newport, R.I. For more information on Johnson, see S. L. Copson, "Johnson, John (1705/6–1791)," *Oxford Dictionary of National Biography*, Oxford University Press, 2004 (<http://www.oxforddnb.com>, accessed June 4, 2006).

70. Sarah Osborn, Diary #14, December 16, 1753, Newport Historical Society, Newport, R.I. See also Hopkins, *Memoirs of the Life of Mrs. Sarah Osborn*, 130. This language was common. For example, David Hamilton claimed that "observing Christians" could "discover God." See Hamilton, *The Private Christian's Witness for Christianity*, 138, 142.

71. Sarah Osborn, Diary #20, March 5, 1757, Newport Historical Society, Newport, R.I.

72. Sarah Osborn, Diary (no number on cover, February 19, 1758–2 April 1758), entry for March 6, 1758, Newport Historical Society, Newport, R.I. For another example, see the entry for March 28, 1760, when Osborn recorded that God had answered her prayer for firewood. Sarah Osborn, Diary (no number on cover, March 1759–April 1760), Newport Historical Society, Newport, R.I.

73. Sarah Osborn, Memoir, Beinecke Library. See Holifield, *Theology in America*, 37.

74. Sarah Osborn, Letter to Joseph Fish, May 3, 1759, Folder 4, in Sarah Osborn, Letters, American Antiquarian Society, Worcester, Mass.

75. Hopkins, *Memoirs of the Life of Mrs. Sarah Osborn*, 185.

76. See Sarah Osborn, Diary #20, cover, Newport Historical Society, Newport, R.I.; and Sarah Osborn, Diary #21, February 2, 1764, Beinecke Library.

77. On Puritan diaries, see David S. Shiels, "The Journal of Spiritual Self-Examination: A History of Personal Diary Writing in New England, 1620–1745" (Ph.D. diss., University of Chicago, 1982); Michael McGiffert, ed., *God's Plot: The Paradoxes of Puritan Piety Being the Autobiography and Journal of Thomas Shepard* (Amherst: University of Massachusetts Press, 1972); and Daniel B. Shea Jr., *Spiritual Auto-biography in Early America* (Princeton: Princeton University Press, 1968).

78. Hopkins, *Memoirs of the Life of Mrs. Sarah Osborn*, 26.

79. Sarah Osborn, Diary #14, July 8, 1753, Newport Historical Society, Newport, R.I.; Hopkins, *Memoirs of the Life of Mrs. Sarah Osborn*, 144, 112. For another example, see Diary #15, January 6, 1754, Newport Historical Society, Newport, R.I. David Bebbington's careful explanation of the difference between Puritan and evangelical understandings of assurance is worth quoting at length: "There was as much desire for confident knowledge of one's own salvation in the seventeenth century as in the eighteenth. But if there was a common preoccupation with assurance, the content of the doctrine was transformed. Whereas the Puritans had held that assurance is rare, late and the fruit of struggle in the experience of believers, the Evangelicals believed it to be general, normally given at conversion and the result of simple acceptance of the gift of God. The consequence of the altered form of the doctrine was a metamorphosis in the nature of popular Protestantism." See Bebbington, *Evangelicalism in Modern Britain*, 43.

80. Sarah Osborn, Memoir, Beinecke Library, 117.

81. Ebenezer Frothingham, *The Articles of Faith and Practice, with the Covenant, That Is Confessed by the Separate Churches of Christ* (Newport: J. Franklin, 1750), 114.

82. Osborn, *Nature, Certainty, and Evidence*, 13.

83. Sarah Osborn, Diary #14, July 29, 1753, Newport Historical Society, Newport, R.I.

84. Jean-Jacques Rousseau, *Emilius, Or a Treatise of Education* (Edinburgh: A. Don-aldson, 1768), 3:74–75, quoted in Linda Kerber, "The Republican Mother: Women and the Enlightenment—An American Perspective," *American Quarterly* 28, no. 2 (Summer 1976): 194.

85. In 1755, there were 1,234 African Americans in Newport, and they made up 18.27 percent of the total population. In 1774, there were 1,246 African Americans, and they made up 13.5 percent of the population. See Elaine Forman Crane, *A Dependent People: Newport, Rhode Island, in the Revolutionary Era* (New York: Fordham University Press, 1985), 52, 76.

86. Sarah Osborn, Diary (no number on cover, 1767), April 7, 1767, Newport Historical Society, Newport, R.I.

87. Ibid., January 27, 1767.

88. Letter from Sarah Osborn to Joseph Fish, August 9, 1766, Folder 6, in Sarah Osborn, Letters, American Antiquarian Society, Worcester, Mass.

89. Norton, "My Resting Reaping Times," 527.

90. *The World of Hannah Heaton: The Diary of an Eighteenth-Century New England Farm Woman*, ed. Barbara E. Lacey (Dekalb: Northern Illinois Press, 2003), 9.

91. On the influence of the Scottish Common Sense tradition on Protestantism, see

Holifield, *Theology in America*; and Mark A. Noll, *America's God: From Jonathan Edwards to Abraham Lincoln* (New York: Oxford University Press, 2002).

92. Judith Butler, *Bodies That Matter: On the Discursive Limits Of "Sex"* (New York: Routledge, 1993).

93. Sarah Osborn, Will, October 5, 1794, Probate Book, no. 3:11, Newport City Hall, Newport, R.I.

94. Hopkins, *Memoirs of the Life of Mrs. Sarah Osborn*, 101; emphasis mine.

5

Beyond the Meetinghouse

Women and Protestant Spirituality in Early America

Janet Moore Lindman

What should American religious historians take as their main subject matter? In this chapter, Janet Moore Lindman urges American religious historians to expand their research "beyond the meetinghouse" in order to explain how religion has shaped lived experience. It is important to understand not only how religion has influenced America's national identity but how it has shaped personal identity as well. Because the majority of church members throughout American history have been women, Lindman argues that historians should pay particular attention to how religious beliefs have shaped women's understandings of selfhood. In an evocative case study of three Protestant women in late eighteenth- and early nineteenth-century America, she explores how Protestantism affected understandings of gender, individuality, and community.

Besides asking American religious historians to move "beyond the meetinghouse," Lindman also urges women's historians to expand their analysis of gender to include other social indices. While women's historians have often asked probing questions about women's racial, economic, and political identities, they have largely ignored religion. As Lindman shows, however, many nineteenth-century Protestant women constructed their sense of selfhood around their spiritual convictions.

Abigail Harris, a New Jersey Baptist, spent a Sabbath evening in March of 1816 visiting friends. Recording this event in her journal, she remarked upon the spirituality of a "Mrs. Wooley": "My Soul is refresh'd in her company, with her excellent conversation, it always appears to be savoury & savour of the things of God . . . , she is A sincere Christian. A strain of piety runs through all her conversation & she introduces it with the greatest ease imaginable & [is] never at A loss for something profitable & new." After conversing together, Harris and Wooley agreed "to intercede for each other at A throne of Grace."[1]

This snippet gives us entrée into the life of a single, white woman of middling status who lived in rural New Jersey in the early nineteenth century; it also evokes the religious world in which she lived and the relational spirituality she created for herself based on female friendships and community networks. Abigail Harris nurtured a religious faith that consisted of more than just her membership in the Salem Baptist Church. She enacted a godly life through a variety of relationships and activities that occurred beyond the meetinghouse. This chapter will discuss the spiritual activism of white women such as Harris in late eighteenth- and early nineteenth-century America to document the ways in which particular women were able to fashion a religion of their own and how they expressed that religion in written accounts. It will also explore the textual production of the female religious self within spiritual narratives and examine the relationship of gender and genre in women's religious writings. Most important, it will argue that Protestant Christianity allowed the pursuit of spirituality, selfhood, and independence for some American women in the eighteenth and early nineteenth centuries.

For many white women in early America, religion not only meant an ideal of spiritual equality but also access to power and activism within their godly communities. As converts or birthright believers, being a female congregant required an individual identity. One's relationship to God was a direct one; a woman's husband, son, or father did not intervene or speak on her behalf when she wanted to join a church. Among evangelicals, the convert stood alone before the church to prove her worthiness by recounting her conversion experience in personal and visceral terms. In a spiritual sense, white women were able to forge a self-identity, which they used to construct an active religious life based on prayer, worship, conversation, and community; for white women of middling or higher status, this translated into a life and religion of their own.

In a literal and figurative sense, we need to look beyond the meetinghouse to fully grasp the spiritual experience of white women in early America. To study women's religious history, we need to look in unlikely places; women are often hard to find in conventional histories of American religion, where a female presence is presumed even if hidden or invisible.[2] Institutional church histories may mention particular women, usually noted for their piety or wifely connection to a famous divine, but women in general are not central to the narrative. While more recent work by religious historians identifies women as active participants, they are often relegated to a particular section or chapter. In most cases, the role of gender and its impact on spirituality, doctrine, and polity is not fully incorporated into the dominant narratives of American religious history.[3] Recent scholarship by women's historians has made great strides in documenting women's contribution to and presence in

American religion, but more can be done to demonstrate that women's history is integral to U.S. religious history.[4]

The presence of white women in church membership and the process of feminization, wherein female members came to dominate Protestant denominations beginning in the late seventeenth century, have been well documented.[5] However, gauging spirituality based on church attendance alone reveals only one part of religious experience. We know that women were in the pews, faithful believers who lived and died without ever being known for anything beyond their church membership. But what did these women do when not in church? What was their relationship to the church leaders? How active were they in the practical affairs of the godly community? We know that Protestant women provided essential services to their congregations, such as supporting ministerial candidates, feeding and housing itinerant preachers, participating in women's and class meetings, donating funds, circulating religious tracts, creating Bible societies, and staffing Sunday schools.[6] But how did they articulate religion in their lives? How did they pursue a godly life as members of the laity? And how did gender interact with their experiences of Protestant spirituality?

By looking beyond the meetinghouse, we can understand the multiple ways religion was consequential to white women's lives in late eighteenth- and early nineteenth-century America. By looking beyond the meetinghouse, we can find out more about how Protestant women lived a spiritual life and became "reproducers of religious culture."[7] We can also gain a fuller sense of religion as a lived experience and the gendering of spirituality in the lives of both women and men.[8] Looking beyond the meetinghouse expands our understanding of American religious history to more than just an institutional or theological enterprise. Consideration of women's religious experience provides a wide-angle view to include myriad spiritual expressions and enactments—embodied spirituality, religious narrative, lay activism, and gender identity—as primary components of American religious history.

The expanse of female religiosity in early America will be explored by discussing three women: a Pennsylvania Quaker, a Virginia Episcopalian, and a New Jersey Baptist—all white, single, literate women who pursued rich spiritual lives, which they recorded in their journals. By analyzing their extant writings, we can see how they formed spiritual identities built upon religious practice, sustained by lay activism, and expressed in their journals. These journals reveal a variety of subjects, including minister's sermons, church polity, familial relations, and female friendships, as well as commentary on the state of religion in their communities, attendance at meetings, and interactions with other believers and denominations. As religious meditations, these journals became a means of identity formation and spiritual manifestation.[9]

Anne Emlen was born a Quaker in Philadelphia in 1755, the youngest child of George and Anne Reckless Emlen. Her father, a wealthy merchant, died in 1776, leaving his widow and his only unmarried daughter, Anne, well provided for in his will.[10] Anne Emlen trod the traditional path to piety among the Society of Friends. She attended meeting; participated in household worship; read the Bible, the church fathers, and Quaker literature; went to the Women's Meeting; and consulted with other Friends on issues of spiritual and congregational import. She monitored her conduct and prayed for help to guard against excess of any kind "in conversation, preaching, reading, writing, working, dressing, etc." She cultivated "plainness and simplicity" and hoped to avoid the follies of youth and all "transitory enjoyments" by dedicating herself to a godly life. After a bout of illness in 1778, Emlen wrote a personal covenant with God in which she agreed "to love, fear and serve thee above all things"; her commitment to a life of "holy conversation" was resolute. Others remarked upon her religious devotion by noting her plain dress and circumspect behavior; she possessed an "innocent simplicity," combined with "good understanding" and a mind that was "a perfect symmetry of heavenly love."[11]

Upon reaching her majority, Emlen took a "very religious turn" and made an important decision related to her spirituality: she decided to remain single. Though privileged and well-connected, Emlen delayed this traditional route to adulthood, a decision many Anglo-American women made in the late eighteenth century.[12] She eschewed marriage to retain her independence and to devote her time to spiritual concerns. Though matrimony was expected for women of her age and status, Emlen rejected at least three proposals of marriage. For example, in 1780, she received a letter from a young man who wanted to marry her in what she called his "mistaken imagination." After this incident, Emlen took time to discuss the institution of marriage in her journal and remarked that polygamy had once been an accepted practice. Recognizing the social evolution of marital customs, she argued that adherence to tradition was not necessary and intimated that remaining single could be a viable choice: "We should not be stumbled at the past."[13] This marital quandary demonstrates adherence to the Quaker tradition of approaching matrimony with the appropriate gravity. Emlen's reluctance to wed was also influenced by Republican rhetoric, which some white women adopted in the Revolutionary era to justify their avoidance of marriage in exchange for a life of liberty.[14] Emlen's religious background and class status allowed her the time and space to carefully consider her future. As she meditated on the secular issue of being single and infused it with religious fervor, she decided she could do God's will by not following the marital path.

Emlen used her journal to debate marriage, challenge religious authority, investigate moral issues, and support her spiritual desire to be a sign to others.[15] Journal writing became a way to gain spiritual insight and to express interiority; the result for Emlen was "sweet serenity which covers my mind whilst thus writing." One aspect of Emlen's narrative self was commanding and self-sufficient and used religious rhetoric to assume a voice of authority. In an undated journal called "Notes on Religious Subjects," Emlen synthesized others' writings to come to her own determinations on issues ranging from church discipline, communion, and baptism, to prayer, preaching, and church music. At other times, she seems more interested in the views of others. She sought the advice of two Friends on the subject of marriage and weighed recent proposals against their suggestion that she avoid the marital state. She found it a great "difficulty to reconcile" the issue of marriage, yet decided that these "turnings and overturnings, siftings and provings," were intended for her good. She credited Friends for intervening on her behalf and worried that she might "be too much absorbed in the cumbers of the world."[16]

Emlen's notebooks are saturated with Christian language and principle, and yet she did not let herself be confined by biblical precedent.[17] Emlen explored the role of women in Christianity by combing the Bible and church commentaries for evidence of female leadership. She outlined the case of the "Exorcis'd Woman" whose enactment of church rituals was recorded in the New Testament. She cited Tertullian, the second-century theologian, who reported that the exorcised woman "performed Ecclesiastical Administrations" and consecrated the elements "with an Invocation not to be despised" (Emlen's emphasis). For Emlen, this demonstrated "that females have a part in the religious exercises of the primitive church."[18] Such evidence strengthened the construction of her religious self while it supported Quaker ideals of female authority. Emlen used biblical texts to justify her position in spite of living in a society that granted most women a negligible role in denominational religion.

Emlen's interest in women's spiritual power reached beyond the Quaker community to include other Protestants. After attending a Methodist service, Emlen discussed the order of worship, meaning of prayer, and public professions of faith with the presiding clergyman. She questioned the extent of religious freedom accessible to Methodists by citing the example of a young woman who, though under extreme soul "exercise," was not allowed to talk about her spiritual crisis because she was in a Methodist Church. Emlen argued that "male and female are one in Christ" and indicated that this woman should have the right to speak. The minister admitted that Methodists "were not all of one mind respecting women's speaking," but added that it was permitted in private meetings. Emlen pointed out the New Testament practice of female prophecy, specifically activity by the daughters of Philip, whose behavior ran counter to Paul's admonition that women remain silent in the church. She contended that prophesying by women was acceptable because it brought on "edifying, exhortation, and comfort." Empowered by the Quaker tradition of female leadership, Emlen tried to convince other Protestants that women could fully participate in their religious communities. Employing a protofeminist hermeneutics to demonstrate the logic of her interpretive analysis, she sought to bolster her own religious beliefs and to help others along the path to righteousness.[19]

Judith Lomax, a Virginia Episcopalian, never married and devoted much of her life to spiritual pursuits. Born in 1774, Judith was the eldest child of Thomas and Anne Lomax and was related to the first families of Virginia. Of Lomax's early life little is known. Her extant journal covers the period from 1819 to 1827 when she was in her forties and fifties. She avoided marriage, whether by choice or circumstance, and dedicated herself to the Lord, because, as she wrote, "who else is capable of filling my vast desires?"[20]

Lomax lived on her father's plantation until his death in the 1816. When her mother and unwed sisters moved in with an aunt, she chose to live alone in a small town called Port Royal. She believed that "Providence" decreed that she separate from her family, even though it meant flouting social convention. Judith wanted to escape the social world she came from because of the earthly temptations it posed to her faith: "Often when I mix with society here and afterwards remember somewhat I have said or done, I blush for having acted, or spoken so." Lomax's elite background allowed her to devote time to spiritual endeavors. Noting the fact that her father's death placed her in "a state of independence," she planned to pursue it as long as possible, asserting God would support and protect her.[21]

Though born into an Anglican family, Lomax shunned interaction with most of her coreligionists, whom she deemed nominal Christians. When some women urged her to attend services with them at St. John's, the local Episcopal church, she replied that "it was impossible" for her to "enjoy" herself there. Labeling herself "the lone Episcopalian," she felt alienated from her own denomination: "In this little village, I am alone; it is true there are some here, who call themselves Episcopalians, but I differ from *them*." Finding a lack of evangelical fervor in her local church, Lomax frequently sought out Methodists and Baptists. She praised the sermons of evangelical ministers and attended prayer meetings. Though these evangelicals were illiterate and working class, she found herself joining them often because "they converse on my favorite subject, the love of God!"[22]

Lomax created a particular faith for herself founded in the Anglican tradition but permeated with the emotionalism of evangelical Christianity. After worshipping at a Methodist Church in the spring of 1820, she remained after services to attend the class meeting, where she "felt a heavenly calm diffused over my mind. . . . I knew what it was to be a Christian!" She enjoyed interacting with Methodists and Baptists and recorded the elation that resulted when Christians forgot their doctrinal distinctions. She constructed an ecumenical outlook and dreamed of a time when Christians would "be one family, one fold in Christ," united by the sacred bond of love. Despite worshipping with evangelicals, Lomax remained an Episcopalian. While she valued her interdenominational relationships, she averred, "I must always give a preference to Christians of *my own* denomination, and aid . . . the institutions in my own Church." Yet she held out little hope that her church would be what she wanted: "I think, the probability is, I may never hear the sound of the gospel from an Episcopal minister, I am determined to extract from *others* all the good I can."[23]

Lomax followed a spiritual regimen of church going, prayer and reading, teaching school, and conversing with Christian friends. She visited the sick and those in mourning, corresponded with missionaries in Africa, read religious tracts in French, and donated money to Bible, prayer book, and tract societies. She attended funerals, even if she didn't know the individual very well, believing it was good for her soul.[24] She invited evangelical ministers to hold prayer meetings in her home. On some Sunday mornings, Lomax held services in her own household; in one instance, she read the liturgy, prayed, sang, and read from the Bible before a congregation of six young black women. She befriended many young people, both male and female, and held informal meetings. On one occasion, "Mr. Pierson, the young Presbyterian," and her "Baptist friend, Miss Timberlake," joined Lomax and another woman for Christian fellowship. Lomax became part of a prayer meeting in which each member shared leadership responsibilities, a prospect she found daunting. While she willingly offered spiritual advice to others, she doubted her ability to do godly work. After visiting a young man dying of consumption, she noted how deficient she felt in speaking to him of God's mercy: "Alas! I always feel myself but a weak soldier of the cross! I fear my own unworthiness, while I am endeavouring to instruct others."[25]

Lomax practiced her faith through journal and letter writing. She believed writing was efficacious to spiritual community and that "Christians, when separated, should write often, and exhort one another, as the mean apostles did of old." This was God's way to "keep alive the heavenly flame" in every Christian heart.[26] Lomax infused letter writing with religious power; through the act of correspondence, Christians became united as one in Christ.[27] She cited sermons by individual ministers and commented on their quality. She remarked especially upon those preachers who addressed her specific theological interests. She not only used her journal to note religious concerns but put it to instructive purpose. In one instance, she shared it with a young man studying for the ministry, who, she hoped, would glean something useful from its pages: "The sweetest honey is sometimes extracted from the most insipid flowers!"[28]

Lomax described herself in gender-appropriate biblical terms: the Lord's handmaiden, one of the ten virgins, and "another Mary at the feet of Jesus." She embraced traditional gender ideology that claimed women were weak creatures. However, as "the favorites of heaven," she believed women were granted special powers by God to overcome secular inadequacies: "With the divine influence resting on us, working in us, to will, and to do, what is it that a woman cannot accomplish!"[29] She exercised religious leadership in many ways and played a singular role in her community: as member of the social elite among the common folk, as an Episcopalian among Baptists and Methodists, as an older woman teaching young people. Yet she employed traditional gender conventions to pursue such activity. When an evangelical minister attacked another church from his pulpit, Lomax wrote an anonymous letter in the hope of squelching the brewing controversy. Her letter used the traditional trope of female self-abnegation: As a "friend of Zion," she reassured the minister that "she would not presume to dictate to one far *better* taught than her in divine things." With "all the diffidence of a female, and with all the humility of a Christian," Lomax recommended biblical passages to heal the crisis, believing that the spirit of God prompted her actions in the name of "*Universal Love!*"[30] Her reluctance to do more than write an anonymous letter fits with the assertion that Southern white women were more conservative than their Northern counterparts in the early nineteenth century.[31] While personally empowered by her faith, Judith Lomax acted with circumspection when it came to public displays of religious authority.

Abigail Harris, the New Jersey Baptist, followed a similar life trajectory to Judith Lomax. Born in 1777, she never married and died in the late 1820s. Though a faithful member of a Baptist congregation, Harris interacted with other evangelicals, frequented Methodist services and yearly meetings, and once attended a black Baptist Church. She combined religious activities and socializing with other believers. One day in November of 1816, Harris attended Sunday services at the Salem Baptist Church in the morning; in the afternoon she traveled with her minister, Mr. Smalley, to Bridgetown, where she heard him preach at the courthouse. She later took tea with some fellow believers and together they went to the evening service at a Methodist meetinghouse.[32]

Harris followed a regimen of religious practice that was both individual and communal. In October of 1808 she rose and, to thank God for her health, read the first two chapters of Psalms; she then ate breakfast and returned to her room to read a religious tract. She engaged in prayer and hoped her soul would stay "in such A frame as this"; [where she could] "sit & sing herself away to everlasting bliss."[33] Abigail Harris strove to be mindful of God at all times; in her desire to be a good Christian, she disliked mindless activity. While visiting a neighbor, she found a company of people engaged in frivolous talk and immediately wished she were at home engaged in prayerful meditation. She judiciously attended worship services and habitually wrote down the sermon's text and major points. As a member of the laity, Harris engaged in intense religious activity. In 1811, she journeyed to a yearly meeting in Wilmington, Delaware, where she heard ten sermons in five days. A month later, she attended the Salem monthly meeting and then went to Cumberland County, where she frequented the women's meeting twice and later went to a night meeting. The next day, she took communion at the Salem Baptist Church.[34]

Harris, like Emlen, contemplated her single state. In 1817, she deliberated on a marriage proposal: "I always despised the idea of being allied to any man, without feeling a very particular attachment to him, but at the age of forty I cannot expect to feel the ardors of one of 18 or 20.—there are several great inducements on which would be such to many, viz., name, honour, wealth, &c." But Harris turned down the offer and instead filled her personal life with family relationships and friendships with other single women. When her close friend, Emma Foster, was wed in 1822, Harris lamented that marriage had disrupted their spiritual connection: "You know not my dearest Emy feelings on resuming my pen again, that has been so long devoted to the service of one so dear to me—but to one who has now assum'd A new name— you know my dear my aversion to wrighting to married women." Harris mourned Foster's infrequent correspondence and hoped Emma's husband would allow her to keep writing, as "he will remember that you were my *friend* before you were *his*."[35]

Harris provided religious leadership to her community, such as traveling to Greenwich to pray for a Quaker woman who was dying.[36] On another occasion, Mrs. Smalley, the minister's wife, insisted that Harris speak "in prayer" at an evening meeting. Abigail Harris agreed but lamented her lack of courage and feared she would be laughed at—or worse, that she would bring "reproach . . . on the good name of Christ." Harris also participated in religious meetings for single women.[37] Only "single sisters of the Church," women "under serious impressions," were admitted as members to this society. Their meetings included Bible readings, hymn singing, and prayer and provided comfort and encouragement to members, who, with "sisterly affection," helped each other avoid worldly temptations.[38] The women's meetings served as a female support system to augment religious faith and engender spiritual leadership.

Like Emlen and Lomax, Harris mulled over spiritual issues in her journal. She avoided secular concerns and hoped to "get above the things of this little world." Harris used writing to relieve her doubts and document her unworthiness. On a Sunday morning in 1813, she prayerfully expressed hopes for herself and the godly community: "O that this day may be indeed a Sabbath day to my soul, that I may not to read & hear & pray but also to feel the influences of the Holy Spirit, witnessing with my spirit that I am thine. . . . O may both preacher & hearer be directed to speak & hear as becometh the word of the people of God, to preach'd & hear'd—may the word be as water Cast on the ground which cannot be gathered but may it be as A well of watering springing up with everlasting Life."[39]

Although Abigail Harris recognized differences among Christians, she had little patience for doctrinal wrangling: "O how much better it is to see Christians live exactly than to hear them dispute subtilly!" She ignored theological debates and posed fundamental questions for all Christians to consider: "How shall we discern the special from the common operations of the spirit? How may A soul discern its first declinings from God? How may A backsliding Christian recover their first Love?" She believed all Christians served one Lord for the same glorious purpose. This belief was born out by behavior; though a Baptist, Abigail Harris formed friendships with Presbyterians and Methodists and attended the services and participated in the rituals of other Protestants.[40] The bonds of Christian love and spiritual connection effaced denominational differences.

The ability of these women to write religious journals was based in a material reality of literacy, money, and, in the case of Emlen and Lomax, servants who could take care of the mundane aspects of life. As Bunkers and Huff point out, the "physical situation of the writer and the production of her text are of especial importance."[41] The single status of these women provided them a degree of personal freedom, which, when combined with material support and social privilege, afforded the means to execute a religious journal. As textual productions driven by spiritual designs, these journals represent a specific time in these women's life cycles when personal independence and narrative output was possible.[42]

Like many women's journals, the ones outlined here conceal as much as they expose.[43] Various subjectivities appear as these writers wavered over their individual desires for a spiritual life, the authority exercised by them as pious women, the dependence imposed on them as gendered subjects, and the social ambitions expected of middle- or upper-class white women. In the textual representation of the self, these women combined internalized models of Christian piety with external expectations of what it meant to be female in their historical time. These religious journals confirm and challenge the gender ideology of the surrounding social context. Though Anne Emlen sought the advice of others, she never asserted that women were especially weak. Judith Lomax stressed the weakness of woman but believed that God's love emboldened and strengthened her.

These journals are written partly in relation to other people, but the textual selves presented are not completely defined by "the Other."[44] They reveal a labored effort to create a moral and social space for their authors as dedicated Christians—to express spiritual interiority. These journals are dominated by the inner quest for spirituality as well as its outer manifestations. Strong religious faith gave these women the ideological means to stake out an autonomous life, even as they inhabited a society that deemed women dependent and secondary. Through the textual creation of a religious self, these women followed a spiritual path that went beyond traditional piety to a life of spiritual authority, singleness, and independence.

Intense focus on one's religious self and writing about one's spiritual experience had been a common practice among Protestants since the Reformation. English and American Protestants alike studied their inner selves regularly, recounting their spiritual triumphs and failures in diaries, journals, and commonplace books. Ruminating about one's spiritual state was a means of finding and confirming religious faith. This internal dialogue helped the believer resolve conflicts and doubts, though constant vigilance was necessary to avoid the toils and snares of worldly enticements. Narrative focus on one's religious belief and behavior was highly individualized, yet it followed Protestant idioms and eventuated into a literary genre called spiritual autobiography. This became a common form of religious writing in the seventeenth and eighteenth centuries, one that allowed Protestant women and men to document their religious journeys from sin to salvation.[45] Formulaic in nature, spiritual autobiographies conformed to the same plotlines and used similar tropes as converts moved from sinner to saint, from despair and confusion to joy and exultation. Spiritual autobiographies not only chronicled individual conversions, they served as exemplars of Christian belief, designed to persuade nonbelievers to follow a godly life.

These women viewed the world through a lens of Protestant spirituality, which became a central motif of their self-identities. Christianity completely framed their writing. As critic Katharine Hodgkin states, "Religion is itself a constitutive principle of speech . . . both in the structure of the narratives of the self and in the very texture of those narratives."[46] They molded spiritual selves with language that was steeped in Christian imagery, biblical reference, and Protestant terminology. Though these journals remained private and unpublished and are fragmented and incomplete, they describe spiritual journeys. Unfettered by literary conventions, they offer more realistic examples of female religious experience. For these women, journal writing became a textual space to create a narrative identity to fit specific needs. They could "write into existence a person otherwise inhibited by conventional and behavioral codes and restrictive practices."[47]

Though unpublished, these journals contain the basic ingredients of a spiritual autobiography to document religious beliefs and practices. These writings are multivalent and attest to selves that are individual and collective, internal and external. The narratives are fluid in construction, which allowed these women to contemplate and demonstrate spiritual leadership, even when obviated by factors such as age, gender, and class. Emlen, Lomax, and Harris experienced their faiths by interacting with others, engaging in household worship, attending meeting, reading and writing, and seeking the advice and support of their fellow believers. To be religious was to be in community with others as these women's selves became active and meaningful in specific relationships. In turn, these religious selves were founded on others' expectations, including coreligionists who admired these women's piety and commitment, and friends and family members who valued their support and affection. Emlen, Lomax, and Harris constructed their religious selves partly in response to what others were doing and thinking—a typical feature of female autobiography.[48]

These three examples demonstrate the ways in which the structure and doctrine of Protestant Christianity inculcated specific gendered roles, narratives selves, and social parameters upon Anglo-American women. The Christian religion, as a multifarious ideology, has the ability to empower and oppress simultaneously. While Protestantism advocated a theology of spiritual egalitarianism, the structure of the institutional church was less accommodating to the lay activism of female members. Women like Emlen, Lomax, and Harris shaped a religion of their own in a world beyond the meeting-house, where Christian fellowship, intimate friendship, and godly community sustained a rich spiritual experience.

To study American women's religious history, we must reconceptualize religion. First, we must identify what is spiritually significant to believers and locate faith within its social and historical context. Second, we must reconfigure women's position relative to church structures. As Ann Braude states, "We should not limit our perception of power to those forms that are publicly recognized within religious institutions."[49] Third, we must be cognizant of the polyvalence of religious experience, of how individuals devise spiritual identities, and of how religion, as lived experience, molds worldviews and motivates behavior. As Ursula King points out, we need to be aware of the "polysemic nature of the concept of religion" and recognize that just as gender is socially constructed, so, too, is religion.[50] The complex and adaptive intersections of religion and gender deserve more scholarly attention to fully document the many permutations of female spirituality in early America.

Notes

1. Abigail Harris Papers, 1801–1827, Cumberland County Historical Society (hereafter CCHS), Greenwich, N.J.
2. Cotton Mather referred to female congregants as "the hidden ones." See Gerald F. Moran, " 'The Hidden Ones': Women and Religion in Puritan New England," in *Triumph over Silence: Women in Protestant History*, ed. Richard L. Greaves (Westport, Conn.: Greenwood Press, 1985), 125–49.
3. Some examples include Rhys Isaac, *The Transformation of Virginia, 1740–1790* (Chapel Hill: University of North Carolina Press, 1982); Christine Heyrman, *Southern Cross: The Beginnings of the Bible Belt* (New York: Knopf, 1997); Russell E. Richey, *Early American Methodism* (Indianapolis: University of Indiana Press, 1991); Randy Sparks, *On Jordan's Storm Banks: Evangelicalism in Mississippi, 1773–1876* (Athens: University of Georgia Press, 1994); and Cynthia Lynn Lyerly, *Methodism and the Southern Mind, 1779–1810* (New York: Oxford University Press, 1998).
4. For an overview of this issue, see Ann Braude, "Women's History *Is* American Religious History," in *Retelling U.S. Religious History*, ed. Thomas A. Tweed (Berkeley: University of California Press, 1997), 87–107. See also Merry E. Wiesner-Hanks, "Women, Gender, and Church History," *Church History* 71, no. 3 (September 2002): 600–620. For some of the literature on women and religion in

early America, see Susan Juster, *Disorderly Women: Sexual Politics and Evangelicalism in Revolutionary New England* (Ithaca, N.Y.: Cornell University Press, 1994); Rebecca Larson, *Daughters of Light: Quaker Women Preaching and Prophesying in the Colonies and Abroad, 1700–1775* (New York: Knopf, 1999); Marilyn Westerkamp, *Women and Religion in Early America, 1600–1850: The Puritan and Evangelical Traditions* (New York: Routledge, 1999); Susan E. Dinan and Debra Meyers, eds., *Women and Religion in Old and New Worlds* (New York: Routledge, 2001); Catherine Brekus, *Strangers and Pilgrims: Female Preaching in America, 1740–1845* (Chapel Hill: University of North Carolina Press, 1998); Mary Ryan, *Cradle of the Middle Class: The Family in Oneida County, New York, 1790–1865* (New York: Cambridge University Press, 1983); Ann Braude, *Radical Spirits: Spiritualism and Women's Rights in Nineteenth-Century America*, 2d ed. (Bloomington: Indiana University Press, 2001); Rosemary Radford Ruether and Rosemary Skinner Keller, eds., *The Nineteenth Century*, vol. 1 of *Women and Religion in America* (New York: Harper and Row, 1981); and Ann Douglas, *The Feminization of American Culture* (New York: Knopf, 1977).

5. The best evidence comes from New England, where female dominance in church membership began in the late seventeenth century. See Richard D. Shiels, "The Feminization of American Congregationalism, 1730–1835," *American Quarterly* 39 (1981): 45–52; Gerald Moran, " 'Sisters' in Christ: Women and the Church in Seventeenth-Century New England," in *Women in American Religion*, ed. Janet Wilson James (Philadelphia: University of Pennsylvania Press, 1980), 47–65; Barbara E. Lacey, "Gender, Piety, and Secularization in Connecticut Religion, 1720–1775," *Journal of Social History* 24, no. 4 (Summer 1991): 799–821; and Harry S. Stout and Catherine A. Brekus, "Declension, Gender, and the 'New Religious History,' " in *Belief and Behavior: Essays in the New Religious History*, ed. Philip R. Vandermeer and Robert P. Swierenga (New Brunswick, N.J.: Rutgers University Press, 1991), 15–37.

6. See Laurel Thatcher Ulrich, *Good Wives: Image and Reality in the Lives of Women in Northern New England, 1650–1750* (New York: Knopf, 1982); Jean R. Soderlund, "Women's Authority in Pennsylvania and New Jersey Quaker Meetings, 1680–1760," *William and Mary Quarterly*, 3rd ser., 44, no. 4 (October 1987): 722–49; Anne M. Boylan, "Evangelical Womanhood in the Nineteenth Century: The Role of Women in Sunday Schools," *Feminist Studies* 4 (October 1978): 62–80; Greaves, *Triumph over Silence*; and Janet Moore Lindman, "A World of Baptists: Gender, Race, and Religious Community in Pennsylvania and Virginia, 1689–1825" (Ph.D. diss., University of Minnesota, 1994), chapter 4.

7. Elizabeth Castelli and James McBride, "Beyond the Language and Memory of the Fathers: Feminist Perspectives in Religious Studies," in *Transcending Boundaries: Multi-disciplinary Approaches to the Study of Gender*, ed. Pamela R. Frese and John M. Coggeshall (New York: Bergin and Harvey, 1991), 115.

8. David D. Hall, *Lived Religion in America: Toward a History of Practice* (Princeton: Princeton University Press, 1997). On evangelical men and religion, see Janet

Moore Lindman, "Acting the Manly Christian: White Evangelical Masculinity in Revolutionary Virginia," *William and Mary Quarterly*, 3rd ser., 57, no. 2 (April 2000): 393–416. On gender and white men in eighteenth-century America, see Kenneth Lockridge, *On the Sources of Patriarchal Rage: The Commonplace Books of William Byrd and Thomas Jefferson and the Gendering of Power in the Eighteenth Century* (New York: New York University Press, 1992); Lisa Wilson, *Ye Heart of a Man: The Domestic Life of Men in Colonial New England* (New Haven: Yale University Press, 1999); Dana Nelson, *National Manhood: Capitalist Citizenship and the Imagined Fraternity of White Men* (Durham, N.C.: Duke University Press, 1998); Mark Kann, *A Republic of Men: The American Founders, Gendered Language and Patriarchal Politics* (New York: New York University Press, 1998); Toby Ditz, "Shipwrecked; or, Masculinity Imperiled: Mercantile Representations of Failure and the Gendered Self in Eighteenth-Century Philadelphia," *Journal of American History* 81 (June 1994): 51–80; and Jane Kamensky, "Talk Like a Man: Speech, Power, and Masculinity in Early New England," *Gender and History* 8 (April 1996): 22–47.

9. See D. Bruce Hindmarsh, *The Evangelical Conversion Narrative: Spiritual Autobiography in Early Modern England* (New York: Oxford University Press, 2005).

10. Will of George Emlen, January 23, 1776, Will Book H, 138, Historical Society of Pennsylvania (hereafter HSP), Philadelphia.

11. "Notes on Religion," vol. 1, 3rd Month, 1778, Emlen Family Papers, HSP, Philadelphia; "Extracts from the Diary of Mrs. Ann Warder," *Pennsylvania Magazine of History and Biography* 17 (1893): 445, and 18 (1893): 57.

12. Eighteenth-century Quakers of the Mid-Atlantic typically married later in life compared to other populations. For marital patterns of the Society of Friends, see Barry Levy, *Quakers and the American Family: British Settlement in the Delaware Valley* (New York: Oxford University Press, 1988), 149, 244, 273; Robert V. Wells, *Revolutions in Americans' Lives: A Demographic Perspective in the History of Americans, Their Families, and Their Society* (Westport, Conn.: Greenwood Press, 1982), 43; and Louise Kantrow, "The Demographic History of a Colonial Aristocracy: A Philadelphia Case Study" (Ph.D. diss., University of Pennsylvania, 1976), 71–73. On white women who remained single in late eighteenth-century America, see Karin Wulf, *Not All Wives: Women of Colonial Philadelphia* (Ithaca, N.Y.: Cornell University Press, 2000); and Lee Virginia Chambers-Schiller, *Liberty, a Better Husband: Single Women in America, the Generations of 1780 to 1840* (New Haven: Yale University Press, 1984).

13. This concurs with George Fox's directive that marriage be a disciplined and spiritualized endeavor. Delaware Valley Quakers expected couples to scrutinize their reasons for marrying and to cultivate unions based on "self-denying, virtuous, Christian love, not romantic lust." See Levy, *Quakers and the American Family*, 71–72, 133.

14. Anne's friend, Hannah Griffitts, used Republican ideology to express similar

sentiments in a 1769 poem: "But to keep my dear Liberty long as I can / Is the Reason I chuse to live single." Poem reprinted in Catherine Le Courreye Blecki and Karin Wulf, eds., *Milcah Martha Moore's Book: A Commonplace Book from Revolutionary America* (University Park: Penn State University Press, 1997), 173.

15. On Quakers as a sign, see Kenneth Carroll, "Early Quakers and 'Going Naked as a Sign,'" *Quaker History* 67 (Autumn 1978): 69–87; and Cristine Levenduski, *Peculiar Power: A Quaker Woman Preacher in Eighteenth-Century America* (Washington, D.C.: Smithsonian Institution Press, 1996), 6.

16. "Notes on Religion," vol. 2, 4th month, 1781, Emlen Family Papers, HSP, Philadelphia.

17. English evangelicals also individualized biblical language and imagery to fit their specific experience of salvation. Hindmarsh, *Evangelical Conversion Narrative*, 309–10.

18. See "Notes on Religious Subjects," undated, Emlen Family Papers, HSP, Philadelphia. Emlen's exegesis follows a pattern used by early Quakers to support their assertion that women could be preachers; see Larson, *Daughters of Light*, 22–23. See also Suzanne Trill, "'Speaking to God in His Phrase and Word': Women's Use of the Psalms in Early Modern England," in *The Nature of Religious Language: A Colloquium*, Roehampton Institute London Papers, ed. Stanley E. Porter (Sheffield: Sheffield Academic Press, 1996).

19. "Notes on Religion," vol. 2, 4th month, 26th, 1781, and vol. 2, 5th month, 1783, Emlen Family Papers, HSP, Philadelphia.

20. Genealogical Notes, Lomax Family Papers, 1776–1960, Virginia Historical Society (hereafter VHS), Richmond, Va.; and Diary of Judith Lomax, 1819–1827, Lomax Family Papers, 1776–1960, VHS, Richmond, Va. See also Laura Hobgood-Oster, *The Sabbath Journal of Judith Lomax, 1774–1828* (Atlanta: Scholars Press, 1999). On Southern white women and religion, see Elizabeth Fox-Genovese, *Within the Plantation Household: Black and White Women of the Old South* (Chapel Hill: University of North Carolina Press, 1988); Jean E. Friedman, *The Enclosed Garden: Women and Community in the Evangelical South, 1830–1900* (Chapel Hill: University of North Carolina Press, 1985); Cynthia Kierner, *Beyond the Household: Women's Place in the Early South, 1700–1835* (Ithaca, N.Y.: Cornell University Press, 1998); Stephanie McCurry, *Masters of Small Worlds: Yeoman Households, Gender Relations and Political Culture of the Antebellum South, 1840–1860* (New York: Oxford University Press, 1995); Richard Rankin, *Ambivalent Churchmen and Evangelical Churchwomen: The Religion of the Episcopal Elite in North Carolina, 1800–1860* (Columbia: University of South Carolina Press, 1993); and Anne Firor Scott, *The Southern Lady: From Pedestal to Politics, 1830–1930* (Chicago: University of Chicago Press, 1970).

21. Undated entry, 1819, Lomax diary, VHS, Richmond, Va.; January 1816 Letter of Judith Lomax to Sarah Tayloe Washington, Louise Anderson Patten Papers, 1729–1970, VHS, Richmond, Va.

22. January 1816 Letter of Judith Lomax to Sarah Tayloe Washington, Louise Anderson Patten Papers, 1729–1970, VHS, Richmond, Va.; August 4, 1819, undated, and January 29, 1820, Lomax diary, VHS, Richmond, Va.

23. May 2, 1820, May 6, 1820, May 26, 1820, and February 11, 1821, Lomax diary, VHS, Richmond, Va.

24. May 1 and 2, 1825, Lomax diary, VHS, Richmond, Va. Bruce Hindmarsh asserts that many attended the dying because "death was a sacred site" where observers could witness a divine presence. Hindmarsh, *Evangelical Conversion Narrative*, 527.

25. Undated entry 1823, July 26, 1824, February 16, 1824, and October 11, 1821, Lomax diary, VHS, Richmond, Va.

26. May 26, 1820, Lomax diary, VHS, Richmond, Va.

27. On letter writing as a spiritual exercise, see Susan Stabile, "A Doctrine of Signatures: The Epistolary Physicks of Esther Burr's Journal," in *A Centre of Wonders: The Body in Early America*, ed. Janet Moore Lindman and Michele Lise Tarter (Ithaca, N.Y.: Cornell University Press, 2001), 109–26. For letter writing as a part of pastoral care, see Hindmarsh, *Evangelical Conversion Narrative*, 151–52.

28. January 13, 1822, November 1822, and April 7, 1821, Lomax diary, VHS, Richmond, Va.

29. Undated, April 7, 1821, and January 28, 1820, Lomax diary, VHS, Richmond, Va.

30. September 27, 1821, Lomax diary, VHS, Richmond, Va.

31. Brekus, *Strangers and Pilgrims*, 131.

32. Undated entry, March 29–30, 1817, August 13, 1809, and November 17, 1816, Miscellaneous Items, Harris Papers, CCHS, Greenwich, N.J.

33. October 12, 1808, Harris Papers, CCHS, Greenwich, N.J.

34. Two undated entries and August 14, 1811, Miscellaneous Items, and September 15, 1811, and January 7, 1817, Harris Papers, CCHS, Greenwich, N.J.

35. January 14, 1817, and May 23, 1822, Letter from Abigail Harris to Emma Foster Ogborn, Harris Papers, CCHS, Greenwich, N.J.

36. July 24, 1816, Harris Papers, CCHS, Greenwich, N.J.

37. Such meetings existed in late seventeenth-century New England. See Mary Maples Dunn, "Saints and Sinners: Congregational and Quaker Women in the Early Colonial Period," in James, *Women in American Religion*; and Charles E. Hambrick-Stowe, *The Practice of Piety: Puritan Devotional Disciplines in Seventeenth-Century New England* (Chapel Hill: University of North Carolina Press, 1982), 140–41. For separate female meetings among English Baptists, see Richard L. Greaves, "Foundation Builders: The Role of Women in Early English Nonconformity," in Greaves, *Triumph over Silence*, 96, 107. A lay meeting of Baptist women existed in Boston in the 1760s; see October 9 and November 8, 1767, entries, Diaries of Hezekiah Smith, 1762–1805, American Baptist Historical Society, Rochester, N.Y.

38. May 24, 1808, Miscellaneous Items, Harris Papers, CCHS, Greenwich, N.J.

39. November 17, 1822, August 10, 1811, August 14, 1811, September 15, 1811, and undated 1813, Harris Papers, CCHS, Greenwich, N.J.

40. August 6, 1809, March 5, 1816, March 29 and March 30, 1817, Harris Papers, CCHS, Greenwich, N.J.

41. Suzanne L. Bunkers and Cynthia A. Huff, eds., *Inscribing the Daily: Critical Essays on Women's Diaries* (Amherst: University of Massachusetts Press, 1996), 20. See also Steven E. Kagle and Lorenza Gramegna, "Rewriting Her Life: Fictionalization and the Use of Fictional Models in Early American Women's Diaries," in ibid., 41.

42. For theoretical discussions of women's writing, see Felicity Nussbaum, "Eighteenth-Century Women's Autobiographical Commonplaces," in *The Private Self: Theory and Practice of Women's Autobiographical Writings*, ed. Shari Benstock (Chapel Hill: University of North Carolina Press, 1988), 149; Felicity Nussbaum, *The Autobiographical Subject: Gender and Ideology in Eighteenth-Century England* (Baltimore: Johns Hopkins University Press, 1989), xii; and Leigh Gilmore, *Autobiographics: A Feminist Theory of Women's Self-Representation* (Ithaca, N.Y.: Cornell University Press, 1994), 3.

43. For the singular attributes of female autobiography, see Domna Stanton, "Autogynography: Is the Subject Different?" in *Women, Autobiography, Theory: A Reader*, ed. Sidonie Smith and Julia Watson (Madison: University of Wisconsin Press, 1998), 12–13; and Nussbaum, "Eighteenth-Century Women's Autobiographical Commonplaces," 149, 167.

44. Mary G. Mason, "The Other Voice: Autobiographies of Women Writers," in *Life/Lines: Theorizing Women's Autobiography*, ed. Bella Brodzki and Celeste Schenck (Ithaca, N.Y.: Cornell University Press, 1988), 22, 44; and Patricia Meyer Spacks, *Imaging a Self: Autobiography and Novel in Eighteenth-Century England* (New York: Cambridge University Press, 1976), 89–91. These journals fit the pattern of discontinuity typically found in women's writings. See Sidonie Smith and Julia Watson, "Introduction: Situating Subjectivity in Women's Autobiographical Practices," in Smith and Watson, *Women, Autobiography, Theory*, 9.

45. On women's spiritual autobiography, see Estelle C. Jelinek, *Women's Autobiography: Essays in Criticism* (Indianapolis: University of Indiana Press, 1980); Estelle C. Jelinek, *The Tradition of Women's Autobiography: From Antiquity to the Present* (New York: Twayne Publishers, 1986); and Virginia Lieson Brereton, *From Sin to Salvation: Stories of Women's Conversions, 1800 to the Present* (Indianapolis: University of Indiana Press, 1991).

46. Katharine Hodgkin, "Conceits of Mind, Conceits of Body: Dionys Fitzherbert and the Discourses of Religion and Madness," in Porter, *The Nature of Religious Language*, 266.

47. See Judy Simons, "Invented Lives: Textuality and Power in Early Women's Diaries," in Bunkers and Huff, *Inscribing the Daily*, 257, 263. On early spiritual journals by women, see Hodgkin, "Conceits of Mind, Conceits of Body," 250.

48. Benstock argues that a woman's self in a narrative is absent or decentered. See Benstock, *The Private Self*, 16; and Levenduski, *Peculiar Power*, 9. See also the introduction to Brodzki and Schenck, *Life/Lines*, 8. On the mythic and experi-

mental nature of the self in autobiography, see Philippe Lejeune, *On Autobiography*, trans. Katherine Leary (Minneapolis: University of Minnesota Press, 1989), 131–32; as well as the introduction in Bunkers and Huff, *Inscribing the Daily*, 4; Katherine R. Goodman, "Elisabeth to Meta: Epistolary Autobiography and the Postulation of Self"; Nussbaum, *The Autobiographical Subject*, 158–60; and James Olney, *Metaphors of Self: The Meaning of Autobiography* (Princeton: Princeton University Press, 1972).

49. Braude, "Women's History *Is* American Religious History," 91.

50. Ursula King, ed., *Religion and Gender* (Oxford: Blackwell, 1995), 4.

6

Unrespectable Saints

Women of the Church of God in Christ

Anthea D. Butler

Many scholars have written about African American women's activism within their Protestant churches, but they have not always taken women's religious beliefs seriously. Instead of exploring women's desire to live as faithful Christians, they have been more interested in how women's religious faith helped them gain "respectability" or paved the way for the civil rights movement. In this chapter about Holiness women in the late nineteenth century, Anthea Butler asks both American religious historians and women's historians to reconsider their assumptions about why African American women were so involved in church work after the Civil War. Like Janet Lindman, whose chapter appears earlier in this volume, Butler asks probing questions about the personal meaning of religious experience.

I was wretched and undone, and was very sinful. My hair was cut in a boyish bob, and my skirts knee high, most of my blouses were without sleeves, and really, after hearing the gospel preached, I became a penitent. One day I decided to alter a garment so that I would not be ashamed to go to the Altar. But before I finished the garment, time came to prepare dinner, and I went to pick green peas. Oh, what a glorious day for me. While in the pea patch, I believed, and my sins were washed away. Then I began to glorify God. The Holy Ghost came upon me and I fell to the ground. I glorified the name of Jesus, and the spirit took full control of my tongue for a time I spoke with other tongues as the spirit gave me utterance. Oh my, how happy I was for I knew that I was saved, and Baptized with the Holy Ghost and fire, and ever since that glorious day my desire has been to walk with god in the beauty of Holiness, and to be of some help, and to assist in some way to improve the character of young women and girls.
—Sallie M. Swan, *A Brief History of the Life and Work of Elder B. S. Lyle*

Sister Minnie Carter's testimony of being filled with the Holy Spirit is a prototypical testimony of becoming Pentecostal. The elements of her testimony hold intriguing clues as to the various means African American Pentecostal women used to construct their religious and social identities within the

Sanctified church tradition. Negotiating the boundaries between respectable behavior for women and unrespectable Pentecostal behaviors such as speaking in tongues, these women defined respectability in religious terms. In her landmark book, *Righteous Discontent: The Women's Movement in the Black Baptist Church, 1880–1920*, Evelyn Brooks Higginbotham argues that black Baptist women adhered to a politics of respectability that equated public behavior with individual self-respect and with the advancement of African Americans as a group. She further contends that African Americans' respectable behavior in public earned them a measure of self-esteem from white America. Women tried to instill in lower-class blacks psychological allegiance to temperance, industriousness, thrift, refined manners, and sexual morals.[1] Although Higginbotham uses this language of "respectability" to explain how black Baptist women negotiated the public sphere, other scholars have borrowed her language to discuss the activities of African American women within their churches and civic organizations.

What is puzzling is how quickly African American religious historians and American religious historians overlook belief as a primary factor when explaining women's activities in the public sphere. Many scholars do not adequately investigate the theology behind the beliefs of their historical subjects and thus miss an important component of explaining some of their actions within the public and private spheres. In the particular case of black Baptist women and, later, black Pentecostal women, their beliefs about holiness and sanctified living formed the moral and political core of how they engaged the world, from their personal appearances to their activism on behalf of the civil rights movement. Their beliefs, especially their belief in sanctification, not only restructured their interior lives but also helped them to overcome the obstacles of class, race, and gender. Women such as Virginia Broughton and Mary Sweet who were involved in the women's movement in the black Baptist church were not solely concerned with respectability from a societal or racial vantage point but also from a religious one.[2] Both Broughton and Sweet were part of a broader network of women who were engaged in the Holiness movement of the nineteenth century. Baptist on the surface, their core beliefs regarding sanctified life and behavior informed them as much or even more than their Baptist upbringings.[3] Their self-respect came from adhering to the Holiness movement's rigorous bodily and religious requirements and not simply from being "race women."

By acknowledging the Holiness background of these women, a new way of interpreting their activities comes into our view. What if their quest for respectability was not about "acting white" but instead about "acting right" for God? Higginbotham's thesis, then, would gain an entirely different meaning. And what if Holiness women were not primarily concerned with political issues, but instead with religious ones? While black theologians have greatly enriched our understanding of the political importance of African American religion, they have sometimes neglected everyday religious life because of their interest in the religious roots of the civil rights movement. Yet, as I will show in this chapter, women who constructed new identities through their embrace of Sanctification were more than prepared to begin new lives after the civil rights movement. Many of them could not have envisioned a day without Jim Crow. By living sanctified lives, they could subvert some of the stigma of Jim Crow by knowing that they possessed sanctified identities within their communities and with God.

What did it mean to become a saint or a sanctified woman? First, it is helpful to understand the theological terminology regarding sanctification. Used throughout the history of Christianity but first articulated as a doctrine of "Christian perfectionism" by John Wesley, sanctification is Wesley's theological term for the instantaneous experience following conversion. The experience of sanctification, which Wesley described as "his heart being strangely warmed," was a second work of grace that allowed converts to pursue the pathway of perfection, which was defined as freedom from sin in one's life and an infilling of God's love.[4] Those who experienced sanctification began to call their shared experiences the "Holiness movement," a synonym for "Christian Perfection," which began to spread in evangelical circles of the nineteenth century.[5] Some Holiness movement adherents who sought proof of their sanctification eventually became Pentecostals who claimed that the ability to speak in tongues was proof that God had bestowed instantaneous sanctification. Holiness and Pentecostal groups that focused on sanctification held in common the desire to live lives of personal holiness that set them apart for service to others and to God.[6] For African American Holiness and Pentecostal women, this attentiveness to their spiritual lives brought about changes that would benefit themselves, their families, and their communities. Their belief in sanctification affected their negotiation of motherhood, marriage, racial issues, and gender roles, providing the foundation for the construction of new identities that were not solely based upon race but also on religion. By becoming "saints," as people who had been sanctified were called, African American women could combat the evils of their personal and public worlds and save both at the same time. This type of respectability did not find its sole locus in societal norms, but rather in living lives focused on the consecration of the self to God and service to the community. The quest for living a sanctified life, and the desire to reform society, made Church of God in Christ (COGIC) women hew to the Bible for examples of prudent and decorous behavior—behavior that Higginbotham has ascribed primarily to racial and societal expectations, or in her words, the "politics of respectability." Yet that prudent and decorous behavior was compelled by the power of the Holy Spirit, and COGIC women who were engaged in the unrespectable behaviors of shouting, speaking in tongues, and the like would have by no means fit the rubrics of respectability focused on societal expectations.

Investigating women's *beliefs* as a source of their agency in the African American church contests the notion that black women were involved in public activities in churches mainly in service to the advancement of the race and the struggle for civil rights. Although black women were intentional about their work of "advancing the race," they were motivated by their religious beliefs and reading of scripture. African American women's desires for individual experiences of God that were transformative of self and the world coincided with the larger historical push in the latter half of the nineteenth century for health, cleanliness, and temperance. By following this trajectory, we can consider the fundamental importance of African American women's evangelical beliefs—beliefs that have been largely ignored in the service of perpetuating an illusive black church homogeneity. For these women, becoming "saints" was the most important element of their religious and social lives. By recognizing that their religious concerns took precedence over their political ones, we can better understand women's motivations. At the same time, we must recognize that their religious concerns embraced race work and educational concerns important to the advancement of the race.

Not only were the middle and upper classes of African American women socially active, but their sisters in lower social strata must be considered part of this uplift history as well. Sanctified women challenged gender norms and class expectations from their religious framework of sanctification to change their lives and communities, renegotiating the boundaries of status and class through the appropriation of spiritual prowess. Sister Minnie Carter's testimony of rolling around in the garden speaking in tongues cannot be termed respectable, but she gained authority and conviction from her experience. Her faith focused her sense of mission and service to others, reframing her identity from merely a sinner to something more.

COGIC and Pentecostal churches offered women another identity that allowed them to gain respect from a different location. By carefully negotiating the boundaries of what women "ought to be and do," these sanctified women worked as missionaries in the roughest parts of the city, created their own standards of beauty and respect in direct antithesis to the stated norms of African American middle- and upper-class women, and embraced aspects of African American slave culture that were shameful to the gentrifying black classes. COGIC women's concern for living holy, and living right, rather than living like whites, gave their belief in sanctified living a subversive edge, allowing them to have greater power than their Baptist and African Methodist Episcopal sisters had. The history of women in COGIC helps to open up alternative narratives for African American women that allow for class mobility, gendered agency, and the reordering of personal identity through religious belief. Women "on the margins" played an important role in reshaping African American religious history.

COGIC women's quest for sanctification began at an unlikely source. A small Bible study magazine called *Hope*, which was published by Joanna P. Moore, the American Baptist Home Missions' first missionary, was integral to the dissemination of Holiness teachings throughout the southern United States and eventually to COGIC women. Moore, raised as a Presbyterian, became connected to a Holiness network of ministers that included both C. P. Jones and Charles Harrison Mason, cofounders of COGIC. Moore became sanctified, according to her account, at the age of twenty-eight after reading Holiness materials and attending a Methodist camp meeting.[7] A short time later, Moore experienced a healing of a tumor that solidified her sanctification experience, since proponents of the Holiness movement closely linked sanctification and healing.[8] Moore's service as a missionary, as she put it, "to the colored people of the south," continued for more than fifty-three years, culminating in her funeral at Ryman Auditorium in 1916, which was presided over by R. H. Boyd, founder of the National Baptist Publishing Board and the *Nashville Globe*. (Her funeral was featured in the *Globe*.) She was buried in Nashville's black Greenwood cemetery, fulfilling her desire to be buried "near the colored people that she had helped."[9] Her story is a rich one, filled with service to a community that was not her own, though she claimed it in life and death.

Moore's magazine *Hope* started as a Bible study for the black Baptist and other women that Moore worked with in Louisiana. Working as a teacher and missionary in the area of Baton Rouge and southern Louisiana, Moore lived with African Americans, helping women learn how to read and establishing "mother's training schools" to teach women "proper" care for children and keeping house. Moore designed *Hope* as a Bible lesson and domestic teaching tool that could be mailed to the places to which she could not travel, as well as read in established Bible Bands. (Bible Bands were Bible-reading groups that taught people how to read and encouraged them to memorize Scripture.) Besides targeting women with her magazine, Moore started the Fireside schools during the period from 1884 to 1886 in order to train mothers and fathers as well as children. Her work became so sought after that it

Joanna P. Moore. From *In Christ's Stead*, 1880.
(Courtesy of American Baptist Historical Society)

gained the attention and derision of the White League, a precursor to the Ku Klux Klan in Louisiana. In an attempt to close Moore's school, the members of the White League painted it with skulls and crossbones and threatened her life, forcing her to leave Louisiana.[10] After moving to Little Rock, Arkansas, she hosted a successful mother's training school and started the Sunshine Band, a Bible study course for children. Later she moved to Nashville, Tennessee, and started a Fireside training school there, eventually turning over the publication of *Hope* for a time to the National Baptist Publishing Board. Moore's work in Nashville proved to be her most important work in terms of the Holiness movement, drawing in such notable women leaders as Mary Sweet and Virginia Broughton, who joined the Fireside school work. By commissioning Bible Band workers and finding missionaries to travel throughout the southern states, Moore's work with black Baptists flourished.[11] Her Holiness beliefs were so prominently affirmed in *Hope* magazine that women who read it began to latch onto her teachings on sanctification. One of the women who responded favorably was the first leader of the COGIC Women's Department, Lizzie Robinson.

Lizzie Robinson's life is an excellent example of how religion helped African American women of meager means to shape new identities. Born into slavery in Dermott, Arkansas, Robinson was a talented child who could read from an early age, but in her early teens, the death of her mother necessitated her marriage. Little is known about her early years, but she met Joanna Moore during Moore's time in Pine Bluff, Arkansas. Robinson recounts her story of being sanctified: "I was Saved and sanctified in the Baptist church. Sister Joanna P. Moore Came to Pine Bluff during this time and taught us how to live. I was converted, but I didn't know how to live. This was the starting point, teaching us how to live."[12]

By emphasizing that Moore had taught people "how to live," Robinson reflected the belief that the pursuit of holiness affected every area of a person's life. In *Hope*, Moore wrote "admonitions" explaining how to live a sanctified life, which she later compiled into an 1898 book used in the Fireside schools, *The Power and Work of the Holy Spirit*. Like most Holiness adherents, Moore viewed holiness as a total experience that encompassed body and soul, enabling one to live a life worthy of God. "You will also be careful to eat only healthy food and be sure not to eat too much, for the drunkard and glutton are classed together. You will also be careful to keep your bodies clean, your clothes clean, your houses in order, because Jesus lives with you all the time through his spirit in your bodies. The women who receive the Baptism of the Holy Spirit are careful to keep themselves and their homes clean and in order."[13] Moore's description of women who are baptized in the spirit emphasized the importance of everyday life. Cleanliness, moderation in food intake, and abstinence from alcohol are all required because of the presence of Jesus within one's very body. For African American women and men whose bodies had been beaten and abused, this belief in divine embodiment was deeply empowering. Since they did not want Jesus or the Holy Spirit to be sullied by their actions, it also made the pursuit of holiness more than just rules to follow.[14] For Robinson and other women embracing holiness, this totality of living in the spirit had a gradual effect upon their self-images and identities. Rather than pushing for cleanliness and abstinence for societal reasons, they wanted to "live right" because of scriptural admonitions and scriptural affirmations that Jesus lived within. Robinson and other women in the rural South were not motivated by their desire for people's approval but by their belief that Jesus literally inhabited their physical space. By identifying with Jesus—the divine within—women like Robinson saw themselves as special and set apart. The rigorous requirements of the pursuit of holiness—for instance, changes in diet, sexual abstinence if unmarried, proper speech, and modest dress—changed their perspective and outlook. Because of their belief that Jesus was living within them, they believed it was of paramount importance to refrain from desires and wants that were not in concert with the Bible.

Robinson's own life was an example. Before meeting Moore, Robinson lived in obscurity, doing housekeeping and taking in laundry, a life that was less than miraculous. After her sanctification, Robinson often referred to how "Sis Moore prayed that the Lord would take my hands out of the wash tubs and fill them with good books and Bibles that I might go from house to house and teach God's people that were lost sheep, that didn't know the way."[15] Moore confirms this story when reminiscing in a later article from *Hope* on their meeting. "Lizzie Wood did not have a good chance for an education and she has passed through many trials. One day several years ago I visited her home in Pine Bluff; she was earning her living by washing; I knelt with her by the washtub and asked God to take her hands out of that tub and fill them with Bibles and send her from house to house to feed hungry souls with the Bread of Life. God has answered my prayer. Glory to his Name!"[16]

Divine intervention was the first step on the pathway toward constructing a new identity. Belonging to God meant that priorities were reordered and new tasks sought. For Robinson, Moore's intervening prayer was the beginning of being led by God. While perhaps not fully giving up washing initially, Robinson began working with the Bible Band system Moore had devised. Traveling door-to-door, selling Bibles and starting up Bible Band groups, her missionary and organizational skills developed. Robinson took to the Bible Band well, and soon her letters to Moore were appearing on a regular basis in *Hope*. It is clear from her words that her newfound sense of purpose gave her a different outlook on her life. As Moore reported: "A Good Sister, Lizzie Woods (nee Robinson), is scattering light in Lexa, Popular Grove, and surrounding country in Ark. She has sold a large number of Bibles and secured subscribers to hope. She says 'Once I loved only to read novels and foolish trash, but now the Bible is to me the best of all books.'"[17]

Robinson's engagement as a local Bible saleswoman, missionary, and teacher acted as a catalyst to expand both her spiritual life and her identity. Instead of treating the church and her work at home as her main focus, Robinson's recognition as Bible Band worker and part-time missionary opened up new possibilities for her, honing her organizing skills and introducing her to other women in her immediate area. Although Robinson and other women were unable to attend Baptist conventions, they met locally with other Baptist women, and their networks enabled them to work together to reconstruct their individual and corporate identities. Because of the constant push to do mission work and their intensive focus on temperance, thrift, domesticity, and piety, women such as Robinson were constantly restructuring and refining their sanctified identities in such a manner that perfection was never attained. The pursuit of sanctification, not its attainment, was what mattered. Becoming sanctified was not merely an individual process but a communal one, in which women had to work together through Bible Bands and scripture study.

The pursuit of sanctification led to competing ideas and interpretations of what it meant to become sanctified. For Robinson and many others at the turn of the century, the crucial issue was whether or not those who had pursued sanctification had genuine proof that sanctification had occurred. While most believed that turning away from "worldly amusements" was enough, others, such as Charles Parham, a prominent Holiness minister and healer, felt that something more had to signal that sanctification had occurred. For Parham, that signal was the ability to speak in tongues, or glossolalia. Parham felt that the ability to speak in tongues, as described in Acts 2, signaled the culmination of the sanctification experience, providing a concrete sign that the Holy Spirit lived inside of a person.[18] Parham's teaching of this new belief culminated in a major revival movement in Los Angeles, California, in 1906, called the Azusa Street revival, which was led by one of his former students, William J. Seymour. This revival movement, which heralded the beginning of the Pentecostal movement, began to spread throughout the Holiness network. One of those who was a recipient of the new "Baptism of the Holy Spirit" at Azusa Street was Charles Harrison Mason, cofounder of the Holiness denomination, Church of God in Christ.

Mason, along with his friend and cofounder C. P. Jones, had been enrolled in a Baptist school in Arkansas before being ejected for his Holiness beliefs. Mason's baptism caused a split between him and Jones, and Mason led the contingent that retained the denominational name.[19] Faced with several dilemmas, including how to organize the abundance of women left in the divided denomination's prayer and Bible Band groups, Mason set out to find a women's leader, and found her in Dermott. Mother Robinson recalls their fateful meeting: "I was sanctified in the Baptist School but did not have the Baptism of the Holy Ghost. Elder Roach was pastoring the Church of God in Christ at Dermott at that time and Bishop Mason came there to preach and came to the school. . . . When Brother Mason came in he asked me where was the other lady. They were upstairs. Mrs. Crow, Mrs. Jones, and Mrs. Cora came downstairs and he began to teach us, I told him that I had been living right for six years but I hadn't been baptized with the Holy Ghost. So, I received the baptism of the Holy Ghost that day, and Mrs. Jones, Mrs. Crow, and Mrs. Stewart looked on and were amazed."[20]

Robinson's speaking in tongues—or receiving the baptism—resulted in both an identity and a status change. As a respected matron of a Baptist academy, she had wielded a considerable amount of authority. Yet, with the advent in her life of the absolutely unrespectable (and often feared) practice of speaking in tongues, Robinson's status plummeted in her community. Recalling the events after Mason's visit, Robinson noted that "two of the Baptist preachers said they would go down yonder (to hell)" before they would let her remain matron of the school.[21] Her attempt to live as a sanctified woman seemed to have been dealt a fatal blow. But although the general public considered Pentecostals to be derelicts or from the "wrong side of the tracks," women such as Robinson and those who would soon join with her in the formation of the COGIC Women's Department would overcome these negative images by linking the sanctified life to the power of the Holy Spirit. Inspired by Pentecostal teachings derived from Joel 2, which indicated that the Spirit would be poured out on "all flesh," women and men revamped their understanding of sanctification and gained both an extra sense of empowerment and a supernatural way to ensure that their personal sanctification was tangible and visible to others. Pentecostals' emphasis on the Spirit pouring out on "all flesh" would play a major role in how Robinson recast her sanctified identity and the identity of the women with whom she would soon work.

Forced out of her position at the Baptist academy, Robinson partnered with another ousted African Methodist Episcopal minister, R. E. Hart, and began holding interracial revival meetings in Tennessee and Arkansas.[22] Hart encouraged Robinson's public speaking but expressed reservations about her desire to travel to Memphis because of the prohibitions within the denomination on women's preaching. "Dr. Hart thought all teaching was preaching. I said to him, I am not a preacher. I have not been called to preach. In Mark 26, he [Jesus] told the women to tell his disciples to meet him in Galilee. Judas killed himself but eleven were there and they came in and the last chapter of Mark, he told the Preachers to go into all the world and preach the gospel to every creature. He, [Jesus] never called a woman's name. He never called a woman to preach."[23]

By making this distinction between preaching and teaching, Robinson could ascend to a position of leadership without disrupting the male leadership inside and outside of COGIC. Although female "teaching" was beginning to gain acceptance in other Pentecostal denominations, Robinson's Baptist heritage died hard. Women were not allowed to preach in black Baptist denominations, and Robinson's early training held fast. Yet her role as teacher would also cause controversy within the ranks of COGIC men. Soon after her arrival in Memphis, Mason asked her to do a Bible study for the pastors, which began rather inauspiciously. She remarked that on her first day of instruction, "Forty-five or Fifty people went out of that house in a solid Prayer line." Yet, by identifying with gendered norms of female subordination, Robinson was able to transcend traditional boundaries with help from men like Mason, who rebuked the group at her next meeting, instructing the men who started to leave to "go back and sit down, go back and sit down and learn some sense, every one of you sit down, go back and sit down!"[24] Walking the fine line of deference to norms of respectability while taking on a "teaching" role allowed Robinson to have influence over men, all the while seeming to pay deference to the norms of respectability and orthodoxy.

By carefully negotiating these gendered boundaries, Robinson was able to develop a unique voice. When Mason asked her to lead the women of the denomination in 1911, she agreed, and Mason appointed her Overseer of Women's Work (later to be termed Women's Department) at the National Convocation Meeting in 1911.[25] Leading this department allowed Robinson to run a broad-scale program that would put the rigors of sanctified identity to the test. Faced with organizing women throughout the South, Robinson began to return to the places that she knew best in Arkansas and Tennessee, as well as traveling to Texas. Such rigorous travel would have been very challenging for a middle-aged African American woman at that time. Limited financial resources, segregated train travel, and nonexistent lodging facilities meant that Robinson had to rely on the networks of COGIC members in each area for assistance. In order to link herself to other women who had the resources and means to help in her organization building, Robinson turned her attention to women who were the spiritual leaders of local congregations, the church mothers. These women, who were often considered the most spiritually mature and were also often the oldest women in the congregation, had the ear of their pastor and the respect of the congregation. In the words of one COGIC church leader, "The role of the local church mother is indeed one of great importance and a 'must' for a growing church. She is to a pastor in the local church what a wife is to her husband in the home. . . . There should be a pastor–church mother relationship going on at all times."[26] Church mothers, who have been part of many African American churches since the nineteenth century, held status and authority within the churches, often handling the disciplinary actions and providing spiritual direction for both men and women of the congregation.[27] By recruiting women with a clear status and identity within the local congregation of COGIC churches, Robinson could ensure that her project of reconstructing identities could be implemented. However, it was clear that not every woman understood what the Prayer and Bible Band was for. As Robinson explained, "The women did not know how to go back home (from the convocation) and start the Bible class, so I went from Church to church and got them started. . . . I went with Mother Chandler for about fifteen or twenty days to organize the Bible Bands in Texas. Mother Chandler was one of the first to get up while I was talking about the Bible and declared that I would never have to say more about it to her. She said 'I am going home to organize Bible Bands and you will know about them when you return.' "[28]

Mother Chandler was one of the first women's appointees of the Women's Department. As a reward for her zeal in establishing Prayer and Bible Bands in churches throughout Texas, she was installed as the Overseer for the women's work in Texas. By choosing church mothers like Chandler who were skilled in organization and had some education, Robinson ensured that COGIC teachings and beliefs would retain their uniformity as she taught them and that the "right kind" of woman would be involved in her women's department. She expected women to be concerned about both their own personal sanctification and the training of workers for furthering the message of sanctification. To ensure that they would use similar processes in constructing new, sanctified identities, Robinson used the Bible Band model wholesale from *Hope*, adapting it to teach COGIC doctrines of sanctification and Holy Spirit baptism, along with admonitions for keeping house. Moore's organizational structure provided a good framework for Robinson's promotion of a sanctified Pentecostal identity, but perhaps it did not provide an adequate framework for women who were "mavericks" or unaccustomed to leadership from either women or men.

Robinson's early missions within COGIC were not without problems, some of which stemmed directly from competing interpretations of what it meant to be a sanctified woman. Both Holiness and early Pentecostalism emphasized the equality of gender in the Holy Spirit's work in an individual. Unfortunately for Robinson, many of the women she encountered on her initial tour were consumed with their "individuality." Some of the women in the church, at least in Memphis, were beginning to question male leadership in general and the denial of women's right to preach in particular. As they understood the Pentecostal hermeneutic of the time—that the Spirit could fall upon all flesh—there should have been no reason to prohibit women from preaching. Recounting how she dealt with a group of women who were embroiled in a conflict with men over women's right to preach, Robinson found herself caught in the middle of the fray. She took a determined stand in order to address the concerns of the women she represented: "I said to the women if the man's time is out, why don't you quit your husbands? Jeremiah said, 'run ye to and fro through the streets of Jerusalem, and see now and know and seek in the broad places thereof, if ye can find a man, if there be any that executeth judgement, that seeketh the truth and I will pardon the city.' God wants a man. Jesus Christ always called himself the Son of Man, and you say you are going to hear a man. They had the biggest fight among themselves you ever witness."[29]

In spite of her sanctification and her Pentecostal experiences, Robinson's Baptist upbringing and Moore's influence locked her into a traditionalist notion of prohibiting women from the pulpit. Robinson's rejection of women's right to preach came from a variety of sources—biblical, cultural, and pragmatic. With former Baptist preacher C. H. Mason leading the church, she had a ready ally in her prohibitions, for despite his empowerment of women, Mason's favorite remark was that "if a woman could be the husband of one wife," she could preach.[30] Because Robinson found herself at every turn facing the question, at times she became quite vituperative in her responses. "The women were turned over to me and I asked, how many preachers are there? Thirty-two stood up. I asked, who told you to preach? I took them right down to the Bible. One said that God had spoken to her out of the cloud and told her to preach, out of the air, I said, well, the devil is the prince of the air and no one told you to preach but the devil. This is the way I started to work in this church. I began to teach. The saints need to be taught."[31]

Although women were and still are prohibited from ordained office in COGIC as preachers, alternative routes to the traditional pastor role arose for women that gave them place and prestige in the denomination. Through Robinson's organization of women's work, church mothers were elevated beyond their spiritual leadership to administrative leadership on local, regional, and state levels. Both home and foreign missionary positions were established, and women could also serve as evangelists who were able to travel and "teach," as opposed to "preach." Women's teaching, much like preaching or exhortation, enabled these women to gain a command of Pentecostal doctrines and beliefs, placing them at times in the unique positions of teaching the very pastors that they were prohibited from becoming.[32]

The controversy surrounding women's preaching was only one area in which COGIC women's identities were redefined. At times, women's missionary or evangelist work led them into a more mainstream definition of their roles. Even when they seemed to follow the logical norms of "what a woman ought to be and do," they deviated enough to make their identities a mixed construction of subversion and conversion.

As a case in point, consider Sister Minnie Carter, the woman who had been sanctified in a pea patch. Her testimony served as a template for the transformed identity that Robinson and later COGIC women saw as the sanctified ideal. A reluctant COGIC member in Belsoni, Mississippi, Sister Carter had a rather developed sense of style before experiencing conversion and sanctification. Her account made much of the fact that she had been sewing a garment to make herself more presentable for church. During her normal "domestic duties," she had an encounter that had left her speaking in tongues on the ground. In the process of doing what was "normal" and expected of women of her day, she had become a saint. Reminding the reader that she had already been converted, she explained that she had begun the process of cleansing her life by altering her clothing, which was not proper for wearing to church. "I became a penitent," she wrote. Sleeveless garments indicated that one was a loose woman, and the sexual nature of showing one's armpits was a definite barrier to becoming sanctified.[33] By drawing her readers' attention to other domestic duties, such as preparing dinner and going out to pick peas, Sister Carter suggested the newfound prominence of domesticity and its connection to sanctification. The process of sanctification involved changing one's lifestyle in stages before speaking in tongues. Living the "sanctified life" meant that one would refrain from practices such as smoking, drinking, immodest dress, coarse language, and immorality. Through sacrifice, consecration, and cleansing, one could attain a sanctified life.[34] The process of sanctification had no specific time frame but took place in the context of protracted prayer meetings, giving, service, and turning away from former "ungodly" practices. Those who attained the sanctified life were called saints, and being a saint meant having a command of scripture, yourself, and everyone else.[35]

Within COGIC, sanctification was more sought after than speaking in tongues, the traditional Pentecostal sign of the baptism of the Holy Spirit.[36] Unlike white Pentecostals who believed that the gift of tongues was given immediately, COGIC and other sanctified churches believed that one needed to attain victory over worldly affectations like bobbed hair and short skirts before the Holy Spirit could inhabit a person. Sister Minnie's conversion, therefore, provided a template for how the conversion, sanctification, and baptism in the spirit should happen. The end result, of course, was not for Sister Minnie's personal edification, but to help other young women. Those who had been sanctified had been instilled with a mission to change the world into a holy place. The faith that one can change the world through living the sanctified life appeals to people who are the "reforming type."[37] Sister Minnie Carter was definitely the reforming type. Her testimony of being filled ends with the phrase that "she wants to assist in some way to improve the character of young women and girls."[38]

Women like Sister Minnie were not only empowered to cleanse themselves but also to cleanse others. The infilling of the spirit did not mean initially that one had become a better class of person. Rather, it was a gift that was supposed to be used to empower others. Sister Minnie's first task was to "improve the character of young women" through her pamphlet on correct behavior for young women. Her account emphasized obvious concerns about dress and behavior, but at times she used an interesting mix of empowerment to put forth her case. "Girls must develop a strong will to resist, and that royal power to pronounce the right and do it, and to say no to every wrong suggestion. You must be firm and possess a sound will to govern your conduct. In the mortal world it is your thoughts that make or mar your character. Self-respect is the source of much power."[39]

The appeal to girls, rather than to men, to control their wills could be understood as sexist. Yet a case could be made that Sister Minnie and other Pentecostal women's spiritual power enabled them to govern themselves as well as the behavior of others. By controlling themselves through living a sanctified life, they also controlled how others behaved toward them. Through her rhetoric, Sister Minnie not only emphasized the emotionality of her religious experience but also the ability of the Spirit to instill strength and character. The rhetoric of sanctified empowerment helped the individual, and in turn helped the "race" by making respect an individual issue of holiness rather than a "public" issue about what others think. As historian Virginia Wolcott notes, "The religious identity of many working class African American women was rooted more in notions of self-respect than in bourgeois public displays of respectability."[40] Modifying behaviors through belief, therefore, was more about private life that modeled a sanctified public persona.

Other COGIC women spread the message of personal empowerment by taking these teachings to the streets of the inner cities. Mother Mary Magrum Johnson and her husband, Brother W. G. "ting a ling" Johnson, set to work upon their arrival in Detroit in what was called "digging out a church." "Digging out" or "plowing the field" and "working the ground" entailed preaching and holding healing services on street corners, in houses of ill repute, in tents, or indeed anywhere else within the cities to gain converts. Mother Mary Johnson's first official "digging out" enterprise was held on Elliot Street in front of a "Bear Trap," a house that got its name from "the class of people who lived within." Bear traps in Detroit were boardinghouses that charged tenants low rent and were havens for illicit activities such as prostitution and gambling.[41] Rather than avoiding these areas, COGIC women saw bear traps and boardinghouses as likely places for converts and evangelistic opportunities. Johnson remarked that her husband "preached" and she "spoke" from Romans 6. This distinction was important because COGIC made a clear distinction between "preaching" and "teaching" or "speaking." Preaching was what men did as ordained elders, and women could "teach or speak" in their roles as mothers and sisters. The distinction would prove to be a problem in urban areas because women who had begun evangelistic meetings were expected to turn over control to ordained men. In Mother Johnson's case, it was perhaps less difficult because the pastor was her husband. She remarked, "I was my husband's helper, stayed in my place, and let God do the work."[42]

For other COGIC women, turning over their ministries prompted feelings that were perhaps not in keeping with being "sanctified." The women who founded Saint's Home Church in Los Angeles in 1914 experienced firsthand the pain of turning over their ministry work. Mother Millie Crawford, from Texas, and Mother Martha Armstrong started a mission in a tent at 14th and Woodson in Los Angeles. Holding daily services that started at 9 A.M. and continued all day long, the women stopped only for lunch. The Southern-style revival "teaching" fared well in the temperate climate of Los Angeles. Men were involved, but the women were described as "standing out as beacon lights" in the leadership of the group.[43] The services were racially mixed, causing a bit of consternation for the first pastor called to Saint's Home, Elder Eddie Driver. Driver was sent from Texas to pastor in Los Angeles partly because of a vision he had had in which "the Lord told him to go to California."[44] Driver was surprised upon his arrival in Los Angeles at the mixed congregation that was attending the services. Described as having a "strong personality," Driver soon had various run-ins with the women who had "dug out" Saint's Home through their tent ministry. After "plowing the field" and "working the ground," the bylaws of COGIC did not allow women to pastor what they had planted. The women who had started Saint's Home either left or stayed within Driver's congregation, attempting to put their ill feelings aside.[45]

Mother Emma Cotton, who migrated to California from Louisiana, tried to live under these rules, but her self-identification as a preacher and leader soon clashed with COGIC norms for being a sanctified woman. Cotton, one of the first state mothers in California, began her evangelistic work alongside her husband in Los Angeles, subsequently moving with him north to the Oakland area. Described by Aimee Semple McPherson as "a little woman with a mighty halleluiah—neatly dressed, unprepossessing and a firebrand," Cotton co-pastored with her husband in the Oakland area, a fact that did not go unnoticed by one COGIC visitor from Memphis.[46] When Elder McKinley McCardell arrived from Texas as a young migrant and boarded at Mother Cotton's home in Oakland for a time, he remarked, "As I approached the door, (to the house) there was a sign, Elder H. C. Cotton, Pastor and Mrs. Emma Cotton, Assistant Pastor; that startled me—looking and thinking; because I had just left a state where women did not pastor churches."[47] Cotton further pushed the boundaries of sanctified women's identity a few years later when she left her husband's new ministry in San Diego to start her own church in Los Angeles. In the *California Eagle*, a small byline heralded her new ministry: "Pentecostal Gospel Mission, 4709 Central Ave. Mrs. Emma Cotton, leader. Gospel meetings every night at 7:30. The purpose of these meetings is to save sinners and have believers receive the baptism of the Holy Ghost and the sick healed. Come and tarry in the fullness of the spirit. All are welcome."[48] Left behind in San Diego, Elder Cotton proceeded to choose perhaps the least likely outcome the following week. As noted in the *California Eagle*, "Rev. H. C. Cotton, pastor of the Church of God in Christ, has gone to Los Angeles for an indefinite stay."[49]

One can only guess at the tensions that may have existed between the Cottons in their dual pursuit of ministry. Unlike Mother Johnson, who partnered with her husband, Mother Cotton's identity was first and foremost as a preacher and evangelist, and her outward actions seem to suggest that marriage was a secondary concern. COGIC men and women imagined the sanctified identity differently. While Mother Cotton left her husband's side to start a ministry in Los Angeles, he remained committed to the marriage and willing to list her as at least associate pastor.

Other women were also faced with making decisions about their pursuit of sanctification that placed their faith in conflict with their personal commitments. Since sanctification meant that women could harness much of the same spiritual energy as men, their quest to reform themselves and others many times interfered in their marriages. COGIC women's marriages, if outside the denomination, were usually frowned upon and not sanctioned from within the COGIC community. If they did marry someone within, they were expected to work alongside their husbands and fill the role of helpmeet.

COGIC women's marital tensions came from various sources. The tensions most often documented came from the practice of what Bishop Mason called "double marriages." The policy of most early Pentecostal denominations was that if one had been divorced, one would be unable to remarry until the former spouse died, and divorced people were prohibited from ministry. Uniquely, COGIC policy not only focused on the issue of divorced persons, but also on those who did not bother to obtain a divorce to remarry. Mason's teaching on what he called "double marriage" emerged from both from a biblical and a pragmatic perspective. "Now You women that have other women's husbands or men that are not yours, and husbands that have other men's wives will have to tell the truth when you meet Jesus. It may be at the well, or on your dying bed, but you will have to tell the truth. The Lord says let not the wife depart from her husband and let not the husband put away his wife. I Cor. 7:10–11. . . . Jesus said whosoever shall put away his wife and marry another committeth adultery against her, and a woman shall put away her husband and marry another, she committeth adultery."[50]

The issue of double marriage had nothing to do with divorce and remarriage, as it did among other Pentecostals. Instead, the policy addressed bigamy. It was not uncommon for persons to simply leave one spouse and take up with another without a legal divorce, a practice that had its roots in the unstructured confines of slave families.[51] The Reconstruction and migration periods did lead to an increase in legalized marriages, but these were for the most part between middle- and upper-class blacks who could afford to do so. For lower-class, impoverished African Americans, common-law marriage and serial relationships were the norm. Migration served to exacerbate the problem, with spouses leaving home ostensibly to find work in the North or West and remarrying in their new locales. Unless someone could identify or notify the previous spouse, chances were that the new spouse would never know that he or she was involved with a bigamist. These resulting pairings led Mason to stand strongly against "double marriages." COGIC leaders involved in a "double marriage" were stripped of their credentials. These types of "family" issues occupied a major portion of the COGIC Convocation minutes in the 1910s and 1920s, resulting in consequences for the guileless and guiltless women involved. For COGIC women, marriage to someone who had another spouse could mean the termination of their positions as evangelists, missionaries, or church mothers. Convocation minutes in the 1920s were filled with stories of evangelists such as Cora Stevens, who lost both her husband and her ministry because of the edict of Mother Robinson and the elders' board, who declared her to be in an "unsanctioned" marriage. Cora's husband had been married previously and had not bothered to obtain a legal divorce from his first spouse, making him a bigamist.[52] He was instructed to leave Cora and go back to his first wife, which he did as a condition of remaining a pastor. Cora, however, lost both her identity as a married woman and her work as an evangelist. Forbidden to remain an evangelist, Cora Stevens was angered by the decision, and for several years she contested the denominational ruling. As a result, Mother Robinson posted a notice in the denominational newspaper, *The Whole Truth*, stating, "Cora Stevens is not a licensed evangelist in the Church of God in Christ. License revoked by Mother Robinson."[53]

Other COGIC women drove their husbands away by being too involved with the church. Lillian Brooks Coffey, successor to Mother Robinson after her death in 1945, lamented in an interview in *Ebony* magazine about her husband leaving her: "I often bare that experience to young women, telling them to be more attentive in their homes and not to let their religious work overlap. . . . [W]e might have reconciled. [Yet] I had gone on and become a little more independent. I was daily gaining national and international influence. This may have made the span too wide to bridge." As the magazine explained, Coffey had "never remarried in deference to her church's stringent rules against divorce."[54] Coffey's dilemma was one that many women within the COGIC ranks faced. The intensity of their sanctified beliefs pushed them into working hard for the church in various evangelistic activities. Although their personal lives at times suffered from following their lives of sanctification, they still upheld marriage as the ideal for the women they led.

That ideal was contradictory. For some, the ideal was "being released" by God from one's spouse, that is, getting rid of them through desertion, divorce, or death. Freedom from the state of matrimony allowed women to use their spiritual and administrative gifts.[55] Marriage was not a prerequisite for leadership as a church mother, and it was perceived at times to be a hindrance, especially if a husband was "less committed" to the faith and the church. Not being married freed women to travel, to take on many speaking engagements, and to pursue other religious and civic activities. In keeping with their sanctified identity, they viewed God or Jesus as a faithful husband, a husband who did not mind if they were away from home. In this way, COGIC women relied not upon husbands, but upon their ultimate husband, God, to fill all of their needs. Outsiders may have thought that sanctified women were unable to keep their husbands, but the truth was that they did not need flesh and blood husbands to spoil their "saintly" identities. Jesus, not approval from a husband or society, was the highest desire for a sanctified woman, and no amount of approval from home or society could compete.

COGIC women, therefore, allow us to rethink the religious roles of African American women beyond Higginbotham's emphasis on respectability. They constructed new sanctified identities by melding together various strands of evangelical belief, Victorian propriety, and progressive feminist activism. For these African American women, pursuing sanctification meant that their public and private lives were filled with tensions that required spiritual rigor, astuteness, diplomacy, and a relentless work ethic. By creating new identities based on the Bible, lower- and middle-class African American women gained status for themselves in a society that ascribed to them only sexual or utilitarian identities. As visible "saints," they valued women's spiritual authority and prowess in a system that recognized the power of women's faith but still affirmed patriarchal leadership. Without the women of COGIC, the ideals of sanctification or holiness perhaps would not have gained such a pervasive hold on both urban and rural African American areas of the nation. As models of sainthood, COGIC church mothers were certain that the world's eyes were upon them and that God's eyes approved.

Notes

1. Evelyn Brooks Higginbotham, *Righteous Discontent: The Women's Movement in the Black Baptist Church, 1880–1920* (Cambridge: Harvard University Press, 1993), 14.

2. Many of the women in Higginbotham's book also had affiliation with loose networks of Holiness ministers and camp meetings in addition to their memberships in black Baptist churches. Virginia Broughton worked closely with Joanna P. Moore, who embraced the Holiness movement. Moore also was good friends with C. P. Jones, cofounder with C. H. Mason of the Church of God in Christ, a Holiness Pentecostal denomination established in 1895 after their disfellowship from the Baptist convention. See Anthea Butler, "A Peculiar Synergy: Matriarchy and the Church of God in Christ" (electronic Ph.D. diss., Vanderbilt University, 2001); David Douglas Daniels, "The Cultural Renewal of Slave Religion: Charles Price Jones and the Emergence of the Holiness Movement in Mississippi" (Ph.D. diss., Union Theological Seminary, 1992); and Virginia Broughton, *Twenty Years'*

Experience of a Missionary, reprinted in Sue E. Houchins, *Spiritual Narratives* (New York: Oxford University Press, 1988).

3. A major controversy among black Baptists prior to the inception of the National Baptist Convention surrounded the issue of sanctification and how it was to be interpreted. The debate was not limited to ministers but affected women as well. See E. C. Morris, *Sermons, Addresses and Reminiscences and Important Correspondence with a Gallery of Eminent Ministers and Scholars* (Nashville: National Baptist Publishing Board, 1901), 32–35; and Daniels, "Cultural Renewal of Slave Religion," 189.

4. Donald W. Dayton, *Theological Roots of Pentecostalism* (Metuchen, N.J.: Scarecrow Press, 1987); Susie Stanley, *Holy Boldness: Women Preachers' Autobiographies and the Sanctified Self* (Knoxville: University of Tennessee Press, 2001), 2.

5. Stanley, *Holy Boldness*, 5. Women involved in the Holiness movement included such figures as Phoebe Palmer, Elizabeth Mix, and Joanna P. Moore.

6. When the Pentecostal movement came into being in the early 1900s, much emphasis was given to and ill will produced from differentiating the beliefs between the two groups. For a summary, see Douglas G. Jacobsen, *Thinking in the Spirit: Theologies of the Early Pentecostal Movement* (Bloomington: Indiana University Press, 2003).

7. Joanna P. Moore, *In Christ's Stead* (Chicago: Women's Baptist Home Mission Society, 1902), 227–28. This camp meeting was perhaps part of a Holiness camp meeting, and attendance at subsequent meetings would have introduced her to a network of ministers that would include C. P. Jones and others.

8. Ibid., 230.

9. Albert W. Wardin Jr., *Tennessee Baptists, a Comprehensive History, 1779–1999* (Brentwood: Tennessee Baptist Convention), 396.

10. Moore, *In Christ's Stead*, 230–31. Moore relates her experience of being healed from a tumor.

11. Broughton, *Twenty Year's Experience*, 108–11. Broughton was the first female graduate of Fisk University and joined Joanna P. Moore's Bible Band movement in Memphis, Tenn.

12. "The Voice of Mother Robinson," in *The Whole Truth* (Memphis, Tenn.) (April 1968): 3, col. 2.

13. Joanna P. Moore, *The Power and Work of the Holy Spirit* (Chicago: Revell, 1912), 26–27.

14. Ibid., 26. More often than not, the scripture to support this is 1 Corinthians 6:19–20: "Your body is a temple of the Holy Spirit within you." Moore goes on to say that "our bodies must be kept pure and clean, for they are the holiest thing on earth, in fact, the only holy thing on earth."

15. Reprint of *Christian Hope Magazine*, April 1937. Mother Lizzie Roberson [Robinson], "History of the Bible Band #333," (n.p., n.d., private collection of Anthea Butler).

16. *Hope* (Nashville, Tenn.) 24, no. 3 (November 1908): 351.

17. *Hope* 22, no. 7 (September 1906): 23.

18. For more information on Parham, see James Goff, *Fields White unto Harvest: Charles F. Parham and the Missionary Origins of Pentecostalism* (Fayetteville: University of Arkansas Press, 1988).

19. Ithiel C. Clemmons, *Bishop C. H. Mason and the Church of God in Christ* (Bakersfield, Calif.: Pneuma Life, 1996).

20. "The Voice of Mother Robinson," 3.

21. Ibid.

22. Charles H. Pleas, *Fifty Years Achievement, 1906–1956: A Period in the History of the Church of God in Christ* (Memphis, Tenn.: COGIC Public Relations, 1956; reprint, 1991), 9.

23. "The Voice of Mother Robinson," 3.

24. Ibid.

25. Lucille J. Cornelius, *The Pioneer History of the Church of God in Christ* (Memphis, Tenn.: COGIC, 1975).

26. Mattie McGlothen, ed., *Women's Department Revised Edition of Organization and Procedure* (Memphis, Tenn.: COGIC Publishing House, 1989), 21.

27. For further explication, see Cheryl Townsend Gilkes, "The Roles of Church and Community Mothers: Ambivalent American Sexism or Fragmented African Familyhood?" *Journal of Feminist Studies in Religion* 2 (1986): 41–59. See also Cheryl Gilkes, *If It Wasn't for the Women—: Black Women's Experience and Womanist Culture in Church and Community* (Maryknoll, N.Y.: Orbis Books, 2001); and C. Eric Lincoln and Lawrence H. Mamiya, *The Black Church in the African-American Experience* (Durham, N.C.: Duke University Press, 1990).

28. Robinson, *The Whole Truth*, Women's Page, 1968, 3.

29. Ibid.

30. Oral interview with Lela Mason Byas, June 1995 (n.p., n.d., private collection of Anthea Butler).

31. "The Voice of Mother Robinson," 3.

32. Butler, "A Peculiar Synergy," 67–68.

33. This allusion was lost on the author until realizing that women mostly did not begin to shave their underarms until after World War II. Prior to that, the underarms were suggestive of a woman's "private" areas.

34. I explicate this more fully in my dissertation; see Butler, "A Peculiar Synergy," 98–110.

35. Cheryl Sanders, *Saints in Exile: The Holiness-Pentecostal Experience in African American Religion and Culture* (Cambridge: Harvard University Press, 1996), 3.

36. Although speaking in tongues is important, it does not carry the same weight as "livin holy." See Vinson Synan, *The Holiness-Pentecostal Tradition: Charismatic Movements in the Twentieth Century*, 2nd ed. (Grand Rapids, Mich.: Eerdmans, 1997), 32.

37. William Clark, "Sanctification in Negro Religion," *Social Forces* 15, no. 4 (May 1937): 545.

38. Sallie M. Swan, *A Brief History of the Life and Work of Elder B. S. Lyle* (n.p., 1944), 29.

39. Ibid., 30.

40. Victoria W. Wolcott, *Remaking Respectability: African American Women in Interwar Detroit* (Chapel Hill: University of North Carolina Press, 2001), 34.

41. Ibid., 9. The Urban League also tried to close up the bear trap on Elliot Street.

42. Mother Mary Magrum Johnson, *Life and Labors* (n.p., n.d.), 15–16, Hammond COGIC Collection, Bentley Historical Library, University of Michigan.

43. Rose Marie Duff, *The Ethnohistory of Saint's Home Church of the Church of God in Christ, Los Angeles, California* (Sacramento: California State University Press), 20.

44. Ibid., 25.

45. Duff, *Ethnohistory of Saint's Home Church*, 39.

46. "Mother Cotton Sounds Bugle," *Foursquare Crusader* (Los Angeles) 2, no. 46 (May 13, 1936): col. 1.

47. 25th Silver Anniversary, Women's Department of California Northwest Jurisdiction, COGIC, May 1982, excerpts from the biography of Elder McKinley McCardell, 11, Mattie McGlothen Library Collection.

48. *California Eagle* (Los Angeles), no title, (church page), February 1, 1935, 4.

49. Ibid., February 8, 1935, 3.

50. Bishop C. H. Mason, "The Whole Truth about Double Marriages," *Minutes of the 1926 Convocation* (reprint, COGIC Publishing House, 1990), 149.

51. Hortense Powdermaker, *After Freedom: A Cultural Study in the Deep South* (New York: Viking, 1939), 156–57. Powdermaker notes that legal divorce in the town of Bronzeville was something "more than a luxury, it savors of pretensions and extravagance."

52. Minutes of the 1924 COGIC Convocation (private collection of Sherry Sherrod Dupree, Gainesville, Fla.), 45.

53. *The Whole Truth* (March 1934): 14, col. 3.

54. Lillian Calhoun, "Woman on the Go for God," *Ebony* 18, no. 7 (May 1963): 84.

55. Butler, "A Peculiar Synergy," 81.

7

Women's Popular Literature as Theological Discourse

A Mormon Case Study, 1880–1920

Susanna Morrill

Historians who write about American theology rarely mention women. Despite evidence that women have often outnumbered men in the pews, historians usually assume that men, not women, made theology. Indeed, the field of American religion continues to be shaped by an implicit dichotomy between male theology—the realm of ideas—and female practice—the realm of bodily practice or behavior.

Similarly, historians who write about Latter-day Saints (more popularly known as the Mormons) usually focus on male leaders such as Joseph Smith or Brigham Young, not female converts. Because of the Mormon practice of polygamy, they also tend to describe Mormonism as a patriarchal faith.

In this chapter, Susanna Morrill challenges us to broaden our understanding of both American theology and Mormonism by taking women's voices seriously. Mormon women in the 1800s never would have described themselves as theologians, but, as Morrill shows, they crafted a popular theology that placed women at the center of the Mormon faith. "Women were making significant theology during this time span," Morrill argues, "but not in the ways we traditionally think about theology."

Sometime between 1880 and 1885, Mormon teenager Colenda Chrilla Rogers Adams recorded in her personal journal a poem written in tribute to her sister, Fannie, who had died in 1880 at the young age of twenty-one. The third verse of the poem best sums up Adams's anguish at her sister's fleeting, delicate, and virtuous mortal life:

> Pale and sweet as the fairest liley.
> Pure as the falling snow
> Oh must thy life as fliting [fleeting?] be
> And quickly must though [thou?] go.[1]

About forty years later, in 1917, the *Relief Society Magazine*, the official publication of the women's auxiliary of the Mormon Church, published an article about Edna L. Smith, the well-respected matron in charge of the "sister workers" in the Salt Lake Temple. The article included an account of Smith's dream about temple genealogical work: "She dreamed she was going into the Temple and as she entered the enclosure, she saw every spot of earth filled with the rarest and most beautiful flowers imaginable. There were lilies of all hues and kinds, but all were luxuriant in growth and beautiful in texture."[2] The leaves of the flowers glowed with spiritual transparency, each flower representing the posthumous temple work performed by members of the Genealogical Society of Utah.

On the surface, these excerpts seem to bear only the most obvious resemblances to each other. They can both be classified as Mormon women's literature—the first was found in a private journal, and the second was published in a well-read women's magazine. One was written by a teenager, and the other arose from the sleeping subconscious of an older woman. Both in some way reflect on the reality and meaning of death. Both rely heavily on the symbol of the flower to express emotion and capture the reader's visual imagination.

But I hope that by the end of this chapter, you will look at these passages with different interpretive eyes. The lines have a much deeper connection with each other—connections that link together these obvious resemblances into a system of extensive and logical female literary argument. The selections are examples of how Latter-day Saint (LDS) women writers used popular literature—particularly poetry, and particularly nature and flower imagery within poetry—to argue for the theological importance of women within the patriarchal home, community, institutional church, and LDS salvational structures. Chronologically, the excerpts come from the beginning and the end of an era of intense activity by Mormon women writers and poets. Adopting and adapting the "culture of flowers" genre from more general Victorian literature, during the years from 1880 to 1920, LDS women writers used the common identification between femaleness, flowers, and other aspects of beneficial nature in order to closely connect women with the divine realm. Employing nature and flower imagery and working within dualistic and literal Mormon theology, on the one hand LDS women writers validated the importance of femaleness as a vital, spiritually material substratum of heaven and earth. On the other hand, they demonstrated the crucial and salvational significance of the specific roles of women as mothers and mediators of liminality within the home, church, and community.

Finally, by means of nature and flower imagery, LDS women writers showed that the central mission of women was to follow the example of Jesus Christ—to be earthly, female christs—and humbly and without public notice dedicate their lives to relieving suffering. In the very act of writing, these authors and poets followed their own advice as they offered their readers moments of revelatory freedom, pleasure, and spiritual uplift. By means of nature and flower imagery, LDS women writers used the authority of a literarily gendered nature in order to prove their points in a persuasive and theological manner.

At base, this was a balancing and supplemental popular theology that was not so much a self-conscious spinning of a feminist argument as it was a result of LDS women writers using available and noncontroversial literary resources within a framework of contemporary, maternalist gender norms in order to communicate women's work and thoughts. While women writers sometimes challenged the status of women within the LDS community, for the most part they employed nature and flower imagery to express a world-view that existed within the range of accepted LDS theology.[3] By means of this imagery, LDS women writers elucidated the theological meanings of female-ness and women for a deliberately patriarchal community that had little to say about the religious significance of women's clearly defined roles as mothers and community caretakers.

Recent scholarship on Mormonism has balanced and shifted the historical focus on the Mormon community. Over the past two decades, there has been an enormous amount of exciting scholarly work written on the history of LDS women. Resources are rich, because, beginning with its founder, Joseph Smith, the LDS Church has had a tradition of personal and institutional record-keeping. Both men and women wrote journals and diaries in order to leave for posterity a private record of their spiritual journeys, and men and women also contributed to church periodicals or published monographs of poetry, literature, and didactic work. Using these sources, scholars such as Lawrence Foster, Todd Compton, Richard Van Wagoner, Jessie Embry, and Kathryn Daynes have illuminated the ideals and realities of nineteenth-century Mormon polygamous families.[4] Scholars including Thomas Alexander, Maureen Ursenbach Beecher, Jill Derr, Lavina Anderson, Maxine Hanks, and D. Michael Quinn have written about the individual and communal lives of Mormon women. In particular, they have elucidated how women's lives intersected with the Relief Society, or with the presently very controversial issue of whether or not women hold the priesthood (the lay apostolic power accorded to all Mormon men in good standing within the church).[5]

When women writers communicated their thoughts through the vehicle of nature and flower imagery, they were simply literarily extending their active home, community, and church lives. They were theologically justifying these active lives for themselves and their communities. As scholars have amply demonstrated, women were vital players within the LDS home, community, and institutional life from the very beginning of the church. They mothered their families. Through the women's auxiliary, the Relief Society, they provided highly organized and self-financed welfare and medical help to those less fortunate.[6] They often worked outside of the home in order to support their large families. They participated in the educational and electoral processes of their communities.

In order to explain this seeming contradiction of active female participation in a self-consciously patriarchal community, we should remember that not far beneath the surface of this overtly male-centered institution, LDS theology and scripture held traditions that encouraged women to explore why women and femaleness were essential to the church. LDS theology was distinct from Protestant and Catholic forms of theology because it held that God was profoundly divine and powerful but also definitely anthropomorphic.[7] The goal for humans was to make it through a phased plan of salvation and divinization and, ideally, to become gods themselves. Individual souls were thought to be born into a preexistent state of being as literal children— spirit children—of God. In order to gain knowledge, in order to ultimately become like their divine father and start this same process on other worlds, these spirits had to be born into mortality without memory of their previous existence. If they proved their mettle in mortality and formed successful family units, male spirits would take on the role of their spiritual father, and female spirits would participate in this process through husbands, or, if not married, less effectively through their male blood relatives.[8]

This plan of salvation highlighted and revised female divinity and Christian scriptural characters in profound ways. In this theological understanding, God the Father had to have a female counterpart or counterparts—a Mother or Mothers in Heaven—in order to physically produce spirit children.[9] Female divinity was a logical, salvational necessity. In addition, in the LDS worldview, Eve became a kind of savior figure because she set in motion the necessary fall into humanity that Jesus would end with his second coming.[10] She was the first woman who, paradoxically, set humanity on the first steps toward divinity by offering to it free will and the knowledge of good and evil, right and wrong.

Though turn-of-the-century women writers contemplated the importance of the Mother(s) in Heaven and Eve within their own work, the more official theology of the church said little about these crucial figures. The foundational scripture of the LDS Church, the Book of Mormon, does not mention the Mother in Heaven and, in fact, has a total of only three named extrabiblical female characters, none of them major players in the overarching religious narrative.[11] LDS women employed nature and flower imagery to explore the meaning of femaleness and women, but they were creatively writing from within the LDS theological tradition. They were encouraged by the presence of significant female scriptural and theological elements and also motivated by the lack of explanation of these same elements.

When LDS women writers employed the theology of nature and flower imagery, they were following a common, nonconfrontational approach to negotiating their position within the church. At the turn of the century, prominent churchwoman Ruth May Fox recorded in her journal an interesting exchange that took place at a meeting of the officers of the Young Ladies Mutual Improvement Association (the church auxiliary for teenagers and young women). At the meeting, the president of the Relief Society, Zina D. H. Young, was asked if women held the priesthood in connection with their husbands. According to Fox, Young replied "that we should be thankful for the many blessings we enjoyed and say nothing about it[.] If you plant a grain of wheat and keep poking and looking at it to see if it was growing you would spoil the root. The answer was very satisfying to me."[12] As the highest-placed woman within the church, Young did not deny that married women held the priesthood, as one might have expected, judging by the modern-day contentious debate on the issue. Rather, by means of nature imagery, she scolded the questioner for potentially subverting this slowly growing reality by drawing attention to it.[13] She felt that women of the church were quietly laying groundwork for a fuller participation of women in the restored apostolic power—whether that was to be at a later date or outside of earthly time is not entirely clear. As LDS women writers used nature and flower imagery, they followed this philosophy. With this popular theology, women were quietly, persuasively, and usually nonconfrontationally advocating for their importance within the church, home, and the plan of salvation.

Why Nature and Flower Imagery?

Victorians loved idealized visions of nature. Jack Goody has pointed out that "culture of flowers" poetry was common within the literary offerings of the Victorian period.[14] And, indeed, as a representative of the genre, the first poem by Adams could have come from the pen of just about any contemporary literary American woman with a religious bent of mind.

However, nature and flower imagery was particularly meaningful and attractive to Mormon women writers for a number of reasons. First, because of church members' intense encounter with nature when they crossed the plains and then settled in the harsh environmental conditions of Utah, nature came to have resonant theological meanings within the community. Second, within the LDS community, poetry, women, revelation, and nature were closely connected, so that women were seen as appropriate purveyors of this imagery during a time when the church was still open to revelation but was seeking order and standardization from sometimes surprising directions.

Joseph Smith was murdered in an Illinois jail in 1844. Brigham Young eventually took over the reins of leadership and, in 1847, led the first group of faithful Mormons into the Great Salt Lake Valley. Over the next two decades and until the transcontinental railroad was completed in 1869, converts streamed across the rugged plains and over the mountains in covered wagons, pulling handcarts, or carrying their possessions on their backs. This extended journey across the plains has taken on epic, mythic qualities within the history and culture of modern Mormonism.[15]

Even in literature of the nineteenth century, writers chronicled the journey as a thrilling and terrible encounter with nature and God. They presented the awesome beauties of nature as embodying the glory of God. Hannah Cornaby made the trip across the plains in the 1850s and, in 1881, published a combined autobiography and book of poems in which she reflected on the experience of her westward journey. She emphasized the great beauties of nature and noted how these beauties brought closer to her the reality of God's love and care.[16] Nature provided both the spiritual support of lovely flowers and the bodily sustenance of wild fruits. This natural encounter probably lasted about three months, but Cornaby felt that it had taught her as much as any part of her life.[17] As experienced on her journey to Utah, nature was a revelation, a scripture, and a sermon, because, for her, nature was God's loving, guiding arm extended during treacherous times to protect and nurture the chosen people.

However, many who made the crossing were not prepared for the exhausting obstacles ahead, and the journey and settlement—difficult under even the best circumstances—also took on painful and terrifying dimensions.[18] Weather and environmental conditions proved overwhelming to farmers and artisans used to the agriculturally more congenial climates of the eastern and southern United States and northern Europe. The most well-known and oft-repeated story about the settlement is how grasshoppers infested and devoured the meager crops that the pioneers were able to coax from the land during their first years in the Great Salt Lake Valley. Though she did not mention the grasshoppers, Elizabeth Horrocks Baxter, born in Utah in 1856, did recount the trying conditions of life in Utah in the 1850s–1860s. According to Baxter, food was often so scarce that she and her father would gather dandelion greens, nettles, and sego lilies (an onionlike root), and her father would butcher starved cattle and preserve them with salt from the Great Salt Lake.[19] Here the nourishing fruits of Hannah Cornaby's journey seem a distant dream as the natural elements provided the most meager and unpleasant harvests: nettles, dying cattle, and salt, only, in abundance.

On the surface, these LDS women writers were simply participating in a nature religion that Catherine Albanese argues has long been a noninstitutionalized part of American culture, predating even European settlement of the land.[20] Yet by the 1880s nature had become an integral strand of the LDS historical and theological narrative. It was an environmental and religious text for the community because of the specific natural history of that community.

LDS women writers most often employed nature and flower imagery within the authoritative and prophetic female discourse of poetry. Within the LDS community, poetry, nature, women, and revelation were closely connected. When women wrote, they tended to write poetry; when they wrote poetry, they tended to employ nature and flower imagery; and when they used nature and flower imagery and poetry they demonstrated that they were receiving revelatory glimpses of the divine realm. The particular LDS connection between poetry, nature, women, and revelation helped to transform this common, popular literature into Mormon theological narrative.[21]

Poetry, women, and revelation were concretely drawn together in the person of Eliza R. Snow, the first and arguably the most important Relief Society president after the church reached Utah in 1847. Within the church, Snow carried the triple title of poetess, prophetess, and priestess, showing the close connections between poetry, prophecy, and even her more formal institutional role of overseer of women's temple work.[22] Snow is well known for writing the poem, "O, My Father," while a plural wife of Joseph Smith or shortly after his death in 1844.[23] This four-verse poem is the best-known exposition of the Mormon theological belief in a Mother in Heaven, and, in the nineteenth century and into the early twentieth century, it was considered to be a revelation.[24] Set to music, the poem became an extremely popular hymn that was sung in church meetings, from local Relief Society gatherings to General Conference assemblies of the entire church body.[25]

Women poets attempted to follow the example of Snow and present spiritually authentic, female-centered messages within their poetic creations. The period that we are concentrating on, 1880 to 1920, was a time of female poetic renaissance within the LDS community. In 1877, Emmeline B. Wells took over the reins of the fledgling *Woman's Exponent*, the semiofficial publication of the Relief Society. From that time until the magazine's demise in 1914, she encouraged other women to contribute their work to the *Exponent*—and always made sure that poetry was well represented in each issue. Women such as Augusta Joyce Crocheron, Hannah Cornaby, Mary Jane Tanner, Sarah Carmichael, Reba Beebe Pratt, Emmeline B. Wells, and Hannah T. King wrote poems for the *Exponent* but also published their own books of poetry during this time span.[26] A daughter of Brigham Young, Susa Young Gates, edited the *Young Woman's Journal*, a periodical first published in 1889 and attached to the church's Young Ladies Mutual Improvement Association. Through this publication, and in her own writings from the time, she advocated that the younger women of the church also have a forum for their literary works.

Unlike Snow, who was seen as participating in Joseph Smith's prophetic authority,[27] these lesser-known Mormon women poets and editors often presented their poems as undergirded by the revelatory authority of nature. Sometimes they configured poetry itself as one of the elements of nature, usually the flower. Equating the process of writing with a kind of literary childbirth, an unnamed poet described her unsuccessful verses as both miscarriage and as a flower dying in an inhospitable environment.[28] Women poets were usually much more explicit about the connections between poetry, revelation, and nature and, in verse, repeatedly expressed their revelatory encounters with the natural surroundings. In one of her poems, Emmeline B. Wells described how voices from the nocturnal mountains disclosed God's truths to her.[29] Nature spoke to Wells of divine reality, and Wells was compelled to communicate these revelations through the most authentic language of nature, female-identified poetry.

Wells and other women writers employed nature and flower imagery at a fortuitous time in their community's history. Focusing on the years from 1890 to 1930, Thomas Alexander has written extensively about how church leaders were seeking theological and institutional standardization as the church entered the twentieth century.[30] Although the term "standardization" implies a period of increasing reification and inflexibility, as Alexander has pointed out, in some ways this was a very creative era when church leaders sought organization and solutions in innovative places. In other words, when women writers employed nature and flower imagery to theological effect during this period, they were following not only the Mormon tradition, but they were part of the larger processes of the Mormon Church. They were seeking answers and structures in an innovative place—popular literature authenticated by experiential encounters with the natural environment—and during an experimental phase of church development. They seized the revelatory and standardizing leeway afforded them as they theologically worked out their places within the home, church, community, and plan of salvation.

Mothers, Heaven, and Home:
The Theology of Nature and Flower Imagery

When LDS women writers used nature and flower imagery, they were not constructing a self-conscious, logical, and thorough theological argument. Women writers built layers of accreted Mormon meaning over an already-existing popular symbolic structure. With each poetic and literary overlay, each author added complexity and LDS theological depth to the popular symbolism. Yet, despite the haphazard and various origins of this popular, supplemental theology, it has remarkable internal logic and consistency.

At the base of this nature theology and all of its incremental arguments lay the identification between beneficial, benevolent nature and femaleness. Sherry Ortner has pointed out that, especially in the modern West, nature was and is often identified as female and degraded.[31] However, in the "culture of flowers" genre—in both mainstream and LDS literature—this gendering of nature was a bit more complicated. Women writers followed closely the Victorian understanding that the female gender was morally superior to the more volatile and uncontrollable male gender. Writers assumed this gendered and value-laden dichotomy within their literary interpretations of nature. For the most part, benevolent and beneficial aspects of nature were seen to be female, while destructive or ambiguous elements of nature were configured as male.

Nature became anthropomorphized Mother Nature, a nourishing orderer of the natural world, as well as an earthly handmaiden and prophet of God. LDS poet and bishop, Orson F. Whitney, speaking to an audience of young women and girls, spoke of nature, femaleness, and the revelatory purpose of nature: "You can learn from nature in all her beautiful forms; they are Revelations from God. . . . Woman as well as man is a symbol of God; she is typical of the earth itself. Earth brings forth as a mortal mother."[32] In this view, female nature, Mother Nature, was the most authentic and effective link between humans and the divine realm. Nature stood as God's mothering, female presence in the mortal world—an earthly, female sacred connected to the heavenly male, father divinity.

Found also in mainstream Protestant literature, this gendering of nature by women writers took on meaningful theological depth in the LDS community. Because Mormonism posited separate and anthropomorphic male and female gods, the very substance of humanity became dualistically separated into essential gender categories.[33] Men were the male godhead in embryo and were, therefore, essentially male, while women were essentially female in their deepest being. In the LDS context, then, a female nature was not simply a literary trope that expressed social expectations about gender; it was also proof of the dualistic and divinely based gendering of humanity and the world.

In Mormon women's literature, writers repeatedly emphasized this dualism. From female nature radiated numerous other female-identified, benevolent aspects of nature that were set against destructive, male-identified aspects of nature.[34] LDS women writers were especially enamored with the female-identified flower. They viewed it as a concentrated form of God's glory and grace—a direct and special messenger from the divine realm sent down to earth to remind all of the higher reality. "Emile," a frequent contributor to the *Woman's Exponent*, wrote about flowers:

> They lead the human soul to look above,
> And make us feel that surely God is near,
> To guide our feet throughout our length of days,
> Yea, if we trust Him, into pleasant ways.[35]

Like nature, spring, and spring months, flowers were female and they were signs of God. They were God's silent but powerful prophets, microcosms of Mother Nature, and friends to struggling mortals.

LDS women writers of this period identified the flower with women on both physical and spiritual levels.[36] But they were most interested in the spiritual qualities that women and flowers shared. In order to connect the spiritually pure substance of femaleness common to both flowers and women, LDS women writers often employed abstract female-identified virtues like charity, mercy, faith, and truth. Augusta Joyce Crocheron made just such a link when she described a bouquet of abstract flowers that she was poetically giving to a friend. Though she included Love and Forgiveness, she offered, first and foremost, Hope as a blooming, illuminating presence that banished all youthful doubts.[37]

Within LDS women's literature, a kind of symbolic triangulation developed between these three literary elements. Femaleness could not be understood apart from benevolent nature, just as benevolent nature could not be understood apart from femaleness. And neither could be fully comprehended without the female-identified, abstract virtues. Each side of the symbolic triangle played off the others and reinforced the others, even if one or both of these sides were not explicitly present in the poem or literary work. The first excerpt of the essay in which Adams compares her sister to a sweet and pure lily is an effective example of this process. Here, Fannie is the anthropomorphic representation of the lily and those characteristics that the lily embodies: sweetness and purity. Each of these triadic elements is, in essence, the same, yet more fully explicated in relationship to the others.

By means of this three-way connection, LDS women writers argued for the centrality and essential goodness of the abstract, divine substance of femaleness. Bequeathed to them by an unseen and largely unknown Mother in Heaven, LDS women writers explicated femaleness by the concrete examples of nature, women, and virtuous action. As represented by nature, femaleness was the sacred that could be grasped and experienced directly—right outside one's kitchen door.

But women writers went beyond simply connecting femaleness with divinity; they also employed nature and flower imagery in order to argue for the theological significance of women's specific roles within the community —the roles of mother and community caretaker or mediator of liminality. In the Mormon understanding, mothers were essential within the plan of salvation because they provided the mortal bodies and early guidance for untested, preexistent spirits.[38] In the *Young Woman's Journal*, Lizzie Smith advocated for the importance of women as mothers: "We must remember that woman is the mold by which the species is perfected or depraved according as the mold is good or bad. The fate of humanity depends, therefore, on woman, since she has all-powerful influence on the fruit she bears."[39] Mothers were the literal portals of the divine realm into the human. And, with their early teachings, mothers could send children toward the highest exaltation in the afterlife, or they could doom them to eternal spiritual disaster.

Mormon women were also expected to direct their mothering behavior outward toward the community. As members of the Relief Society, and under the local church representative, the bishop, women looked after the less fortunate of their localities. In particular, Relief Society workers were expected to be present at times of birth, sickness, and death. They helped to bring each spirit child into the world and also witnessed the mature spirit return back to its final, sacred abode: women assisted members of their community to negotiate the tricky entrances and exits to mortality.[40] Extending their roles as mothers, women were to stand at the portals of mortality as the mediators of these times of extreme liminality for their extended church family.

LDS women writers demonstrated the crucial nature of familial and community motherhood by using nature and flower imagery—specifically garden imagery—to connect motherhood, the home, Zion, preexistence, and heaven. Mormon women writers argued that the home was the premier realm of women and that it was here that women formed children's characters for better or for worse. In this literature, the home was often described as a garden for the raising of heaven-sent children.[41] This imagery of the home fits well with actual physical descriptions of the home. In these physical descriptions, LDS women writers presented the home as an idyllic dwelling surrounded by gardens and flowers. These gardens signaled to the reader that the homes were truly spiritual and nourishing places for the inhabitants. A poet portrayed one such home in this way:

> With blooming flowers and ample lawn;
> In background rose an orchard old,
> And 'round the cottage porch festooned
> Sweet honeysuckles; roses wreathed
> Around the windows wide, and told
> Home's praises by ev'ry perfume breathed.[42]

For LDS women writers of this period, the ideal home was incomplete without a garden filled with flowers and other emblems of female-identified benevolent natural elements to provide a nourishing, spiritual backdrop for the development of embodied spirit children.

LDS women writers showed that these garden-surrounded, mother-centered homes were the building blocks of Utah, considered to be the earthly Zion, the land of the chosen people. Usually Mormon women writers glorified their Zion by describing the great change that came over the land when the pioneers entered the valley. Initially filled with barren, male-identified, forbidding elements, the LDS community changed the very landscape with their virtuous lives and homes.[43] The land became an earthly, female-identified Eden. In an oft-repeated phrase, the pioneers made the desert bloom as a rose:

> They found a desert—made a garden fair,
> Where luscious fruits bend low on the clustering trees,
> And flowers of every tint perfume the air,
> Where towns and cities broad equal blessings share.[44]

This "fair garden" of Zion was made up of individual, mother-tended gardens. Mother-centered homes were the microcosms of the larger, God-ordained community. Physically and spiritually, these homes were the backbone of the community.

LDS women further validated the importance of motherhood by linking these earthly, garden-surrounded, female-centered homes with the highest divine realms of preexistence and heaven. Emmeline B. Wells repeatedly argued in her work that beneficial nature and the garden-surrounded homes awakened distant, deeply hidden memories of one's spiritual childhood in the gardens of the Father and Mother Gods. In a poem praising the beauties of summer, Wells described the fields of flowers, scented breezes, and bird songs of summer. She ended the poem wondering why this scene evoked a longing for the lost and forgotten part of herself, the preexistent life in the sacred realm. The answer:

'Tis a heritage, surely, "Our Father" has given,
Which links us unseen to a happier sphere;
A faint recollection of what was in heaven,
That clings to us ever while lingering here.[45]

In this literature, the preexistent memory evoked by beautiful nature was directly parallel to the memories of earthly home that were awakened by earthly gardens—or floral tokens from earthly gardens. When women writers remembered their happy homes of childhood, they remembered the gardens most of all. Ruth May Fox described how faded sprigs of violet and myrtle brought the woman protagonist of her poem back to the flower-filled fields of her childhood home and her carefree wanderings with her future husband.[46] Beneficial, female-identified nature served as a trigger for the memory of women's first spiritual homes and their second earthly homes. Using nature and flower imagery, women writers demonstrated that the mother-centered earthly home paralleled in physical reality and spiritual heft the importance of the preexistent home. In the overall plan of salvation and as shown by their similar flower-filled environments, both were places of birth and beginning—both were crucial places of nourishment and development for each individual soul.

Heaven was the final and eternal stopping place; it was physically the same place as the preexistence, but this time experienced by the matured spirit. For women writers, benevolent nature was both the link between and the separator of the earthly home and heaven. LDS women writers presented heaven as a garden, but a garden of flowers that would never wilt and die, as did their earthly equivalents.[47] In the literature and as befitted their liminal, spiritual makeup, women repeatedly crossed between heaven and earth in what today would be termed near-death experiences. In one such story, a girl about to die from scrofula had a dream in which a recently deceased cousin showed her the place she would go upon her death. In her dream, she longed to stop and pick the flowers and enjoy the water and gardenlike environment of this beautiful land.[48] Heaven was beyond the reach of mortality, but mother-centered homes—as indicated by their heavenly, gardened surroundings—were the closest earthly representation of the highest sphere. Edna Smith's dream exemplifies this conflation of mother, home, and heaven by means of garden imagery. The heavenly, temple environment glows with the literal spiritual flowers of women's community mothering, in this case, genealogical work. In Smith's subconscious, women's earthly work and home were simply extensions of the ideal, heavenly home that was women's primordial home and the environment that shaped their essential femaleness.

By means of garden and home imagery, LDS women writers demonstrated that the roles of mother and mediator of liminality were divinely connected and crucial parts of the plan of salvation. As creators of home and humanity, women stood at the center of the eternal progression that drove forward the plan of salvation.

In their literature, writers themselves modeled the work that women were expected to do in order to maintain this central place in the home and community. When LDS women writers used nature and flower imagery to describe the importance of femaleness and women within the plan of salvation, they were actively engaging in and enriching the communal, religious life of Mormon women.

Women writers argued that a key part of testing or probation on earth was intense and purifying suffering.[49] By living through this suffering and by freely making the right choices during one's mortality, a faithful Mormon could advance to a higher existence in the afterlife. LDS women writers often emphasized that the most sorely tested would be the most highly exalted. An unnamed poet described two married sets of spouses, one a poor and weary polygamous quartet and one a happy monogamous couple.[50] Only the poor, polygamous group made it into heaven because they had toiled and kept faith through very difficult times.

Though suffering was a necessary, purifying obstacle for both men and women, LDS women writers saw that suffering was the peculiar lot of women as familial and social mothers within the church. Specifically, women were to follow the example of Jesus Christ and take on a surfeit of suffering in order to relieve the troubles of those around them. This assumption appears throughout LDS women's literature of the period. Perhaps the clearest statement of it was made by Edward Tullidge, who gathered the writing of the leading Mormon women of the day and produced *The Women of Mormondom* as an extended explanation of and apologetic for the practice of polygamy. Closely connecting women and Jesus Christ, Tullidge wrote: "From woman, the love of Jesus for humanity. From her his sympathies for the race. 'Twas she, in her son, who forgave sin; she who bade the sinner go and sin no more; she who wept over Jerusalem as a mother weepeth over her young[.] And it was woman, in her son, who died upon the cross for the sins of the world."[51]

Women writers further argued that women should perform these acts of self-sacrifice humbly and in secret. They were to be like the modest violet hidden under the forest's leaves: unseen, but quietly shedding fragrance for all to enjoy.[52] Women were to follow the example of Jesus Christ, but they were to take on suffering quietly, penitently, and invisibly.

Although we can see the most obvious expression of these assumptions in the Relief Society work that women performed, LDS women writers turned their literary talents to the same task. Women writers were not simply producing popular nature and flower poetry to fit the tastes of the time, or to argue for the importance of women and femaleness. They were motivated by a deep belief that their gifts were God-given and that their work, unheralded and unacknowledged by necessity, should have a salutary effect on the religious lives of their readers. When writers invoked the spirit of poesy—a common theme in this poetry—they were asking for God's inspiration and guidance so that their words would become literary extensions of women's work in the community.[53] In praising the books of Hannah T. King and Hannah Cornaby, another poet appropriately used nature and flower imagery to describe how these poetic works—works that themselves liberally employed nature and flower imagery—inspired her to follow Jesus' example in her poetic creations. She felt her words bloomed and "shed sweet fragrance 'round" to all. For her, both the writing and the reading of these words were religious acts: "One enjoys the planting—others the bloom, / 'Tis joy to both—a blessing to each."[54] LDS women writers expected that their words would have practical, beneficial effect for their sisters in faith. As they wrote, they lived their religion and their theology.

For these writers, the revelatory power of nature and flowers served as the catalyst for creating in readers a similar revelatory moment of release from suffering. Writers were attempting to tap into their readers' primeval memory and experience of preexistence, and then extend it forward as a promise of the eternal natural beauties that were to come in the next life. When LDS women writers described the scent or the appearance of a flower, or the beauty of a sunset, or the sounds of a mountain stream, they were trying to evoke in their readers a vision and experience of the highest reality. Ideally, for a moment, these poems lifted readers out of the thorns and stones of suffering and allowed them to catch glimpses of the eternal realm. Like the dying and returning poetic flowers with which they were identified, readers were to experience a moment of internal resurrection that experientially assured them of a future and final resurrection. Ideally, reading nature and flower poetry was to have been a kind of literary, ritual act of release for women from everyday cares and worries. With this moment of release, women readers could return refreshed to their religious mission in a world of suffering and sorrow.

For a time, judging by the ubiquity and popularity of nature and flower poetry, LDS women writers succeeded, in some measure, at this poetic mission of spiritual fortification. The period from 1880 to 1920 stands as the high-water mark for this popular, theological expression. While nature and flower imagery continues to have theological and symbolic meaning in the LDS community, by 1920 its energy and authority as a female, theological mode of expression was largely spent. In some ways, nature and flower theology declined as an inevitable result of changing tastes. It was the tool of the first and second generations of LDS women who were raised in Victorian literary culture and then lived in a young church that was fueled by revelatory power. The generation that came of age in the early twentieth century was much more interested in scientific, practical approaches to organization and communication.

Added to the generational gap, and as Thomas G. Alexander has shown, by the 1930s, church leaders increasingly abandoned more experimental projects of institutional standardization and embarked on a thoroughgoing centralization of the church.[55] The Relief Society eventually lost its status as something like a female parallel to the priesthood, as it became very clearly a church auxiliary and more fully under the control of the central, male church leadership. If nature and flower theology was one expression of women's active, independent church, home, and community lives, its decline was evidence that Mormon women lost some institutional status and authority as the twentieth century progressed.[56] The seeds of women's priesthood, so carefully tended by Zina Young and her contemporaries, bore, perhaps, somewhat different fruit than intended.

LDS women writers used nature and flower imagery to balance and occasionally forthrightly challenge the male focus of their theology. Scholars of American religion can look to the nature and flower theology for a different kind of balance and challenge—a popular, meaningful, literary remedy for the relative invisibility of women within formal, scholarly theological developments in nineteenth-century America. Women were making significant theology during this time, but not in the ways we traditionally think about theology. Literary historians Jane Tompkins and Ann Douglas have already demonstrated, in rather different ways, the crucial role that popular literature played for American women in discussions about gender during the nineteenth century.[57] In the case of Mormon women, popular literature was a vital and accessible theological narrative and, therefore, now provides an elucidating window into this particular religious community. We see a very different, female-focused side of Mormon religious history—and add some balance to institutional, theological American religious histories that tend to pass over less-institutionalized, female theological contributions. The Mormon community was not simply a patriarchal institution situated within a patriarchal society and theology that looked to male prophets for spiritual and religious guidance. This is a narrow view and, if strictly adhered to, it is a misleading historical vision. This was also a community with an active women's culture and a rich, female-centered theology that supported this culture.

This chapter demonstrates the complexity and contradictions that inevitably exist within religious communities, especially around issues of women and gender. This popular theology stands as an example of how the important places of meaning-making within religions are often found outside of the institutional structures of religious communities. Members of cultures and religions are endlessly creative in finding ways to close the gap between the ideals and the reality of their religious beliefs and their lives. As did these LDS women writers, members of religious communities live, sometimes comfortably, sometimes not so comfortably, within tensions and sometimes outright contradictions. They often accept and reject beliefs and practices according to their own purposes and interests. In this case, a "safe," popular literary tool became a catalyst for extensive and often subtextual theological discussion and expression. This expression lends complexity to our understanding of the LDS community—but also to the history of women within institutionally based religious communities in general. By seriously considering this popular theology, we make American religious history more complicated and, therefore, richer and more reflective of women's and men's religious lives.

Notes

1. Colenda Chrilla Rogers Adams, journal, first page, Archives and Manuscripts Division of the Historical Department, Church of Jesus Christ of Latter-day Saints.
2. "A Friend of the Helpless Dead," *Relief Society Magazine* 4, no. 9 (September 1917): 485.
3. For a discussion that critiques the position of women more generally within American society, see Phebe C. Young, "Reasons Why," *Woman's Exponent* (hereafter *WE*) 18, no. 12 (November 15, 1889): 93–94.
4. Lawrence Foster, *Religion and Sexuality: The Shakers, the Mormons, and the Oneida Community* (Urbana: University of Illinois Press, 1984); Todd Compton, *In Sacred Loneliness: The Plural Wives of Joseph Smith* (Salt Lake City: Signature Books, 1997); Richard S. Van Wagoner, *Mormon Polygamy: A History* (Salt Lake

City: Signature Books, 1986); Jessie L. Embry, *Mormon Polygamous Families: Life in the Principle* (Salt Lake City: University of Utah Press, 1987); Kathryn M. Daynes, *More Wives Than One: Transformation of the Mormon Marriage System, 1840–1910* (Urbana: University of Illinois Press, 2001).

5. Thomas G. Alexander, *Mormonism in Transition: A History of the Latter-day Saints, 1890–1930* (Urbana: University of Illinois Press, 1986); Eliza Roxcy Snow, *The Personal Writings of Eliza Roxcy Snow*, ed. Maureen Ursenbach Beecher (Salt Lake City: University of Utah Press, 1995); Jill Mulvay Derr, Janath Russell Cannon, and Maureen Ursenbach Beecher, *Women of Covenant: The Story of Relief Society* (Salt Lake City: Deseret Book Company, 1992); Maureen Ursenbach Beecher and Lavina Fielding Anderson, eds., *Sisters in Spirit: Mormon Women in Historical and Cultural Perspective* (Urbana: University of Illinois Press, 1992); Maxine Hanks, ed., *Women and Authority: Re-emerging Mormon Feminism* (Salt Lake City: Signature Books, 1992); D. Michael Quinn, "Women Have Had the Priesthood since 1843," in ibid.

6. For details of this work and the participation of women in the Mormon community more generally, see Derr, Cannon, and Beecher, *Women of Covenant*.

7. Joseph Smith most famously explicated this view of the Mormon God, as well as the Mormon understanding of progressive salvation, in the King Follett discourse, a funeral sermon delivered in Nauvoo, Illinois. Stan Larson, "The King Follett Discourse: A Newly Amalgamated Text," *BYU Studies* 18, no. 2 (Winter 1978): 193–208.

8. For a description of the ultimate role of women in the plan of salvation, see the Patriarchal Blessing of Jane Kartchner Morris. Jane Kartchner Morris, journals and reminiscences, October 1916–February 1971, vol. 3, 8–12, Archives and Manuscripts Division of the Historical Department, Church of Jesus Christ of Latter-day Saints.

9. For scholarly discussions about the Mother(s) in Heaven, see Linda Wilcox, "The Mormon Concept of a Mother in Heaven," *Sunstone* 22, nos. 3–4 (June 1999): 78–87; and John Heeren, Donald B. Lindsey, and Marylee Mason, "The Mormon Concept of Mother in Heaven: A Sociological Account of Its Origin and Development," *Journal for the Sociological Study of Religion* 23, no. 4 (December 1984): 396–411.

10. For nineteenth-century discussions about the reinterpreted Eve, see "Answer to Woman and Sin: In the Cincinnati Enquirer," *WE* 19, no. 12 (March 1, 1884): 145; Julia A. MacDonald, "One Phase of the Divine Mission of Woman," *WE* 20, no. 13 (January 1, 1892): 97; and S. W. Richards, "Woman's Exponent," *WE* 22, no. 11 (January 15, 1894): 81–82.

11. Abesh/Abish (Alma 19), Isabel (Alma 39), and Sariah (1 Nephi) are the three named Book of Mormon women characters.

12. Ruth May Fox, diaries, March 7, 1896, Archives and Manuscripts Division of the Historical Department, Church of Jesus Christ of Latter-day Saints.

13. On many occasions, Young and other Relief Society leaders very publicly and

forcefully instructed the women of the church to obey the male priesthood. See "Ladies Semi-Monthly Meeting," *WE* 26, no. 24 (May 15–26, 1898): 286; and "R.S., Y.L.M.I.A., and Primary Reports," *WE* 9, no. 9 (October 1, 1880): 71.

14. Jack Goody, "The Secret Language of Flowers," *Yale Journal of Criticism* 3, no. 2 (1990): 139.

15. For a full discussion of the modern interpretation of this extended event, see Eric Eliason, *Celebrating Zion: Pioneers in Mormon Popular Historical Expression* (Joseph Fielding Smith Institute for Latter-day Saint History and Brigham Young University Studies, 2004).

16. She wrote: "Admiring nature, we had abundant opportunities of beholding its varied beauties. . . . The delicious wild fruits met with at different stages of the journey were much relished, and afforded a wholesome variety to our diets." Hannah Cornaby, *Autobiography and Poems* (Salt Lake City: J. C. Graham, 1881), 33.

17. Ibid.

18. For a description of some of the requirements and difficulties attached to the journey across the plains, see *Brigham Young's Homes*, ed. Colleen Whitley (Logan: Utah State University Press, 2002), 70–73.

19. Elizabeth Horrocks Baxter, Pioneer Personal History, 3, Federal Writers' Project, Utah State Historical Society.

20. Catherine Albanese, *Nature Religion in America: From the Algonkian Indians to the New Age* (Chicago: University of Chicago Press, 1990).

21. For a general discussion of the role of women as revelators within the LDS community, see Ian G. Barber, "Mormon Women as 'Natural' Seers: An Enduring Legacy," in Hanks, *Women and Authority*, 167–84. For an explicit identification of poetry as female and as a form of revelation, see Orson F. Whitney, "Poetry and Poets," *WE* 15, no. 11 (November 1, 1886): 81–86.

22. For the use of these titles, see L. G. R., "A Delightful Meeting," *WE* 16, no. 9 (October 1, 1887): 68.

23. George D. Pyper, *Stories of Latter-day Saint Hymns: Their Authors and Composers* (n.p.: George D. Pyper, 1939), 4.

24. Ibid., 1. The third verse of the poem reveals the existence of a Mother in Heaven. Writing of the preexistent state, Snow explained:

> I had learned to call Thee Father,
> Through Thy spirit from on high;
> But until the Key of Knowledge
> Was restored, I knew not why.
> In the heavens are parents single?
> No; the thought makes reason stare!
> Truth is reason, Truth eternal
> Tells me I've a Mother there.

25. Polygamous wife and Salt Lake City resident Florence Dean loved this hymn and recorded several times when it was put into a new arrangement or provided

particular comfort and solace. See Florence Ridges Dean, journal, August 1893–
June 1896, 13, 29, Archives and Manuscripts Division of the Historical Department, Church of Jesus Christ of Latter-day Saints.

26. Augusta Joyce Crocheron, *Wild Flowers of Deseret* (Salt Lake City: Printed at the
Office of the Juvenile Instructor, 1881); Cornaby, *Autobiography*; Mary J. Tanner,
A Book of Fugitive Poems (Salt Lake City: J. C. Graham, 1880); Sarah E. Car-
michael, *Poems* (San Francisco: Towne and Bacon, 1866); Reba Beebe Pratt, *The
Sheaf of a Gleaner* (Salt Lake City: Jos. Hyrum Parry, 1886); Emmeline B. Wells,
Musings and Memories (Salt Lake City: Deseret News, 1915); Hannah T. King, *The
Women of the Scriptures* (Salt Lake City: Dernford House, 1878).

27. Pyper, *Stories*, 2, 4.

28. "Embryo," *WE* 28, nos. 22 and 23 (April 15 and May 1, 1900): 123.

29. Wells, "The Voices of the Mountains," *Musings*, 98–99.

30. Alexander, *Mormonism in Transition.*

31. Sherry B. Ortner, "So, Is Female to Male as Nature Is to Culture?" in *Making
Gender: The Politics and Erotics of Culture* (Boston: Beacon Press, 1996), 173–80.

32. Ray Evans, "R.S., Y.L.M.I.A. and P.A. Reports: Box Elder," *WE* 18, no. 4 (July 15,
1889): 31–32. See also Emily Pfieffer, "Wearied," *WE* 19, no. 2 (June 15, 1890): 11.

33. For a fuller discussion of this essentializing gendering, see O. Kendall White,
"Ideology of the Family in Nineteenth Century Mormonism," *Sociological Spectrum* 6 (June 1986): 289–305.

34. LDS women writers presented spring, summer, and autumn as female and op-
posed these seasons to male winter. Writers especially focused on the season of
spring as showing God's promise of eternal life. See Wells, "Welcome to Spring,"
Musings, 54. For examples of female-identified spring months, see E. B. Wells,
"Coquettish April," *WE* 18, no. 22 (April 15, 1890): 173; Martha A. Gaulton, "May:
Addressed to Bishop O. F. Whitney," *WE* 12, no. 1 (June 1, 1883): 3; and Emily H.
Woodmansee, "Joyful June," *WE* 12, no. 2 (June 15, 1883): 9.

35. Emile, "A Summer Reverie," *WE* 11, no. 10 (October 15, 1882): 23.

36. Writers often compared the physical appearances of young women to the flower.
See Ruby Lamont, "Wedding Bells," *WE* 24, no. 5 (August 1, 1895): 33; Ruth May
Fox, "A June Rose," *WE* 36, no. 1 (June 1907): 1; and L. M. H., "Lost Rosabell," *WE*
28, no. 3 (July 1, 1899): 17.

37. Crocheron, "To Annie Llewellyn," *Wild Flowers of Deseret*, 123–24. See also L. M.
H., "Violets," *WE* 20, no. 17 (March 1, 1892): 123; and "The Children's Jubilee," *WE*
25, no. 18 (March 15, 1897): 116.

38. Augusta Joyce Crocheron described in wonder the process whereby a young
spirit—her son, Royal—chose her as his vehicle and guide to mortality. Crocheron,
"To Royal," *Wild Flowers of Deseret*, 124–25. For other descriptions of the preexistence or preexistent spirit children, see Romania B. Pratt, "Hygiene," *Young
Woman's Journal* (hereafter *YWJ*) 1, no. 1 (October 1889): 29–31; C. L. Walker,
"Lines . . . ," *WE* 16, no. 18 (February 15, 1888): 143; and E. T., "Number Nine," *WE*
18, no. 16 (January 15, 1890): 121.

39. Lizzie Smith, "The Equality of the Sexes," *YWJ* 1, no. 6 (March 1890): 176.

40. A Relief Society president argued that these communal functions of women made them equal to their husbands in the priesthood: "Woman is entitled to be equal with man, every key of the priesthood that man has, woman can enjoy with her husband, women are our first and last friends, we could not do without them, we go side by side." C. Daniels, "Utah Stake," *WE* 18, no. 17 (February 1, 1890): 136. See also Lu Dalton, "Woman," *WE* 21, no. 14 (January 15, 1893): 107.

41. See Annie, "Make Home Beautiful," *WE* 10, no. 9 (October 1, 1881): 65; "Make Your Home Beautiful," *WE* 18, no. 21 (April 1, 1890): 165.

42. "Helen and Virginia," *WE* 13, no. 5 (August 1, 1884): 35.

43. For descriptions of barren, pre-Mormon Utah, see "Pioneer Day: In the Large Tabernacle," *WE* 15, no. 5 (August 1, 1886): 36; Ellen Jakeman, "The Pioneers," *WE* 21, no. 3 (August 1, 1892): 17; and Hyacinth, "Freedom's Echo," *WE* 21, no. 15 (February 1, 1893): 113.

44. R. M. F., "The Year of Jubilee," *WE* 25, no. 13 (January 1, 1897): 89.

45. Wells, "A Song of Summer," *Musings*, 24.

46. R. M. F., "Myrtle and Violets," *WE* 24, no. 23 (May 1, 1896): 145–46.

47. For a heaven filled with immortal flowers, see Aunt Em, "Souvenirs of Lilac-Time," *WE* 11, no. 1 (June 1, 1882): 2. See also L. M. Hewlings, "To Bereaved Friends," *WE* 15, no. 3 (July 1, 1886): 19; and L. M. Hewling, "Requiem," *WE* 18, no. 5 (August 1, 1889): 33.

48. Lu Dalton, "Back from the Borderland," *YWJ* 1, no. 5 (February 1890): 129. See also Lydia D. Alder, "In Loving Memory of Little Margaret," *WE* 23, no. 17 (April 1, 1895): 241.

49. Prolific poet Emily Hill Woodmansee used a winter landscape to express the terrible sadness and suffering of life, while poet and first *Exponent* editor L. Lula Greene Richards employed thorns, weeds, and storms to the same effect. Emily Hill Woodmansee, "Our Hopes Are in Thee," *WE* 9, no. 18 (February 15, 1881): 137. L. Lula Greene Richards, "M. I. Horne's Seventy-Fifth Birthday," *WE* 22, no. 9 (December 1, 1893): 70. See also Hyacinth, "Childhood," *WE* 27, nos. 1 and 2 (June 1 and 15, 1898): 298; and Maud Baggarley, "Weariness," *WE* 35, no. 3 (September 1906): 17.

50. Augusta Joyce Crocheron, "Nothing on the Books," *WE* 12, no. 19 (March 1, 1884): 147. See also "A Dream," *WE* 13, no. 1 (June 1, 1884): 6.

51. Edward W. Tullidge, *The Women of Mormondom* (New York: Tullidge and Crandall, 1877), 540.

52. In her book, Hannah Cornaby lauded another lowly spring flower, the tulip, as the harbinger of spring and a promise of the resurrection. Cornaby, "To a Tulip," *Autobiography*, 93–94.

53. For examples of invocations to some form of inspiration or revelation, see Crocheron, "My Harp," *Wild Flowers of Deseret*, 4; "Thoughts Within," ibid., 112–13; Hannah T. King, "Silent Voices," *WE* 11, no. 20 (March 15, 1883): 155; and Emile, "Beauties of Nature," *WE* 13, no. 1 (June 1, 1884): 1.

54. E. S. D., "Thoughts," *WE* 11, no. 2 (June 15, 1882): 11.

55. Alexander, "The Church Auxiliary Organizations," in Alexander, *Mormonism in Transition*, 125–56.

56. For arguments about how and why women's authority declined, especially in relation to the priesthood, see Linda King Newell, "The Historical Relationship of Mormon Women and Priesthood," in Hanks, *Women and Authority*, 23–48; and Quinn, "Mormon Women Have Had the Priesthood since 1843," 365–409.

57. Jane Tompkins, *Sensational Designs: The Cultural Work of American Fiction, 1790–1860* (New York: Oxford University Press, 1985); Ann Douglas, *The Feminization of American Culture* (New York: Anchor Books, 1988).

8

The "New Woman" at the "University"

Gender and American Catholic Identity in the Progressive Era

Kathleen Sprows Cummings

Until fairly recently, the history of Catholicism tended to focus on leaders and institutions. But in the wake of Vatican II, the great Roman Catholic council (1962–65) that modernized the church's teachings, many historians began to turn their attention away from priests and bishops to the experiences of ordinary Catholic believers. Inspired by Pope John XXIII's emphasis on the church as the entire "people of God," they resolved to write more inclusive stories about the Catholic past. Yet the new Catholic social history of the 1970s and 1980s still had little to say about Catholic women, not even the remarkable sisters who founded hundreds of hospitals, schools, and charities in the nineteenth and twentieth centuries.

In this case study of the Sisters of Notre Dame de Namur, Kathleen Sprows Cummings argues that writing Catholic history from the perspective of Catholic sisters sheds new light on two of the most vexing issues in Catholic historiography: the relationship between Catholicism and Progressivism in the early twentieth century, and the Americanist controversy. Using the tools of both social history and gender history, she shows that historians have missed the influence of Progressive ideals on Catholicism because of their exclusive focus on men. She also shows that the Americanist controversy involved anxieties over the "new woman."

In 1897, Sister Julia McGroarty, the American superior of the Sisters of Notre Dame de Namur, announced the beginning of her community's latest and most ambitious project: the founding of Trinity College for Catholic women in Washington, D.C. Trinity, which opened three years later, was not the first Catholic women's college; that distinction belongs to its Baltimore neighbor, the College of Notre Dame of Maryland. Trinity was, however, unique among early Catholic women's colleges in that it did not evolve from a preexisting academy.[1]

Founding Trinity presented Sister Julia with an array of challenges. Other founders were able to transform academies into colleges simply through revised charters and adjusted curricula, but the Sisters of Notre Dame needed to raise money, purchase land, design buildings, recruit students, and train faculty. Moreover, although its peer institutions invariably made inconspicuous transitions from girls' academies to women's colleges, Trinity attracted a great deal of attention. Deprived of the luxury of unobtrusiveness, Sister Julia was forced to justify higher education for Catholic women to a much greater extent than her counterparts at other Catholic women's colleges and was left much more vulnerable to criticism as a result.

Several years after Trinity opened, Katherine O'Keeffe O'Mahoney included a biographical sketch of Sister Julia, an Irish immigrant, in a collection entitled *Famous Irish Women*. Interviewing an unnamed Sister of Notre Dame about Sister Julia's efforts in founding Trinity, O'Mahoney had received this response: "Sister Superior prayed and Trinity was started."[2]

O'Mahoney had no doubt been hoping for a less-abbreviated version of events. Like many who seek to examine the historical contribution of American sisters, however, she had run up against the characteristic humility and self-effacement that was part and parcel of Catholic women's religious life.[3] One does not have to search far to discover the source of the anonymous nun's reticence. In 1901, Sister Julia herself had passed along to the community the advice of Rev. Philip Garrigan, the vice rector of nearby Catholic University. Garrigan had reminded her that, "like the dear Blessed Mother, the Sisters were chosen to do great things and like her too, they should be satisfied that he alone be witness of their cooperation with His grace. The Blessed Virgin did not publish her history to the world; neither should we be concerned whether people know what we do or not."[4] Ironically, it would be Garrigan who proved to be the beneficiary of his own advice. Replicating a familiar pattern in Catholic women's history, he and other clergy at Catholic University are often described as the prime movers in Trinity's founding.[5]

Adjusting the historical narrative to reflect women's achievements and influence represents the first step in taking Catholic women's religious experience seriously. Ultimately, though, this alone is an insufficient measure if one is to make a more convincing case that women's history matters to the study of American religion. This chapter approaches the founding of Trinity College from the perspective of women's history in its more sophisticated states of conceptualization.[6] By examining the college's connection to Americanism, a late nineteenth-century ideological conflict in the Catholic Church, this chapter illuminates broader connections between the construction of gender and the articulation of religious identity in the Progressive-era United States.

Americanism refers to a series of controversies that sharply divided the Catholic hierarchy between the convocation of the Third Plenary Council of Baltimore in 1884 and the appearance of Pope Leo XIII's *Testem Benevolentiae* in 1899. At issue was the question of how the church should relate to American culture and society. On one side of the debate stood liberals or "Americanists," who promoted greater Catholic integration into the American political and social mainstream. Seeking to "unite Church and age," Americanists advocated rapid assimilation of Catholic immigrants, more participation of Catholic laity in public life, and stronger cooperation between parochial and public schools. They also believed that the United States, with its constitutional protection of religious freedom, provided the ideal conditions for the flourishing of Catholicism. Members of the opposing group, called conservatives, generally supported a more insular Catholic community in the United States. Wary of the Americanists' exuberant patriotism, they believed that the American church should keep barriers intact to shield its members from the evils of the United States. Conservatives also advocated closer ties between the American church and the Vatican.[7]

Throughout the 1880s and 1890s, liberals and conservatives disagreed about Catholic participation in the labor movement, the assimilation of Catholic immigrants, the education of Catholic children, and the extent of Vatican influence on the church in the United States. In 1896, the controversy crossed the Atlantic when some European Americanists claimed that the church in the United States should serve as a model for the church throughout the world. In 1899, Pope Leo XIII settled the conflict with an apostolic letter. *Testem Benevolentiae* condemned as heresy a series of propositions under the heading of "Americanism," the most noteworthy of which was the claim that the American church was intrinsically different from the Church Universal.

The controversy over Americanism has been considered one of the most significant episodes in U.S. Catholic history, and its underlying cause—disagreement over what it meant to be Catholic and American—might even be described as the central organizing principle of the discipline. At the outset, it may be difficult to imagine what links the men of Americanism—extremely powerful and deemed significant—with the women of Trinity—largely powerless and dismissed as tangential. But the college and the controversy have an intriguing, if little-known, connection. In their quest to open a Catholic women's college, the Sisters of Notre Dame unwittingly landed in the middle of the conflict, and their alleged alliance with the

Americanists placed the entire endeavor in jeopardy. Indeed, Trinity would never have been founded had not a crucial phase of the controversy ended in favor of Sister Julia's supporters—an outcome over which she had virtually no control. The story thus initially appears to confirm perceptions of Catholic women as powerless figures who operated at the mercy of male authority figures.

But while the early days of Trinity demonstrate the constraints placed on the female faithful of the Catholic Church, the rest of the story shows that it was indeed possible to accomplish authentic work on behalf of women within the context of a male-dominated institution. At a time when the identity question was paramount, what it meant to be a woman in the Catholic Church largely depended on perceptions of what it meant to be a Catholic in American culture.

The case of Trinity offers three revisions to historical interpretations of late nineteenth-century Catholicism. First, it illustrates that while Catholic identity was often marshaled in support of traditional gender roles, so too could it serve as a vehicle through which women contested and renegotiated the parameters of their experience. Second, it reveals that anxieties over gender roles intensified the controversy over Americanism. Conservatives assailed liberals not only for raising challenging questions about the relationship between Catholicism and democratic culture, but also for challenging women's prescribed place in church and society. Third, it calls into question assumptions about the place of U.S. Catholics in Progressive-era America. The defeat of the Americanists in 1899, coupled with the more emphatic condemnation of modernism by Pope Pius in 1907, has led to a historical understanding of Catholics as uniquely insulated from broad currents of Progressive reform that swept the United States in the early years of the twentieth century.[8] But the women who founded Trinity were profoundly influenced by the expansion of women's higher education in American society, a key development of the Progressive era. In founding a Catholic women's college, the sisters used selective appropriation to negotiate between the Old and the New Worlds, bringing themselves and their students into an unprecedented level of engagement with non-Catholic American culture.

Early Days at Trinity

Although all final decisions regarding Trinity fell to Sister Julia in her capacity as head of the American province, she often designated Sister Mary Euphrasia Taylor, the superior of Notre Dame's convent in Washington, as her representative in the capital.[9] Their private correspondence reveals that both women appreciated the significance and magnitude of their undertaking, but they often denied taking the initiative. "We did not seek the work," Sister Julia wrote; "it came to us from a Higher Authority."[10] Though her capitalization clearly indicates a reference to a divine mandate, Trinity's founding has usually been ascribed to a *temporal* higher authority: most historical accounts suggest that it was officials at Catholic University who persuaded the sisters to open a college instead of an academy.[11] The sisters' own records suggest that Sister Julia had intended to open a women's college all along. While the inveterate self-effacement of nuns probably explains the discrepancy in part, it may also have resulted from deliberate calculation, as it undoubtedly served the sisters' purposes to say that the idea had originated with a prelate rather than with themselves.[12]

But no matter who provided the immediate impetus, it is clear that Sister Julia had been preparing to open a Catholic women's college since the early 1890s. She was one of the first American superiors to recognize that middle-class daughters of Irish Catholic immigrants would need college degrees to compete for access to professional occupations. Accordingly, she redesigned the curriculum of Notre Dame's academies to prepare students to study at the college level and established two Normal Schools to train Catholic women to be teachers.[13]

Opening a Catholic women's college was also a matter of congregational pride. As of 1897, the Sisters of Notre Dame taught at only one parish school in Washington, D.C. Sister Mary Euphrasia argued that it was imperative that Notre Dame increase its visibility in the city. Otherwise, visitors would receive the inaccurate impression that parochial schools were "the principal work of our society, for which *alone* the sisters were *fitted* [emphasis in original]." A superior Catholic women's college, she argued, would more adequately represent Notre Dame's mission in Washington. To underscore the need for decisive action, she pointed out that Eckington College, a Protestant institution, had recently opened near Catholic University.[14]

According to Sister Mary Euphrasia, Philip Garrigan received the sisters' proposal with the "warmest and most cordial approbation." He explained why. Two years before, Catholic University had announced plans to allow women to attend lectures as "special students." Bishop John Keane, then the rector of the university, declared that the university had no plans to admit women as regular students. Undeterred, twenty women applied in the fall of 1895. Although these applications were rejected, they testified to a growing desire for higher education among Catholic women. Garrigan went on to speculate that those twenty female applicants, rejected by Catholic

University, had presumably enrolled in "Protestant or infidel" institutions of higher learning.[15]

Garrigan's reasoning highlighted the two most compelling arguments in favor of Catholic women's colleges. The twenty female applicants to Catholic University contributed to increasing anxiety in the Catholic community over the prospect of coeducation. Among Catholics, there was virtually unanimous agreement that men and women be educated separately. Any Catholic women's college would need to avoid even the suggestion of coeducation if it were to succeed. According to Garrigan, that taint had already thwarted two other proposals. He reported that two other religious orders, the Ladies of the Sacred Heart and the Sisters of the Holy Cross, had each contemplated building "a women's annexe [sic]" to Catholic University. Cardinal Francis Satolli, the apostolic delegate in Washington at the time, had vetoed both plans because they had seemed perilously close to coeducation.[16]

As Garrigan's second comment indicated, providing an alternative to "Protestant or infidel" schools was also a matter of concern. By the 1890s, American women had a variety of options to pursue a college degree. Oberlin College in Ohio had admitted women since 1833, and eight state universities had become coeducational during the Civil War years. The founding of all-female Vassar College in 1865 initiated another trend. Other women's colleges followed: Wellesley in 1870, Smith in 1871, Bryn Mawr in 1885, and Mount Holyoke in 1888. In the early 1890s, Radcliffe College and Barnard College opened as affiliated institutions of Harvard and Columbia, providing a third type of American women's college. These early women's colleges are collectively known as the Seven Sisters.[17]

Although Catholics were not expressly prohibited from attending non-Catholic institutions, they were discouraged from doing so because of fears about the potential damage to their faith.[18] Some believed that Catholic women would be more susceptible than Catholic men to Protestant proselytizing. Austin O'Malley, a medical doctor and professor of literature at Notre Dame, explained why secular education would put the souls of Catholic females in greater jeopardy: "The life in a non-Catholic women's college, where attention to the 'evils of Popery' is more absorbing than in colleges for boys, is not the best atmosphere in the world for the growth of a Catholic girl's faith. . . . the girl in the non-Catholic college is exposed to stronger temptations than those experienced by a Catholic boy in a similar position, because the emotional preacher is more potent in the girls' college than in the boys."[19] O'Malley claimed that "Catholic girls in large and increasing numbers are flocking to non-Catholic colleges, to the injury of loss of faith."

Since Catholic men's colleges were prohibited—he described coeducation as an "abomination"—he argued that the only remedy was to open Catholic colleges for women. By the late 1890s, many Catholics who would otherwise oppose higher education for women agreed with O'Malley: Catholic women's colleges were a necessary defense against coeducation and mass apostasy.[20]

Although the sisters understood both of these arguments, neither had formed their primary rationale. Coeducation never surfaced in their discussions, and although they were keenly aware that Catholic women had the option to attend secular schools, their students' potential loss of faith did not seem to be a leading concern. Sister Mary Euphrasia's uneasiness over the proximity of Eckington College, at least, stemmed from her fears that Notre Dame's prestige would suffer by comparison. After this conversation with Garrigan, however, both she and Sister Julia recognized that the twin goals of preventing coeducation and the loss of faith constituted the most persuasive—and not coincidentally, the least controversial—arguments in favor of establishing a Catholic women's college. Subsequently these objectives would figure more prominently in arguments that they would make on Trinity's behalf.

Before they could proceed, the sisters needed permission from James Cardinal Gibbons, the archbishop of Baltimore, under whose jurisdiction Trinity would fall. After meeting with Sister Mary Euphrasia, Gibbons authorized the project, specifying that the proposed institution would work "in union with though entirely independently of the Catholic University." Gibbons admitted in a later letter that he was delighted because Trinity's founding would "relieve the University authorities from the embarrassment of refusing women admission."[21] Although the project did not require official approval from Rome, Gibbons advised Sister Mary Euphrasia to visit Archbishop Sebastian Martinelli, Satolli's replacement as apostolic delegate, to keep him informed of the plans. She called on Martinelli in late April and they had an amiable conversation.[22] The sisters also required sanction from Mother Aimee, the superior general at Namur, before they could begin. Mother Aimee cabled her consent on April 1.[23]

After canvassing the Washington suburbs for appropriate sites for the new college, the sisters purchased twenty acres at the intersection of Michigan and Lincoln avenues in the northeastern suburb of Brookland. This plot was located approximately one-third of a mile from Catholic University. The sale would not be final until later that summer, and the nuns had agreed to postpone a public announcement until then. Because Sister Julia knew that "everything would depend on the first impression," she wanted time to carefully formulate a statement that would include Gibbons's official letter of endorsement. She lost the opportunity to control the nature of the revelation in mid-June, when the news leaked to the press. The newspapers sensationalized the story and misrepresented some of the facts. Some reported that the college was slated to open in 1898, when the actual target date was two years later. Others erroneously described Trinity as a wing of Catholic University. Sister Julia sent statements to secular and religious newspapers to correct these mistakes.[24]

Sister Julia had anticipated that the proposal to open a college would anger traditional opponents of higher education for Catholic women, who predicted disaster for the family and the church should Trinity open. But by 1897, the twin specters of secular education and coeducation had significantly undermined this resistance. Although there was by no means universal support, most agreed that Catholic women's colleges should open as a matter of expediency. What Sister Julia had not foreseen was that far-more-menacing attacks on the college would emerge from a debate over Catholic identity rather than one about gender roles. The most dangerous threat to Trinity came from Catholic prelates and intellectuals, who viewed the problem of higher education for women as symptomatic of a more grievous sin: Catholic capitulation to American culture.

"The War of 1897"

In mid-July 1897, Archbishop John Ireland of St. Paul wrote a letter to Sister Julia in which he congratulated her on her work but warned that difficulties might lie ahead: "I am afraid," Ireland cautioned, "things will not go as smoothly as you expect."[25] It was fitting that this prophetic warning came from Ireland, the unofficial leader of the "Americanists" and the one who had coined its slogan, "Church and Age Unite!" This group also included Cardinal Gibbons; John J. Keane, the first rector of Catholic University; Denis O'Connell, the rector of the North American College in Rome; and John Lancaster Spalding, bishop of Peoria and the brightest intellectual among the American hierarchy. Archbishop Michael Corrigan of New York and Bishop Bernard McQuaid of Rochester, New York, led the conservatives. This group also included many German-American priests and bishops who were suspicious of Irish-American dominance among the American hierarchy.

Discussions about Catholic education from the elementary to the university levels deepened the division between the two groups. At the parochial level, Americanists thought that Catholic schools should promote assimilation, while German-American Catholics viewed them as the means to preserve both language and ethnic culture. In 1891, Archbishop Ireland implemented a compromise plan between parochial and public schools in his diocese, prompting a "school controversy" that lasted two years and further divided the hierarchy.[26]

Catholic University, which opened in 1889, was intertwined with the Americanist controversy in several ways. Early discussions about the institution had helped divide liberals and conservatives. Quarrels did not always emanate from ideological differences; Archbishops Corrigan and McQuaid, favoring a New York location for the university, resented the eventual choice of Washington. The conservatives were further alienated by the close involvement of several key Americanists in the planning process. Keane of Richmond was designated the first rector of the university; Ireland served on its organizing committee; and it was located in Gibbons's jurisdiction. Bishop Spalding's progressive talk at the cornerstone-laying ceremony further irritated conservatives by explicitly identifying the university with the liberal group.[27]

Monsignor Joseph Schroeder, a German-born professor of dogmatic theology, was the leading conservative at Catholic University and an outspoken enemy of the Americanists there. He led a faction of German-American Catholics based primarily in the Midwest and attacked the Americanists through the St. Louis–based paper, *Das Herold des Glaubens* (The Herald of Faith). Schroeder had disproportionate influence in Rome through his friendship with Cardinal Francis Satolli, the former apostolic delegate to the United States (who had earlier vetoed proposals to incorporate a "women's annexe" to Catholic University). When Satolli had arrived in the United States in 1892, he allied himself with the Americanists. But by the time he returned to Rome four years later, he had moved into the conservative camp. With help from Schroeder, Satolli began to undermine Keane at the Vatican, criticizing the rector for his liberal views and his close association with American Protestants. In September of 1896, Satolli used his influence with the pope to orchestrate the dismissal of Keane as rector of Catholic University. Keane's departure represented a stunning defeat for the liberals.[28]

Early discussions of Trinity came on the heels of this particularly bitter episode in the Americanist debate. Both sides recognized the college as a potential weapon. For the Americanists, Trinity demonstrated the promise of Catholic acculturation to American society. Ireland's enthusiastic support, for example, stemmed from what he perceived as the need for college-trained teachers in parochial schools. In his own diocese of St. Paul, he would encourage his sister, Mother Seraphine of the Sisters of St. Joseph, to open the College of St. Catherine in 1905.[29]

Other Americanists praised Trinity. Cardinal Gibbons described the college as a "blessing to our country" and a "glory to our Church."[30] Reverend Thomas Conaty, Keane's successor as rector of Catholic University, emphasized Trinity's "utmost importance to Church and state. . . . the age demands scholarship, and women's responsibilities urge that intellectual and moral development unite in fitting her to do her full duty to society."[31] Spalding of Peoria became one of Trinity's staunchest supporters. In a lecture about the college, he affirmed one of Americanism's central tenets, the belief that the United States provided the most favorable conditions for moral perfection.[32] Reverend Edward Pace, a Catholic University professor of philosophy, agreed that Catholic women's colleges were needed because the American "democratic spirit" had given Catholic women in the United States more potential for achievement.[33]

For Americanists, then, Trinity symbolized all the good that would result from a union between church and age; for Schroeder and his supporters, the college represented the perils of such an alliance. As early as mid-April, before the sisters had even chosen a site, Schroeder had, through Satolli, reported to the Vatican that the Sisters of Notre Dame had purchased property near Catholic University and they planned to have the same teachers and the same classes as male students. Just before his late-April meeting with Sister Mary Euphrasia, Archbishop Martinelli received a letter from Pope Leo XIII, in which he asked for clarification about these rumors. After hearing more about the plans for Trinity, the apostolic delegate had denied that the nuns planned to sponsor coeducation. He did not mention the correspondence to Sister Mary Euphrasia, thinking he had heard "the end of it."[34]

The Sisters of Notre Dame did not learn about negative rumors until Schroeder and his supporters publicly attacked them through *Das Herold des Glaubens* in late summer. Editor John Enzelberger wrote one of the most damaging critiques, entitled "The 'New Woman' at the 'University.'" The word choice was provocative. While "University" raised the specter of coeducation, the phrase "New Woman" presented equal cause for alarm. Coined by Henry James, it referred to those who had availed themselves of new opportunities open to middle-class women at the end of the nineteenth century. By attending college, earning a living, working in a settlement house, or otherwise participating in activities outside the home, the New Woman challenged the Victorian ideal of female domesticity. Financially independent from either a father or a husband, she exercised control over her own life.[35]

Because of her independence and self-sufficiency, the New Woman was routinely depicted as the antithesis of the true Catholic woman.[36] By invoking her in his article about Trinity, Enzleberger claimed that the sisters "wanted to imitate Protestants and unbelievers." Describing Trinity as a "wing" of the Catholic University, Enzleberger contended that the nuns did not care about the danger that higher learning would pose to the students' faith. As evidence of Trinity's blatant disregard of Catholicism, he pointed out that Trinity's admission requirements did not include religion. He described Trinity as a nondenominational institution masquerading as a Catholic one and concluded that the college had only served to strengthen his "old-fashioned conviction that, for the present, man's world should stand at the pinnacle of learning."[37]

Sister Mary Euphrasia responded to the accusations in a letter to the editor of *Das Herold des Glaubens*. She emphasized that Trinity would be no "annex or wing" of Catholic University. While she admitted that Trinity did not stipulate religion as an entrance requirement, she caustically reminded the editors that such a prerequisite would exclude the very students that Catholic colleges hoped to benefit, those who had attended secular secondary schools. She did assure the editors that the curriculum would have a number of religion requirements.[38] Her rejoinder came too late, however, to repair the damage that had already been done. By the time these attacks were made public, Schroeder and his cohort had succeeded, with the help of Satolli, in convincing Pope Leo XIII that something was amiss at Trinity.

On August 15, Satolli wrote to Gibbons: "I have learned also of the project of a University for the weaker sex . . . ; this affair, as mentioned in the newspapers, has made a disagreeable impression here, particularly so because it was described that it would be a dangerous addition and amalgamation of Institutions, for the teaching of students of both sexes."[39] A week later, Martinelli informed Gibbons that the Holy Father had heard of the matter "from sources unknown to me." He suggested that the sisters should seek approval from the Holy See before they continued their plans.[40]

This development brought an immediate halt to progress on Trinity. Cardinal Gibbons summoned Sister Mary Euphrasia to Baltimore and, blaming "the German element in the West," told her that she and Sister Julia must stop work on Trinity until the matter was resolved.[41] With characteristic aplomb, Sister Mary Euphrasia assured the cardinal that she would not lose heart and that she had "every confidence that God would himself carry through a work in which his Hand had been visible from the beginning." Later, in recounting this exchange in a letter to her superior, she reflected on the humor of "giving what seemed to be a lecture on confidence in God to the Cardinal Archbishop of Baltimore."[42]

After the news leaked that Schroeder had succeeded in thwarting plans, reporters descended on the Notre Dame convent on North Capitol Street.[43] In what one sister later described as an "impromptu press conference," Sister

Mary Euphrasia attempted to correct those reports by explaining the purpose and plan of Trinity.[44] On the advice of Cardinal Gibbons, she decided to pay a personal visit to the apostolic delegate, to convince him to intercede on Trinity's behalf. She arrived at Martinelli's Washington residence only to discover that he was vacationing in Atlantic City. Undaunted, she visited him at the ocean resort a few days later, traveling half a day for an audience that lasted a little over an hour.

It was during this meeting that Martinelli told her about the papal letter he had received prior to their April conversation. He promised to tell the Vatican, once again, that the Sisters of Notre Dame were not promoting coeducation. Martinelli also explained the exact nature of the prohibition on the college, which involved the distinction between a college and a university. A university would require papal consent, but a college needed only the permission of the local bishop. Martinelli did tell her, though, that Gibbons was unlikely to approve of any plan discountenanced by the Holy Father.[45] In saying this, Martinelli was being somewhat disingenuous, in that he himself was the one who had advised Gibbons to stop the sisters until they resolved matters with Rome.

Sister Julia was initially cheerful. In an early letter to Sister Mary Euphrasia, she claimed to be "not in the least troubled. . . . I would much rather have the storm before we begin than a breeze later which might insure a feeling of distrust and thus injure the work."[46] But her frustration increased as she recognized the assault as a thinly veiled attack on the Americanists. Though she believed that the accusations against the college were unwarranted, she had little recourse to defend herself. At one point, she lamented the inaction to which her sex confined her, vowing that "if she was a man, she could put on her hat and go off to see the pope."[47]

Unable "to go off and see the pope," the sisters petitioned the Vatican through mail, using letters to make three points. First and foremost, they dismissed the erroneous reports about coeducation. Sister Julia attributed these rumors to "the spirit of opposition in the Western Churches."[48] In another letter, she wrote that "anyone who knows the order [Notre Dame] will recognize [the rumors about coeducation] as gratuitous."[49] The nuns also emphasized the need to prevent a loss of faith should Catholic women enroll at secular colleges. Sister Julia reminded Cardinal Rampolla that in the United States, education was the "cry of the age." If Catholic girls were not provided with a Catholic alternative, they would "continue to frequent godless schools." She claimed that there were a dozen Protestant, anti-Catholic women's colleges in the United States; in those institutions, the "anti-Catholic interpretation in Science, Philosophy, History, and the Arts" caused its Catholic students widespread moral injury.[50] Sister Mary Euphrasia dramatized the impending disaster by reporting that, over the last four years, eleven Catholic students had "lost the faith" at Colombian University (later George Washington University), a Baptist University in Washington, D.C.[51]

Finally, the sisters disassociated themselves from modern women by emphasizing Trinity's connection to the past. Sister Mary Euphrasia reminded Satolli that religious teaching had long been the "alpha and omega" of Notre Dame's philosophy of education.[52] Sister Julia assured Cardinal Rampolla that "the memory of Italy's renown in its women saints and scholars" would be "the law and guide" of Trinity College.[53] Establishing this connection to a Catholic past not only differentiated Trinity from its secular counterparts, but also refuted any suggestion that the nuns were behaving like New Women.[54]

Meanwhile, Gibbons defended the sisters. He promised Martinelli that the college would have "no official or organic connection whatever with the Catholic University" and pointed out that they were separated by one-third of a mile. Georgetown College and the Visitation Convent were even nearer to each other, he noted, "yet no inconvenience has resulted though they have been in existence there for a hundred years." Writing to Satolli, Gibbons assured him that "the reports which have reached Rome with regard to a new female school of higher studies are utterly false or greatly exaggerated, and are the offspring of ignorance and malice."[55]

The Paulists, a religious order of men who shared Americanist views, published an "authoritative statement" about Trinity College in the September issue of *Catholic World*. Attempting to correct reports about the college that had been "prematurely circulated," the author testified to the impeccable credentials of the Sisters of Notre Dame de Namur, both in matters of faith and in teaching ability. Emphasizing that the project had been approved by Gibbons and Conaty, he argued that Trinity would "offer to its students all the advantages of the best American colleges, and will have, in addition, those benefits that come from education given under the direction of experienced religious teachers." Proximity to Catholic University would help Trinity's students achieve academic excellence by giving them the benefit of the university's public lecture courses. Finally, he argued that by seeking "friendship" with the university, the sisters were not challenging Catholic teaching; on the contrary, they were showing their "desire to be in close touch with the bishops of the Church."[56]

The nuns put their plans on indefinite hold for the next several months, during which one young sister observed that "waiting is more tiresome than work."[57] Good news arrived in November, when Rampolla wrote to Martinelli in the name of the pope: "His Holiness, after having considered the matter well, thinks that there should be nothing more said considering the difficulties in the way of the project of the erection of an Institution for females in the vicinity of the Catholic University."[58] Three days later, Gibbons summoned Sister Mary Euphrasia to Baltimore to dictate a translation of this letter.[59] Conaty, also present at the meeting, advised the sisters not to gloat over their victory: "Do not exult too loud, but proceed joyfully in secret, grateful that this great difficulty has been so happily overcome."[60] The nuns did rejoice privately: "Glory be to God in all things!" one young sister wrote. "We can build our college as soon as we have money enough, and go right on without minding what anyone says to us."[61]

What led to the Vatican's reversal? The sisters' lobbying efforts undoubtedly helped, as did the support of influential prelates such as Martinelli and Gibbons. But it is unclear whether these measures alone would have sufficed. What was probably the most significant factor in the decision was Schroeder's rapidly declining influence at Catholic University and in Rome. In what Archbishop Ireland dubbed the "War of 1897," the Americanist contingent at Catholic University launched an offensive against Schroeder and collected witnesses who testified that he regularly stayed out until dawn, frequenting disreputable saloons. In October, they presented this evidence to the Vatican, and the university's Board of Trustees voted for dismissal. At the request of the pope, Schroeder was permitted to resign.[62] Rampolla's letter to Martinelli linked Schroeder's fall from grace to the Trinity question. After assuring the apostolic delegate that "the University would receive no further annoyance" from Schroeder, Rampolla wrote that the pope would no longer listen to "disadvantageous reports" about Trinity.[63]

In retrospect, it is clear that the Sisters of Notre Dame de Namur were not in league with the Americanists; Sister Julia once claimed never even to have heard of Americanism until she was accused of it.[64] Given their proximity to Catholic University, and their timing, it was unlikely that the sisters would have remained completely unaffected by the conflict. But that Trinity became intertwined with the controversy to such a great extent is significant, because it demonstrates how easily gender could be manipulated to serve other purposes. Members on both sides of the debate used gender to either impugn or defend the Americanist position. Supporters exalted them as true women; opponents assailed them as new women. This remarkable affair shows how vulnerable Catholic women became when they attempted to renegotiate gender boundaries within the church.

But the Sisters of Notre Dame were never mere pawns in a larger power struggle, and their story represents much more than an interesting footnote in the tangled history of Americanist politics. Trinity's founders experienced the same tensions that had prompted the debate over Americanism, and long after the "war of 1897" was over, the challenge of adapting Old World Catholicism to American culture awaited them. Their response offers an illuminating window into Catholics' efforts to negotiate between religious and national identities that were often in competition with each other at the beginning of the twentieth century.

"Conspicuously American, Conspicuously Catholic"

In his perceptive study of Catholics and Progressivism, Joseph McShane, s.j., observed that every aspect of Catholic life in the early twentieth century was affected by the struggle to balance conflicting sets of expectations. "As a mission church under the supervision of the Congregation for the Propagation of the Faith," he notes, "the Catholic Church had to be conspicuously loyal to Rome and its directives; as a suspect Church in a host culture, she had to be conspicuously American." Lacking the intellectual tools to reconcile ethnic Catholicism with American ideals, the church was unable to develop a coherent response to the problems of industrialization until 1919, when American bishops issued their Program of Social Reconstruction.[65]

Like other American Catholics, the Sisters of Notre Dame felt compelled to be at once "conspicuously American and conspicuously Catholic." But unlike their friends among the liberal clergy, who eventually paid the price for tilting the balance too heavily toward the "American" side of the equation, the women who founded Trinity proved to be very deft at reconciling the expectations of the Old World with the exigencies of the New.

One of the most obvious arenas where these tensions surfaced was in the negotiations between the American sisters and their European counterparts. Sister Julia had always intended to minimize Namur's influence on Trinity. She placed Trinity under the direct supervision of the provincial superior in Cincinnati, rather than the authority of the Superior General at Namur, and resolved to hire faculty who "have been rigidly trained in American educational methods."[66] To a certain extent, Sister Julia's emphasis on the autonomy of the American province was representative of what was happening in other women's religious congregations with European roots. Like many other women's religious communities with origins on the continent, the Sisters of Notre Dame had grown increasingly Irish and American over the second half of the nineteenth century.[67] Since a larger percentage of the congregation had little or no connection to a European motherhouse, a strain in the relationship was perhaps inevitable. But Trinity's founding undoubtedly accentuated the transatlantic tension.

Reports of the sisters' alleged involvement with the Americanists had reached Mother Aimee in Belgium and dampened the superior's initial enthusiasm for the project. Disputes over financing the college increased her suspicion of the endeavor. At issue were two different approaches to fundraising. Mother Aimee urged Sister Julia to delay actual construction of the college until they had accumulated sufficient funds. Cardinal Gibbons, on the other hand, encouraged them to start building immediately. When construction had not begun by April 1898, Gibbons correctly guessed that Namur was behind the delay, and he threatened to remove his support for Trinity as a result. With this in mind, Sister Julia decided that it would ultimately be more effective to work and raise money simultaneously.[68] Although Mother Aimee never retracted her official endorsement of the college, her friendship with Sister Julia permanently soured. Both women celebrated their golden jubilees in the summer of 1898, and Sister Julia traveled to Belgium for the commemoration ceremonies. Although she anticipated that the personal visit would provide her with an opportunity to clear up the misunderstanding, her hopes were in vain.[69] While evidence suggests that the cooling of the relationship genuinely saddened Sister Julia, her effort to distance the American sisters from Namur was both deliberate and necessary. Because Belgium was known for its conservative brand of Catholicism, it was in Trinity's best interest to deemphasize any foreign taint. Sister Julia had repeatedly assured her progressive supporters that the American sisters had been "singularly free from European influence."[70]

In addition to showing the sisters' increased autonomy from Namur, Trinity's founding also evinced, albeit in an unexpected way, a move away from Roman influence. When the machinations of Schroeder and Satolli raised the possibility of a papal prohibition on the American nuns' work, Sister Julia was well aware that a public rebuke from Rome would suggest to other Americans that Catholics were under the thumb of the Vatican. As Sister Julia wrote to Cardinal Ferrata, "Personal convictions do not generally influence us, but we cannot but be alive to the fact that this has now become a national affair, fixing the eyes of the whole country upon us."[71] In the long run, however, Schroeder and Satolli's attempt to assert Vatican influence actually produced an opposite effect.

Recall the wording of Rampolla's letter to Martinelli on the resolution of the Trinity question: "His Holiness . . . thinks that there should be nothing more said . . . of an Institution for females." Now that the question had been settled, Sister Mary Euphrasia hoped for an official statement from the Vatican that was a bit less tepid. She wanted to ask the apostolic delegate for a formal blessing of the project. Frederick Rooker, one of Martinelli's aides, refused to allow her to submit the request. With astute logic, Rooker argued that Rome, having "stuck its finger in the pie" in the wake of Schroeder's and Satolli's accusations, would not admit publicly that it had been in error. But neither would the Vatican interfere again. Once Trinity opened, Rooker predicted that Trinity could "get any amount of blessings and approbations direct from His Holiness himself." Until then, Rome would be silent on the matter. As the official representative of the Vatican, Martinelli would be unable to publicly endorse Trinity. Though he supported the sisters, he would have to refuse Sister Mary Euphrasia's request. Because of the damage that would do, Rooker pointed out, it was wiser not to put the apostolic delegate in that position. As it happened, Rooker was correct in predicting that Rome would wait until Trinity opened to send its formal blessing.[72]

If careful negotiations with superiors in Namur and Rome provided the sisters with one avenue to become "conspicuously American," finding new ways to reach out to non-Catholics offered another. This is most clearly seen in the relationships that developed between the sisters and secular educators. Early on, the sisters planned to model their college on the Seven Sisters schools, emphasizing that Trinity would be "of the same grade as Vassar, thus giving young women an opportunity for the highest collegiate instruction."[73] As she promised in Trinity's prospectus, it would be the "object and life of the Sisters of Notre Dame de Namur to provide the safeguards to faith and morals while they offer to women courses of study which will be equal if not superior to those of our best non-Catholic colleges."[74]

Sister Julia and other members of the Notre Dame community studied the catalogs of Wellesley and Bryn Mawr to familiarize themselves with their curricula. Later, she and several other sisters traveled to Bryn Mawr, Mount Holyoke, Radcliffe, Smith, and Wellesley.[75] During these visits, the nuns met with deans and presidents, attended classes, visited Catholic students, and acquainted themselves with campus life. These visits forged mutual admiration between secular administrators and the Sisters of Notre Dame that would endure even after Trinity opened. M. Carey Thomas, the president of Bryn Mawr, attended the dedication ceremony in November 1900 to support her "sister college."[76] Cooperative efforts between Trinity's founders and their secular counterparts resulted in a curriculum that was virtually identical to that of Vassar and Bryn Mawr.[77]

The Ladies Auxiliary Board of Regents, a group of women who coordinated fund-raising for Trinity, also attested to the sisters' increasingly American orientation.[78] The sisters deliberately recruited prominent women in Washington, many of whom were converts to Catholicism. Representative regents included Ella Lorraine Dorsey, a Daughter of the American Revolution and an employee at the U.S. Patent Office; Olive Risley Seward, adopted daughter of the former secretary of state; and Mollie Eliot Seawell, the grand-niece of former president John Tyler. At their first meeting in the spring of 1898, the Ladies Board rejected a proposal to solicit donations from foreign sources and resolved to appeal only to Americans for aid.[79] In addition to raising funds and publicizing the college, members of the Ladies Board also recruited students from across the United States. Consequently Trinity's pioneer class was more geographically diverse than its peer institutions.[80]

Classes began at Trinity on November 8, 1900, and the college was dedicated on November 22. Martinelli celebrated Mass at the dedication ceremony, and Gibbons blessed the first building. Bishops from Brooklyn, New York, Richmond, and Wheeling were present, as were representatives of other women's religious communities. Members of the diplomatic corps, senators and congressmen, and presidents of secular colleges also attended. Conaty delivered the principal address, in which he described Trinity's students as having the potential to be both "the glory of the Church" and the "Salvation of the State."[81]

Other supporters echoed Conaty in their own endorsements of the college. One observer remarked that because the Catholic girl was "as truly an American girl as any other, of an equally democratic and independent spirit . . . it was not to be expected that there should be any difference in thirst for knowledge."[82] Another prelate commented that Trinity's founding gave the Sisters of Notre Dame a "distinctly American line" by proving that they were as "in love with country as they were with God."[83]

As this rhetoric indicates, there is ample evidence to suggest that the sisters went to considerable lengths to accentuate their Americanness. What should not be overlooked, however, is the fact that the sisters' accommodation to American culture was largely facilitated by their efforts to emphasize their Catholicity. During their first discussion about Trinity, Garrigan told Sister Mary Euphrasia that he hoped that Trinity would do for *Catholic* women what "Vassar and Wellesley and Bryn Mawr are doing for American women."[84] The nuns readily understood Garrigan's distinction. When Sister Mary Euphrasia assured Cardinal Satolli that she was trying to "counteract the tendencies of the times," she was obviously defending the sisters against the accusation that they were emulating Protestants.[85] But she was not being dishonest in making this claim. Emphasizing Catholicism as Trinity's raison d'etre, the sisters understood that there were important distinctions between their college and its secular counterparts.[86]

Despite their proclamations of Americanness, for example, the sisters obviously valued retaining the connection to their European roots. Although Sister Julia had insisted that she would only use teachers who would be familiar with the new American methods, she ensured that faculty would also be well-versed in Catholic techniques. In fall 1899, she sent two sisters to Namur in order to prepare them to teach at the college level. The next summer, she gathered the ten sisters who would become Trinity's first faculty at the Notre Dame summer school in Waltham, Massachusetts.[87] Furthermore, despite the goodwill that existed between themselves and the administrators of non-Catholic colleges, Sister Julia was determined that Trinity's curriculum would be distinguished from that of secular colleges through the addition of requirements in religion and church history. An early catalog stated that because the history of Christianity was the "story of the true emancipation and elevation of womankind," it is eminently proper that "the history of the Catholic Church, the divinely appointed custodian and interpreter of the will and the spirit of Jesus Christ, should be thoroughly taught in any school of higher studies for Christian women."[88]

Campus life varied only slightly from life on non-Catholic campuses. Mass was celebrated every morning and, although it was not required, the majority attended. Retreats occurred regularly, and sodalities existed along with organizations such as the glee club and the athletic association.[89] All members of Trinity's first class were either Catholic or preparing to become Catholic. The class included several Catholic transfer students from Wellesley and Barnard, which was interpreted as vindication of the argument that Catholic women would not choose secular colleges if they had a Catholic alternative. The student body was also ethnically distinct. Along with most of the other early Catholic women's colleges, Trinity helped put a uniquely Irish-American stamp on Catholic women's higher education.[90] Perhaps the most vivid testament to Trinity's Irishness comes from its first class roster, which included the names Dooley, Gavin, O'Mahoney, McEnelly, Linehan, O'Connell, and Kennedy.[91] Significantly, the sisters avoided becoming too explicit about their ethnic heritage. At one suggestion that they choose a shamrock for Trinity's emblem, they politely demurred, saying it would be "too expressive."[92]

What is perhaps more striking than these actual differences in faculty, curriculum, campus life, and student body was the way that the sisters, their supporters, and their students presented Trinity as distinct from non-Catholic women's colleges. The most obvious manifestation of this sense of difference was the repeated emphasis on Trinity's connection to an Irish and Catholic past. Like many other Catholic women, Sister Julia envisioned herself as part of a long and venerable tradition, and she declared this sentiment in most of her discussions about the college. In Trinity's first catalog, for example, she expressed her hope that Trinity would "give the women of our day every facility for becoming as brilliant lights in the intellectual world as those who have shone in ecclesiastical history in bygone ages—the Hildas, the Liobas, the Marcellas, the Paulas, the Eustochiums, the Catherines, and a host of others."[93] Sister Mary Euphrasia also believed that modern Catholic women's college students were merely following in the tradition of "St. Catherine of Sienna [sic] in the fourteenth, and St. Theresa in the sixteenth century . . . each in turn the glory of the age in which she lived." She also pointed to the women scholars at Padua, reminding her sisters that the Catholic Church had educated women at Padua three centuries before Harvard, Cornell, or Yale opened their doors to women. In a letter to Sister Julia, she wrote, "Now *the Church approves that we take up the work of Padua!* [emphasis in original]."[94] One supporter of the sisters used a visit to Namur to observe that "in working for Heaven we always plant or build better than we know; and the evolution of the work of the Sisterhood of Notre Dame from the poor schools of France to the State schools of Belgium, the normal schools of England, and Trinity College of America is perfectly logical, religiously and socially."[95] By anchoring Trinity securely to a Catholic past, the sisters were able to present their college as a "perfectly logical" evolution of the historic commitment of their congregation. In so doing, they implicitly refuted any suggestion that Trinity represented a radical innovation, a far more dangerous proposition for Catholic women.[96]

Trinity's students were often reminded that they, too, were following in the footsteps of ancient Catholic women. Lelia Hardin Bugg, a popular Catholic writer who became a member of Trinity's inaugural class, acknowledged that the college began "a new course in the cause of higher education of Christian women." Bugg cautioned her readers, however, that Trinity College was "but reviving an old privilege conferred by the Church on women centuries before the discoverer of America was born, the privilege of being learned and good." To underscore this connection to their Catholic past, statues of "St. Paula, St. Katherine, Laura Bassi, wearing the cap and gown of the University of Bologna, Helena Bisopiagia, the sunny-haired Venetian, first among the philosophers of her time, and Novella d'Andrea" greeted the students when they walked on the terrace of Trinity's main building.[97] Of course, the college's publicity materials explicitly distinguished Trinity's students from the threatening "New Woman": "While the New Woman, with her head full of vagaries, is reconstructing the Universe, Trinity College will offer to her Catholic sisters an opportunity to accrue knowledge which, though adapting itself to all rightful demands of the period, is firmly wedded to that unchanging faith which has lifted women of all ages to her true position."[98] The women of Trinity—founders, students, supporters—constructed a usable past that allowed them to follow in the footsteps of the New Woman, while convincing themselves and others that they were headed in an opposite direction. By declaring themselves the spiritual sisters of female scholars at medieval Catholic universities rather than of contemporary educators and students at Wellesley or Bryn Mawr, the women of Trinity redefined themselves from potential threats into acceptable women. By combining selective retrieval of Catholic tradition with cautious borrowing from American culture, the women of Trinity managed to become "conspicuously American" without jeopardizing their standing within the church. It was, in other words, through the articulation of a distinctive Catholic identity that they discovered the means to subvert a rigid ideology of gender that often circumscribed women's lives and choices.

Conclusion

In her profile of Sister Julia McGroarty, Katharine O'Keeffe O'Mahoney observed that Trinity "was no new departure in that Ever-Living Church that is ready to meet the needs of all places and all times."[99] Like the comment that appeared earlier in her sketch—"Sister Superior prayed and Trinity was started"—this statement must be subjected to further scrutiny. Trinity, along with the thirteen other Catholic women's colleges founded between 1896 and 1918, *did* represent a new and important departure for American Catholics.

Trinity's founding thus has broader implications for the study of U.S. Catholicism. Perched at an important intersection between Catholic culture and American society, its leaders blended tradition and innovation in ways that made sense to them as American Catholics. By effectively straddling the boundaries between the Old and the New Worlds, the women of Trinity produced a much timelier response to the demands of a modernizing America than did the institutional church. Their story therefore suggests that some American Catholics may have been more attuned to and affected by developments in Progressive-era United States than historians have previously understood.

Notes

1. Sister Mary Cameron, SSND, *The College of Notre Dame of Maryland, 1895–1945* (New York: Declan X. McMullen Company, 1947), 56–58; Mary Oates, CSJ, "The Development of Catholic Colleges for Women, 1895–1960," *U.S. Catholic Historian* 7 (1988): 414; Mary Hayes, SND de N, "The Founding of Trinity College, Washington, D.C.: A Case Study in Christian Feminism," *U.S. Catholic Historian* 10 (1991): 84.

2. Katharine O'Keeffe O'Mahoney, *Famous Irish Women* (Lawrence, Mass.: Lawrence Publishing Company, 1907), 127.

3. As Suellen Hoy observed in her history of Irish nuns, "Obscurity and invisibility, though not uncommon in the study of women's lives in general, are particularly troublesome when they are sought after and considered measures of success." Suellen Hoy, "The Journey Out: The Recruitment and Emigration of Irish Religious Women to the United States, 1812–1914," *Journal of Women's History* 6 (Winter 1995–96): 65.

4. Sister Julia (hereafter SJ) to the Sisters of Trinity, February 1901, "Founding Years," Trinity College Archives (hereafter TCA), Washington, D.C.

5. Carol Coburn and Martha Smith note that nuns' achievements and influence are routinely attributed to "Father" or "beloved Bishop." *Spirited Lives: How Nuns Shaped Catholic Culture and American Life* (Chapel Hill: University of North Carolina Press, 1999), 223.

6. Gerda Lerner, *The Majority Finds Its Past: Placing Women in History* (New York: Oxford University Press, 1979), 145–59.

7. Jay P. Dolan, *The American Catholic Experience: A History from Colonial Times to the Present* (Notre Dame, Ind.: University of Notre Dame Press, 1992), 309–11; Thomas McAvoy, *The Great Crisis in American Catholic History, 1895–1900* (Chicago: H. Regnery, 1957); Philip Gleason, "The New Americanism in Catholic Historiography," *U.S. Catholic Historian* 11 (Summer 1993): 4–5. All of the essays in this issue are devoted to the Americanist controversy.

8. Walter Nugent, "A Catholic Progressive? The Case of Judge E. O. Brown," *Journal of the Gilded Age and Progressive Era* 2, no. 1 (2003): 5.

9. Sister Mary Euphrasia (hereafter SME), "In the Midst of Things," *Notre Dame Quarterly* (2 September 1910), copy in TCA, Washington, D.C.

10. SJ to SME, September 2, 1897, copied into SME, "A Sketch of the Foundation of Trinity College for Catholic Women, Washington, D.C.," unpublished manuscript, 1897, TCA, Washington, D.C., I:236. This manuscript is recorded in two books. The first is numbered 1–259, and the second 1–133. Subsequent references will specify which book is being cited, I or II.

11. Trinity's first historian, Sister Mary Patricia Butler, SND, wrote that Garrigan and Thomas Conaty, the rector of Catholic University, "entered into the project with such zest and wisdom as wholly to change and exalt the nature of the enterprise. They pointed out clearly and with excellent reasoning that what was needed was not an academy but a college for women." Mary Patricia Butler, *An Historical Sketch of Trinity College, 1897–1925* (n.p.: Read Taylor, 1925), 10. Modern historical accounts also credit the rectors of Catholic University with convincing the sisters to set their sights on a higher goal. Philip Gleason, *Contending with Modernity: Catholic Higher Education in the Twentieth Century* (New York: Oxford University Press, 1995), 28, 89.

12. SME, "Sketch of the Foundation," I:1–3.

13. Annie Toler Hilliard, "An Investigation of Selected Events and Forces That Contributed to the Growth and Development of Trinity College, Washington, D.C., from 1897–1982" (Ph.D. diss., George Washington University, 1984), 62–64.

14. SME, "Sketch of the Foundation," I:3.

15. Ibid., 8, 10; Lucy M. Cohen, "Early Efforts to Admit Sisters and Lay Women to the Catholic University of America," in *An Introduction to Pioneering Women at the Catholic University of America*, ed. E. Catherine Dunn and Dorothy A. Mohler (Washington, D.C.: Catholic University Press, 1990); Gleason, *Contending with Modernity*, 28.

16. SME, "Sketch of the Foundation," I:8. Most Catholic colleges were single sex until the 1970s.

17. Sara M. Evans, *Born for Liberty: A History of Women in America* (New York: Free Press, 1989), 139.

18. It is not exactly clear how many Catholic women were attending secular schools at the time of Trinity's founding. Father John Farrell, the Catholic chaplain at Harvard, conducted a survey in 1907 and found that 1,557 Catholic women were attending secular colleges. Gleason, *Contending with Modernity*, 25.

19. Austin O'Malley, "College Work for Catholic Girls," *Catholic World* 68 (1898): 162.

20. For a discussion of the consensus in the Catholic community with regard to women's higher education, see Kathleen A. Mahoney, "American Catholic Colleges for Women: Historical Origins," in *Catholic Women's Colleges in America*, ed. Tracy Schier and Cynthia Russett (Baltimore: Johns Hopkins University Press, 2002), 28.

21. Gibbons to SJ, June 21, 1897, TCA, Washington, D.C.

22. Sister Columba Mullaly, SND, *Trinity College, Washington, D.C.: The First Eighty Years* (Westminster, Md.: Christian Classics, 1987), 26.

23. SME, "Sketch of the Foundation," I:63.

24. Mullaly, *Trinity College*, 30.

25. Archbishop John Ireland to SJ, July 16, 1897, TCA, Washington, D.C.

26. Ibid., 273–75.

27. Gleason, *Contending with Modernity*, 7–12.

28. Gerald P. Fogarty, S.J., *The Vatican and the American Hierarchy from 1870–1965* (Collegeville, Minn.: Liturgical Press, 1985), 158–59; Peter E. Hogan, SSJ, *The Catholic University of America, 1896–1903: The Rectorship of Thomas J. Conaty* (Washington, D.C.: Catholic University of America Press, 1949), 6.

29. Karen M. Kennelly, CSJ, "Ireland, Mother Seraphine [Ellen]," in *European Immigrant Women in the United States: A Biographical Dictionary*, ed. Judy Barrett Litoff and Judith McDonnell (New York: Garland, 1994), 149.

30. Gibbons to SJ, June 21, 1897, TCA, Washington, D.C.

31. Lelia Hardin Bugg, "Trinity College," *Rosary Magazine* (April 1901): 379.

32. Right Reverend J. L. Spalding, D.D., Bishop of Peoria, "Woman and the Higher

Education," in *Higher Education for Catholic Women: A Historical Anthology*, ed. Mary J. Oates, CSJ (New York: Garland, 1987), 25–47.

33. Rev. Edward Pace, Ph.D., "The College Woman," *Donahue's Magazine* 52 (1904): 287.

34. Mullaly, *Trinity College*, 27.

35. Nancy F. Cott, *The Grounding of Modern Feminism* (New Haven: Yale University Press, 1987), 39.

36. "Occupations for Women," *Donahue's Magazine* 39 (1898): 289; Kathleen Sprows Cummings, " 'Not the New Woman?' Irish American Women and the Creation of a Usable Past," *U.S. Catholic Historian* 19 (2001): 37–39.

37. J.N.E., "The 'New Woman' at the 'University,' " August 11, 1897, *Das Herold des Glaubens*, translation in "Founding Years," TCA, Washington, D.C. Evidence that Schroeder was behind this letter can be found in a letter from Sister Angela Elizabeth, SND, to Sister Sheila Doherty, June 2, 1972, TCA, Washington, D.C. "J.N.E." is most likely John N. Enzelberger, a German priest from Illinois and the editor of *Das Herold des Glaubens*.

38. SME to editors of *Das Herold des Glaubens*, August 28, 1897, copy in TCA, Washington, D.C.

39. Satolli to Gibbons, August 15, 1897, translation in Hogan, *Catholic University of America*, 97 (original in Italian in Baltimore Archdiocesan Archives).

40. Martinelli to Gibbons, August 23, 1897, quoted in Hogan, *Catholic University of America*, 97.

41. SME, "Sketch of the Foundation," I:195.

42. SJ to SME, September 2, 1897, in ibid., I:236.

43. See clippings file, TCA, Washington, D.C.

44. Mullaly, *Trinity College*, 36.

45. SME, "Sketch of the Foundation," I:209–16.

46. Ibid.

47. Sister Agnes Loretto to Sister Superior [Sister Mary Borgia], September 15, 1897, TCA, Washington, D.C.

48. SJ to Cardinal Ferrata, September 8, 1897, copy in TCA, Washington, D.C.

49. SJ to Cardinal Alois Mazzella, September 1897, copy in TCA, Washington, D.C.

50. SJ to Cardinal Rampolla, September 8, 1897, copy in TCA, Washington, D.C.

51. SME to Cardinal Satolli, August 26, 1897, copy in TCA, Washington, D.C.

52. SME to Satolli, August 26, 1897, copy in TCA, Washington, D.C.

53. SJ to Rampolla, September 8, 1897, copy in TCA, Washington, D.C.

54. This tactic was widely employed by Catholic women. See Cummings, "Not the New Woman?" passim.

55. Gibbons to Satolli, September 5, 1897, quoted in Hogan, *Catholic University of America*, 98.

56. M.C.M., "The Columbian Reading Union," *Catholic World* 65 (September 1897): 861–62.

57. Sister Agnes Loretto to Sister Superior, September 15, 1897.

58. Rampolla to Martinelli, November 13, 1897. Letter was received at the Apostolic Delegate on November 30. Translation quoted in Hogan, *Catholic University of America*, 98.

59. SME, "Sketch of the Foundation," II:17.

60. Ibid.

61. Sister Agnes Loretto to Sister Superior [Sister Mary Borgia], October 26, 1897.

62. Schroeder officially resigned on December 29, 1897. Gleason, *Contending with Modernity*, 10; Fogarty, *Vatican and the American Hierarchy*, 158–59.

63. SME, "Sketch of the Foundation," II:16. Letter dictated by Gibbons to SME.

64. Sister Angela Elizabeth Keenan, SND, *Three against the Wind: The Founding of Trinity College, Washington D.C.* (Westminster, Md.: Christian Classics, 1973), 112.

65. Joseph M. McShane, S.J., *"Sufficiently Radical": Catholicism, Progressivism and the Bishop's Program of 1919* (Washington, D.C.: Catholic University of America Press, 1986), 1–2.

66. Minutes of LAB [Ladies Auxiliary Board], April 3, 1899, TCA, Washington, D.C.; "A Summary of Questions Most Frequently Asked, 28 November 1899," pamphlet, "Founding Years," TCA, Washington, D.C.

67. Hasia R. Diner, *Erin's Daughters in America: Irish Immigrant Women in the Nineteenth Century* (Baltimore: Johns Hopkins University Press, 1983); Hoy, "The Journey Out," 64–98.

68. Keenan, *Three against the Wind*, 129. As it happened, the declaration of the Spanish-American War would delay the groundbreaking for over a year.

69. Sister Helen Louise, SND, *Sister Julia*, 281.

70. Hayes, "Founding of Trinity," 81; SJ to Dr. Garrigan, April 18, 1898, SJ correspondence, TCA, Washington, D.C.

71. SJ to Cardinal Ferrata, September 8, 1897, copy in TCA, Washington, D.C.

72. Mullaly, *Trinity College*, 40.

73. M.C.M., "Columbian Reading Union," *Catholic World* 65 (1897): 862.

74. Trinity College Prospectus, in "Founding Years," TCA, Washington, D.C.

75. SJ to SME, April 1897, copied into SME, "Sketch of the Foundation," I:63; Minutes of the Ladies Auxiliary Board (hereafter LAB), May 10, 1899, TCA, Washington, D.C.; Keenan, *Three against the Wind*, 124.

76. Bugg, "Trinity College," 377.

77. Mullaly, *Trinity College*, 266.

78. SJ to SME, n.d. (April), in SME, "Sketch of the Foundation," I:62.

79. Minutes of LAB, March 31, 1898, TCA, Washington, D.C.

80. Twenty-two students represented eighteen different states. Minutes of LAB, May 9, 1901, TCA, Washington, D.C.

81. Butler, *Historical Sketch*, 35; Bugg, "Trinity College."

82. M. McDevitt, "Trinity College and Higher Education," *Catholic World* (June 1904): 389.

83. Rev. Thomas Beaven, Archbishop of Springfield, to SJ, July 14, 1897, TCA, Washington, D.C. Excerpts of this were reprinted in a publicity pamphlet.

84. Garrigan to SME, in "Sketch of the Foundation," I:27.

85. SME to Cardinal Satolli, August 26, 1897, copy in TCA, Washington, D.C.

86. SJ to SME, August 11, 1897, in SME, "Sketch of the Foundation," I:187.

87. Sarah Willard Howe, "Trinity College," *Donahue's Magazine* 44 (1900): 323; Bugg, "Trinity College," 382.

88. Trinity College Catalogue, 1898, TCA, Washington, D.C.

89. Minutes of the Advisory Board, May 9, 1901, TCA, Washington, D.C.; Mullaly, *Trinity College*, 314.

90. Sister Julia was one of a host of Irish-born founders of Catholic women's colleges. Mother Seraphine of the Sisters of St. Joseph of Carondolet (formerly Ellen Ireland), who was born in Kilkenny in 1842, founded the College of St. Catherine in St. Paul. Mother Irene Gill of the Ursulines, born in Galway in 1860, founded the College of Saint Angela in New Rochelle, New York (later called College of New Rochelle). Mother Marie Joseph Butler of the Sisters of the Sacred Heart of Mary, born in Kilkenny in 1860, founded Marymount College in New York City in 1918.

91. Butler, *Historical Sketch*, 22. Irish surnames predominated on later class rosters as well. "Degrees Conferred, 1904–1925," Trinity College Catalogue, TCA, Washington, D.C.

92. Sister Agnes Loretto to Sister Superior, September 15, 1897, TCA, Washington, D.C.

93. Trinity College Catalogue, 1898, TCA, Washington, D.C. For a discussion of female scholars of the Middle Ages, see Mahoney, "Historical Origins," 28–36.

94. SME to SJ, May 25, 1897, in SME, "Sketch of the Foundation," I:135–36.

95. Katherine E. Conway, *New Footsteps in Well-Trodden Ways* (Boston: Pilot Publishing Company, 1899), 210.

96. See Cummings, "Not the New Woman?"

97. Bugg, "Trinity College," 388.

98. Mary T. Waggaman, "Catholic Life in Washington," *Catholic World* 66 (March 1898): 837–38.

99. O'Mahoney, *Famous Irish Women*, 123–24.

9

Faith, Feminism, and History

Ann Braude

Ann Braude has been at the forefront of efforts to create new, more inclusive histories of American religion—histories that recognize, in her words, "female presence." In this chapter, she urges scholars to reconsider how assumptions of incompatibility between faith and feminism have distorted historical narratives. In contrast to those who have portrayed the women's movement of the late 1960s and 1970s and institutional religion as antithetical, she argues that feminism took place within churches and synagogues as well as against them. Besides offering a new interpretation of the feminist movement, she shares her personal reflections on the intellectual difficulties—and rewards—of narrating women's presence in American religion.

When I left the University of Chicago in 1978 after receiving my master's degree, the scholarly literature on the religious history of American women fit between two bookends on my desk. When I returned twenty-five years later in the fall of 2004 for the first national conference on the topic (the conference that gave rise to this book), that literature had grown to exceed the grasp of any individual.

There is no question that we have come a long way as a field in those twenty-five years. During my first year of graduate school (1977), two texts appeared that opened up a world: Nancy Cott's *The Bonds of Womanhood* and Ann Douglas's *The Feminization of American Culture*. These works set terms of discussion that we still learn from, struggle with, and critique. They joined articles by Carroll Smith-Rosenberg and Barbara Welter, as well as Kathyrn Kish Sklar's biography of Catherine Beecher, in demarcating powerful connections between religion and gender in American culture.[1]

The number of exciting forthcoming titles and works-in-progress by young scholars included in this volume testifies to the proliferation of serious explorations of multiplying questions. Yet as rich as the resources and as talented as the workers, formidable challenges still confront efforts to bring our work to bear on larger questions of American history. All historians ground their work in larger narratives. How do we ensure that women's history and the study of gender not only utilize, but also influence, syntheses of American religious history? How do we use what we have accomplished to shift the terms, the periodization, and the interpretation of American religious history, so that women are not only included but are also instrumental to the stories we tell? How do we implant women's presence in the architecture of history, rather than in the finishes that ornament narrative facades?

These questions provoked my essay "Women's History *Is* American Religious History." That essay called on scholars to take as their point of departure the fact that women constitute the majority of participants in all sizable religious groups throughout American history. In order to refocus attention on female majorities, my essay drew into question three interpretive motifs— declension, feminization, and secularization—all of which, I argued, misdirect the focus of American religious history toward the absence of men, away from its most consistent feature, the presence of women.[2]

In this chapter, I will briefly introduce my current research on religion and modern feminism and then view it through the lens of "Women's History *Is* American Religious History." The advice I dispensed in that essay is not always easy to live by. To encourage other women's historians to assist in the reformulation of larger narratives, I want to offer some suggestions from my own research about how this process might take place.

My current project concerns religion's interaction with second-wave feminism. This movement, whose beginnings are often dated to the publication of *The Feminine Mystique* in 1963, is called "second wave" in order to relate it to and distinguish it from the nineteenth-century movement that culminated with the passage of women's suffrage in 1920. The end of second-wave feminism has been frequently reported over the last two decades, and a third wave was announced in the 1990s; but in fact no clear terminus to the second has yet appeared. The evidence from the world of religion suggests that, although the second wave has subsided in some settings, it continues to appear with new vibrancy in others, and that its appearance often, but not always, leads to permanent change.[3]

For many years after writing my first book, *Radical Spirits*, which focused on the overlap between religion and the first wave of women's rights activism in the nineteenth century, I shied away from studying advocates for women. I was concerned that they were overrepresented in historical treatments, in contrast to the many women for whom faith intertwined with a religious focus on the family and with the embrace of distinctive, if sometimes problematic, gender roles. While I shared with many colleagues the desire to recover a usable past, I did not want to run the risk of turning history into a search for individuals who share the values of the present. When I wrote a brief survey, *Women and American Religion*, I started with pious matrons Margaret Winthrop and Anne Bradstreet, not with Anne Hutchinson or the Salem witchcraft trials.[4]

I was eventually convinced to return to the study of religion and women's rights not because of its historical importance, although it is very important, but because I became convinced that the assumption of an inherent conflict between faith and feminism, an intellectual claim dating at least back to the French Revolution, had become erroneously embedded in narratives of U.S. history. Although historians of seventeenth-, eighteenth-, and nineteenth-century women acknowledge the instrumental role and cultural richness of women's piety, this is rarely the case in twentieth-century history, as Margaret Lamberts Bendroth and Virginia Brereton noted in their project on twentieth-century Protestantism.[5] Massive efforts of women across denominations to equalize women's access to ritual, language, and leadership, and, in many cases, to make their religious communities forces for women's equality in the wider world, are conspicuously absent. The writing of women's history itself seemed to incorporate assumptions about the incompatibility of religious outlooks with the movement that gave it birth as a field of study—the movement for women's liberation. I suspect that polarized perspectives emerging in the 1980s, often labeled the "culture wars," distorted the history of this period in ways that have serious consequences not only for historians but also for religious communities and for society at large. And so I decided to focus directly on the relation of religion to the feminist movement.

Let us consider an image that could be interpreted as reinforcing the stereotype I hope to depose. This photo depicts an event that occurred at Catholic University in Washington, D.C., in 1971. On the right in the photograph, the radical feminist, Ti-Grace Atkinson, deflects a slap from the conservative Catholic, Patricia Buckley Bozell, sister of columnist William F. Buckley Jr. and Senator James Buckley. Addressing a capacity audience of Catholic students and educators, Atkinson had described the Virgin Mary as being "knocked up" with an involuntary pregnancy. At that point, Bozell, seated in the press box, rushed the podium and raised her hand to Atkinson. Far from downplaying her apparent incivility, Bozell trumpeted it on the cover of *Triumph*, the conservative Catholic periodical she edited with her husband, along with an excerpt from the article inside explaining her action: "Miss Atkinson was, in my presence, defaming the Mother of God and God himself in the vilest possible manner; and I am a Catholic. I have been brought up to believe that intolerance of blasphemy is a Christian duty."[6]

Cover of *Triumph* magazine, April 1971.
(Courtesy of Widener Library, Harvard University)

This photograph, which also appeared in the *Washington Post* and the *New York Times*, encapsulates a common interpretation of American history, in which religion and feminism are seen as inherently antithetical, as opposing forces in American culture. On this one point, Atkinson and Bozell were in complete agreement. "The struggle between the liberation of women and the Catholic Church is a struggle to the death," Atkinson told the audience.[7]

On one hand, some feminists depict religious women as apologists for patriarchy whose allegiance to religious communities conflicts with authentic advocacy on women's behalf. On the other, social conservatives often portray feminism as an agent of secularism or as destructive of religious values. They assume that those who work to enhance women's status lack authentic faith. Ti-Grace Atkinson and Patricia Buckley Bozell justified the worst fears of both camps. Bozell held up intolerance as a religious virtue justifying violence; Atkinson called for the destruction of marriage, motherhood, and religion.[8]

But a second glance at the celebrated slap muddies the view of religion and feminism as a binary opposition. Comparable numbers of Catholics applauded Atkinson's speech and protested it at the nearby Shrine of the Immaculate Conception. Catholic students sought Atkinson out and invited her to address them. When the university president barred her from campus, the students went to court, successfully defending their right to hear her. Perhaps because of her Catholic upbringing and outspoken criticism of the Catholic Church, Atkinson was a popular speaker at Catholic institutions. "It is the greatest honor of my life to be here tonight," she wrote in her speech at Catholic University, before indicting the church for murder, political conspiracy, enslavement, prostitution, incitement to rape, and obscenity for its treatment of women.[9]

Several priests on the faculty of Catholic University were outspoken advocates for women's rights, such as Father Charles Curran, who had been threatened with dismissal for challenging the prohibition on birth control in the papal encyclical *Humanae Vitae*. The founder and chair of the sociology department, Monsignor Paul Hanly Furfey, was another ardent advocate who, like Ti-Grace Atkinson, was an early member of the board of directors of the National Organization for Women (NOW). "It seems to me to be every Christian's sacred duty to join NOW," wrote Monsignor Furfey.[10] On second glance, the controversy at Catholic University suggests a debate *within* a religious community more than a conflict between religious and secular forces.

Furfey's understanding of feminism as a Christian duty points toward another set of narratives in which religious values are seen as promoting the full humanity and equal rights of women. This approach also represents a strong tradition in historical writing, particularly regarding nineteenth-century movements for temperance and Christian missions. These movements naturally lend themselves to such interpretations because they served as springboards for women to both denominational and political leadership, and because a view of Christianity as liberating to women served as a foundational rationale for their work. Although Christian women's groups continued to be motivated by this view in the twentieth century and similar patterns appear in Jewish organizations, among historians this perspective on the twentieth century has generally been limited to denominational histories, although important new studies are beginning to appear.

My larger project seeks to historicize *both* the presumed antagonism of religion and feminism *and* their presumed sympathy. In this chapter, I will emphasize the first, which dominates the historiography of the twentieth century. Narratives of opposition are reflected in the relative absence of religion from the growing body of literature chronicling second-wave feminism. Religion tends to be absent, that is, except when it is a roadblock to women's rights. There the Catholic Church is often included as an opponent of legal abortion or of the Equal Rights Amendment to the U.S. Constitution. During the last decade, although scholars have emphasized the plurality of feminisms and the importance of difference as a category, references to distinctive religious feminisms in the United States have diminished, even as they have increased with regard to international feminisms.[11]

The women who transformed American religion, particularly in the 1960s and 1970s—who led campaigns for women's equality within religious settings, for changes in language and liturgy, in polity and practice—understood their efforts as part of the larger social movement of second-wave feminism. Their efforts confound the categories used to portray religion and feminism in opposition.

An early photograph of the founders of the National Organization for Women begins to tell the story. Taken at the first national meeting in 1966, it shows a nun in full habit standing next to United Methodist Anna Arnold Hedgeman, an African American lay leader who was coordinator of the Commission on Religion and Race of the National Council of Churches, with both standing next to Betty Friedan.

Before saying more about each of these figures, a few observations are in order. First, NOW provides a useful point of departure for this discussion because it epitomizes the secularism of the women's movement both for religious conservatives and for feminist historians. This photograph both reinforces and contradicts common assumptions from both camps about

Founders of the National Organization for Women at the first national meeting in 1966.
Left to right: Dorothy Haener, Sister Joel Read, Anna Arnold Hedgeman,
Betty Friedan, Inez Casiano, Richard Graham, and Inka O'Hanrahan.
(Courtesy of Schlesinger Library, Harvard University)

NOW. Bourgeois trappings abound—pumps, pearls, and professional titles adorn the subjects of the photograph. But the group also displays more diversity than is commonly attributed to the organization, including a man (Richard Graham), a nun (Sister Joel Read), an African American church-woman (Anna Arnold Hedgeman), and two labor leaders, one of them Hispanic (Dorothy Haener and Inez Casiano). (The other figure is probably Inka O'Hanrahan.)

It should also be observed at the outset that in addition to including religious women among its founders, NOW from its earliest years included religion as an arena of feminist activism, sponsoring an ecumenical task force, the Women and Religion Task Force. The task force organized worship services, mobilized an informational picket when the General Convention of the Episcopal Church voted on the ordination of women, circulated petitions sponsored by the Adrian Dominican Congregation for the ordination of Catholic women, and campaigned for new editions of the Bible to provide translations accurately expressing women's roles, as well as supporting women's rights in a variety of religious contexts—a strange agenda indeed for an agent of secularization. Approval of the task force's actions at national conferences of NOW meant that the organization was on record as viewing equality within one's faith as one of the rights women needed in order to achieve equality within American society.

The agenda of NOW's Women and Religion Task Force reflected concerns of church members active in the organization. By 1969 the language of women's liberation could be heard at the national meetings of most liberal Protestant denominations. The United Presbyterian Church in the U.S.A. and the American Baptist Convention each passed sweeping resolutions calling for the churches to work toward equality for women both within their own structures and in every aspect of social and economic life. A study authorized by the 1968 conference of the United Methodist Church led to formation of a General Commission charged with addressing discrimination against women at all levels of the denomination. Feminist foment led to decisions by the Lutheran Church in America and the American Lutheran Church to ordain women in 1970. Church Women United, the women's branch of the National Council of Churches, endorsed both the Equal Rights Amendment and the legalization of abortion in the same year. A group of Episcopal women deemed their church "racist, militarist, and sexist" and called for it "to remedy the historical discrimination against women and its destructive effects in the Christian community" by ordaining women and by enforcing Title VII of the Civil Rights Act of 1964 with regard to employment in the church.[12] Martin Marty, one of the most trusted observers of American Protestantism, wrote in 1973, "The liberation of women may be a more hopeful sign of Christian renewal than are the statistics of religious awakenings."[13]

One could cite many more examples of the presence of women's liberation within religious settings, but we return now to the photograph of the founders of NOW, in order to approach this story through the individual women depicted there. Let us focus on three figures standing next to each other at the center of the photograph: one a Protestant, one a Catholic, and one a Jew.

First, consider the most overtly religious figure in the photograph—the nun in full habit. While Betty Friedan is a well-known figure whose name—if not face—most of us would recognize, this figure is most identifiable by the floor-length robe meant to obscure her individuality in a year in which the knee-length skirt was (judging by the other figures pictured) de rigueur. She is not technically in full habit. The loose collar and the little bit of hair she shows indicate that her habit has already been modified as a result of the reforms of Vatican II. Sister Joel Read, a School Sister of St. Francis who taught history at the congregation's Alverno College in Milwaukee, Wisconsin, was one of two members of her order to join in the founding of NOW—the other was Sister Austin Doherty.

In her own memories of the founding of NOW, Betty Friedan frequently foregrounds Roman Catholic religious, whose presence in their habits juxtaposed a visual icon of female subservience with the possibility of change represented by the new organization. "They were liberated nuns," she recalled, "who were personally moving more and more out of wearing their habits, but I used to insist they wear them when we visited members of Congress or had our pictures taken and they agreed for the cause."[14] This view contrasts with the memory of Sister Austin Doherty that the habits she and Read wore afforded them a level of protection from risks undertaken by the founders of NOW.[15]

According to Friedan, Sister Joel Read had more than a symbolic role in the birth of NOW. At the first meeting, competing priorities and personalities threatened the fledgling effort. "A young Catholic nun," Friedan recalled, was "particularly eloquent and commonsensible, breaking through the quibbling over details that could have kept the organization from getting born." Interestingly, Joel Read recalls no such role and does not even recall speaking during the meeting. Perhaps the lessons of life in a religious community in which the individual's needs are secondary to those of the group were so obvious to her that she did not find such contributions memorable. Read recalled that her role was mainly symbolic, that she attracted Friedan's attention primarily because of her habit. But in Friedan's memory, the role of women religious loomed large. They commanded Friedan's respect for the distance they traveled from vows of obedience to feminist consciousness. Joel Read, Friedan recalled, "like so many of the militant nuns who have been at the heart of our movement while they were liberating themselves from the cloister, abandoned [the] habit, [and] revolutionized the order and the college she now heads."[16]

Joel Read represents a group that rarely appears in histories of feminism or in larger narratives of religion and politics in this period (a lacuna addressed elsewhere in this book). Catholic women's religious orders were perfectly positioned to provide participants in the developing movement for women's liberation. Reaching their peak of membership at 180,000 in the year this photo was taken, they had raised sisters' educational levels significantly as a result of the Sister Formation Movement during the 1950s. When women's liberation hit the scene, women's religious orders constituted a formidable community of educated, employed women who had just been encouraged by Vatican II to leave their convents and engage the social issues of the day. Profoundly affected by their involvement with the civil rights movement, the peace movement, and movements for liberation in Latin America and elsewhere, they were also intimately familiar with patriarchal authority in its most overt form. When they applied concerns for justice to themselves and to other women, many found feminism. Committed to habits of daily prayer and reflection and to biblical mandates to work to end oppression, the conversion of Roman Catholic sisters to feminism brought a disciplined and energetic cadre to the movement.

Standing next to Sister Joel Read is the African American civil rights activist Anna Arnold Hedgeman. Hedgeman was a distinguished Methodist churchwoman, best known for having recruited 30,000 white clergy to join the 1963 civil rights march on Washington. A veteran of the professional ranks of the YWCA, she had broad experience with ecumenical and interracial endeavors, as well as with race-based institutions. At the time she served on NOW's founding board, she was employed by the National Council of Churches' Commission on Religion and Race.[17]

Hedgeman represents two important groups that are just beginning to appear in accounts of modern feminism: ecumenical women's organizations and Protestant liberals. Both embodied continuity with the optimistic social gospel of the Progressive era, and both represented huge memberships. Women's organizations institutionalized ongoing work toward egalitarian ideals in YWCA programs and in both domestic and foreign missions. Those institutions bridged generations of activists.

According to Dorothy Haener (who stands to the left of Joel Read), when the founders of NOW lined up for this photo, Pauli Murray stepped back and pushed Anna Hedgeman forward. This story sounds plausible because Murray would have been an obvious choice for the historic photograph. She was one of the first to propose the idea of a national women's rights organization, and she sat with Friedan while Friedan scribbled the "Statement of Purpose" adopted at NOW's first meeting on a paper napkin. However, she chose not to serve on the founding board because she feared a conflict of interest between her role in the new women's rights advocacy organization and her work as a consultant for the federal government's Equal Employment Opportunity Commission. She might well have opted out of the photo for the same reason, but no such concern precludes our attention to her as one of the founders of NOW.[18]

Already the veteran of a distinguished career in law and public affairs, Pauli Murray was a professor at Brandeis University when she joined in the founding of NOW. A lifelong Episcopalian, Murray traced her roots in the church back six generations in her 1956 book, *Proud Shoes*, which documented the baptism of her enslaved grandmother in the church patronized by her slave-holding great-grandfather. Her feminist consciousness emerged in the context of black organizations that she felt ignored women's issues and of a church that excluded women from ordination. In 1966 she experienced a crisis while witnessing the exclusively male clergy consecrate the host during a Eucharistic service at St. Mark's in New York City. "An uncontrollable anger exploded inside me, filling me with such rage I had to get up and leave." Murray called sexism "a stumbling block to faith" but never wavered in her loyalty to the Episcopal Church. Three months after she walked out of St. Marks, she helped found NOW.[19]

Continually angered by her church's refusal to recognize the principle of human equality that she viewed as central to the teachings of Jesus, Murray nevertheless made an astounding decision in 1973. She resigned her tenured chair at Brandeis to become a full-time student at General Theological Seminary. "I have felt increasingly inadequate as both a lawyer and a teacher in addressing myself to these social issues. The missing element in my training and experience is theological," she wrote, explaining her decision.[20] At the age of sixty-two, this prominent woman attorney and senior faculty member sat in classrooms composed almost exclusively of young white men to study amid the all-male hierarchy of the Episcopal Church of which she had been so critical. This gave her a front-row seat to the coming struggles over the ordination of women that nearly destroyed her church in the mid-1970s. She attended the noncanonical ordination of the "Philadelphia eleven" in 1974 but was not herself ordained until the denomination finally voted to ordain women in 1977. Then, at sixty-six, she became the first African American woman to be ordained as an Episcopal priest. She spent the remaining nine years of her life serving small Episcopal parishes.

Most of the African American women who served on NOW's early boards of directors also played leadership roles in their Protestant denominations.[21] As a group, this distinguishes them from other board members and suggests that narratives of opposition between religion and feminism have the effect of excluding women of color. Continuity between the religious content of the nineteenth-century black women's club movement and groups that contributed to the second wave is evident in the overlapping on the boards of directors of the National Council of Negro Women, the YWCA, and other denominational, ecumenical, and civil rights organizations. Historian Susan Hartmann argues that African American women played a larger share in the leadership of feminist initiatives associated with the National Council of

Churches than in secular feminist organizations (including NOW), and that, as a result, racial issues were more central to the agendas of these groups. Pauli Murray, in fact, linked these two issues. Complaining that both African American and religious women played diminishing roles in NOW, she withdrew from active involvement in order to focus her feminist activism within the Episcopal Church.[22]

We turn now to Betty Friedan, the central figure in the photograph of the founders of NOW, who may initially seem to have little to do with religious history. But her book *The Feminine Mystique* and her role as the first president of NOW unquestionably make her a pivotal figure in modern women's history.

Friedan received a Jewish education but rejected belief in God while preparing for confirmation at the reform synagogue in Peoria, Illinois. Deeply scarred by the social ostracism her family experienced in Peoria, she attributed her passion for justice to her "feelings of the injustice of anti-Semitism."[23] Yet religious groups did play a role in the reception of her book, a role that may be obscured by presuppositions.

Religious groups were the largest and best-organized women's groups in the country when *The Feminine Mystique* was published in 1963. Friedan's lecture tours following publication included Protestant, Catholic, and Jewish audiences. For example, consider an advertisement for Friedan's appearance at the sisterhood luncheon at Temple Emanu-El, a Reform synagogue in Dallas, Texas. "What kind of woman are you? Betty Friedan will help you decide," the invitation reads, listing as one set of options qualities resembling those of the stereotyped Jewish mother: "Frantic cook? Chauffeur? Smothered Mother? Too involved? Restless?" On the other side was a different set of ideals: "Interesting? Informed? Responsible Parent? Motivated? Satisfied?" Friedan's book sold three million copies between 1963 and 1970, but the top-grossing nonfiction title in 1965 was Dan Greenburg's humor book, *How to Be a Jewish Mother*. There, according to anthropologist Riv-Ellen Prell, Greenburg articulated a cultural image in which Jewish men turned internalized anti-Semitism outward onto their wives and mothers, depicting them as avaricious and acquisitive, as backward and embarrassing, as they used excesses of food and criticism to infantilize their sons, impeding efforts at assimilation, success, adulthood, and happiness.[24] This document suggests that members of the Temple Emanu-El sisterhood had specifically Jewish reasons for interest in Friedan's book.

The Feminine Mystique was required reading for the 175 national leaders of Methodist women at their 1963 annual meeting, entitled "Women in a New Age." Returning to their home communities, those 175 brought the fruit of

WHAT KIND OF WOMAN ARE YOU?

FRANTIC COOK?

Chauffeur?

Smothered Mother?

TOO INVOLVED?

Restless?

Interesting?

Informed?

Responsible Parent?

Motivated?

Satisfied?

BETTY FRIEDAN
author, "THE FEMININE MYSTIQUE"

Betty Friedan will help you decide when she speaks on

"A NEW IMAGE OF WOMAN"

Attend Temple Emanu-El Sisterhood

DONOR LUNCHEON

Tuesday, October 29, 1963

Sherry - 11:30 a.m.   Luncheon - 12:15 p.m.

Advertisement for Betty Friedan's visit to Temple Emanu-El in Dallas, Texas, on October 29, 1963. (Courtesy of Schlesinger Library, Harvard University) their reading and discussion back to the 1.2 million members of United Methodist Women. In contrast, it would be three years before Friedan and others would found NOW to advance the concerns raised in her book. NOW's membership climbed steadily from the 300 it started with in 1966 but would never match that of United Methodist Women.

Many religious women applied *The Feminine Mystique* directly to their experiences within their denominations. "I could hardly believe what I was reading because it reflected so much of my own experience," recalled Lois Wilson. After a young woman in her church group gave her a copy of the book in 1965, Wilson went on to seek ordination and become the first female moderator of the United Church of Canada, as well as a president of the World Council of Churches. According to Betty Bone Schiess, one of the "Philadelphia eleven" ordained in an irregular ceremony before the Episcopal Church finally approved the ordination of women, "It was Betty Friedan and the National Organization for Women which changed the Episcopal Church." She credited Friedan's book, and the founding of a local NOW chapter after Friedan lectured in Syracuse, with inspiring her pursuit of the priesthood and her efforts to seek change in the Episcopal Church.[25]

As these brief examples illustrate, narratives portraying religion and feminism as opposing forces represent a misreading of America's past. But the question remains: how might the removal of this assumption lead to rethinking narratives of American religious history?

The foregoing discussion suggests the theme of continuity, a narrative theme that implicitly departs from secularization as an organizing principle. I noted this specifically with regard to African American women's organizations, a point emphasized in Judith Weisenfeld's study of the Harlem YWCA.[26] But it can be usefully applied to religious women in general—not to say that they are static or ahistorical in any way, but only to note that attention may be drawn more easily to those who participate in new trends, so that the salience of continuing belief systems is ignored. As anthropologist Mary Douglas has observed, social change is easy to explain in comparison to the complex mechanisms necessary to reproduce cultural values and practices. Women are often seen as cultural conservatives, perpetuating hallowed traditions on behalf of entire communities. This means that even while participating in a new trend like feminism, not all will do so in the same way as the most vocal or visible spokeswomen.

There is no question that the women's liberation movement, along with other movements of the 1960s and 1970s, had the feeling of a revolution, of a moment when old verities crumbled before irresistible forces of truth and justice. From the vantage point of the twenty-first century, it appears that

that experience, which shaped the perspectives of the founders of women's history, may have prevented attention to currents flowing from earlier periods. We are all inevitably influenced by our own moment in time. But it is clear that the founding generation of women's historians was deeply shaped by the feminist movement itself. Sara Evans, in a pivotal work that takes steps toward including religious women in the history of the women's movement, gives voice to this perspective in the name of her book, *Tidal Wave*, evoking a monumental force sweeping away everything in its path. While it is difficult to disagree with the title's implication that the second wave of women's rights created sweeping permanent changes in America's landscape, it is worth pondering its significance for the majority of Americans who considered themselves to be church members, and who therefore experienced those changes in the context of communities whose survival depended on continuity with ancient beliefs and practices.[27]

But the changes of the 1960s should not be understood exclusively *as a contrast to* the continuities of religious groups. Looking backward from the sixties, a narrative of continuity calls our attention to earlier actors combining the terms of the false binary of religion and feminism. When historian Susan Lynn looked for groups that bridged the social movements of the 1960s with pre–World War II progressive reform, she, not surprisingly, found Christian organizations, the YWCA and the American Friends Service Committee, at the center of a loose coalition of activist groups including the National Council of Jewish Women and the National Council of Negro Women. Her book, *Progressive Women in Conservative Times*, chronicles the two post–World War II decades but focuses on organizations formed well before that, dating, in most cases, to the late nineteenth century. In *Gender and the Social Gospel*, Wendy Edwards and Carolyn Gifford place these groups in a longer historical trajectory, arguing that a focus on women's presence expands the scope, chronology, and geographic reach of the social gospel. The essays in their volume push the social gospel backward into the women's temperance movement, forward into the work of Faye Wattleton and Marian Wright Edelman, and southward into states where, as John McDowell has shown, women's organizations addressed poverty and racism when other groups did not.[28]

Extending a trajectory of continuity combining religion and women's rights even further backward lands us in the women's missionary movement, a movement ably chronicled in Dana Robert's book, *American Women in Mission: A Social History of Their Thought and Practice*. This book offers a model for the project of reimagining the large arcs of religious history from women's point of view for several reasons. First, it covers a 200-year period,

1792 to 1992, making it possible to observe major transitions as well as continuities. Second, it treats a broad swath of Christian women, from Protestant liberals to Pentecostal faith missions, as well as Roman Catholic sisters, enabling Robert to distinguish gender as a variable from denominational or local differences.

Given these features, Robert's approach to the fundamentalist-modernist controversy is especially salient. Noting that the demise of powerful women's mission boards in the 1920s coincided with the fracturing of American Protestantism over the issue of modernism, she concurs with Betty DeBerg and Margaret Bendroth that anxieties about women's emerging claims to self-determination lay at the heart of the fundamentalist agenda. Fundamentalists criticized women's missions for their focus on education, health, and social conditions and argued that women missionaries themselves opposed the Word of God by usurping male roles and authority. However, Robert *also* sees the modernist position as problematic for the deeply biblical theology of women's missions. Here she disagrees, for example, with Patricia Hill, who attributes the demise of the women's missionary movement solely to the modernist impulse toward professionalization. "The fundamentalist modernist controversy," Robert writes, "struck at the very heart of the women's missionary movement by pitting the Bible against the ministry of women," a development that would reverberate throughout the culture wars of the 1980s and into the twenty-first century. In her account, the women's missionary movement, under the leadership of Helen Barrett Montgomery, articulated a third alternative, affirming both the liberal focus on the Kingdom of God and the conservative concern for the urgency of spreading "the good news" to every land. Montgomery attempted to hold the middle ground by producing a new translation of the Bible, the first English edition that translates Phoebe's role as "minister" rather than as "deaconess."[29]

Montgomery's story could be one pivot point for a narrative of U.S. religious history that is based on women's presence and that refuses to see women's piety at odds with their assertions of their rights to act on their piety. A friend and coworker of Susan B. Anthony, Montgomery was elected president of the Northern Baptist Convention in 1922. Propelled to the pinnacle of lay leadership by the extraordinary success of the gender-based women's missionary movement, she was greeted with an ovation by the 5,000 Baptists in attendance. She then took the podium to preside at the very convention at which fundamentalists and liberals battled for control of the denomination. Devoting her presidential address to a plea for tolerance and unity and against doctrinal tests, she apparently aligned herself with the liberals. But she framed her plea in decidedly unmodern terms, recalling the faith of the women that built her movement: "Satan is here," she told the convention. "He longs to divide us. . . . Nothing but prayer can defeat him."[30]

While William Bell Riley agitated unsuccessfully to purge Baptist colleges of modernist thought and to impose a doctrinal test on the denomination, the convention adopted a key plank endorsed by a coalition of religious and secular women's groups following World War I: a resolution calling for the abolition of war as a means of settling international disputes and for the formation of a league of nations "outlawing any nation that resorts to arms to further its own interests."

This moment serves as an effective narrative pivot because it includes in one snapshot so many strands of theological debate, gender politics, and religious culture, all pulling in different directions at the same time. Rather than more univocal markers, the event describes a messy historical intersection. For while Helen Barrett Montgomery's liberal allies carried the day at the Northern Baptist Convention, the women's missionary movement that brought her there was in trouble, weakened both by attacks on women's ministry by fundamentalists and by liberal concepts of efficiency and professionalization.[31]

The process of dismantling powerful missionary organizations that had functioned as the women's arm of many denominations for fifty years was well under way. Women leaders would spend decades regrouping, usually resulting in multipurpose women's organizations for which missions were one of several agendas. And those organizations, in turn, would repeatedly face the kind of reorganizations that diminished women's leadership and autonomy by subsuming them into "general" organizations. In the 1960s, reorganization became a spur to feminist activism. This is a continuing narrative that merits a full treatment—beginning with Rufus Anderson's refusal to permit a nondenominational women's mission board in 1830 and extending to current challenges to United Methodist Women, Church Women United, and, perhaps most dramatically, the Southern Baptist Women's Missionary Union.[32]

As early as 1961, before the rise of the field of women's history, Gladys Gilkey Calkins offered an insightful analysis of women's relationship to the large themes of American religious history. In *Follow Those Women*, she chronicled one hundred years of women's work in the ecumenical movement, ending in 1961:

> The fact that in churches as a whole there was little interest in the Social Gospel in the nineteen-twenties did not particularly affect women's con-

cerns about these questions. Their approach to social issues was essentially pragmatic and not doctrinaire. Women were concerned about the welfare and needs of individuals; while this had made them sympathetic to the preaching of the Social Gospel, it had not made them dependent upon it. . . . The battle of Fundamentalism versus Liberalism might rage in the pulpits, and the Scopes Trial make headlines in the newspapers, but these would not throw the women off course. There was too much that needed to be done.[33]

Calkins's insider perspective presenting women as "sympathetic to but not dependent on" the preaching of prominent theologians provides a superb provocation for the project of grounding religious history in women's presence. Indeed, it offers us a model—a model of sympathy for, but independence from, categories derived from the history of the male minority. Her claim that the concerns of organizations constituted of the most active church members are distinct from those of "the church as a whole" speaks eloquently to recent methodological suggestions about the study of "lived religion"—and to the idea that the meaning of a faith resides with those who enact it as much as with those who preach it. It also reminds us that the subplot of power discrepancies must always accompany a focus on women's presence.

The narratives of American religious history presented by both Dana Robert and Gladys Gilkey Calkins, and reinforced by the presence of religion in NOW, suggest that in many cases it is sexism, not feminism, that can be associated with secularization. History shows that women's presence is central to the story of American religion. Where women's presence is discouraged, so is religious faith.

Notes

I am grateful to Catherine Brekus for inspiring this chapter and to Tracy Wall for assistance with the photographs.

1. Nancy Cott, *The Bonds of Womanhood: "Woman's Sphere" in New England, 1780–1835* (New Haven: Yale University Press, 1977); Ann Douglas, *The Feminization of American Culture* (New York: Knopf, 1977). Pathbreaking essays were later collected in Barbara Welter, *Dimity Convictions: The American Woman in the 19th Century* (Athens: Ohio University Press, 1976); and Carroll Smith-Rosenberg, *Disorderly Conduct: Visions of Gender in Victorian America* (New York: Knopf, 1985). See also Kathryn Kish Sklar, *Catherine Beecher: A Study in American Domesticity* (New Haven: Yale University Press, 1973); Nancy F. Cott, *Root of Bitterness* (New Haven: Yale University Press, 1978); and Janet Wilson James, ed.,

Women in American Religion (Philadelphia: University of Pennsylvania Press, 1978).

2. Ann Braude, "Women's History *Is* American Religious History," in *Retelling U.S. Religious History*, ed. Thomas Tweed (Berkeley: University of California Press, 1996). Reprinted in David Hackett, ed., *Religion and American Culture: A Reader*, 2nd ed. (New York: Routledge, 2003). Since then, the premise that female majorities are normal, not deviant, has been affirmed by the statistical analysis of sociologist Rodney Stark, in "Physiology and Faith: Addressing the 'Universal' Gender Difference in Religious Commitment," *Journal of the Scientific Study of Religion* 31, no. 3 (September 2002): 495–507.

3. See, for example, Susan Bolotin, "Voices from the Post-Feminist Generation," *New York Times Magazine* (October 17, 1982): 28–31, 103, 106; and John McLaughlin's television magazine, "One on One," was titled "Is Feminism Dead?" on March 14, 1992. Also "Is Feminism Dead?" *Time* magazine, June 29, 1998. In 2004, Lisa Jervis questioned the continued utility of the wave metaphor, in "The End of Feminism's Third Wave," *MS* magazine (Winter 2004). Available at <http://www.msmagazine.com/winter2004/thirdwave.asp>.

4. Ann Braude, *Radical Spirits: Spiritualism and Women's Rights in Nineteenth-Century America* (1st ed., New York: Beacon Press, 1989; 2nd ed., Bloomington: Indiana University Press, 2001); Ann Braude, *Women and Religion in America* (New York: Oxford University Press, 2000).

5. Margaret Lamberts Bendroth and Virginia Lieson Brereton, eds., *Women and Twentieth-Century Protestantism* (Urbana: University of Illinois Press, 2002).

6. Ti-Grace Atkinson, *Amazon Odyssey* (New York: Links Books, 1974), 191–97; Patricia Buckley Bozell, "God and Woman at Catholic U," *Triumph* 6, no. 4 (April 1971): 22–23.

7. Accounts by Atkinson, Bozell, the *New York Times*, and the *Washington Post* are remarkably consistent, agreeing in virtually every detail. *Washington Post*, March 11, 1971, B1, and March 12, 1971, B1–2; *New York Times* (March 12, 1971). All printed the same photograph from the *Washington Post*.

8. Bozell's views pervade *Triumph*, of which she was the managing editor and a frequent contributor during the time her husband, Brent Bozell, was editor. See, for example, "The Sexual Dialectic" *Triumph* 6, no. 1 (January 1971): 36–37; "The Wages of Pluralism" *Triumph* 6, no. 3 (March 1971): 18–20; and "The Misogyny of It All" *Triumph* 8, no. 4 (April 1973): 17. For Atkinson's views, see, for example, "Movement Politics and Other Sleights of Hand," in Atkinson, *Amazon Odyssey*, 98.

9. Atkinson, *Amazon Odyssey*, 191–97.

10. Als Paul Hanly Furfey to Elizabeth Jane Farians, February 7, 1969. Elizabeth Farians, Papers of NOW officers, Schlesinger Library, Radcliffe Institute, Harvard University. Furfey was elected to the NOW board of directors in 1969. See *NOW Acts* 2, no. 1 (Winter/Spring 1969): 37.

11. The best account of religious feminism remains the work of journalists Judith

Hole and Ellen Levine, *Rebirth of Feminism* (New York: Quadrangle Books, 1971). See also Winifred Wandersee, *On the Move: American Women in the 1970s* (Boston: Twayne, 1988); and Blanche Linden-Ward and Carol Hurd Green, *American Women in the 1960s: Changing the Future* (New York: Twayne, 1993). For recent accounts excluding religion, see Ruth Rosen, *The World Split Open* (New York: Penguin, 2001); Susan Brownmiller, *In Our Time: Memoir of a Revolution* (New York: Dial Press, 1999); Rachel Blau DuPlessis and Ann Snitow, *The Feminist Memoir Project: Voices from Women's Liberation* (New York: Three Rivers Press, 1998); and Florence Howe, ed., *The Politics of Women's Studies: Testimony from Thirty Founding Mothers* (New York: Feminist Press, 2000). On international feminism, see Estelle Freedman, *No Turning Back* (New York: Ballantine Books, 2002).

12. Margaret Shannon, *Just Because: The Story of the National Movement of Church Women United* (Corte Madera, Calif.: Omega Books, 1977), 280–83; "Graymoor Resolution," in Sarah Bentley Doely, ed., *Women's Liberation and the Church* (New York: Association Press, 1970), 113–14.

13. Martin Marty, *The Fire We Can Light* (New York: Doubleday, 1973), 195.

14. Betty Friedan, *Life So Far* (New York: Simon and Schuster, 2000), 178. See also pp. 175, 181, 189, 201, 212, 219.

15. "Step by Step: Building a Feminist Movement," video recording produced by Joyce Follet, Wisconsin Public Television, 1998.

16. Betty Friedan, *It Changed My Life: Writings on the Women's Movement* (New York: Random House, 1976), 85. Telephone interview with Sister Joel Read, August 21, 2003.

17. Anna Arnold Hedgeman wrote two autobiographies: *The Trumpet Sounds* (New York: Holt, Rinehart and Winston, 1964); and *The Gift of Chaos* (New York: Oxford University Press, 1977). Nancy Marie Robertson provides a helpful summary in Susan Ware, ed., *Notable American Women: A Biographical Dictionary, Completing the Twentieth Century* (Cambridge: Harvard University Press, 2004), 285–86.

18. Pauli Murray, *Song in a Weary Throat: An American Pilgrimage* (New York: Harper and Row, 1987), 362, 365, 368.

19. Ibid., 370.

20. "Christmas Letter," 1973, Pauli Murray Papers, Schlesinger Library, Radcliffe Institute, Harvard University.

21. Pauli Murray, Anna Arnold Hedgeman, Coretta Scott King, and Eliza Paschall.

22. Susan Hartmann, "Expanding Feminism's Field and Focus: Activism in the National Council of Churches in the 1960s and 70s," in Bendroth and Brereton, *Women and Twentieth-Century Protestantism*, 152; Susan Hartmann, "Pauli Murray and the 'Juncture of Women's Liberation and Black Liberation,'" *Journal of Women's History* 14, no. 2 (2002): 76.

23. Susan Weidman Schneider, *Jewish and Female: Choices and Changes in Our Lives Today* (New York: Simon and Schuster, 1984), 504. On the relationship between

Friedan's feminism and her Judaism, see Joyce Antler, *The Journey Home: How Jewish Women Shaped Modern America* (New York: Schocken Books, 1997), 259–67; Betty Friedan, "Women and Jews: The Quest for Selfhood," *Congress Monthly* 52, no. 2 (February/March 1985); Betty Friedan, "Jewish Roots: An Interview with Betty Friedan," *Tikkun* 3, no. 1 (January/February 1988): 25–29; and Francine Klagsbrun, "Marching in Front," *Hadassah Magazine* 75 (November 1993).

24. Riv-Ellen Prell, *Fighting to Become American: Assimilation and the Trouble between Jewish Men and Women* (Boston: Beacon Press, 1999), 145–51.

25. Lois Miriam Wilson, *Transforming the Faiths of Our Fathers: Women Who Changed American Religion*, ed. Ann Braude (New York: Palgrave, 2003), 13–14; Betty Bone Schiess, *Why Me, Lord: The Story of One Woman's Ordination* (Syracuse, N.Y.: Syracuse University Press, 2003), 28.

26. Judith Weisenfeld, *African American Women and Christian Activism: New York's Black YWCA, 1905–45* (Cambridge: Harvard University Press, 1997).

27. The title is from a poem by Seamus Heaney, "The Cure at Troy": "History says, Don't hope / On this side of the grave. But then, once in a lifetime / The longed for tidal wave / Of justice can rise up, And hope and history rhyme." Evans's book, while it goes further than most treatments in including religious feminists, generally uses them as an indication of how widespread certain developments had become, not as instrumental in charting the course of the women's movement.

28. Wendy J. Deichman Edwards and Carolyn de Swarte Gifford, eds., *Gender and the Social Gospel* (Urbana: University of Illinois Press, 2003); Susan Lynn, *Progressive Women in Conservative Times: Racial Justice, Peace, and Feminism, 1945 to the 1960s* (New Brunswick, N.J.: Rutgers University Press, 1992); John Patrick McDowell, *The Social Gospel in the South: The Women's Home Mission Movement in the Methodist Episcopal Church, South, 1886–1939* (Baton Rouge: Louisiana State University Press, 1982).

29. Dana Lee Robert, *American Women in Mission: A Social History of Their Thought and Practice* (Macon, Ga.: Mercer University Press, 1996), 281; Helen Barrett Montgomery, *Centenary Translation of the New Testament* (Philadelphia: American Baptist Publishing Society, 1924).

30. *New York Times*, June 15, 1922, 26.

31. Patricia Ruth Hill, *The World Their Household: The American Woman's Foreign Mission Movement and Cultural Transformation, 1870–1920* (Ann Arbor: University of Michigan Press, 1984).

32. Leon Howell, *United Methodism at Risk: A Wake-Up Call* (Kingston, N.Y.: Information Project for United Methodists, 2003); Catherine B. Allen, "Shifting Sands for Southern Baptist Women in Missions," in *Gospel Bearers, Gender Barriers*, ed. Dana L. Robert (New York: Orbis Books, 2002), 113–26.

33. Gladys Gilkey Calkins, *Follow Those Women: Church Women in the Ecumenical Movement* (New York: Published for United Church Women, National Council of the Churches of Christ in U.S.A. by the Office of Publication and Distribution, 1961), 19.

10

"Are You the White Sisters or the Black Sisters?"

Amy Koehlinger

Women Confounding Categories of Race and Gender

Standard narratives of U.S. religious history often portray Catholic sisters either as objects of anti-Catholic hatred or as victims of bishops' ecclesiastical power. In this essay, Amy Koehlinger turns the tables and explores one chapter in the history of Catholic women religious from their perspective. Documenting the experience of Catholic sisters who worked to promote racial justice in the 1960s, Koehlinger argues that their story should change how American religious historians and women's historians write about social reform. Contrary to what many scholars have assumed, Catholic as well as Protestant women were deeply involved in reform movements, including the civil rights movement.

On a more theoretical level, Koehlinger argues that historians of American religion should approach the analytical categories of race and gender as vulnerable social constructions rather than as concrete ontological realities. Sisters who participated in the "racial apostolate" were uniquely positioned to do this work because their religious status had complicated their gender.

Koehlinger's case study of Catholic sisters raises provocative questions about the fields of both women's history and American religious history. What do scholars mean when they say that they study "women's history"? Historians tend to use the word "women" as if its meaning is self-evident, but as Koehlinger argues, the singular category of "women" often obscures the complicated reality of women's lives.

In a 1966 essay on new forms of apostolic service by Catholic women religious, Sister Mary Peter Champagne, csj, stated a question that had consumed her generation of vowed women in the Catholic Church. "Among the questions being asked in this age of questioning," she began, "the one concerning the relevance of religious life in the modern world is among the most frequent. Is there still a need within the church for the religious state? Could not the work being done by sisters be done just as effectively by lay women?"[1]

In the early 1960s numerous voices within the Catholic Church—both sisters and nonsisters—asked whether women religious had become irrelevant to modern society. Critics charged that sisters were naive, insular, and increasingly out of touch with a world that was growing ever more complex and perilous. Sequestered in convents and parochial schools and set apart by their medieval dress and ideals of religious perfection, sisters were dismissed by some as little more than quaint but useless artifacts of a bygone era. To American sisters in the early 1960s, these challenges to the relevance of their institutes were not just abstract, rhetorical musings: they were urgent and very real criticisms that gave a particular urgency to the ongoing postconciliar conversation among sisters about the status and purpose of vowed women in the Catholic Church and the relationship of sisters to the world outside convent walls.[2] In renewal chapter meetings, in private conversations, and even in print, sisters debated about how to make the religious state germane to modern times. They argued over which elements of their life were essential and which were dispensable. They experimented with formation practices, modified habits, and new kinds of apostolic activities. Often the "relevance conversation" took the form of a debate over whether sisters' differentness from other women was an impediment to effective ministry, as critics charged, or whether sisters' differentness was a resource that helped them make a unique contribution to the church and to society.

Sister Champagne's question was a rhetorical nod to this debate, and her essay presented a robust argument supporting the perspective that women religious still had something unique and indispensable to contribute to the postconciliar church and, by extension, to the modern world. The church still needed sisters, she argued; it needed women who were categorically distinct from laywomen. Sister Champagne proposed that modern sisters, *as sisters*, were uniquely positioned to address modern society's problems; all they needed was the opportunity and freedom to do so. Like many American sisters in the mid-1960s, Sister Champagne responded to the pervasive "relevance question" by emphasizing the practical utility of religious vows. Sisters holding this view contended that the problem lay not in sisters' differentness from other women—indeed, they argued, the habit and the vows were indispensable components of effective ministry. Rather, the problem lay in sisters' isolation within Catholic enclaves, away from the outside world and its problems. Noting that the Second Vatican Council had provided a theological affirmation of the relevance of religious life to the human family beyond convent walls, Sister Champagne reasoned that "the same answer could be derived" more directly by considering the new, experimental forms of apostolic service that a number of American sisters recently had taken up in non-Catholic areas. According to Sister Champagne, these "new works of new nuns" (as they were called by sisters at the time) constituted a powerful argument for the utility of the religious state and the distinctions that separated sisters from other laywomen. In various projects across the country, Catholic sisters were addressing society's most pressing social and spiritual needs by taking their distinct way of life into unlikely, non-Catholic places like inner-city slums, secular college campuses, and the poorest corners of the Jim Crow South.

In the early 1960s, a significant number of Caucasian women religious left the relative insularity of Catholic convents, schools, and hospitals in largely white and increasingly suburban Catholic neighborhoods to pursue "new works" in African American enclaves in Northern urban centers and in the rural South. There, sisters established a wide range of programs addressing the myriad social effects of racial discrimination, including poverty, joblessness, hunger, drug addiction, lack of access to education, political disfranchisement, and insufficient health care. These sisters who worked to promote racial justice created a "racial apostolate," one that reoriented the distinctive mission of vowed religious life in active orders toward work among African Americans, promoting racial justice. In the racial apostolate, sisters volunteered to teach at traditionally African American colleges in the South. They held racial sensitivity training sessions in parish neighborhoods experiencing integration. They counseled persons struggling with addiction in recovery programs in Harlem. They sustained urban parochial schools after white students had left for segregated suburban neighborhoods. They ran summer schools and playground groups in Chicago housing projects and tutored adults how to read in Cleveland. They marched in the civil rights protests in Selma.

The racial apostolate of the 1960s was not without precedent among American sisters. Several homegrown orders of religious founded in the United States in the late nineteenth century claimed a specific charism (or gift of ministry) to live among, serve, and in some cases convert, African Americans and Native Americans. African American Catholic women who felt a call to religious consecration responded to the substantial barriers that prevented them from joining European orders by forming their own religious congregations in the mid- and late nineteenth century. Through congregations like the Sisters of the Holy Family and the Oblate Sisters of Providence, African American sisters created their own "racial apostolate" serving enslaved and free people of color, both Catholic and non-Catholic, through a system of schools, orphanages, and hospitals located primarily in Southern Catholic enclaves like New Orleans and Baltimore.[3] The efforts of African American sisters were mirrored by members of predominantly Caucasian congregations like Katherine Drexel's Sisters of the Blessed Sacrament, who also lived and worked among people of color, providing education and health care to minority groups.[4] As Suellen Hoy has documented, in the early twentieth century, congregations like the Sisters of the Good Shepherd, the Franciscan Missionaries of Mary, and the Daughters of Charity found creative ways to engage with newly arrived African Americans in their city, often in marked contrast with lay Catholic perceptions that the migration amounted to a "Negro invasion."[5] Despite a shared concern for the physical and spiritual welfare of African Americans, sisters of European ancestry who crossed the "color line" and sisters of color rarely cooperated with each other in their apostolic efforts. Though there were noteworthy exceptions, for the most part congregations of American women religious were racially segregated in their founding and remained so even through the civil rights era, pursuing separate apostolic activities in separate institutions.[6]

Despite these antecedents, the racial apostolate of Caucasian sisters in the 1960s was a significant departure from established patterns of apostolic activity for white women religious at the time. At the dawning of the civil rights era, interracial apostolic work by white religious was the exception rather than the rule; the majority of sisters lived and worked almost exclusively among Catholics of the same skin color. The Code of Canon Law promulgated in 1918 framed consecration and apostolate as unequal components of the religious state, defining sisters' identities primarily in terms of convent-centered prayer. Thus a "cloistral mentality that stressed separation from the world as the norm" was embedded in the revised constitutions of most orders at the end of World War I, creating an insular "convent culture" that dominated religious life for women from the 1920s through the 1950s.[7] Religious regulations and restrictions, customs surrounding mobility and contact with the laity, modes of dress, daily schedules, and limitations on activity all worked collectively to underscore the separateness of religious from the profane world. This ethos of monastic separation significantly restricted the apostolate of American women religious between the wars, confining sisters to Catholic institutions and then limiting their activities within even the narrow confines of Catholic schools and parishes, lest sisters be contaminated by contact with the world.[8] One unintended effect of religious enclosure was that the apostolate of Catholic sisters became as segregated as the Catholic communities in which they labored and ministered during the first half of the twentieth century.

The racial apostolate of the 1960s was one way that American Catholic women religious of European descent responded to the contradictory imperatives that emerged from their interstitial position within the structure of the American church. As outsiders both to the clergy and the laity, sisters in all periods of American history found themselves in the unenviable position of having to carefully negotiate between parishioners and the magisterium. In their professional roles as teachers and nurses, sisters represented the public face of the church's teachings to the lay Catholics they served. Yet their work also required them to understand and respond sympathetically to the perspectives and practical needs of lay Catholics. In the tumult of the 1960s, this interstitial location meant that sisters stood at the junction where mounting racial tensions and strong resistance to racial integration in American Catholic parishes collided with new theologies of human solidarity and universal human dignity issuing from the Second Vatican Council in Rome. Caught between these contradictory trends in Catholic life, "new nuns" responded to their situation by harnessing the conciliar approbation for racial justice to create a new apostolate that directly confronted the deepening segregation in the postwar American church: they left segregated Catholic enclaves to promote racial justice among non-Catholic people of color. In doing so, they laid bare the problematic gap between the church's progressive reform ideology and the inert traditionalism held by the majority of its American members in the conciliar era. They also crafted a model of apostolic relevance that was a powerful challenge to the culture of religious enclosure.

Sister Champagne's perceptive observation that the religious state was central to sisters' "new works" proved correct in powerful ways for white sisters who engaged in the racial apostolate. Indeed, the apostolic work of Catholic sisters promoting racial justice in the 1960s and early 1970s constitutes a striking example of how the differentness of women religious facilitated and assisted their apostolic work. The religious state was essential to Caucasian sisters' work in the racial apostolate. Specifically, sisters' status as vowed religious effectively camouflaged and even complicated their gender, thereby expanding the spheres of movement and activity that were available to them as white women in the racially charged atmosphere of segregated America. Put another way, sisters were able to go places and do things that nonreligious white women could not, and this gave sisters particular advantages in their efforts to redress the sources and consequences of white supremacy. And it sometimes produced effects that were surprising even to them.

In this chapter, I will make two arguments. First, I will argue that the history of Catholic sisters should change both the way that women's historians write about social reform movements and the way that American religious historians write about the religious experience of women. American history and American religious history both have privileged the public activism of Protestant women, often to the exclusion of Catholic women and especially Catholic women religious. Early women's historians in the 1970s and 1980s focused on Protestant women's social reform in the United States, documenting the public activism of women in the abolition, temperance, suffrage, and settlement house movements.[9] Similarly, women most often appear in standard historical narratives about America's religious past either as religious innovators or as social reformers, women for whom religion provided a socially legitimate avenue for entering and influencing the public sphere. Protestantism overwhelmingly dominates these narratives, standing either as the source of the public moral authority wielded by reforming women like Frances Willard and Carrie Nation or as the foil against which female innovators like Ann Lee or Mary Baker Eddy created new religious movements. Textbooks in American religious history rarely discuss Catholic varieties of reform, and Catholic sisters, unlike Protestant reformers such as Jane Addams, are barely mentioned. When sisters do appear in historical accounts they often are cast as either exotics or incompetents, women whose experience is too peculiar to illuminate larger trends. This is unfortunate because Catholic sisters in all historical periods, no less than their Protestant counterparts, occupied overtly public roles as social activists and reformers. Catholic women religious addressed social ills through an elaborate and influential system of schools, hospitals, and relief organizations. In many cases, sisters single-handedly founded, financed, managed, and staffed these institutions.[10] As such, the experience of sisters represents an important, often unique, slice of the history of the public activism of women in the United States.

While the recent development of "lived religion" as an interpretive category within the field of North American religion has corrected the artificial narrowness of previous scholarly models that recognized women's religiosity only in its public manifestations and Protestant incarnations, lived religion remains, at best, a partial solution to the historiographical elision of Catholic women. Lived religion's attention to questions of practice and meaning, and its attendant focus on the cultural, devotional, and extraecclesial facets of religious experience, has substantially broadened the historical portrait of religion in the United States to include previously overlooked facets of the intimate religious worlds created and inhabited by women.[11] This much-needed expansion of the kinds of religious expressions considered legitimate subjects for historical inquiry has, by extension, created new avenues for the integration of Catholic, Jewish, and other non-Protestant women into narratives about American religious history. Despite these important contributions, this new mode of historical inquiry, taken by itself, risks resurrecting a new version of Barbara Welter's "feminization" thesis by overemphasizing

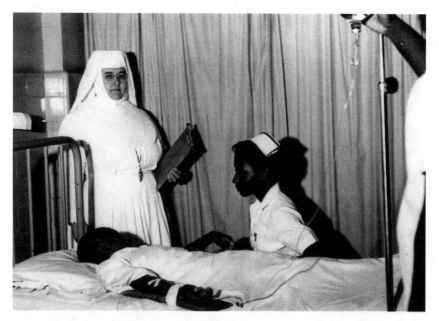

Sister Louis Bertrand Dixon, ssj, assisting a nursing student and patient at the congregation's Good Samaritan Hospital in Selma, Alabama. "Good Sam" was one of the few hospitals in Alabama that treated African American patients without restriction before civil rights reforms. Civil rights marchers wounded during the violent "Bloody Sunday" attack in March 1965 were taken directly from the Edmund Pettis Bridge to Good Sam for treatment. (Courtesy of the Archives of the Sisters of Saint Joseph, Rochester, New York)

the domestic and devotional aspects of Catholic women's religious experience at the expense of a fuller rendering of the diverse ways that Catholic women interpreted and enacted religious faith.[12] While Protestant women like Willard and Addams were waging pitched political battles against exploitation, drunkenness, and injustice, so the emerging narrative suggests, Catholic women imagined change largely in familial and domestic terms. Lacking the social ambitions and political entitlements wielded by Protestants, Catholic women tried to change circumstances within their families rather than within society at large, preferring devotional practices like intercessory prayer to public demonstrations. While this narrative is not entirely inaccurate, it is certainly incomplete, eliding the perspective and activities of Catholic women, like sisters, who pursued change on institutional and social levels. Sisters like the ones in this study—devout Catholic women who also were outspoken social critics, social reformers, and public activists—

challenge emerging narratives within the field of American religious history to include and represent the broad spectrum of religious expressions by Catholic women.[13]

Second, I will argue that American religious historians must be more sensitive to the complexity of human experience that lies beneath seemingly straightforward markers of social identity like gender and race. As I will demonstrate, Catholic sisters inhabited a flexible and at times surprisingly malleable social identity. Their practical gender, as well as their ecclesiastical status, often was unclear or uncertain in Catholic settings, and sisters purposely manipulated this ambiguity to increase the effectiveness of their ministries. When Caucasian sisters entered the Jim Crow South, this uncertainty about their gender, coupled with their close associations with the African American community, created similar uncertainty about their race. "Women's history *is* American religious history" (to borrow an influential phrase from Ann Braude), but this interpretive frame needs to better accommodate situations in which females weren't precisely "women" and thus fell outside binary models of gender.[14] As historians continue to grapple with the scholarly implications of the transformation of "women's history" into "gender history," the Catholic sisters in this study remind us of the inherent limits of abstract, analytical categories to fully capture the awful, lovely, messy experience of being human in a particular place and time.

Protean Gender, Complex Identity

Like generations of vowed women before them, American sisters at midcentury experienced gender as a complex, if not profoundly unstable, component of their identities. The proposition that American sisters in the 1960s possessed complex gender is not as radical as it seems on the surface. American sisters and their unstable, interstitial gender are part of the larger history of vowed and ascetic women within Christianity.[15]

In *The Body and Society*, Peter Brown's seminal work on gender and Christianity in antiquity, Brown reminds us that sexual renunciation—the refusal by early Christian women to participate in procreation and heterosexual households—stood as a radical critique of the dominant social order. Vowed celibacy challenged the very basis of Roman society, namely the household and its views of the body, power, and sexuality. In the ancient world, Christian female sexual renouncers stood in open defiance of the powerful household system within Roman society.[16] In many cases, early sexual renouncers were seen as a "third sex," neither male nor female but rather something entirely different, as "female men of God." Brown argues that sexually renouncing women in the ancient world were "gateways" from one social group to another: they could make headway into pagan families that men could not, could nurture children and so influence them, and could be present in public spaces with less risk of martyrdom.[17]

Similarly, *Sisters in Arms*, Jo Ann McNamara's impressive chronicle of the 2,000-year history of women religious, also reminds us that women religious at various times have transcended rigid categories of gender. Third-century virgins, for example, experimented with the claim that their purity elevated them beyond gender, transforming them into functional men. "Virgins and honorary virgins had their own ideas about their status," McNamara writes. "They saw themselves transformed and lifted beyond the constrictions of the gender system."[18] McNamara contends that monastic theorists conceptualized these consecrated virgins as a third gender, believing that without active sexual and reproductive activity, gender did not exist.[19]

American Catholic sisters in the twentieth century represent the modern equivalent of Brown's sexual renouncers in antiquity and McNamara's medieval consecrated virgins. Because women religious were neither sexually available to men for marriage nor candidates for childbearing, they stood outside the Catholic ideal of the period that held up Marianism as a model of female identity, equating womanhood with motherhood. Though Catholic Church doctrine at times did associate women religious with Mary through the trope of virginity,[20] and though members of the male hierarchy often infantilized sisters in much the same way as they did other women, *in actual practice* in noncloistered settings, sisters often were understood to be unwomen, and were treated as such. Considered to be neither male nor entirely female, sisters constituted a third gender within the American church. Certain conventions of religious life reinforced this view of the interstitial gender of sisters. The substantial religious habit sisters were obligated to wear obscured their physical characteristics, hiding corporeality generally and sexual characteristics specifically. Furthermore, sisters often were given male names-in-religion. Thus a woman religious was as likely to be called "Sister Bernard" as she was "Sister Bernadette." One sister recounted how as a graduate student at Catholic University in the mid-1960s she was reminded of her unusual gender whenever she visited the university pool, where she confronted not two but three dressing room options: one marked "men," one marked "women," and a third marked "nuns."[21]

The complex gender of sisters was amplified by a similar uncertainty about their ecclesiastical status in the church. In the Catholic cosmology that divided the world into distinct categories of sacred and profane and thus bifurcated the church into laity and clergy, sisters fit easily into neither category. As nonclergy, technically, women religious were laity. However, the Catholic tradition in this period carefully cultivated specific practices that differentiated vowed women from their noncelibate or unvowed lay counterparts, complicating sisters' inclusion in the broad category of laity. As one sociologist of religious life observed, a sister was viewed by the laity as "a 'holy person' with special gifts and access to the spiritual realm."[22] Deference to sisters was deeply embedded in Catholic social practice. Such deference was instilled in parochial school classrooms, performed in social rituals and gestures, and perpetuated in social institutions like the parish and devotional societies. This lay deference to women religious reified perceptions that sisters were not quite human. Regulations of enclosure that prohibited sisters from engaging in rudimentary tasks of human maintenance such as eating or sleeping in the presence of laity further reinforced the unearthliness of their image and provided a rationale for their segregation from laity. In practice, especially in settings like schools and hospitals where sisters enjoyed professional authority over other laity, the ecclesiastical status of women religious was, at best, unclear. Most Catholics (including women religious) considered sisters to be a category unto themselves in the structure of the church, distinct from both laity and clergy and positioned somewhere between them. For many American Catholics, women religious continued to occupy this interstitial position between laity and clergy even after the Second Vatican Council officially clarified their status as laity.

The interstitial gender and complex identity of sisters in American Catholicism was a double-edged sword for them. It posed certain obstacles for their autonomy and the success of their ministries. Sisters at times felt like freakish outsiders among lay Catholics and were treated as such in parish settings. Catholic laity regarded sisters as markedly different from themselves. Confined by enclosure to Catholic spheres and then separated from Catholic laity within those spheres, sisters often felt isolated within parish settings in which their social contacts were limited to the other sisters in the convent and the children in the school. "We the sisters seldom relate to the people here. We are involved in school only," wrote one sister of her experience in a white Catholic parish. She continued: "I was thinking of holding a day of recollections for all the women of the parish. I want so badly to get involved in this parish."[23] But nonreligious laywomen often were hesitant to confide in or trust sisters, believing that these nonmothers (of doubtful womanhood) could not understand the practical—much less spiritual—trials faced by women in households. Children, too, often feared sisters and drew away from physical contact with them.

If the complex identity of sisters made it difficult for them to fit easily into Catholic spheres oriented toward binary categories of male and female, lay and clergy, it nonetheless provided women religious with certain advantages. Specifically, the interstitial gender of sisters enabled them to transgress boundaries that Catholic women, traditionally defined, could not. For example, sisters were admitted to Catholic schools that otherwise denied admission to women. They were able to pursue advanced degrees at a time when very few women had access to higher education, much less graduate study.[24] Sisterhood also offered women opportunities for professional development and accomplishment that were not available to their nonvowed female contemporaries. Cultural stereotypes portray sisters as harried, bitter, naive women confined to overcrowded parochial school classrooms. These images ignore the equally accurate historical portrait of sisters as competent and confident administrators who founded, managed, financed, and sustained large institutions like hospitals and colleges and who mastered subtle negotiations with powerful bishops and secular authorities. Thus, by not fitting into a recognizable category of gender, sisters often were able to transcend the restrictions associated with femaleness both in the Catholic Church and in American society generally. Additionally, Catholic sisters learned to manipulate their interstitial position between maleness and femaleness. They became adept at the strategic management of their identities and the conscious performance of ambiguous gender when doing so enhanced their mobility or their ministries.

Thus, though asceticism often is characterized as a withdrawal from the world, for many American sisters in active congregations in the 1960s, holy vows were a way of moving *into* the world in ways that were not otherwise permitted to women. Though sisters' interstitial gender tended to isolate them in Catholic settings where they were outsiders both to laywomen and to the male magisterium, in non-Catholic settings, like the "new works" of the racial apostolate, the complexity of sisters' gender enhanced their work by making it possible for them occasionally to transcend other fundamental social divides. Specifically, the unclear gender of American women religious enabled them, at times, to similarly confound the binary construction of race at the heart of Jim Crow segregation.

Portrayed in starkest terms, the cultural "logic" of Jim Crow rested on a particular understanding of the relationships between race, gender, and sex in which a hardened racial hierarchy was constituted and justified through the naturalization of a gendered one.[25] American white supremacy in late Jim Crow enforced binary categorizations of whiteness and blackness, insisting that all people and all institutions could, and indeed must, be classified as either black or white, in order, it claimed, to "protect" vulnerable white womanhood from "polluting" sexual contact with black men. Threatened by ambiguity, this perverse cultural logic resisted nuance, denied exception, and punished transgression—in most cases. But within such contexts of hardened racial polarization and racial segregation, the protean gender of sisters provided them with a form of camouflage that gave them a measure of freedom to manipulate these categories, as well as the boundaries that they implied. If sisters were not clearly women—because, as in the Catholic context, they were not candidates for heterosexual relationships or motherhood—then they also were not white women (that especially laden category under Jim Crow) and thus did not need the sexual protection that racial segregations purportedly offered to white women. Thus, sisters' in-betweenness, their position outside binary categories of male and female, also placed them outside of the central categories of Jim Crow, allowing them at times to "fly below the radar" of white supremacy and to interact with and live in close proximity to African Americans, particularly African American men, without eliciting violent responses from white supremacists. And, as it turns out, the interstitial gender of women religious sometimes rendered Catholic sisters in the racial apostolate "inconclusively white" (to borrow a phrase from Matthew Frye Jacobson) as well.[26]

Sisters and "Sistahs"

In 1971, Sister Benedicta Claus sent greetings "from the deep South," as she called it, to friends in her religious community in Ferdinand, Indiana. Reflecting on the experience of teaching literature at an African American college in South Carolina as part of the racial apostolate, Sister Claus's letter invited her fellow sisters to imagine themselves in an environment where they were strange—so strange, in fact, that even the name "sister," a word to which they responded tens of times a day, was problematic. She wrote: "Benedict is a Baptist College, 1400 students, all black. Just imagine what an enigma I was on campus last September: northerner, white skin, fast speech, and a Catholic. To call me 'Sister' was nearly incredible for these students, since all members of the black community call each other BROTHER and SISTER. By being white I was the one person in the classroom that should be Miss, Mrs., Dr., or anything but definitely not 'Sister.'"[27]

In South Carolina, Benedicta could not rely on the similarities of race and religion that framed her relationships with students in the Catholic college where she usually taught, and that gave a flat, taken-for-granted quality to the title "sister." Rather, in North Carolina, Sister Benedicta was "enigmatic, northern, white, Catholic" (to use her own words), an exotic outsider whose formal title made an odd and arresting pun on the word that usually meant "familiar, included, female, African-American, Black, one of us."

The "sister" pun was startling to Catholic sisters in the racial apostolate like Benedicta precisely because it contrasted so sharply with their awareness that, as religious and also as whites, they were outsiders to the overwhelmingly Protestant, African American institutions in which they served. Most assignments in the racial apostolate required sisters to leave convents in Catholic neighborhoods and live either in the rural South or in predominantly African American neighborhoods in the urban North. For many sisters, the racial apostolate was their first significant interaction with African Americans. "We really lived in the black community," one sister explained. "We had very, very little to do with any white people because we lived among black people, and white people didn't like it."[28] The work of the racial apostolate took sisters outside the familiar dynamics of parochial school classrooms, often placing them in unfamiliar, informal situations with non-Catholics. "How can you capture on paper the wide-eyed greeting of little children who are curious to see whether the ladies in white are really women beneath their habits?" commented one sister of the response of children to their first encounter with nuns.[29]

In their correspondence, sisters often chose to describe their increasingly complicated racial status through anecdotes about their relationships with African American children (for whom sisters' race might well have been confusing, given the strangeness of the habit and the fact of sisters' residence in segregated neighborhoods). In some stories, children are uncertain about a sister's race, as when a convent chronicle reported that "little Shirley Mae George" interrupted a hand game she was playing with a sister and "taking Sister's hand in both her tiny ones, she held it up close to her face and said, 'Sister, why yo hand white?'"[30] In other accounts, children bluntly resisted the possibility of sisters' whiteness, as when one girl approached her teacher after class and said, "Sister, if you get much lighter, folks are going to think you are a white lady."[31] Another sister recalled a student who took her finger and said, "'Sister Megia, you fittin to turn white?' She responded, 'Johnny, I am white.' I was covered up in the habit and he never realized I was white."[32]

If the race of sisters was unclear to their youngest students, it outright confused the white power structure. Sisters in the racial apostolate often were considered black, or at least were treated as such by local whites. In Selma, for example, the two Catholic churches in town were identified by the racial composition of their congregations rather than by the respective parish names—St. Elizabeth's was "the black church" and Assumption was "the white church." Segregated classifications were applied also to the sisters who staffed each parish school: the Sisters of Mercy at the white parish were more commonly known as "the white sisters" and the Sisters of St. Joseph at the black mission parish were called "the black sisters." These labels were applied contrary to the obvious, visual fact that the color of sisters' habits contradicted their designation. Thus, despite the fact that in most locations orders of religious are casually identified by the color of their religious garb—Maryknolls are frequently referred to as "grey nuns," for example—in 1960 Selma, the "white sisters" wore black, and "the black sisters" frequently wore white.[33]

The designation "black sisters" complicated sisters' experiences of themselves as religious and further destabilized the already volatile religious and gender identities that women religious inhabited and performed. Thus, sisters' race—or, more precisely, their experience of their own race—was in some circumstances obscured or complicated by their status as religious and their identifications with African Americans. "We most definitely are NOT neutral," wrote Sister Mary Paul Geck from Selma in 1965. "For all practical purposes we are 'Negroes' living in a Negro community."[34] The designation "black sister" marked these women not only as ones who were integrated into African American spheres; it also sometimes marked white sisters as no longer entitled to the privileges attached to whiteness in a racist society. In Selma, sisters grew accustomed to the more benign expressions of racism that some white Selma residents directed at them as "the black sisters," including hard stares on the streets and taunts from passing motorists. Sisters Remigia and Louis Bertrand reported that as they were shopping one day in Selma they were approached by a clerk who tartly inquired whether they were "the white sisters or the black sisters."[35] Sisters in Chicago were denied service at the local Woolworth's lunch counter once it was known that they were active in the nearby housing projects. In some extreme cases, sisters in the racial apostolate used segregated facilities and in the South were subject to harassment when attempting to register and to vote.[36]

Similar to the ways that in lay settings sisters used their interstitial gender to gain certain ends, sisters in the racial apostolate consciously exploited confusion about their race to further their apostolic work. Sisters learned to manipulate the malleability of their complex racial position and to move strategically between black and white worlds and black and white identities. Sisters embraced their association with the black community in situations where they needed to cultivate the trust of African Americans or when such trust attributed legitimacy to their mission. They also learned to claim whiteness in situations of duress, or while fund-raising, or when acting in professional medical capacities. This strategic deployment of whiteness was

Sister Ligouri Dunlea, ssj, with nursing students in Selma on a rare snowy day. Because of their close association with African Americans in Selma, the Sisters of Saint Joseph were casually referred to as "the black nuns" by Selma residents, despite the fact that they were white women wearing white habits. (Courtesy of the Archives of the Sisters of Saint Joseph, Rochester, New York)

particularly helpful when sisters faced religious and civil authorities such as the bishop or the police, especially when they believed that they could leverage concessions from the white power structure.

Sisters' manipulation of racial categories found its clearest expression at the voting booth. By the time the Southern Christian Leadership Conference voter registration drive accelerated in Selma in the early 1960s, the Sisters of St. Joseph in a mission there had learned to use their racial malleability to attempt to leverage small political concessions for African Americans. Sisters from the convent often went to the voter registration office in the company of black neighbors and colleagues from the hospital.[37] The sisters' reputation of close associations with African Americans sometimes followed them to the county registrar and ultimately to the ballot box, so that "the black sisters" were subject to experiences of harassment and stalling at the hands of voting officials. Sisters believed that at times their unclear racial status introduced temporary ambiguity into the registration and voting process and perhaps undermined the wholesale disfranchisement of African Americans. Sisters assumed that their presence in the registration line, witnessing the actions of white officials, occasionally influenced registrars to refrain from more extreme tactics of intimidation. Sisters employed their racial ambiguity at the polls, too, and thus encountered discrimination. "We were voting over at the firehouse," Sister St. Joseph recalled, "so, what did they hand out, but pencils that could be erased and we had to write leaning on the fenders of firetrucks. We stayed until all the people who could vote were done. We weren't very popular."[38]

There were, of course, limits to sisters' ability to subvert the racial categories of Jim Crow. The tensions inherent in sisters' complicated social location, between the black and white worlds, were intensified on occasions when they entered public spaces in the company of black colleagues. There, sisters encountered limits to their identification with African Americans. In their mission hospital in Selma, for example, sisters often were in the presence of white doctors and white police in the emergency room. In the hospital setting, sisters were expected to tolerate, if not follow, racist social conventions, and they were sharply reprimanded by doctors when they failed or refused to draw symbolic distance between themselves and African Americans.[39]

Sisters did not tell stories about harassment in order to suggest that they endured levels of racial discrimination similar to African Americans. The sisters I interviewed readily acknowledged that encounters like the ones I have described gave them a limited and relatively benign taste of the experiences of discrimination endured by their African American neighbors and colleagues. Sisters also did not tell these stories to suggest that they made any remarkable progress toward undoing the power of Jim Crow. Rather, tales of being the object of racism served a narrative function for sisters, helping them to describe the effect of their interactions with African Americans on them, particularly on their identities and their later perspectives about religious life.

Because sisters often felt like outsiders within Catholic parish settings, they longed for inclusion in the black communities where they worked in the racial apostolate. Their search for solidarity with African Americans was subtly supported by the fact that sisters' strangeness in these locations destabilized their identities as vowed religious. A sister arriving at the housing projects of Chicago's Cabrini Green, for example, faced the task of maintaining her religious identity in a context where few of her neighbors immediately understood what her sisterhood meant, much less how to address her. Sisters told and retold stories about how children addressed them informally, with a "Hello Veil" or "Hiya Sistahs."[40] The rituals that reinforced sisters' religious identities—daily mass, community prayer, the deference (or condescension) of lay Catholics, the "Yes, sister" and "No, sister" of Catholic schoolchildren—these elements were conspicuously absent in most forms of the racial apostolate. And in their place, sisters found themselves at the center of a remarkable pun.

Sisters reported with astonishment the fact that, contrary to the traditional Catholic use to which sisters were well accustomed, young people used the word "sister" as an affectionate term within the black community. A sister reported that her presence had precipitated "ecstasy" among her students. "My name is 'Sister Campbell,'" she wrote to other sisters. "Apparently, 'Sister' has Soul, and the students give me a big unearned grin when they say Sistah!"[41] The power of the overlapping meaning of the word "sister" for Catholic women religious should not be underestimated; in their correspondence sisters in diverse projects and locations referred to this coincidence frequently and with absolute wonder.

Sisters derived affirmation both from being included in black communities and from the convergence of black and Catholic cultures in the title "sister." Many sisters in the racial apostolate interpreted the title as an affirmation that they had achieved the acceptance and belonging they sought within the black community. Some implied, further, that the designation "sister" effectively concealed, if not eradicated, their race (a complicated claim, to be sure).[42] Thus, when sisters in Chicago's Cabrini Green proudly reported that a student had expressed her trust in them by exclaiming, "You-all ain't whites. You is Sistahs!," they were trying not only to describe the experiences of inclusion but also the growing complexity of their own racial identities within the racial apostolate.[43] Some sisters even went so far as to internalize their identifications with African Americans. In a striking instance of this dynamic, a deeply unhappy sister who had returned to her community in North Dakota after a summer in Chicago explained, "It is virtual hell to be here. I can't get those West Side people out of my heart & head. I feel black. I look at everything through Negro eyes—Negro emotions & Negro pain."[44]

The sister pun also provided women religious with a much-desired entreé into black culture, allowing them to form unique connections with black students, particularly with young black women. Women in the racial apostolate reported that the term "sister" also sometimes altered the tone of interactions between sisters and students. As Sister Benedicta observed in the passage I quoted earlier, sisters believed that being able to call a white teacher "sister" may have diffused or subverted the pressure black students felt to respond to women religious with patterns of racial deference otherwise enforced in segregated America. The term introduced humor and irony into conversations between black youth and white women religious, opening space for improvisation and play and allowing sisters to participate in gender-specific conversations with laywomen. One nun reported that female students felt comfortable enough to ask her "Sister questions" about her lay attire. "The word 'Sister' seems to mean something special to the girls," she noted.[45]

The term "sister" also opened space for revisions to ways of being a Catholic sister. The double meaning of the word positioned women religious in the middle of an ever-widening gap between traditional and revised visions of religious life. Service in the cause of racial justice bridged familiar patterns of apostolic and religious life with a new vision of what the religious life could be. And when African American young women addressed them as "sister," a woman religious experienced simultaneously a traditional Catholic and a racial activist identity.

Sisters' complicated experiences of race in the 1960s shaped the internal reforms they implemented after the Second Vatican Council, with far-reaching effects. When sisters saw themselves as part of the human family rather than as ones set apart from human experience—as "sistahs" rather than as sisters—they began to believe that they were entitled to the same human rights in the church that African Americans had sought from American society in the civil rights movement. When sisters experienced the fluidity of their racial identities, specifically the arbitrariness of the privileges and stigmas attached to whiteness and blackness in American society, many sisters recognized a similar arbitrariness to the privileges and stigmas attached to maleness and femaleness in the Catholic Church. When the church opened a period of experimentation and reform for religious orders through the Second Vatican Council, American sisters borrowed experience and rhetoric from the civil rights movement to justify their demands for radical shifts in the rules and authority structures that governed religious life. In the resulting transformation of religious congregations, women religious distanced themselves from traditional apostolic works in Catholic schools and hospitals and traditional models of dress, living arrangements, and community governance. Sisters' increasing autonomy from male hierarchical authority and escalating critiques of institutional misogyny in the church sharpened a postconciliar crisis of Catholic magisterial authority.

Catholic scholarship on the Second Vatican Council often traces the institutional changes among American women religious to the mandates from the Council, erroneously assuming that in reforming their orders sisters were simply responding to initiatives and directives that came from the male hierarchy. The story of sisters in the racial apostolate documents one particular example of the deep, preconciliar roots of sisters' reforms, suggesting that Vatican II merely accelerated complicated processes of transformation that already were under way among American sisters well before the Council began. Put another way, causality for the dramatic changes to religious life of women religious in the 1970s started with sisters' experiences of the slipperiness of categories of race and gender, not with the male magisterium and its rigid assumptions about gender and power.

Standing with Women Religious

What is the significance of sisters' racial ambiguity for our collective work as historians of American religion? What does this unusual chapter in Catholic history contribute to our understanding of women in North American religion?

At a very basic level, scholars of religious life in America have largely overlooked women religious and their activities. There has been a disturbing tendency within Catholic historiography to not "see" sisters who built, inhabited, and staffed the institutions about which history books are written. Traditional histories of Catholic diocesan life describe the elaborate systems of schools, hospitals, and social service delivery that characterized nineteenth- and twentieth-century Catholicism as if they were created by the wave of a bishop's hand rather than through the concrete diligence and ambition of Catholic sisters. The emergent wave of new scholarship on women religious will change our understanding of American religion in several important ways. Recent work on Catholic women religious challenges historians of American religion to incorporate Catholicism into narratives about the religious roots of social reform that too often have privileged the reform activities of Protestant women. Long before the racial apostolate, Catholic sisters were central to and engaged in work to redress inequities in education and health care, labor and poverty. I would like for recent scholarship on sisters to have the effect that when people in the field think of female social reformers they are as likely to think of Catholic sisters as they are to think of Jane Addams.

When I teach students in my American Catholicism class about gender, I often frame our discussion by explaining that women religious were "the exception that proved the rule" that Catholicism historically offered women a maternal ideal of what it means to be female, one that equated womanhood with a vocation to motherhood. I explain to students that women have been primarily perceived by the church in terms of their biological capacity to bear children—as mothers—and the primary role model held up again and again for women was, of course, Mary. Then I point out that we can look at the woman-equals-mother equation in Catholicism from another angle when we consider the gender experience of women religious—women who were, by definition and by vow, celibate and thus not candidates for motherhood. The equation goes like this: if woman equals mother, then not mother equals not woman. And, as we have seen, sisters often were not considered to be women or were not treated like them in practice within the American church.

And it is at about that point in the lecture that some bright or mischievous student will raise a hand and say, "Well, if sisters weren't considered women, then did people think they were men?" "No," I say (usually with a grin, because I know where this is headed). "Well, if sisters weren't women, and they weren't men," the now impatient student persists, "then what *were* they?" My use of sisters as an "exception to the rule" of Catholic gender perplexes students because with few exceptions they think of gender in binary terms: there are two possible categories, male and female.

Many of us, as historians of American religion, operate within a similarly restricted (albeit more subtle) intellectual world of analytical categories when it comes to thinking about the experience of gender. Though much of the current historical work on women at least nods in the direction of gender theorists like Judith Butler, our narratives about the past still often fail to reflect the unstable and complex ways that people live the experience of gender. Many of the stories we tell about gender and American religion are simplistically straightforward: women either reify ideals of gender or they subvert them. Traditional narratives of American religious history often divide women into categories of those women who reinforced and those who contradicted gendered norms. So, women either participate in domestic piety, decorate their homes with religious symbols, frame public work in terms associated with nurturing and mothering and thus perform gendered ideals, or, like Sojourner Truth or Aimee Semple McPherson, religious women stand toe to toe with male religious authority, staring it straight in the eye and daring it to confine them to the limited spheres reserved for women. Like my students, our categories of analysis within the field of North American religion often leave us little room to consider other more complicated ways that gender might operate in the lives of the people we study.

In her essay "Women's Stories, Women's Symbols," Caroline Walker Bynum challenged scholars to write from the perspective of standing *with* women, rather than looking at them.[46] Too often historians of religious life in the United States have failed to approach Catholic women religious as full subjects. Rather, standard narratives of American religious history often render sisters as objects—or perhaps even victims—of the historically significant behavior of others. From convent burnings to the manipulations of bishops, women religious most often appear in narratives of American religion when things are done to them or despite them. Put another way, Catholic women religious don't initiate action or do anything historically noteworthy other than stand as targets for the oppressive or intolerant behavior of others (usually either Protestants or the male hierarchy). I'd like to challenge American historians to stand *with* women religious, and to add them to the narrative as full subjects, taking seriously the ideas and perspectives that sisters brought to the task of making sense of the world—and of changing it.

How does the historical picture change when we stand with women religious and try to see their context and actions in ways that would have made sense to them? My research leads me to believe that when we stand with women religious we see that the categories of race and gender that historians sometimes use cavalierly, as if they had explanatory power or concrete reality, are a lot more slippery in actual human experience than they appear in the historical narratives we construct about human experience. Returning to the double use of the term "sister" and the phenomenon of "the black sisters," the example of Catholic sisters in the racial apostolate challenges the field of American religion to be more cautious about the binary categories that often structure our own thinking and analysis. Sisters slipped through the cracks of race and gender, and in so doing they challenge us to use caution when employing categories of white, black, male, and female as ontological realities rather than as vulnerable social constructions and changeable historical experiences—and I stress the words vulnerable and changeable here. Catholic sisters in the 1960s lingered in the gap between maleness and femaleness, temporarily slipping through cracks in America's racial polarization and playing those positions to their advantage to increase the effect of their ministries. Catholic sisters teach us an appreciation for the margins, for the liminal, for in-between states of being, for historical actors who defy categories and blur boundaries. And they teach us the radical potential that lies in transgressing or confounding the very categories that lie at the heart of social organization and thus of social power.

Notes

1. Sister Mary Peter Champagne, CSJ, "Newman Communities," in *New Works of New Nuns* (St. Louis: B. Herder, 1968), 95.
2. This conversation predated the 1960s. It began in the early 1950s with Pope Pius XII's exhortation to sisters to examine their institutions for out-of-date rules and customs, intensified with the reforms that the Sister Formation Conference implemented in the educational practices of American congregations through the 1950s and early 1960s, and peaked with the 1962 publication of Leon Joseph

Cardinal Suenens's *The Nun in the World* (Westminster, Md.: Newman Press, 1962) and the Second Vatican Council's promulgation of the Decree on the Renewal of Religious Life (*Perfectae Caritatis*) in 1965. For further reading on this process, see Lora Ann Quinonez, CDP, and Mary Daniel Turner, SND, *The Transformation of American Catholic Sisters* (Philadelphia: Temple University Press, 1992); the chapter "Inside Outsiders," in Mary Jo Weaver, *New Catholic Women: A Contemporary Challenge to Religious Authority* (San Francisco: Harper and Row, 1986); and Rebecca Sullivan, *Visual Habits: Nuns, Feminism, and American Postwar Popular Culture* (Toronto: University of Toronto Press, 2005).

3. For further reading on congregations of African American women religious, see Cyprian Davis, *The History of Black Catholics in the U.S.* (New York: Crossroad, 1992); Tracy Fessenden, "The Sisters of the Holy Family and the Veil of Race," *Religion and American Culture* (2000): 187–224; Diane Batts Morrow, *Persons of Color and Religious at the Same Time: The Oblate Sisters of Providence, 1828–1860* (Chapel Hill: University of North Carolina Press, 2002); and Louis Marie Bryan, *History of the National Black Sisters' Conference, Celibate Black Commitment* (Pittsburgh: National Black Sisters' Conference, 1971).

4. Dana Robert, *American Women in Mission: A Social History of Their Thought and Practice* (Macon, Ga.: Mercer University Press, 1997), 332.

5. Suellen Hoy, *Good Hearts: Catholic Sisters in Chicago's Past* (Urbana: University of Illinois Press, 2006), 73.

6. Sisters who attempted to racially integrate racial apostolate programs ran headlong into logistical barriers linked to the profound segregation of religious congregations in the United States. Writing to inform Sister Margaret Traxler that her congregation would not release her to participate in a particular racial apostolate program, Sister Mary Antona Ebo, FSM, an African American woman religious, tied the racial segregation of apostolic programs to the legacy of white supremacy in American congregations of religious. "Perhaps you can use this as a reply to some of the people who criticize you for not having Negro sisters on the team," Ebo offered, "not only the lack of generosity of those orders who may have a sister to contribute . . . but also the orders who have for so long taken a 'lily-white' attitude toward God-given vocations. Perhaps, some of the rest would have Negro sisters to contribute if the attitude would have been different" (ellipses in original text). Sister Mary Antona Ebo, FSM, to Sister Margaret Ellen (Mary Peter) Traxler, SSND, typewritten letter, May 13, 1967, series 4, box 1, National Catholic Conference for Interracial Justice (NCCIJ) papers, Marquette University archives, Milwaukee.

7. Mary Ewens, OP, "Women in the Convent," in *American Catholic Women: A Historical Exploration*, ed. Karen Kennelly, CSJ (New York: Macmillan, 1989), 36–37.

8. Patricia Byrne, "Saving Souls and Educating Americans, 1930–1945," in *Transforming Parish Ministry: The Changing Roles of Catholic Clergy, Laity, and Women Religious* (New York: Crossroad, 1990), 140. The essays by Byrne collected under the heading "In the Parish but Not of It: Sisters" in the above volume make up an

unparalleled narrative of the history of American women religious in the twentieth century. Byrne's subtle and detailed essays are a good starting point for further reading on the patterns of change and continuity among American sisters in this period.

9. This rich body of literature is too large to list, but exemplary studies on the public roles of women from the first generation of women's historians include Catherine Clinton, *The Other Civil War: American Women in the Nineteenth Century* (New York: Hill and Wang, 1984); Nancy F. Cott, *The Bonds of Womanhood: "Woman's Sphere" in New England, 1780–1835* (New Haven: Yale University Press, 1977); Sara Evans, *Personal Politics: The Roots of Women's Liberation in the Civil Rights Movement and the New Left* (New York: Alfred A. Knopf, 1979); Jacqueline Jones, *Soldiers of Light and Love: Northern Teachers and Georgia Blacks, 1865–1873* (Chapel Hill: University of North Carolina Press, 1980); Kathryn Kish Sklar, *Catherine Beecher: A Study in American Domesticity* (New Haven: Yale University Press, 1973); and Carroll Smith-Rosenberg, *Disorderly Conduct: Visions of Gender in Victorian America* (New York: Oxford University Press, 1985).

10. Some recent works documenting public roles and social reform activities of Catholic sisters include Carol K. Coburn and Martha Smith, *Spirited Lives: How Nuns Shaped Catholic Culture and American Life, 1836–1920* (Chapel Hill: University of North Carolina Press, 1999); and Mary Oates, *The Catholic Philanthropic Tradition in America* (Bloomington: Indiana University Press, 1995).

11. Noteworthy early monographs on the "lived religion" of American women include R. Marie Griffith, *God's Daughters: Evangelical Women and the Power of Submission* (Berkeley: University of California Press, 1997); Jenna Weissman Joselit, *The Wonders of America: Reinventing Jewish Culture, 1880–1950* (New York: Hill and Wang, 1994); Colleen McDannell, *The Christian Home in Victorian America, 1840–1900* (Bloomington: Indiana University Press, 1986); and Robert Orsi, *Thank You, St. Jude: Women's Devotion to the Patron Saint of Hopeless Causes* (New Haven: Yale University Press, 1996).

12. See Barbara Welter, "The Feminization of American Religion: 1800–1860," in *Clio's Consciousness Raised: New Perspectives on the History of Women*, ed. Mary Hartman and Lois Banner (New York: Harper and Row, 1974). Ann Braude carefully and authoritatively refuted this argument in her influential 1997 essay "Women's History *Is* American Religious History," in *Retelling U.S. Religious History*, ed. Thomas A. Tweed (Berkeley: University of California Press, 1997). Braude's essay also explores the anti-Catholic and antiwoman bias of the "feminization" concept as it has been applied to American religion.

13. Leslie Woodcock Tentler's *Catholics and Contraception: An American History* (Ithaca, N.Y.: Cornell University Press, 2004) is an excellent example of historical scholarship that explores the complex relationship between private and political matters of faith for Catholic women.

14. See Braude, "Women's History *Is* American Religious History."

15. In addition to works by Brown and McNamara, cited below in notes 16 and 18, my

thinking on the gender of women religious has been influenced by Caroline Walker Bynum's work, particularly *Fragmentation and Redemption: Essays on Gender and the Human Body in Medieval Religion* (New York: Zone Books, 1992); and Dyan Elliott, *Fallen Bodies: Pollution, Sexuality, and Demonology in the Middle Ages* (Philadelphia: University of Pennsylvania Press, 1998).

16. Peter Robert Brown, *The Body and Society: Men, Women, and Sexual Renunciation in Early Christianity* (New York: Columbia University Press, 1988), 100.

17. Ibid., 153.

18. Jo Ann McNamara, *Sisters in Arms: Catholic Nuns through Two Millennia* (Cambridge: Harvard University Press, 1996), 43.

19. Ibid., 144.

20. For the most recent statement of this principle, see John Paul II, *Mulieris Dignitatem.*

21. This particular example comes from a conversation with Cecilia Murray, OP, but several sisters have related similar stories about bathroom facilities in other places.

22. Helen Rose Ebaugh, *Women in the Vanishing Cloister: Organizational Decline in Catholic Religious Orders in the United States* (New Brunswick, N.J.: Rutgers University Press, 1993), 26.

23. Typewritten letter from Sister Mary James to Sister Margaret Ellen (Mary Peter) Traxler, SSND, February 20, 1967, NCCIJ correspondence, Series 4, Box 3, "I–Q" file, NCCIJ papers, Marquette University archives, Milwaukee.

24. In fact, 68 percent of American women religious held a bachelor's degree in 1966, and by 1986 that figure had risen to 88 percent. See Ebaugh, *Women in the Vanishing Cloister,* 19.

25. Though both books deal with an earlier period than this chapter does, my thinking on the gendered history of Jim Crow segregation has been influenced by Jane Dailey, *Before Jim Crow: The Politics of Race in Postemancipation Virginia* (Chapel Hill: University of North Carolina Press, 2000); and Glenda Gilmore, *Gender and Jim Crow: Women and the Politics of White Supremacy in North Carolina, 1896–1920* (Chapel Hill: University of North Carolina Press, 1996).

26. On racial malleability, see Matthew Frye Jacobson, *Whiteness of a Different Color: European Immigrants and the Alchemy of Race* (Cambridge: Harvard University Press, 1998).

27. Typewritten letter from Sister Benedicta Claus to Benedictine Sisters, copy with handwritten addendum to Sister Margaret Ellen (Mary Peter) Traxler, SSND, February 1971, Series 19, Box 13, "CHOICE" file. National Catholic Conference for Interracial Justice papers, Marquette University archives, Milwaukee.

28. Sister Mary Paul Geck, SSJ, interview with author, December 13, 2000, Rochester, N.Y.

29. "Marymount College Self-Help Program," *Nuns' Newsletter* (September 1966), National Catholic Conference for Interracial Justice papers, Marquette University archives, Milwaukee.

30. Convent chronicle, 6/16/41, Selma series, "Convent Chronicle, 1940–1960," archives of the Sisters of St. Joseph, Rochester, N.Y.

31. Typewritten letter to (Monsignor) Very Reverend John S. Randall, Rochester N.Y., February 21, 1951, Selma series, box G-13-1-2, "Selma, 1940–68," Archives of the Sisters of St. Joseph, Rochester, N.Y.

32. Sister Remigia McHenry, typewritten memoir, Selma series, box G-13-1-5, "Year of the South," archives of the Sisters of St. Joseph, Rochester, N.Y.

33. Convent chronicle, 12/23/40, Selma series, "Convent Chronicle, 1940–1960," archives of the Sisters of St. Joseph, Rochester, N.Y.

34. Typewritten letter from Sister Mary Paul (Geck) to "My dear Sisters and friends, in the Rochester, N.Y., Motherhouse, February 7, 1965, Selma series, box G-13-1-2, "Selma, 1940–68," archives of the Sisters of St. Joseph, Rochester, N.Y.

35. Quoted in Patricia Cavanaugh Creighton, "What Were You Doing in Selma, Sister?" (unpublished B.A. thesis, Department of History, SUNY–Purchase, May 1988), 10, with corrections added by the SSJ archivist to the passage in question, p. 24, archives of the Sisters of St. Joseph, Rochester, N.Y.

36. Sister Barbara Lumm, SSJ, interview with author, December 14, 2000, Rochester, N.Y.

37. Sister Mary Paul Geck, SSJ, interview with author, December 13, 2000, Rochester, N.Y.

38. Creighton, "What Were Doing in Selma, Sister?," 37.

39. Sister Mary Paul Geck, SSJ, interview with author, December 13, 2000, Rochester, N.Y.

40. Project Cabrini Newsletter #4, July 4–10, 1965, Series 19, Box 2, "Project Cabrini" file, NCCIJ papers, Marquette University archives, Milwaukee.

41. Handwritten letter from Sister Joan Campbell, SL, to Sister Margaret Ellen (Mary Peter) Traxler, SSND, February 18, 1970, Series 19, Box 13, "CHOICE" file, NCCIJ papers, Marquette University archives, Milwaukee. In her letter, Sister Campbell continued her explanation: " 'Campbell' is the name of the main street through the honky-tonk section of the black community, and this fact secured the value of my student stock immediately!" I don't have time in this chapter to explore the meaning of sister's racializations of African American voices, but I'd like to note that I do address this troubling complication at length in the forthcoming *The New Nuns: Racial Justice and Religious Reform in the 1960s* (Cambridge: Harvard University Press, 2007).

42. It should be noted that a few sisters described a different, less accepting reaction from African Americans. These infrequent accounts stress that African Americans, regardless of sisters' perceptions of them, may have had quite complicated reactions to the presence of white sisters within their neighborhoods, particularly with the emergence of the Black Power movement and separatist ideologies. Sisters' accounts of the openness of African Americans to their presence should be understood purely as sisters' perspectives on the issue and not as a reflection of African American experience.

43. Project Cabrini Newsletter #8, August 1–12, 1965, Series 19, Box 2, "Project Cabrini" file, NCCIJ papers, Marquette University archives, Milwaukee.

44. Handwritten letter from Sister Peter to Sister Margaret Ellen (Mary Peter) Traxler, SSND, September 19, 1967, NCCIJ Correspondence, Series 4, Box 4, "R–Sh" file, NCCIJ papers, Marquette University archives, Milwaukee.

45. Handwritten letter from Sister Joan Campbell, SL, to Sister Margaret Ellen (Mary Peter) Traxler, SSND, February 18, 1970, Series 19, Box 13, "CHOICE" file, NCCIJ papers, Marquette University archives, Milwaukee.

46. See Caroline Walker Bynum, "Women's Stories, Women's Symbols," in Bynum, *Fragmentation and Redemption*, 50–51.

11

Engendering Dissent

Women and American Judaism

Pamela S. Nadell

Many of the most important controversies in American Jewish history—the ordination of female rabbis, the introduction of mixed seating in the synagogue, the innovation of bat mitzvah—have involved gender. Yet when historians of Judaism have written about these controversies, they have relied almost entirely on male voices. Instead of treating Jewish women as historical agents, scholars have assumed that male leaders were solely responsible for the most significant changes in Jewish belief and practice.

Who are the female actors in the great controversies concerning gender in the history of American Judaism? This is the question that has inspired much of Pamela Nadell's research on Jewish women, including her groundbreaking book, Women Who Would Be Rabbis: A History of Women's Ordination, 1889–1985. *In this chapter, Nadell reflects on the historical silence surrounding Jewish women—a silence that only recently has been broken. As she illustrates, Jewish women have indeed been lively historical actors, and yet, because scholars have ignored them for so long, she and other women's historians have found it both personally and professionally difficult to restore them to the historical record. Women's stories, however, offer a crucial perspective on the transformations that have shaped modern Jewish life.*

In the mid-1970s, a reporter for the Jewish press announced: "With the ordination of Rabbi Sally Priesand in 1972, Judaism learned that a great religious debate over women in the pulpit had been settled before it began."[1] I opened my book, *Women Who Would Be Rabbis: A History of Women's Ordination, 1889–1985* (1988), with this conceit because it baldly states a trope familiar to those of us who write women's history. It repeats what many, including some among our scholarly colleagues, advanced at one time with great certainty: that there was little for us to pursue. After all, conventional wisdom taught that history was made by men. Therefore, to write the history of American religion was to study its leaders, the men who led its seminaries, who guided its churches (in my case, its synagogues), and who shaped its teachings and articulated its theologies.

In fact, when I edited a special issue for the scholarly quarterly *American Jewish History* on women's history, I introduced the volume by responding to a colleague who had called to tell me that "he was thinking of venturing into American Jewish women's history, [b]ut first he wanted to make certain that everything had not already been written."[2] I responded to him then, in 1995, just as I would today: "Hardly!"

A decade before *Women Who Would Be Rabbis* appeared, I had, in fact, written a book, a history in the guise of a reference volume, about the men who had shaped Conservative Judaism in America.[3] For that project I had researched the major institutions of the Conservative movement—its seminary, its rabbinical conclave, and its synagogue association. I had described Conservatism's theology through the prism of the movement's controversies over reinterpreting the historic body of Jewish law. I had sketched biographies of 130 significant Conservative leaders, men whose intellectual and spiritual leadership had placed them in the forefront of this American Jewish denomination and often of American Jewish life writ large. Only a single woman, Mathilde Roth Schechter, founding president of what today is called the Women's League for Conservative Judaism, merited her own biographical sketch. With the exception of references to a prominent female educator and to the first woman who became a Conservative rabbi, the other women appearing ever so briefly in this history did so because they had married prominent men, the rabbis and scholars I named.

Even as I was writing *Conservative Judaism in America*, I knew my approach was deeply problematic. I even hinted at this in the introduction.[4] But sometimes career choices are driven by practicalities. I recall announcing, even as I signed the contract with the publisher who had asked for this book, that when I was finished, I would write what I really wanted to write, namely, a book about American Jewish women.

In retrospect, I now know I was not alone in deciding early in my career not to turn to the history of Jewish women. As Paula Hyman, the pioneering scholar in Jewish women's history, has observed trenchantly, what Jewish historians deemed significant to study was "defined by the parameters of male experience." Even as late as 1994, she asserted that "graduate students in Judaic studies have gotten the message: if you want to succeed in this field, do not write your dissertation on a woman's topic. Wait until you have tenure."[5] And that was exactly the road I had taken.

Now, a decade later, I sense that Professor Hyman's statement is no longer true. The study of gender has finally won acceptance in most fields of Jewish studies. But I am convinced that her caveat reflected the reality of Jewish historical scholarship well into the 1990s. Not until 1991 did a volume of scholarly articles on the history of Jewish women appear.[6] When I was choosing essays for my edited book *American Jewish Women's History: A Reader*, which was published in 2003, I made a similar observation: all but two of the eighteen articles in this anthology were written after 1990.[7]

Thus, the emergence of a significant body of literature writing women into the history of the Jewish people is a project a little more than a decade old.[8] Yet already that literature, to which I and so many others have substantially contributed, has propelled a more nuanced understanding of the history of the subfield of American Judaism.

In fact, that was the goal that led Brandeis University Professor Jonathan D. Sarna and me to edit the volume *Women and American Judaism: Historical Perspectives* (2001). Here we collected new essays, written by both senior and emerging scholars. Not surprisingly, a number of our authors were graduate students when they presented their papers at the consultation that shaped our book. The essays disclose women negotiating Judaism "in four different venues: in the home, in the synagogue, within the Jewish community, and among Christians in the larger community." They also show how, over time, ideals of proper Jewish womanhood in each of these venues changed. Ultimately, we concluded "that from the colonial era to the close of the twentieth century, American women, committed to Judaism and to their own Jewish communities, repeatedly reshaped Judaism and helped to redefine the place of men and women within it."[9]

In *Women and American Judaism* Sarna and I considered Ann Braude's justly celebrated article "Women's History *Is* American Religious History," just as so many of the other authors in this volume have done. Despite Braude's persuasiveness, Sarna and I felt that we dare not make quite so bold a claim that women's history is also the history of American Judaism. Nevertheless, we accepted Braude's challenge to focus on "the presence of women" in American religion, and we agreed that doing so compels a major reevaluation of the themes and narratives of American religious history, in this case of American Judaism. We argued that the essays in our book affirmed that uncovering the history of women in American Judaism would revise and expand our understanding of the historical experience of American Jewish religious life and thus transform our perception of the past.[10]

Let me reflect then upon the ways in which both my scholarship and that of some of my colleagues, who have also cast a gendered lens upon American Judaism, have revised its history.

I will begin with my own *Women Who Would Be Rabbis*. Despite the myopia of the 1970s Jewish press, the question of women's ordination was hardly settled before it was raised. In fact, it was first introduced by the

Philadelphia writer Mary M. Cohen on the front page of a Jewish newspaper in 1889. Crafting a Jewish response to the nineteenth-century woman's rights movement and its demand for women's access to the professions, including the ministry, Cohen helped launch a debate that swirled for over a century in Jewish life, and which indeed would cease in a particular Jewish denomination only when women won the right to rabbinical ordination.

Women Who Would Be Rabbis follows that debate. In the 1890s, an "era of rising expectations for women's ordination" was fueled partly by the 1893 Congress of Jewish Women at the World's Columbian Exposition and by the career of Ray Frank, the "girl rabbi of the golden west." In the 1920s and 1930s, five women spent enough time in rabbinical seminaries to force their students, faculty, and boards of trustees—and Jews more broadly—to contemplate seriously the notion of a woman in the pulpit. One of these, in Germany, ultimately received private, not seminary, ordination, but she shared the tragic fate of her people and perished at the hands of the Nazis. The others all failed to be ordained, but each came later in her life to raise the question once again.

Changes in seminary education in the 1950s and 1960s unexpectedly brought more women to rabbinical school. Ultimately, one of them, Sally Priesand, riding the crest of the new wave of American feminism, was ordained a Reform rabbi in 1972. That event and the surrounding publicity sparked a highly public and painful debate in Conservative Judaism in the 1970s and early 1980s. When that denomination, in 1983, decided too in favor of ordaining women rabbis, the Orthodox began asking, "Will there be Orthodox women rabbis?"

Others before me, including Rabbi Sally Priesand and religion scholar Ellen Umansky, had uncovered strands of the debate,[11] but in *Women Who Would Be Rabbis*, I connected the threads. I traced its trajectory, as it had waxed and waned in American Jewish life since 1889. I analyzed the arguments advanced by both sides—by those who decried this break with tradition, as well as by those, especially the women who would have been rabbis if they could have become rabbis, who argued that women were utterly capable and worthy of taking on this role. Criticized for seeking to overturn the tradition that, as rabbis, they would be bound to uphold, these women, and those who opposed them, turned again and again to the same sources in Jewish tradition and in the history of Jewish women.

For example, they read the same classical texts of Jewish law and found no statement specifically prohibiting female rabbis. They paraded long lists of the learned Jewish women of the past, especially those who had used their sacred study and learning to teach and to rule. Arguing that these women functioned just like rabbis, the women who would be rabbis sought to climb on their shoulders, to claim their places as rabbis, teachers, and preachers in American Judaism. Yet, because the women who would be rabbis lacked any sense of the collective history of the question, each had to discover on her own, and as if de novo, arguments to advance.

In uncovering the cycles of debate over women's rabbinic ordination, I relied upon Gerda Lerner's *The Creation of Feminist Consciousness.* Lerner had demonstrated the grave consequences of the failure to recount women's history. Whereas men, with their written histories, had benefited from transmission of knowledge from one generation to the next, she knew that "women were denied knowledge of their history, and thus each woman had to argue as though no woman before her had ever thought or written. Women had to use their energy to reinvent the wheel, over and over again, generation after generation."[12] I showed how this held true for the women who wanted to become rabbis and how they were unable to build upon the strategies and creativity of those who had discovered before them the very same arguments for why women should become rabbis.

Women Who Would Be Rabbis thus stands, I believe, among the "new narratives" Braude called for in "Women's History *Is* Religious History."[13] Because of the vagaries of publishing, the manuscript for *Women Who Would Be Rabbis* was in press by the time Braude's article appeared. Nevertheless, Braude and I were thinking along parallel tracks, for *Women Who Would Be Rabbis* revolves around the "themes of female presence and male power" that Braude argued were essential for a reconceptualization of American religious history.[14] The women who sought ordination constituted the "female presence," and they challenged the powerful men who guarded the gates to ordination.

Women's rabbinic ordination thus became another arena in which Judaism encountered modernity and forged new adaptations and syntheses, and its history expands our understanding of modern Judaism. *Women Who Would Be Rabbis* also points us, I think, to another theme Braude briefly raised in her seminal article, but one which she has explored in greater depth elsewhere. In "Women's History *Is* Religious History," she wrote that women "have played a prominent role in religious dissent."[15] That holds true for the debate over women's rabbinic ordination. In fact, as Sarna and I argued in *Women and American Judaism,* "many of the central themes and controversies in American Jewish religious life have revolved around the position of women in Judaism both literally and figuratively."[16]

Standard accounts of the history and sociology of American Judaism have paid only limited attention to how gender has long been a source of dissent.

Instead, American Judaism has generally been presented as the evolution of its denominations: Reform, Orthodox, Conservative, and later Reconstructionist. These older narratives take one of two approaches. Some trace the waves of Jewish immigrants, in which males continue to remain the norm, and how their impulses to reform, with both a lowercase and a capital R, reflected their acculturation. Others focus specifically upon denominational evolution, analyzing the emergence of national institutions and evolving ideologies. Women receive little mention; gender as a category of analysis is largely absent.[17]

But dissent is front and center. Newer immigrants rejected the syntheses of American life and Judaism crafted by those who came before in order to fashion their own synagogues, institutions, and religious ideologies. As the denominations evolved, they implicitly and explicitly asserted that the expressions of Judaism shaped by others were inauthentic. Dissenting visions within each denomination caused internal strife. Dissent is thus a paramount theme of American Jewish religious history.[18]

In *Women and American Judaism*, Sarna and I listed some of the arenas in which gender provoked dissent. Long before the question of women's ordination was raised, we knew that American Jews had argued over whether Judaism permitted men and women to sit together during worship. These men and women had debated whether their daughters should receive the same educations as their sons. They had wrestled with whether or not girls should celebrate their passage into adolescence as Jewish boys did in the bar mitzvah. They had struggled over what roles women could take on in the service. And they had agonized, and continue to agonize, over how to help the *agunah*, the woman chained, under Jewish law, to an untenable marriage because her husband no longer lived with her but would not grant her a divorce. Sarna and I concluded: "These questions and many others relating to the position of women within American Judaism evoked passionate debates, deep communal conflicts, and enormous anxiety as Jewish men and women renegotiated the boundaries of gender in American Jewish life."[19]

Reconceptualizing the history of American Judaism requires exploring these and other topics relating to gender in greater depth. To illustrate what I mean, consider a contemporary synagogue service. In most, but by no means all, male and female congregants sit together. In many congregations, women worshippers now wear the ritual garb (head coverings and prayer shawls) traditionally worn only by men. Some female worshippers take leading roles in the service, reading from the Torah and chanting the prophetic reading known as the Haftarah. This contemporary synagogue service is dramatically and visibly transformed, not only from the synagogues of the colonial era where women sat and gossiped or prayed in a raised gallery, but also from those of the mid-twentieth century when the only time females ascended to the *bimah*, the raised platform at the front of the sanctuary, was on the day of their bat mitzvah or that of their daughter. How this occurred, and where and how it caused conflict is part of the history of American Judaism.

Scholars Jonathan Sarna and Karla Goldman have both written about one of the most visible of the shifts in the religious service, the adoption of mixed seating or family seating patterns in the American synagogue. Deviating from the traditional separation of men and women during Jewish worship became, in Karla Goldman's felicitous phrase, one of the "gender frontier[s] in the synagogue."[20] In 1851, Reform rabbi Isaac Mayer Wise introduced mixed seating in Albany, New York. Although he later described this step as an important ideological reform, it was surely driven at the time by practicalities. Wise's new congregation consecrated an old church for its first synagogue, and the building had pews. Rather than reconfigure the church to separate the sexes in worship, the members decided to sit with their wives in the pews. Even if adopted as a matter of convenience, the shift, Goldman reminds us, reflected the worldview of its Americanizing congregants.[21] By the 1860s, the seating of men and women together in worship had increasingly become a hallmark of reforming synagogues in America, although not in Europe, a perceptible adaptation of American middle-class gendered norms.[22]

As Sarna has shown, mixed seating became a test of Judaism's embrace of modernity. Proponents believed mixed seating countered the charge of Judaism's Orientalism and backwardness. It showed modern Judaism standing for family togetherness and women's equality and keeping in step with the times for its youth. Opponents believed family pews allowed Jews to abandon tradition, violate Jewish law, and imitate Christians.[23]

As Conservative Judaism evolved in the twentieth century, mixed seating became the norm in its congregations too, although not in its seminary. By mid-century, mixed seating had become "the most commonly accepted yardstick for differentiating Conservatism from Orthodoxy."[24]

As a symbol of women's equality, it should not surprise us that mixed seating caused friction. Sarna describes several nineteenth- and twentieth-century synagogue disputes that landed in U.S. courts when one group of congregants sued another to prevent the adoption of mixed seating. After women were accepted as candidates for ordination at the Conservative movement's Jewish Theological Seminary, seminary leaders faced a dilemma. The seminary synagogue separated men and women in worship. Now that women were about to become rabbis, what were they to do? Seminary officials decided to compromise by retaining the traditional prayer service and adding an egalitarian one for those who wanted it.[25] Even the Orthodox who do not permit mixed seating show their sensitivity to how this violates American norms. I recall an Orthodox rabbi in the late 1980s boasting to me that when his congregation built its new synagogue, its sanctuary would offer men and women separate but completely equal seats.

What I find particularly striking about the history of the dissension over mixed seating in the American synagogue is that, contrary to the debate over women's ordination in which we can point to specific female historical actors, women are largely absent from the debate. Instead, we hear only of the men invested in this concession to women's new status in American Jewish life. For example, Sarna writes of a dispute over mixed seating in 1861 that led "several of the old members: of a Cleveland congregation, including its treasurer, to resign." Since women did not then hold synagogue membership and since the treasurer was named Benjamin, this dispute about gender, interpreted as a harbinger of women's emancipation in the synagogue, appears decidedly androcentric. Sarna's lengthy discussion of the lawsuit, *Israel J. Solomon v. the Congregation of B'nai Jeshurn*, names only the men engaged in the court case. In fact, in none of his examples of strife over mixed seating are women present.[26] They appear only implicitly as an anonymous and amorphous female body whose synagogue seats would change if their congregations allowed them to sit with their husbands.

But what did the women want? Were they at all invested in the debate? Did they urge their husbands, fathers, and sons, the men named, to champion this reform? Or to fight it? How did women feel the first time they changed seats to join their husbands in the pews? What did this mean to the family? What did it mean to their daughters? Unfortunately, because of an absence of sources or of the great difficulty at ferreting them out, female voices do not surface in the narrative. Thus, while the debate about mixed seating is literally about women's place in the synagogue, it is nevertheless scarcely reflective of the study of women's presence that Braude has challenged us to write.

A survey of other controversies in American Jewish religious life revolving around the position of women in Judaism demonstrates just how often women's presence is absent in controversies involving gender. In fact, I would argue that much of the historiography on how gender caused dissent in American Judaism—and I criticize here too some of my own earlier work— is marked far less by women's presence than by their absence. Therefore, scholars of American Judaism have much work yet to do before we can begin to conceptualize a history that fully incorporates gender as a category of analysis.

For example, in *Women Who Would Be Rabbis*, I wrote briefly about a new role offered to Conservative Jewish women in the mid-1950s, the honor of an *aliyah*, of being called up to bless the Torah scrolls, a role also related to the growing acceptance of the increasingly common female rite of passage, the bat mitzvah. In 1954, Rabbi Ira Eisenstein, then president of the Conservative movement's rabbinical conclave, the Rabbinical Assembly, challenged his colleagues: "We are still operating upon the Orthodox assumption that the basic inequality of the woman must be preserved in law." Referring specifically to the wider American "struggle to emancipate the woman from the domination of the man in political and social life," he urged his colleagues to consider "the equalization of the status of women in Jewish law as a true expression of a Torah of justice." A year later, two rabbis wrote legal opinions giving their colleagues permission to invite women to bless the Torah. One would allow women to do so only on special occasions, like the day of a son's bar mitzvah. The other felt females could have this synagogue honor at any time.[27] Thus, Conservative rabbis came proudly to embrace *aliyah* for women as a new marker of their dedication to women's equality.

But, a half century ago, when the rabbis debated these *responsa* (legal briefs), one articulated the concern I raise now about women's absence as historical actors. About women's *aliyah*, Rabbi Gershon Winer asked: "Is there a crying need of privileges being denied? Are our women folk asking for these particular privileges?"[28]

The renowned sociologist Marshall Sklare also pointed to the complacence of Conservative Jewish women. In his classic study, *Conservative Judaism*, published in 1955, he wrote briefly about the position of women in both Conservative and Orthodox Judaism. He knew women's inferior position in Judaism went against Western norms, and he believed that this would become "perhaps the single most disruptive force, or strain, to American Jewish Orthodoxy." He felt that "even though change will entail a serious violation of the religious code and the overcoming of much resistance, a status quo position would mean organizational suicide." Yet so far the women themselves had not clamored for change: "There has been no widespread agitation for perfect equality. Conservative women have generally been satisfied with their limited status—a great advance over the age-old segregation."[29] The result was that debates over gender in the synagogue in the 1950s were about what the men thought and had to say. Once again, women's presence is not felt.

The same is largely true for accounts of the emergence of bat mitzvah. If we visit again the contemporary synagogue service discussed above, we will see how bar and bat mitzvah, the rite of passage to adolescence in American

Jewish life—but to maturity earlier in Jewish history—lie at the center of so many Sabbath morning services. Whereas the notion of bar mitzvah, the passage to adult responsibilities in the synagogue for boys, appears in rabbinic sources, bat mitzvah in America was a twentieth-century innovation.[30] Nevertheless, it has become "one of the most common ceremonies in contemporary American synagogues" since 1922 when Judith Kaplan was invited to celebrate her bat mitzvah by her father, Jewish Theological Seminary professor and founder of Reconstructionist Judaism Mordecai M. Kaplan. Typically, after mentioning Judith Kaplan's bat mitzvah, the histories of the evolution of the bat mitzvah turn back to the rabbis, the men who debated and finally agreed to introduce it into their congregations.[31] Once again, the historical actors are almost exclusively male.

Finally, this is also true of the writing on the thorny legal issue of the *agunah*, and here again I turn to my own work on the subject. Conservative rabbis, who viewed themselves as bound to uphold Jewish law, found the plight of the *agunah* to be "one of the most distressing and painful conditions" of modern Jewish life. Under Jewish law, a woman whose husband's death cannot be established with certainty or whose husband refuses to grant her a *get*, a Jewish divorce, is prohibited from ever remarrying. She remains bound by the Jewish laws of marriage to a husband who no longer lives with her. (Jewish law imposes no such constraint upon abandoned husbands.) The calamity of the women who become *agunot* remains a deeply disturbing problem in any Jewish society whose members abide by Jewish law, including those in Orthodox Jewish communities in the United States and all Jews in the state of Israel.[32]

As early as 1929, Conservative rabbis sought solutions to the plight of the *agunah*. In fact, they spent the next forty years advancing various legal proposals to resolve this particularly gendered imbalance in Jewish law.[33] Yet, once again, women are absent from the history. Instead, when I wrote of this controversy involving gender, I wrote of the rabbis who crafted legal subterfuges to prevent women from becoming *agunot* and of the Orthodox scholars who vehemently objected to their solutions. But, on the women whose lives were affected by this law, I was silent.

Although Marshall Sklare was certainly correct in noting that at midcentury there was no "widespread agitation for perfect equality" among Conservative women, I am no longer convinced, if I ever was, that women were not historical actors in these gendered controversies in American Judaism. And I wonder if—just as I uncovered women's voices in the debate on ordination—we could find other women similarly engaged in these other controversies. I see glimmers of possibility. For example, in *To the Golden*

Cities, Deborah Dash Moore names a woman involved in the introduction of women's *aliyot*. She writes about the furor that ensued, however briefly, in the middle of synagogue services, when, in the mid-1950s, Aaron Wise, rabbi of Los Angeles's Valley Jewish Community Center, called his wife, Miriam, to bless the Torah during High Holiday services.[34] In 1963, Trude Weiss-Rosmarin, author and editor of the *Jewish Spectator*, who has been described as one of the "other" New York Jewish intellectuals, railed against the "obsolete Jewish laws of divorce," giving us one woman's perspective on the gendered controversy.[35]

In the important study *The Other Feminists*, historian Susan Hartmann uncovered the women she called "lively characters," key players, who, in the decades before the second wave of American feminism, propelled their establishments to advance feminist aims. Hartmann's examination of the "sea change in attitudes, practices, and policies regarding gender roles" in organizations as diverse as the International Union of Electrical Workers, the Ford Foundation, and the National Council of Churches turned up small cohorts of central female players pushing from within to raise feminist consciousness. In the case of the American Civil Liberties Union, she found that "the ACLU began its support for women's rights primarily because of the passion and labor of one woman."[36]

I would assert that in order to reconceptualize the study of American Judaism to incorporate women's presence and not just to expand our history by incorporating debates involving gender, we need to uncover a similar history of female "lively characters" in American Jewish life. I took this approach in my recent article, "An Angle of Vision: Jewish Women's Studies in the Seminaries," in which I focused on the introduction of women's and gender studies into rabbinical schools following women's ordination in the liberal movements of American Judaism.[37] But, of course, I was looking at very recent history and the sources were easy to discover. I did the same in uncovering the "lively characters"—although I did not then use that term—who shaped the Reform sisterhoods early in the twentieth century.[38]

Consequently, I challenge myself and my colleagues to bring women's presence forward for other aspects of the history of American Judaism. I know just how difficult this is. I spent ten years working on *Women Who Would be Rabbis*. Lucky for me, because of the attention of the press to any question dealing with the advance of women in society, I was successful in discovering new sources, including press reports about women in the ministry going back to the nineteenth century that helped bring women's voices forward. Furthermore, I found scrapbooks and other records from women who were pivotal actors in this debate. These did not exist in any archive.

Rather they had remained in the possession of the women or of their daughters, and I tracked them down. (I never came across sons who had held onto their mothers' scrapbooks.) Invaluable primary sources to me, these were generally deemed historically insignificant by others. In fact, for another project, when I tried to find the papers of one woman, Anita Libman Lebeson, who began writing Jewish women into history before women's history emerged as a new and leading field of study, I was told by her daughter that her mother's papers were all gone. The daughter claimed that she had tried at one time to give them to the American Jewish Historical Society, but they were declined.

I know that some, and I suspect many, of the female actors were intimately connected to the men whose names already surface in the historical records of gender engendering controversy. Therefore, their names are a good place to start. When Rabbi Aaron Wise first gave an *aliyah* to a woman, it was his wife, Miriam, who caused such a furor when she came up to bless the Torah. Ira Eisenstein, the rabbi who charged his Conservative colleagues to rectify the status of women in Jewish law, was married to Judith Kaplan Eisenstein, the bat mitzvah girl of 1922. For *Women Who Would Be Rabbis*, I interviewed Toby Fink, who had begun studying for the rabbinate as an undergraduate at the University of Cincinnati in 1957. We both knew that she was the daughter of Rabbi Joseph I. Fink, former president of the Reform movement's rabbinical conference, but only I knew that he had led a committee of rabbis that, in its "Report on the Ordination of Women," affirmed that women could be ordained while his daughter was still in high school.[39]

My concern with women's presence is also reflected in my most recent work, the edited volume *American Jewish Women's History: A Reader*. Even as I was working on *Women and American Judaism*, I was rereading my way through the scholarship that has appeared on American Jewish women's history and trying to conceptualize a reader in this new literature. Influenced again by Gerda Lerner, who wrote, "My commitment to women's history came out of my life, not out of my head,"[40] I used the overarching theme of agency to guide my choices for this anthology. I sought articles that showed how Jewish women had acted and exerted power to sustain and to shape Jewish life in America. These articles highlight American Jewish women in their multiple roles—"as daughters, wives, and mothers; students and teachers; workers and entrepreneurs." I chose articles that positioned Jewish women "in their kitchens and in their synagogues, at their writing tables and behind the counters of general stores, hunched over sewing machines and dancing in front of the mirror. [The articles] consider their volunteer activities and political crusades. They examine their interior lives and the stereotypes imposed on them. They take up their piety and the roles they played in shaping American Judaism. They show American Jewish women with their Christian neighbors and see them working to better their own lives and the lives of Jews everywhere." In short, in this anthology, Jewish women stand front and foremost as historical actors.[41]

There are many fine studies that, like so much of the literature on the gendered controversies in American Judaism, including, of course, my own writing, explore the evolution of men's ideas abut Jewish women and their roles.[42] But, in making my decisions about what to include in *American Jewish Women's History: A Reader*, I deliberately excluded those works. Instead, by emphasizing Jewish women's agency—whether it was exercised by colonial matrons or club women, turn-of-the century garment workers or late-twentieth-century feminists—women emerged as historical actors molding the contours of American Jewish life. Their presence is thus manifest. And uncovering the history of that presence is the first step to reconceptualizing a history of women in American Jewish life and American Judaism.

Notes

1. Pamela S. Nadell, *Women Who Would Be Rabbis: A History of Women's Ordination, 1889–1985* (Boston: Beacon Press, 1998), ix.
2. Pamela S. Nadell, "Introduction," *American Jewish History* 83 (1995): 147–51, 147.
3. Pamela S. Nadell, *Conservative Judaism in America: A Biographical Dictionary and Sourcebook* (New York: Greenwood Press, 1988).
4. I explained the decision behind my androcentric focus, in ibid., x.
5. Paula E. Hyman, "Feminist Studies and Modern Jewish History," in *Feminist Perspectives on Jewish Studies*, ed. Lynn Davidman and Shelly Tenenbaum (New Haven: Yale University Press, 1994), 120–39, 120, 134.
6. Judith R. Baskin, ed., *Jewish Women in Historical Perspective* (Detroit: Wayne State University Press, 1991).
7. Pamela S. Nadell, ed., *American Jewish Women's History: A Reader* (New York: New York University Press, 2003).
8. Long before the acceptance of women's history in the last quarter of the twentieth century as a legitimate field of study, a few female historians tried to interject women into Jewish history. Elsewhere I have written about three twentieth-century independent female scholars, all of whom held Ph.D.s, lived in the United States, and wrote Jewish women's history. All three were marginalized both during their careers and by those who would develop the new scholarship on gender and Jewish women. Pamela S. Nadell, "Women on the Margins of Jewish Historiography," in *The Margins of Jewish History*, ed. Marc Lee Raphael (Williamsburg, Va.: College of William and Mary, 2000), 102–12.
9. Pamela S. Nadell and Jonathan D. Sarna, "Introduction," in *Women and Ameri-*

can Judaism: Historical Perspectives, ed. Pamela S. Nadell and Jonathan D. Sarna (Hanover, N.H.: Brandeis University Press, 2001), 1–14, 3, 12; italics in original in the latter quotation.

10. Ann Braude, "Women's History *Is* Religious History," in *Retelling U.S. Religious History*, ed. Thomas A. Tweed (Berkeley: University of California Press, 1997), 87–107, 90, 88; Nadell and Sarna, *Women and American Judaism*, 1.

11. Sally Priesand, *Judaism and the New Woman* (New York: Behrman House, 1975); Ellen M. Umansky, "Women in Judaism: From the Reform Movement to Contemporary Jewish Religious Feminism," in *Women of Spirit: Female Leadership in the Jewish and Christian Traditions*, ed. Rosemary Ruether and Eleanor McLaughlin (New York: Simon and Schuster, 1979), 339–42.

12. Gerda Lerner, *The Creation of Feminist Consciousness: From the Middle Ages to Eighteen-Seventy* (New York: Oxford University Press, 1993), 166.

13. Braude, "Women's History *Is* Religious History," 91.

14. Ibid., 107.

15. Ibid., 89. She explores this in Ann Braude, *Radical Spirits: Spiritualism and Women's Rights in Nineteenth-Century America* (Boston: Beacon Press, 1989).

16. Nadell and Sarna, *Women and American Judaism*, 2–3.

17. See, for example, Nathan Glazer, *American Judaism* (1957; rev. ed., Chicago: University of Chicago Press, 1972); and Marc Lee Raphael, *Profiles in American Judaism: The Reform, Conservative, Orthodox, and Reconstructionist Traditions in Historical Perspective* (San Francisco: Harper and Row, 1984). I wrote this before the publication of Jonathan D. Sarna's *American Judaism: A History* (New Haven: Yale University Press, 2004) and Hasia Diner's *The Jews of the United States* (Berkeley: University of California Press, 2004). Both of these histories do incorporate new scholarship on women and gender.

18. Dissent is obviously a major theme of religious history. Note that my "Ordaining Women Rabbis," in *Religions of the United States in Practice*, vol. 2, ed. Colleen McDannell, Princeton Readings in Religion (Princeton: Princeton University Press, 2001), 389–417, appears in the section titled "Persuading: Witnessing, Controversies, and Polemics."

19. Nadell and Sarna, *Women and American Judaism*, 2.

20. Karla Goldman, *Beyond the Synagogue Gallery: Finding a Place for Women in American Judaism* (Cambridge: Harvard University Press, 2000), 93–99, 129–33, quotation, 93.

21. Ibid., 94.

22. Jonathan D. Sarna, "The Debate over Mixed Seating in the American Synagogue," in *The American Synagogue: A Sanctuary Transformed*, ed. Jack Wertheimer (Cambridge: Cambridge University Press, 1987), 363–94.

23. Ibid., esp. 378.

24. Ibid.; Sarna quotes Marshall Sklare on p. 380.

25. *JTS: Campus Life* (accessed August 15, 2003), <http://www.jtsa.edu/life/>.

26. Sarna, "The Debate over Mixed Seating in the American Synagogue," esp. 372–78.

27. Nadell, *Women Who Would Be Rabbis*; for references to this discussion and the following paragraphs, see 184–85 and the notes.

28. Quoted in ibid., 184–85.

29. All quoted in ibid.

30. Bat mitzvah has earlier origins in nineteenth-century Europe; see Norma Baumel Joseph, "Ritual Law and Praxis: Bat Mitsva Celebrations," *Modern Judaism* 22, no. 3 (2002): 234–60, 256n10.

31. The following all focus especially on male responses to bat mitzvah: Regina Stein, "The Road to Bat Mitzvah in America," in Nadell and Sarna, *Women and American Judaism*, 223–34, quotation, 223; Paula Hyman, "The Introduction of Bat Mitzvah in Conservative Judaism in Postwar America," *YIVO Annual* 19 (1990): 133–46; and Joseph, "Ritual Law and Praxis: Bat Mitsva Celebrations." One of the few to ask the question "what happens to the girl" (p. 254) is Erica S. Brown, "Bat Mitzvah in Jewish Law and Contemporary Practice," in *Jewish Legal Writings by Women*, ed. Micah D. Halpern and Chana Safrai (Jerusalem: Urim Publications, 1998), 232–58. Still, the subject merits only a single paragraph in this article.

32. For a recent case, see Oren Rawls, "In Other Words," *Forward*, July 25, 2003: <http://www.forward.com/issues/2003/03.07.25/otherwords.html>. Nadell, *Conservative Judaism in America*, 7.

33. I discuss this in the introduction to Nadell, *Conservative Judaism in America*, 7–14.

34. Deborah Dash Moore, *To the Golden Cities: Pursuing the American Jewish Dream in Miami and L.A.* (New York: Free Press, 1994), 120–21.

35. Trude Weiss-Rosmarin, "Women without Legal Rights," *Jewish Spectator*, October 1963; Deborah Dash Moore, "Trude Weiss-Rosmarin and the *Jewish Spectator*," in *The "Other" New York Jewish Intellectuals*, ed. Carole S. Kessner (New York: New York University Press, 1994), 101–21.

36. Susan M. Hartmann, *The Other Feminists: Activists in the Liberal Establishment* (New Haven: Yale University Press, 1998), 1, 174, 57.

37. Pamela S. Nadell, "An Angle of Vision: Jewish Women's Studies in the Seminaries," *Conservative Judaism* 55, no. 1 (2002): 3–10.

38. Pamela S. Nadell and Rita J. Simon, "Ladies of the Sisterhood: Women in the American Reform Synagogue, 1900–1930," in *Active Voices: Women in Jewish Culture*, ed. Maurie Sacks (Urbana: University of Illinois Press, 1995), 63–75.

39. Nadell, *Women Who Would Be Rabbis*, 143.

40. Gerda Lerner, "Women among the Professors of History: The Story of a Process of Transformation," in *Voices of Women Historians: The Personal, the Political, the Professional*, ed. Eileen Boris and Nupur Chaudhuri (Bloomington: Indiana University Press, 1999), 1–10, quotation, 1.

41. Nadell, *American Jewish Women's History*, 2.

42. An important example is Karla Goldman, "The Ambivalence of Reform Judaism: Kaufmann Kohler and the Ideal Jewish Woman," *American Jewish History* 79 (1990): 477–99.

12

Little Slices of Heaven and Mary's Candy Kisses

Mexican American Women Redefining
Feminism and Catholicism

*Kristy Nabhan-
Warren*

In this chapter, Kristy Nabhan-Warren asks historians to reimagine two narratives that rarely converge: the narrative of the feminist movement and the narrative of Catholic history. Like Ann Braude, whose chapter appears earlier in this volume, Nabhan-Warren argues that historians must craft richer, more complex accounts of the relationship between religion and the modern feminist movement. Because many scholars have defined feminism narrowly as the desire for autonomy, they have largely ignored women who have defined themselves in relationship to their families, communities, and churches. Catholic women in particular, who venerate the Virgin Mary as the model of ideal womanhood, have often been depicted as reactionary or antifeminist. Yet, as Nabhan-Warren shows in her case study of Estela Ruiz, lay Catholic women have been empowered by their faith to reform their families and society.

Besides urging historians to develop a more capacious understanding of feminism, Nabhan-Warren illustrates that Catholic women, despite their subordinate status in the official church, have transformed Catholic culture through their determined lay activism. Too often, Catholic historians have explained historical transformations by pointing to papal encyclicals and bishops' letters. As Nabhan-Warren illustrates, however, scholars who are intrigued by the changing character of Mexican American Catholicism—a Catholicism that has become increasingly evangelical in recent years—must also pay close attention to women's grassroots organizations. Although the "official" church is run by a celibate male clergy, laywomen have been crucial actors in redefining Catholic identity.

According to Estela Ruiz, a Mexican American woman in her mid-sixties who claims to both see and hear the Virgin Mary, the Virgin of the Americas changed her life when she first appeared to her in her bedroom on the night of December 3, 1988. She was praying especially hard for youngest son Reyes Jr., who was battling a drug addiction, and for a mending of daughter-in-law Leticia and son Fernando's troubled marriage. Estela was clutching her rosary tightly as she stared at a print of the Sacred Heart of Mary, which hung in front of her. She fingered the crystal beads and prayed to the Blessed Mother to take care of her family. As she was reciting the last decet of the rosary, she saw a light emanating from the portrait; it grew brighter and brighter and she had to close her eyes. Estela describes this as a profoundly moving moment:

> I began to see this cloud form around the bottom of the Blessed Mother, but before the cloud, a bright light appeared. I tried to let go of the rosary to rub my eyes but I couldn't; it's like it was stuck to my hand. I felt like I was paralyzed, but not in a bad way. . . . My heart was going bum bum, bum bum. . . . I *knew* that we were praying the rosary, I *knew* what was going on. . . . Then She spoke to me and said 'don't you know that I am going to take care of your children?' I was praying for my children and She was listening *the whole time*! . . . After She spoke I knew it was Her. I began to cry "La mujer bonita! She's here! Oh my God She's so beautiful!" I was crying and tears were rolling down my face.[1]

When she describes this moment today, Ruiz says that this Virgin of the Americas enabled her to find a balance between self and family, being "in the world" but not "of the world," and most importantly, she says, led her and her family to a more profound Catholic and spiritual life. Describing the Lady as a "demanding" Virgin who asks much of her and her family, Ruiz says that she welcomes the challenges because they have made her "a better person than I was before." She says that the Virgin "melted my heart and warmed my soul," turning her into a better mother, wife, and leader in her faith and in her community.

Since the onset of her apparitions and messages, Ruiz has become the matriarch of an evangelizing Catholic community, Mary's Ministries, based at her home in South Phoenix, as well as an inspiration to women in her community and in Latin America, where Mary's Ministries is currently expanding.[2] About 80 percent of the approximately 2,000 members are women who ethnically self-define as Hispanas, Mexican Americans, and Latinas. These women define themselves as Catholics, Mexican Americans, mothers, daughters, wives, girlfriends, evangelists, and urban warriors. All of them claim that the Virgin of the Americas, the Virgin who appears to Ruiz, enables them to balance these multiple identities with a greater ease, and they credit this bicultural *mestiza* Virgin with their renewed confidence in themselves and in their abilities. They invert what has been interpreted as an oppressive symbol, reclaiming the Virgin as a powerful symbol of liberation, spiritual renewal, and model for community reform; they in turn redefine empowerment and what feminism does and does not mean for them. Estela

Ruiz and the other women of Mary's Ministries not only draw on a rich Mexican history of reimagining the Virgin Mary as an empowering, liberating symbol, but they are redefining Catholicism.

Ruiz and the women of Mary's Ministries challenge feminist scholars' assumptions that Mary is at best a weak and at worst a useless symbol for women.[3] The main problem with these feminist critiques is that these scholars have not gone outside the confines of the Catholic Church and Catholic theology to see how the Virgin is being interpreted and reimagined by Catholic women. These women turn to the Virgin as a source of inspiration and hope and, most importantly, as a *fellow woman*—a mother, daughter, and friend, who understands their struggles and pain. Mary's Ministries women are neither anomalous nor are they unique. When we look at other Mexican American communities, we find that women are crafting their own relationships with the Virgin Mary and that they find deep love and meaning in their *María*.[4] These women would find it deeply offensive to be told that their symbol is demeaning and/or useless; through their devotion, they make the Virgin Mary a dynamic, relevant, and flexible symbol.

The Mariology—the theology of Mary—that these women promote combines messages of ethnic, social, and religious empowerment. As a result of Estela Ruiz's apparitional experiences, Mary's Ministries is devoted to furthering the Virgin's messages and to promoting community activism through its ESPIRITU Community Development Corporation. Women in this organization are profoundly moved and are motivated by what they see as Mary's grace bestowed upon them. They give thanks for what they interpret as her blessings. Mary gives them "candy kisses" and "little slices of heaven"—heavenly gifts that help them endure their everyday struggles and attain their hopes and dreams.

There has clearly been an institutional bias in the study of Catholicism in the United States, and this has influenced studies of Hispanic Catholicism, in which, until recently, only church-based organizations have been documented. Although most studies of Mexican American Catholics address the role of women, they tend to focus on higher-profile groups connected to the church, like Las Hermanas, Hijas de María, and the Guadalupanas. These groups have undoubtedly made an impact in Hispanic Catholic communities in the United States, but there have been others, too, that have been overlooked, especially those that have been community organized and/or based outside of the Catholic Church.[5] Groups such as Mary's Ministries, Catholic and grass roots in origin, are largely absent from the historical narratives, not because they did not exist but because they were deemed "popular" and therefore not really Catholic.[6] As historian of American religions Robert Orsi has recently noted, "The designation *popular religion* served to seal off certain expressions of religious life from an unspecified but obviously normative 'religion.'"[7] This dichotomy, which separates Catholicism into two distinct, separate categories, the Catholicism of the church and the Catholicism of the people, has been perpetuated by scholars and has only recently begun to be challenged.[8] As shown by Mary's Ministries, a lay-initiated, Marian shrine–based organization, these categories are blurred. Grassroots groups can work effectively with the institutional church, but they are not dependent on church finances and support for their success. By using ethnographic methods, we can better grasp the rich history of Mexican American women and can understand how their stories redefine American Catholicism. By evangelizing in their communities and linking the church and the people, these women are at the forefront of lay efforts to transform the Catholic Church.

Estela Ruiz and the women of Mary's Ministries are faithful churchgoing Catholics, but they are also devotees of a backyard-based "popular" movement that merges Marian devotion with aspects of evangelicalism. Infusing their piety with evangelical pronouncements and embodied religion, they speak in tongues and lay their hands on each other in the effort to heal. As Catholics—*católicas*—and as evangelicals—*evangélicas*—they help organize and run weeklong "faith courses" that blend conservative Catholicism with evangelical Christianity, and that promise to offer initiates a new life in Mary and Christ. The "official" church has struggled to find ways to speak to the Mexican American faithful, but Ruiz and the women of Mary's Ministries have begun to craft a new, popular form of Catholicism that both the laity and the clergy have found deeply meaningful.

Liberated by la Virgen

Ruiz describes her encounter with the Virgin Mary as the single most transformative moment in her life. A self-described "lukewarm" Catholic prior to her apparitions and subsequent conversion, Ruiz says she just "went through the motions" at mass and thought about what she would do after the service. She ridiculed her spouse for his devotion to the Virgin of Guadalupe and thought that he was "one of those crazies, you know, those religious nuts." The safe distance Ruiz had created between herself and the Catholic Church and her faith was shattered, as she emphasizes, during the fall of 1988 when she was visited by the Virgin in dreams and when the Virgin spoke to her through a painting that hung on her living room wall. Ruiz says that she now realizes that the Virgin was getting her ready for her first apparitions and for her and her family's conversions that were to follow: the Virgin was "warming my heart and melting my soul."

According to Ruiz, she was her own toughest critic. Before her apparitions of Mary she was a "true American," one who was immersed in the material rather than in the spiritual world. "I was truly in the world. I desired all the things America wanted. I tried to get prestige through knowledge—the knowledge of the world. I pushed my family and God to the side but I didn't push God totally away because I thought I might need Him! [She laughs.] I was in the women's liberation movement. I loved it and wanted to be liberated; I don't know what from, but I wanted to be liberated."[9] Ruiz describes herself in unflattering terms here, as greedy, headstrong, and confused. Her involvement with the women's liberation movement, created distance between herself and her family, and any "liberation" she may have experienced was illusory at best. She began to worry about her own mortality, she recalls, and about what would happen to her if she died: "I was woman—I was 'liberating' myself, so I thought, and had just begun to live. But I also saw my hair turning gray and my face starting to droop. I feared death and didn't know where I'd go if I died."[10]

Estela Ruiz was reaching a "crisis" in her life: her salary and career successes as a school administrator were starting to lose their appeal, and she began to think about "the state of my soul." She also missed her deceased mother terribly and felt like her life was "empty." As the historian David Blackbourn has indicated, the stories of Marian visionaries have deep psychological roots: the absence of a mother, feelings of intense emotional loss, and the reality of an unhappy family are common threads that link them. In addition, "long term anxiety and a sense of neglect" is common among visionaries, the majority of whom have been girls and women.[11]

Estela Ruiz's narrative fits Blackbourn's description of visionaries, and her anxieties, loss of her mother, and awareness that she was not connecting with her family led to what she calls a "real emotional breakdown[.] I guess you could technically call it a nervous breakdown, but it was more than that—it reached into the depths of my soul." She says that the Virgin appeared to her as a major "wake-up call" to resurrect her relationship with her family.

Ruiz's Virgin and her experiences with her do not encourage the kind of oppression and misogyny that Marina Warner and Kari Børresen would claim the Virgin Mary represents. Nor do her experiences resonate with what Martha Cotera has called Marianismo, an ideology centered on the supposed disempowering qualities of the Virgin Mary that encourages women's passivity, submissiveness, and virtuousness and that sets a double sexual and moral standard for women.[12] In her personal messages to Ruiz, the Virgin acts like a mother, counselor, and spiritual guide and has not, according to her, encouraged passivity or meekness on any level. "She has always encouraged me to go out there and be the best I can be, no matter what I do." When Ruiz wanted to quit her master's program in education to focus her attention on the apparitions, it was Mary, she says, who encouraged her to finish her degree. When Ruiz doubted herself as a wife and mother, it was the Virgin, she says, who made her feel worthwhile. Indeed, for her as well as for other women in the community, this Virgin takes on the multiple roles of counselor, therapist, mother, spiritual role model, and model of Catholic womanhood. Under the Virgin of the America's guidance and tutelage, Ruiz is able to maximize her roles as wife, mother, educator, public visionary, and evangelizer, and, according to her, it is the Virgin herself who gives her encouragement and approval for her to thrive in all these capacities. Ruiz says that the Virgin is the ideal mother—one who listens and counsels and who is a pillar of love and support.

If we take Warner's, Børresen's, and Cotera's critiques of the Virgin Mary as a symbol a step further, Ruiz, in leaving her administrative position and devoting herself full time to the Virgin and to her ministry, has capitulated to familial, cultural, and religious chauvinism. But the reality and context for Estela Ruiz's decisions are far more complicated than that. Because of her intimate relationship with the Virgin of the Americas, she has been able to overcome past fears and insecurities and is today ensconced in a world of devotion that honors her motherhood and family life, as it respects her role as a Marian visionary. She is now able to feel good about being a wife, mother, and grandmother as well as a "career woman," because her work now falls within acceptable cultural and religious boundaries and is seen as enhancing her maternal and wifely roles. In terms of power, Ruiz has more than she did prior to the onset of her apparitions. She is a famous Marian visionary, highly sought after for public appearances, and her shrine to the Virgin of the Americas was one of the busiest shrine sites in the United States in the 1990s. Her work is not that much different than it was before her self-proclaimed conversion, but it is now validated within a family-run enterprise, Mary's Ministries and ESPIRITU. Ruiz once exclaimed, "The children call me grandma and they call Reyes grandpa and I just love that!" When I have been with her on the school's campus, I have watched as the children confirm these proclamations; they run up to her in their starched shirts and throw their arms around her. She says that she loves to hug the children, "especially because many of them don't get any affection at home." Ruiz's new career complements her wifely and motherly roles, and when she talks about it, she emphasizes her nurturing qualities. But when she talks about her early

Mercy and Terésa at Estela Ruiz's backyard shrine, 2002. (Photograph by author)

days as an administrator, it is evident that she enjoyed those years thoroughly, and her eyes gleam with pride: "You know that the manual that I wrote on bilingual education was used for many years in the Phoenix school system and still is in many schools." Over the years I have witnessed Estela Ruiz greet the crowds who flock to her shrine. She is happy and is in her element. She enjoys talking to pilgrims and counseling them, or, as she puts it, "sharing the Blessed Mother's love" with them.

Ruiz's roles as a Marian visionary, wife, and mother complement her work at the school and in Mary's Ministries—all are deeply intertwined. She describes her career before the visions as "a job." But her new occupation as a visionary and Montessori school administrator she sees as a vocation, a "calling." "When I work with the children at the school and the teachers I am doing the Blessed Mother's work, just as when I help organize a faith course for Mary's Ministries—this is all for the Blessed Mother." As a woman who says she was "chosen" by the Virgin Mary herself to do this important work in her community, Estela Ruiz is what Latina theologian Gloria Ines-Loya calls a *pasionaria* and *pastora* in her community; as a visionary and evangelizer with Mary's Ministries she "takes responsibility" for the evangelization of her community and seeks to change the way the church perceives Hispanics and specifically Mexican Americans.[13] Her efforts have inspired other women in her community to follow in her footsteps; they interpret Ruiz's Marian messages as calls to reform their own families and neighborhoods.

When her apparitions began, the first thing the Virgin told her to do, according to her, was to "get a spiritual advisor, a priest." Ruiz initially worked with Father Jack Spaulding, formerly of St. Maria Goretti Catholic Church, and, later, at the prompting of the former bishop of Phoenix, Thomas O'Brien, Father Doug Nohava was chosen as the spiritual director for Mary's Ministries. Ruiz and her family met with Father Jack, and later, Father Doug, on a regular basis. Both Father Jack and Father Doug became ardent supporters of Ruiz and her claims, even though the diocese's investigation resulted in a published statement that there were no miracles taking place. But although she may not have had the support of the bishop, who was known for his skepticism of apparitions, she did have the support of several area priests, who invited her to their churches to speak, and who attended the backyard rosary prayer sessions and annual retreats. After Mary's Ministries was formed in the mid-1990s and members began evangelizing in Latin America, the organization was supported by priests throughout Latin America, including the former Bishop José Ignacio Alemany Grau of Chachapoyas, Peru, who attended the retreat in December 2000. During his weekend-long visit, the bishop met privately with Ruiz and members of her family, blessed the shrine, administered the Eucharist, and gave his formal blessing to Mary's Ministries' work. So while Estela Ruiz's apparitions may not have garnered the support of the Phoenix Diocese, local as well as international priests supported the claims of the apparitions and had Mary's Ministries–sponsored faith courses held in their parishes.

Ruiz's Marian shrine site became one of the most active in the United States during the late twentieth century, part of the tightly linked worldwide apparition circuit that includes Medjugorge, Lourdes, Fatima, and the Mexico City Basilica. Estela Ruiz and her husband, Reyes, founded Mary's Ministries in 1992, and they describe it as a Catholic evangelizing organization, according to Estela Ruiz, "inspired by the Virgin Mary herself." U.S. diocesan priests have supported Mary's Ministries since its inception—-throughout the 1990s faith courses were sponsored and held in parishes ranging from Arizona to Chicago to Hawaii. And since 1998, Latin American priests have been active players in Mary's Ministries and in the evangelization process in countries that include Mexico, Belize, Chile, Peru, and Guatemala. Hispanic men and women are attracted to the organization and to what they see as "breathing new life into the church," as one South Phoenix female member told me. The Mexican American members of Mary's Ministries with whom I have worked believe that Mary is calling them to improve not only their own lives but the lives of others, and since the late 1990s there has been a conscious turn toward evangelizing and reaching out to Latin American Catholics.

Ruiz's apparitions, subsequent backyard rosary gatherings, and creation of Mary's Ministries have created an alternative space of American Catholicism —one that offers institutional connectedness but also a haven for Catholics to praise the Virgin Mary on their own terms. The shrine site is itself a bridge between the church and the laity—priests, laymen, and laywomen regularly pray at the shrine, and annual December retreats link the Virgin's messages to the Catholic church hierarchy. Estela Ruiz has been a role model for the thousands of Catholics who have visited the shrine since 1989; her conversion story is well known and serves as inspiration to pilgrims to fortify their prayer lives and increase their church attendance. Yet even though Mary's messages encourage her "children" to attend church, she is not owned by the Catholic Church—she speaks to the pilgrims on a personal level and makes their experiences at the shrine intimate. The shrine is meant as a complement to the church, not as a substitute, and Estela and her family members are quick to point this out. Yet the men and women who journey to the shrine have experiences that they have not had anyplace else, and this is what makes the shrine distinct from the church. Mary's presence, and, moreover, Ruiz's authoritative presence as one who both sees and hears the Virgin, have made the shrine an alternative Catholic space that is defined by lay Catholic Hispanic women.

A "Tough" Virgin

According to Estela Ruiz, the Virgin of the Americas is a "tough lady" who appears to bring hope "to the world" and "to my children." She beseeches her "children" to embrace Jesus, to attend church regularly, to pray the rosary, and, above all else, to take the Eucharist as often as possible. The Virgin draws a clear line between following "God's ways" and following "the ways of the world." Although she acknowledges that following Satan is much easier than following God, she peppers her messages with hope and encouragement. She spoke to her children on April 25, 1992: "I am with you, my little ones, to comfort you when in need, to guide you when you seem to feel confused. If you allow me to, I will guide you to your salvation, who is my Son, Jesus."[14] In each of her nearly 300 messages, she emphasizes her role as a loving and concerned mother who wants to guide her children to heaven. As she beseeched her children on July 3, 1993, "I see the devastation of my children on earth and my heart cries for you, my little ones, whom God has given to me because of His love for you."[15]

But this Mary is also a stern mother, and she chastises her children when they have not been praying hard enough, when their prayers have been "lukewarm," or when they seem to have veered towards the "ways of the world." We see that this Virgin is capable of impatience. On January 1, 1994, she showed her irritation with her children, tempered with proclamations of love: "Your decision to turn to God is the only salvation for you, my beloved. I cannot continue to say it over and over."[16] Mary grows irritable as she watches her children veer toward destruction and Satan's open arms, and she hit a low point in her patience with her children on June 4, 1994: "My children in the Americas cannot tolerate or deal with pain, physical or emotional, because your spirits, your souls are empty of that which allows you to deal with pain and suffering. You are far from God who is your source and strength, who gives you the courage to endure all in the world."[17]

The Virgin of the Americas is an exacting woman indeed. In her messages to Ruiz between 1988 and 1998, she implored her children to take up her cause and to be her "soldiers" and to do battle against "Satan and his legions." As she stated in a July 28, 1990, message, "Do not let the world lure you into its falseness. Become strong through prayer and love of God through the sacraments and become my soldiers, willing to help me wage war against the sin and evilness of Satan."[18] Waging war against evil, according to the Virgin of the Americas, means making an easy decision to choose God over Satan. Members of Mary's Ministries take it one step further: they become self-proclaimed "Mary's soldiers" and go out to do battle with Satan through evangelization.

The women of Mary's Ministries use the classic Christian language of "conversion," "rebirth," and "awakening" to describe their first experiences of visiting the shrine to the Virgin of the Americas, and they explain that their powerful experiences have filled them with the imperative to share Mary's love and power with others. They see their new selves as a way to improve their families, their communities, and their churches. In their various duties as administrators and teachers at ESPIRITU's charter school, in their capacities as mothers and wives and as community leaders fighting for urban reform, the women of Mary's Ministries and ESPIRITU are determined to fight stereotypes of Mexican Americans and to make the world a better place for their sons and daughters. All of these women have experienced dark periods in their lives in which they were forced to face their "sins" and realize that they were "of the world."[19] As with Estela Ruiz, they say that they needed to reform themselves before they were capable of helping others in their community. Each of the thirty women I interviewed between 1993 and 2002 in South Phoenix claimed that the Virgin Mary—Guadalupe and the Lady of the Americas—had enabled them to become better individuals, mothers, wives, daughters, and Catholics. These women refer to Mary's graces bestowed on them as "candy kisses"—divine *besos de María* that helped them get through the tough times in their lives and to look toward a more hopeful, confident future.

María, a Mexican American Catholic woman in her fifties and a core member of Mary's Ministries, says that her life has been profoundly changed by the Virgin of the Americas. Divorced and a single mother to three grown children, María told me during one of our interviews: "You are looking at a miracle. I am one of those conversions that Estela talks about." Describing her life as "a mess" before she became involved with Mary's Ministries, she had been filled with anger and bitterness toward her alcoholic husband, who spent most of his paycheck on liquor and drugs and who was a "weekend dad," available and sober for his children only on weekends. María's conversion began after she divorced her husband and made her *Cursillo*, a short course in Christianity popular among Hispanic Catholics in the Southwest.[20] Recounting her first time at the shrine, María told me, "It was a special place; I felt that something was different here, something good." She says that she was moved to tears during this visit; she "cried and cried" because she felt a sense of peace wash over her. When she joined Mary's Ministries that year, in 1993, she was attracted by the community of faithful believers and felt as though her life was finally worth something. In addition to her involvement with Mary's Ministries South Phoenix outreach initiatives, María is also heavily involved in the organization's evangelization in Latin America and has helped set up faith courses in Peru, Guatemala, Mexico, and Belize. She wants, she says, for the Virgin of the America's mantle to touch "all of her children in the Americas." María also thinks that Mary's Ministries evangelization is a "good thing" for the church that sometimes lacks enthusiasm in its outreach to Hispanics.

These faith courses in which María is involved set Mary's Ministries apart from other Marian apparition–based organizations in the United States and in the Americas. These courses are a combination of Catholic apologetics, the enthusiasm of Charismatic Catholicism, and Pentecostal-style evangelicalism. The events of a typical Mary's Ministries faith course reflect broader American evangelical concerns, as do the Virgin of the Americas' messages on which the organization is based.[21] The faith courses that have been established in the United States, and more recently in Central and South America, emphasize a personal encounter with Jesus Christ, the receiving of the Holy Spirit, receiving "gifts" of speaking in tongues, and healing through a version of laying on of hands (praying "with" instead of "over"). A specific language of conversion is used. Being "saved" and becoming a "new man/woman" is an integral part of the discursive world of the faith courses. The conservative Catholicism, social activism, and evangelicalism that is emphasized in Mary's Ministries faith courses and at the shrine finds its origins in the Virgin's messages to Estela Ruiz. The source for this syncretic blend of piety and praxis has its roots in a *mestiza* Virgin who speaks directly to a contemporary Mexican American woman, Estela Ruiz, and whose messages are an important source of strength and encouragement to the women of Mary's Ministries.

It is women who have been the most active members of Mary's Ministries and who have committed themselves to evangelization and neighborhood revitalization. The faith courses emphasize the classic evangelical battle between good and evil, God versus Satan, at the same time that they invoke the Catholic Virgin of the Americas' invitation to her children to be her "warriors" in the "fight against Satan." Margaret's 1998 testimony epitomizes these themes. With her voice straining under the weight of emotion, she spoke about the "living hell" she and her spouse had to endure. Their son, who has been incarcerated off and on since he was in his teens, has caused them a tremendous amount of grief and suffering: "It has taken me a long time to heal and it is still happening," she said. Margaret shared with the faith course attendees the trials her son put her family through with gang activity and drugs and said she was "so grateful" to the Virgin Mary for helping her cope with her son's waywardness. She read aloud the story of the mustard seed, Mark 4:30–33, and commented, "We're all the mustard seeds and Mary asks us to close our eyes and to put our trust in Jesus. . . . all it takes is to have faith." Margaret talked about her mother's lifelong devotion to the Blessed Mother and to Santo Niño de Atocha and about the impression the older woman made on her when she was a young girl: "My mother watered my mustard seed and let it grow." Her mother, Margaret said, nourished her own "seed" her entire life, to be rewarded at death by the arrival of Mary, whose presence "filled the room with the smell of roses. . . . She had come for my mother because of her great faith." Margaret's testimony was typical of Mary's Ministries testimonies, which emphasize the Devil's pull, turning to the Blessed Mother for guidance, and joining a community of faith such as Mary's Ministries. Margaret says that she has found hope and comfort in the organization, and that because of the many gifts that Mary has bestowed on her, she is committed to evangelization in her community.

This Virgin of the Americas promotes both Catholicism and evangelical Christianity, and women like María and Margaret have taken up her "call" with intense fervor. In her messages to Estela Ruiz, the Virgin calls for Catholic praxis—specifically Catholic social action. Although she demands that her

Women of Mary's Ministries taking a break at the 2001 December retreat.
(Photograph by author)

"children" start going to mass each day, she says that even this is not enough. Instead of being content with her "children's" participation in private piety, she asks that they join her legion of warriors to make their Catholic faith socially relevant. She wants Catholics to be more than "pew-warmers," to borrow a phrase from Little Rey Ruiz, Estela's youngest son. The Virgin of the Americas goes beyond the mild manneredness of the Church Mary and incites her children to "spiritual warfare," and to fight the battle against Satan in places outside of the church—in the streets, schools, and homes of South Phoenix and beyond. Ruiz once admitted to me, "Sometimes I am just *so tired* that I don't want to listen to the Blessed Mother anymore because she wants us to do *so much*, but I know in my heart that she is right and I keep on working because I am her soldier, her soldadera." Mary's Ministries trains soldiers to "do Mary's work" in the K–12 grade charter school founded by the organization in 1995, in Mary's Ministries faith courses, and in community outreach.

Like María and Margaret, Terésa is committed to "fighting for her community" and calls herself an urban "warrior for God." Terésa was one of the first to sign up for the Rio Vista Block Watch and Neighborhood Association; for Terésa, carrying her flashlight through the streets of South Phoenix is a political act, one that she is quite proud of. A longtime resident of South

Phoenix, Terésa, a widow, knew that she had to do something to make her neighborhood a safer place for her daughter and two granddaughters, who live with her. Terésa says that two events in the past five years have had a lasting effect on her life. The first was the experience of being threatened at knifepoint by a drug dealer and "gangbanger" in her former residence at Brighton Place apartments; the second was meeting the Ruiz family, who introduced her to the Virgin of the Americas and to the goals of Mary's Ministries and ESPIRITU. Like María, Terésa remembers her first visit to the shrine of the Virgin of the Americas as a moving and cathartic moment: "I cried and cried because I had felt that things in my life were not going to work out, but when I prayed to *María* I knew, I just *knew* that my life would get better." Teresa felt "at peace" and says that a warmth came over her—for the first time in many years she felt "safe and loved."

Soon after her first encounter with the Virgin Mary at Ruiz's shrine, Terésa discovered that she could be outspoken. She took the apartment management to court and accused it of gross neglect. Terésa's actions led to an investigative report by a local news station, and as a result Brighton Place was forced to invest money in the apartments. She told me with a voice shaking with emotion that she never would have had the courage to fight the management if it had not been for the help and encouragement of the Ruizes and for her new faith in God and the Virgin. "I owe my life as it is now to the Ruiz[es] and most of all to God and to the Blessed Mother." Because of the strength that she receives from the Virgin, Terésa now feels "called" and morally obligated to clean up the rest of her neighborhood. With Brighton Place in clear view from her current dwelling, she patrols the streets every weekend at nightfall, carrying her walkie-talkie and flashlight.

All of these women say that they have a deeper relationship with their Catholic Church and Catholic faith as a result of Mary's messages to Ruiz. Moreover, they feel as though they finally have "something to offer" their church, as one female member of the ministry told me. What they can offer is evangelization and the possibility of renewing the Catholic faith. The women of Mary's Ministries see themselves at the forefront of renewal, and they take their roles as evangelizers seriously. They see themselves as reaching out to the Hispanic community in effective ways, and they in turn experience spiritual growth and renewal.

Empowered, but Not "Feminists"

Estela Ruiz, now in her sixties, has been able to liberate herself from the contesting powers and demands of *la familia* and her own desires for success and individualism because of her relationship with the Virgin. Though she claims she is no longer a feminist, she holds fast to feminist principles that women should be fulfilled human beings and that their concerns are deeply intertwined with their communities and families. Estela's narrative resembles the stories of evangelical women in sociologist Judith Stacey's pathbreaking study on late-twentieth-century American families. Like evangelical women, Estela Ruiz points to a complex feminism, a "postfeminism" that makes room for competing interests and demands.[22] She blends political and social liberalism with religious and gendered conservatism—thus creating a complex mixture of stances. On some issues, such as her strong advocacy of women's higher education, Ruiz would be considered "liberal," yet on others she would be called "conservative," such as her stance against birth control and abortion. Women like Estela Ruiz and those Stacey interviewed challenge our perceptions of the boundaries of feminism because they make the boundaries malleable. The term "postfeminism" is an attempt to put into language the inherent contradictions within women's lives. Through and because of her apparitions, Estela has been able to create a space for herself within traditional expectations of Mexican American women and womanhood. By bridging the gulf that separated her from her society's and her family's expectations, her apparitions have enabled her to forge a more legitimate status in her family and community. The Virgin, like Estela Ruiz, balances "feminist" and more "traditional" demands and concerns. She tells Ruiz to achieve her educational goals, but at the same time she encourages a kind of submission to her husband and her family—much as she takes a backseat to her father and his son, Jesus. After all, it was the Virgin, according to Estela Ruiz, who told her to finish her degree and her term as school administrator before "devoting myself to Her one hundred percent." The Virgin wanted a well-educated, well-connected Mexican American woman to deliver her messages to South Phoenix and "to the world," and in Estela Ruiz she found that kind of messenger. Despite their deep commitment to religious and social change in their communities, none of these women call themselves feminists; they reject the term and are troubled by feminism, which they perceive as a movement that is divorced from God and spirituality, that causes serious damage to relationships between men and women, and that is deeply offensive to the Catholic Church with its pro-choice and birth control stances.

It is within the communal, familial setting of the faith courses that Mexican American men and women are able to form relationships with others and craft meaningful roles for themselves. Spiritually energized by the Holy Spirit, they seek to help others know Christ as intimately as they do. Faith courses offer Mexican American men and women a performative space through which they can explore gendered codes and different options for themselves.[23] The courses teach postfeminism, the "dominant gender ideology of contemporary evangelicals," which "selectively incorporates and adapts many feminist family reforms."[24]

Men and women are taught that heterosexual relationships are to be based on marriages of mutual submission. Mary's Ministries' version of mutual submission is practiced by candidates when they are "joined in a union with Christ" for the day of evangelization—a man is paired with a woman and the two are told they are "wedded" for the day in a "holy marriage." This exercise puts into practice the evangelical notion of mutual submission in Christ. Estela Ruiz is a strong advocate for mutual submission and says that she counsels her daughters-in-law on how to be successfully mutually submissive with their husbands. She tells them that they must trust their husbands and openly discuss their concerns with them, and, in turn, their husbands should trust and confide in them. Ruiz interprets mutual submission as essential for strong relationships and marriages because "trust is the basis of a successful relationship." Her gender ideology, reflected in Mary's Ministries rhetoric and in the faith course dynamics and skits, emphasizes the need for men and women to be mutually respectful—a teaching in line with other contemporary evangelical groups such as Women's Aglow, Global Ministries, and the Promise Keepers. For these groups, submission does not equal subjugation, and marriage is likened to a "loving teamwork" in which both members work for the collective good of the marriage and the family.[25]

Mary's Ministries encourages women, many of whom have experienced trauma and abuse in their lives and who have never been in a position to delegate authority, to take leadership roles. Unlike women in the contemporary Mexican American evangelical organization Alcance Victoria, who are not allowed to be leaders in the movement, women in Mary's Ministries can and do lead faith courses in and outside the United States.[26] Mexican American women's involvement is crucial to the success of the faith courses, and they participate on numerous levels. It is Mexican American women who run the kitchen, cook the meals for the faith course participants, give their testimonies, tend to children of the participants during the course, and help to clean up after the course. Although both men's and women's work is important to the success of each faith course offered, it is women who perform a wider variety of tasks and who contribute their many skills and gifts. In addition to their involvement in the courses, the majority of these women hold full-time jobs, and several are pursuing college degrees.

During the faith courses held in Phoenix, Ruiz serves as a role model for

Mexican American women. Her intelligence, visionary status, motherhood, and outwardly professed humility are greatly admired by the many Mexican American women who attend. Women are drawn to her and seek her company and advice on everything from marital to child-raising issues. Ruiz's children came of age during the Chicano movement, and her entry into the university and workforce also coincided with the *movimiento,* as well as with the feminist movement. Her career as a school administrator coincided with the Chicana movement, which has clearly had an impact on her as she managed to maintain her roles as mother, wife, and career woman.[27] Estela Ruiz is a firm believer in women achieving their career goals, and she serves as a role model for mothers and career women alike. Yet she denounces the feminist movement and insists that she is "not a feminist." The danger of feminism, she says, is that it becomes like a god for many women and "takes over." As the acknowledged matriarch of Mary's Ministries, she interweaves evangelicalism with liberating messages for the women who take the faith courses and who volunteer their efforts. Besides emphasizing women's duties to their husbands as partners in marriage, she defends the right of women to be educated and to succeed in their careers. Ruiz has been a major influence in daughter-in-law Leticia's decision to pursue her doctorate. Yet she cautions women to be careful not to allow their careers to "take over" family and marital life, as hers once did. God, Ruiz emphasizes, must be foremost in women's minds as they succeed in their careers "in the world" and as mothers and wives—feminist leanings are tempered by evangelical Christian messages. So long as women realize that they must put God first in their lives, everything else will "fall into place," she says.

Even though the women of Mary's Ministries believe that the feminist movement hurt relations between men and women and they refuse to be called feminists, their language and beliefs have been informed by a feminist-inspired gender ideology. The majority of the women who attend the faith courses have experienced hard times and seek the friendship and comfort of other women. They share similar life histories and are able to discuss the challenges of being wives and mothers in a supportive environment where they will not be judged. Although these women's problems do not simply disappear because of the faith courses, they gain a sense of empowerment that equips them to reenter family life armed with self-confidence.

What Gloria Anzaldúa calls "whitewomen's feminism" has unintentionally worked to perpetuate traditional narratives and misinformed notions of women of color because it sees history through a white lens.[28] Latina cultural critic Elizabeth Martínez writes: "Feminism does not understand how, for a colonized racial/ethnic people, cultural integrity is profoundly interwoven with survival. Or how the family can be seen primarily as a key weapon of self-defense in a hostile world rather than as an oppressive institution." Chicana historian Vicki Ruiz also writes about Chicanas recoiling against "the middle-class orientation of liberal feminists; the anti-male rhetoric of radicals; and the condescending, dismissive attitudes expressed by both."[29] I wanted to call these women feminists many times during the course of my fieldwork, but they rejected my attempts to link my struggles with theirs—my own white feminist lens at times blinded me to their realities and desires. These women have displayed a courage and conviction in the face of a history of racism and sexism, and they turn to the Virgin Mary for inspiration, hope, and guidance. As faithful Catholics, they work with the church but also challenge it to better meet the needs of Hispanic Catholics.

As the women of Mary's Ministries respond to their community's needs, they can be said to lead "objectively feminist lives," to borrow a phrase from Elizabeth Martínez.[30] Although they cannot be called "feminists," these women embody, through their beliefs and actions, a core tenet of feminism— that women must be given the opportunity to become truly fulfilled human beings. The women of Mary's Ministries and ESPIRITU have willingly given themselves over to God and the Virgin Mary, whom they credit for their new, converted selves, and they are able to see what they call the "fruits" of their renewed faith in God in their daily lives. These women put themselves in danger and in difficult situations because of their commitment to their children and their neighbors' children, and they use motherhood as a "political weapon" to fight the social ills in their community.[31] They also demonstrate sociologist Carol Hardy-Fantana's observation that "politics" for Latina women is "an interpersonal, interactive process—building bridges and making connections between people."[32]

Mary's Ministries provides the physical and emotional space for women to heal from the suffering they have endured; it provides a setting where the pain of divorce or the anguish of having imprisoned children or children killed as a result of gang battles can be healed. Women are encouraged to take on a new and important task that will help to reduce their pain, maybe even overcome it, and they willingly dedicate themselves to doing God's and Mary's work. These women are doing the best they can to overcome the obstacles and complicated realities of their lives, and they are nourished by the community and fellowship offered to them by members of Mary's Ministries. Above all else, they learn to surrender their wills to God and place their hearts in Mary's "open arms." Like Protestant evangelical Aglow women, the women of Mary's Ministries understand that inner healing begins with surrendering themselves to Jesus and, in the case with Catholic Mary's Ministries, to the Virgin Mary as well.[33] The faith courses allow the space and time for these women to vent their fears and frustrations and to "give it up" to Jesus and Mary.

All of these women have a conversion story to tell, a story that acknowledges the suffering that they have endured but also their role in their own dramas of suffering. These women take responsibility for their actions, and their personal resolve and strength is increased through their involvement in a supportive group. What we are able to see when we look at their narratives is that through their active participation, and in a particular kind of place, women are able to get beyond their pain and are even able to start to feel alive again. After handing over their sin and suffering to Jesus and the Virgin, they feel an incredible kind of relief. As María S., a Mexican mother of four, said, "En este lugar estoy feliz y muy contente. Es possible sentir mejor sobre mis problemas. Gracias a Dios y a la Virgen! Gracias a la familia de Ruizes!"[34] ("In this place, I am happy and very content. I can feel better about my problems. Thank you God! Thank you Virgin [Mary]! Thank you to the Ruiz family!") As María S.'s comments indicate, the perceived presence of Jesus and Mary, the familial setting of the faith course, and the Ruiz family all help to create a geographic and spiritual zone where spiritual healing can take place.

These women's activism also reflects their familial commitments: they view their activism as integrally related to their roles as mothers and as wives.[35] They are self-described "warriors for God and Mary," motivated by strong religious faith. The women involved in Mary's Ministries demonstrate that it is possible to become an empowered, liberated woman through belief in the power of the Virgin—a female symbol who is not always seen as liberating for women. These women turn to the Virgin of the Americas and the Virgin of Guadalupe for the strength to continue in their struggles. Whether they are teaching at Mary's Ministries charter school, helping to set up a faith course, or participating in their neighborhood's block watch, these Mexican American women draw on their multilayered identities as modern women, mothers, Catholics, and Mexican Americans and have chosen to dedicate their lives to a heavenly mandated reform of their community. In Mary's Ministries and in ESPIRITU, these women find a place where they are able to come to a better understanding and acceptance of their ethnic and religious identities.

Estela, Margaret, María, and Terésa have turned to the Virgin Mary, a liberating figure for them, who has helped them become the confident women they are today. Though they do not wish to be called feminists, as a result of the relationships they have formed with *la Virgen*, these women have gained the courage and confidence to work toward the betterment of not only themselves, but also for their church, their families, and their communities. While these women find spiritual nourishment when they attend mass, it is through their extrachurch devotions, like those in Ruiz's backyard, that their faith finds its deepest and fullest expression. Through their efforts they are creating a new kind of evangelical American Catholicism. Those who have received "Mary's candy kisses" and "little slices of heaven" not only feel called to proclaim their devotion to her, but also to spread their hopes and dreams for their families, communities, and the Catholic Church.

Notes

1. Estela Ruiz, interview with author, South Phoenix, Arizona, October 27, 1993.
2. Mary's Ministries has teamed up with Latin American dioceses and has sponsored faith courses in central Chile (Linares and San Bernardo); south, central, and northern Peru (Sulyana and Lima); eastern Ecuador (Cuenca); southern Colombia (Hirador); northern Brazil (Franca); Guatemala; and Chihuahua, Coahuila, Durango, and Hermosillo, Mexico. The priests and bishops who work with Mary's Ministries are of mixed orders. Bishop José Alemany of Peru is currently Mary's Ministries' spiritual director. There are approximately one hundred Mary's Ministries missionaries today, the majority of whom are Peruvian and Mexican women. There are about fifteen Mexican American missionaries from South Phoenix who have each given a year's commitment to do mission work in Latin American communities supported by local dioceses. During their stay, they live in Mary Houses, paid for by Mary's Ministries.
3. Marina Warner, in *Alone of All Her Sex: The Myth and Cult of the Virgin Mary* (New York: Random House, 1976), claims that the Virgin Mary has been used to keep women subordinate and that the ideal of virginity has been stifling for women and men. Kari Børresen also disputes that the Virgin Mary can be a useful symbol for women because the discourse surrounding her is controlled by the Catholic Church. Kari Børresen, "Mary in Catholic Theology," in *Mary in the Churches*, ed. Hans Küng and Jürgen Moltmann (New York: Seabury Press, 1983).
4. A new wave of scholarship on women and their relationship to the Virgin Mary is focusing on women's empowerment through their devotion to the Virgin. Deidre Sklar has shown how Mexican American women in New Mexico have forged meaningful relationships with the Virgin Mary, in *Dancing with the Virgin: Body and Faith in the Fiesta of Tortugas, New Mexico* (Berkeley: University of California Press, 2001). Karen Mary Davalos has shown how Mexican American women in Pilsen turn to Mary as inspiration and hope, in "'The Real Way of Praying': The *Via Crucis, Mexicano* Sacred Space, and the Architecture of Domination," in *Horizons of the Sacred: Mexican Traditions in U.S. Catholicism*, ed. Timothy Matovina and Gary Riebe-Estrela (Ithaca, N.Y.: Cornell University Press, 2002), 41–68. Jeanette Rodriguez, in *Our Lady of Guadalupe: Faith and Empowerment*

among *Mexican-American Women* (Austin: University of Texas Press, 1994), focuses exclusively on women's devotion to the Virgin and takes seriously women's stories about the power of *la Virgen* for them. See also Kristy Nabhan-Warren, *The Virgin of El Barrio: Marian Apparitions, Catholic Evangelizing, and Mexican American Activism* (New York: New York University Press, 2005), for additional narratives of Mexican American women's self-proclaimed empowerment through the Virgin.

5. In Antonio M. Stevens Arroyo, ed., *Prophets Denied Honor: An Anthology on the Hispanic Church in the United States* (Maryknoll, N.Y.: Orbis Books, 1980), for example, Las Hermanas, a group of women religious of Hispanic ethnicity, is the only women's organization accorded a chapter, and the Hispanic church is portrayed primarily as a male-led institution. Women's voices are, for the most part, absent. On the other hand, several of the chapters in the recently published *Horizons of the Sacred: Mexican Traditions in U.S. Catholicism*, ed. Timothy Matovina and Gary Riebe-Estrella (Ithaca, N.Y.: Cornell University Press, 2002), explore how women's faith is intricately tied to a community's needs. See especially Davalos, "The Real Way of Praying"; and Luis D. León, " 'Soy una Curandera y Soy una Católica': The Poetics of a Mexican Healing Tradition," in Matovina and Riebe-Estrela, *Horizons of the Sacred*, 95–118. Roberto R. Treviño pays special attention to Mexican American women's vital roles in shaping Mexican American ethno-Catholicism. See Roberto R. Treviño, *The Church in the Barrio: Mexican American Ethno-Catholicism in Houston* (Chapel Hill: University of North Carolina Press, 2006).

6. C. Gilberto Romero has argued that Hispanic practitioners of popular piety have an "intuitive insight," and he provides an apologetics of Hispanic popular piety, in *Hispanic Devotional Piety: Tracing the Biblical Roots* (New York: Orbis Books, 1991), 40, 41. Stephen Holler's work also privileges Hispanic popular piety. He has referred to Hispanics who attend Catholic mass regularly as "losing their identity." Latino Studies lecture, Indiana University, April 9, 1999. His published work does acknowledge that there is a relationship between U.S. Hispanic popular piety and the Catholic Church, but he does not explore the relationship in depth. Holler, "Exploring the Popular Religion of U.S. Hispanic/Latino Ethnic Groups," *Latino Studies Journal* 6, no. 3 (September 1995): 3–29.

7. Robert A. Orsi, *The Madonna of 115th Street: Faith and Community in Italian Harlem, 1880–1950*, 2nd ed. (New Haven: Yale University Press, 2002), xiv.

8. In addition to Robert Orsi's more recent critique of the dichotomization of religious experience into categories of "popular" and "official," see Robert Wright, "If It's Official, It Can't Be Popular? Reflections on Popular and Folk Religion," *Journal of Hispanic/Latino Theology* 1 (May 1994): 47–67; and Robert Wright, "Popular and Official Religiosity: A Theoretical Analysis and Case Study of Laredo-Nuevo-Laredo, 1755–1857" (Ph.D. diss., Graduate Theological Union, 1992). See also Orlando O. Espín, "Popular Catholicism among Latinos," in *Hispanic Catholic Culture in the U.S.: Issues and Concerns*, ed. Jay P. Dolan and Allan

Figueroa Deck (Notre Dame, Ind.: University of Notre Dame Press, 1994), 308–59. Treviño, in *The Church in the Barrio*, also challenges the easy categorization of religious experience.

9. Estela Ruiz, interview with author, South Phoenix, Arizona, December 6, 2000.

10. Ibid.

11. David Blackbourn, *Marpingen: Apparitions of the Virgin Mary in Bismarckian Germany* (Oxford: Clarendon Press, 1993), 23–24.

12. Martha Cotera, "Marianismo," in *Dona Doormat no esta aqui!*, ed. Irene Dominguez (Washington, D.C.: U.S. Department of Education, 1985), 147.

13. Gloria Ines-Loya, "The Hispanic Woman: *Pasionaria* and *Pastora* of the Hispanic Community," in *Frontiers of Hispanic Theology in the United States*, ed. Allan Figueroa Deck (New York: Orbis Books, 1992), 125.

14. *Our Lady of the Americas: The Messages of the Blessed Virgin Mary as Received by Estela Ruiz of South Phoenix, Arizona* (McKees Rocks, Pa.: Pittsburgh Center for Peace, 1994), 127.

15. Ibid., 189.

16. "Our Lady of the Americas' Messages from November '94–Present," Mary's Ministries, 30 East Cody Drive, Phoenix, Arizona 85040.

17. Ibid.

18. *Our Lady of the Americas*, 35.

19. The phrase "of the world" was repeatedly used, with very little variation, by the women I interviewed and spoke with in South Phoenix in fall 1998. These women all felt that they had become immersed in consumerism and materialism and had fallen away from God. Most still attended Catholic mass but described going to church as going through the motions. Like Estela Ruiz's description of herself prior to the onset of her apparitions of Mary, women affiliated with Mary's Ministries talk of their lives as before and after they let Jesus "into their hearts."

20. *Cursillos* are weekend retreats held for Catholics who want to deepen their relationship with God. *Cursillo de Christianidad* is Spanish for "short course in Christianity." The weekend-long course was popularized by Mexican Americans in the Southwest during the 1960s and 1970s. Originally a lay-initiated movement, the *Cursillo de Christianidad* was brought from Majorca, Spain, to the southwestern United States in the 1950s and has been an enduring component of faith formation among Mexican American Catholics in the Southwest and Midwest ever since.

21. For a good overview of American evangelicalism, see James Davidson Hunter, *Evangelicalism: The Coming Generation* (Chicago: University of Chicago Press, 1987). See also James Davidson Hunter, *American Evangelicalism: Conservative Religion and the Quandary of Modernity* (New Brunswick, N.J.: Rutgers University Press, 1983); David Harrington Watt, *A Transforming Faith: Explorations of Twentieth-Century American Evangelicalism* (New Brunswick, N.J.: Rutgers University Press, 1991); Randall Balmer, *Mine Eyes Have Seen the Glory: A Journey into the Evangelical Subculture in America* (New York: Oxford University Press, 1993);

and Robert Wuthnow, *The Struggle for America's Soul: Evangelicals, Liberals, and Secularism* (Grand Rapids, Mich.: Eerdmans, 1989), for careful coverage of the main issues and concerns for evangelicals. For a comparative look at American evangelicalism, see Donald W. Dayton and Robert K. Johnston, ed. *The Variety of American Evangelicalism* (Knoxville: University of Tennessee Press, 1991).

22. Judith Stacey, *Brave New Families: Stories of Domestic Upheaval in Late Twentieth Century America* (San Francisco: Basic Books, 1991).

23. There are several excellent sources that explore the ability of women to transcend everyday gender restrictions and to create a space for themselves. Lila Abu-Lughod, *Writing Women's Worlds: Bedouin Stories* (Berkeley: University of California Press, 1993); Karen McCarthy Brown, *Mama Lola: A Vodou Priestess in Brooklyn* (Berkeley: University of California Press, 1991); Carolyn Walker Bynum, *Holy Feast and Holy Fast: The Religious Significance of Food to Medieval Women* (Berkeley: University of California Press, 1987); R. Marie Griffith, *God's Daughters: Evangelical Women and the Power of Submission* (Berkeley: University of California Press, 1997); Laurel Kendall, *Shamans, Housewives, and Other Restless Spirits* (Honolulu: University of Hawaii Press, 1985); Elaine J. Lawless, *God's Peculiar People: Women's Voices and Folk Tradition in a Pentecostal Church* (Lexington: University Press of Kentucky, 1988); and Elaine J. Lawless, *Women Preaching Revolution: Calling for Connection in a Disconnected Time* (Philadelphia: University of Pennsylvania Press, 1996).

24. Stacey, *Brave New Families*, 145.

25. Ibid., 134–35.

26. Luís León discusses Alcance Victoria, Victory Outreach, at length in "Born Again in East LA: The Congregation as Border Space," in *Gatherings in the Diaspora*, ed. R. Stephen Warner and Judith G. Wittner (Philadelphia: Temple University Press, 1998), 163–96.

27. The Chicana movement grew out of the larger Chicano movement. Mexican American and Hispanic women began to realize that their needs were being largely overlooked by the Chicano movement, which was led by men. In the eyes of Chicanas, a term that Mexican American women adopted for themselves at this time, the larger feminist movement, dominated by Anglo Protestant women, was also not addressing Mexican American women's concerns. Women drawn to the Chicana movement tended and tend to be well educated and political activists, as were and are Chicanos. Most Chicanas do not see their movement as taking away from the Chicano movement, since their concerns parallel those of their male counterparts. For in-depth discussion of the Chicana movement, see Maxine Baca Zinn, "Political Familism: Toward Sex Role Equality in Chicano Families," *Aztlán: Chicano Journal of the Social Sciences and the Arts* 6 (Spring 1975): 13–26; Irene I. Blea, *La Chicana and the Intersection of Race, Class, and Gender* (New York: Praeger, 1992); and Alfredo Mirande and Evangelina Enriquez, *La Chicana* (Chicago: University of Chicago Press, 1979).

28. Gloria Anzaldúa, ed., *Making Face, Making Soul: Haciendo Caras* (San Francisco: Aunt Lute Foundation Books, 1990), xvi.

29. Elizabeth Martínez, "In Pursuit of Latina Liberation," *Signs* 20, no. 4 (Summer 1995): 1026; Vicki Ruiz, *From Out of the Shadows: Mexican Women in Twentieth-Century America* (Oxford: Oxford University Press, 1998), 110, 111.

30. Martínez, "In Pursuit of Latina Liberation," 1024, 1025.

31. Patience A. Schell, "An Honorable Avocation for Ladies: The Work of Mexico City Unión de Damas Católicas Mexicanas, 1912–1926," *Journal of Women's History* 10, no. 4 (Winter 1999): 94.

32. Carol Hardy-Fanta, *Latina Politics, Latino Politics: Gender, Culture, and Political Participation in Boston* (Philadelphia: Temple University Press, 1993), 189.

33. R. Marie Griffith talks about this "openness" to Jesus: "As in Helen's story about Ryan, healing is perceived as requiring 'openness' to its very possibility, a leap of faith against despair. Often in describing these kinds of emotional or spiritual healings, a woman will write of suddenly realizing she had a choice between remaining in her pain and embracing the life held out to her by Jesus. Making the choice for life, and thus moving out of the darkness and into the light, is perceived as a simple surrender, a taking hold of something freely offered, an opening up of the heart to its deepest desires and their fulfillment" (*God's Daughters*, 98).

34. María, an October 1998 faith course graduate, spoke openly and passionately about her many troubles. A single mother, she works all day as a housekeeper and goes home to take care of her children. She says that she is tired all the time and that she does not feel very well. She is extremely grateful to the Ruizes and to her "nuevos hermanas y hermanos" (new sisters and brothers) that she made in the course. María took the faith course with her sister, and both had to be driven to the faith course by friends, as neither has a car.

35. Mary Pardo discusses the interrelated roles of motherhood and social justice for Mexican American women activists in Los Angeles, suggesting that family and work are interrelated for Latina activists. Mary Pardo, *Mexican American Women Activists: Identity and Resistance in Two Los Angeles Communities* (Philadelphia: Temple University Press, 1998), 1–16; Mary Pardo, "Mexican American Women Grassroots Community Activists: 'Mothers of East Los Angeles,'" *Frontiers* 20, no. 1 (1990): 1–6; Mary Pardo, "Creating Community: Mexican American Women in Eastside Los Angeles," in *Community Activism and Feminist Politics: Organizing across Race, Class, and Gender*, ed. Nancy A. Naples (New York: Routledge, 1998), 275–98.

Acknowledgments

During one of our many conversations about American history, W. Clark Gilpin asked me, "What difference does it make to include women in our narratives of American religion?" If not for his thoughtful question and his intellectual engagement with my work, this book never would have been written. He has been a crucial conversation partner, an exemplary colleague, and a good friend.

Many other historians also helped me to imagine what this book should look like. For sharing their research and their insights, I am grateful to Ann Braude, Anthea Butler, Julie Byrne, Cathleen D. Cahill, Yvonne Chireau, Emily Clark, Elizabeth Flowers, Karin Gedge, Karla Goldman, R. Marie Griffith, Susan Juster, Amy Koehlinger, Janet Moore Lindman, Daisy L. Machado, Susanna Morrill, Kristy Nabhan-Warren, Pamela S. Nadell, Elizabeth Reis, Judith Weisenfeld, Marilyn Westerkamp, Ruth Bloch, Edith Blumhofer, Kathleen Conzen, Rosemary D. Gooden, Sandra Gustafson, Rosalind Hinton, Suellen Hoy, Pamela Jones, Cynthia Jurisson, Rosemary Skinner Keller, Janice Knight, Kathryn Long, Laurie Maffly-Kipp, Rowena McClinton, Rosemary Radford Ruether, Ellen Skerrett, Susan Sleeper-Smith, Julia Speller, and Sarah McFarland Taylor. Two anonymous readers for the University of North Carolina Press helped me to sharpen my argument. Elaine Maisner, my editor, encouraged me to pursue this project and offered invaluable advice every step of the way. Dorothea Anderson made this a much stronger book through her judicious copyediting. I owe a special debt of gratitude to Kathleen Sprows Cummings, who not only contributed an excellent essay to this volume but also offered encouragement when I most needed it.

I shared the introduction to this volume with many of my colleagues at the University of Chicago Divinity School during our annual faculty retreat. I would like to thank Richard Rosengarten, Martin Marty, Bernard McGinn, Chris Gamwell, Matthew Kapstein, Kathryn Tanner, and especially Malika Zeghal for helping me to clarify my ideas. I also discussed my introduction with members of the Feminist Theories of Religion workshop at the University of Chicago, who proved to be particularly engaged and astute readers. I owe special thanks to Larisa Reznick, Sarah Imhoff, Annette Bourland Huizenga, and Jennifer Schuberth for their suggestions. Other friends and colleagues also generously offered advice and encouragement, especially Amy

Hollywood, David Hackett, Elizabeth Alvarez, Amy Artman, Jonathan Ebel, Wendy Cadge, Kathryn Lofton, and, as always, Harry Stout and Thomas Tweed.

The research for this book was funded by a generous bequest from Ruby Lyles, a Divinity School alumna who was fascinated by American religious history, and the Martin Marty Center at the University of Chicago. Seth Perry and Ross Eiler, my research assistants during the early stages of this book, provided invaluable help. Working on this project would have been much less fun without them. I am also grateful to Jenny Quijano Sax and Sandra Peppers for all of their work on my behalf. Philippa Koch helped create the index.

I did much of the work on this book at home, where I can hear my children playing while I'm thinking about American religious history. If not for Carrie Lakey, who takes excellent care of my daughters while I'm writing, I would have found it much more difficult to finish this book. Her friendship has graced our lives in many ways.

Family and friends have sustained me with their care. The support of my parents, Trudy and Gordon Brekus, has meant the world to me. Ellen Curtis Boiselle has been a steadfast friend for more than seventeen years, enriching my life with her generous spirit and her quiet wisdom. Erik Sontheimer, my husband, has believed in me—and the importance of my work—since we fell in love in graduate school. Our life together has been a gift.

This book is for our daughters, Claire and Rachel.

Selected Readings

Beecher, Maureen Ursenbach, and Lavina Fielding Anderson, eds. *Sisters in Spirit: Mormon Women in Historical and Cultural Perspective.* Urbana: University of Illinois Press, 1987.

Bendroth, Margaret Lamberts, and Virginia Lieson Brereton, eds. *Women and Twentieth-Century Protestantism.* Urbana: University of Illinois Press, 2002.

Blumhofer, Edith. *Aimee Semple McPherson: Everybody's Sister.* Grand Rapids, Mich.: Eerdmans, 1993.

Braude, Ann. *Radical Spirits: Spiritualism and Women's Rights in Nineteenth-Century America.* Boston: Beacon Press, 1989.

Brekus, Catherine A. *Strangers and Pilgrims: Female Preaching in America, 1740–1845.* Chapel Hill: University of North Carolina Press, 1998.

Clark, Emily. *Masterless Mistresses: The New Orleans Ursulines and the Development of a New World Society, 1727–1834.* Chapel Hill: University of North Carolina Press, 2007.

Cott, Nancy F. *The Bonds of Womanhood: "Woman's Sphere" in New England, 1780–1835.* 2nd ed. New Haven: Yale University Press, 1997.

Diner, Hasia R., and Beryl Benderly. *Her Works Praise Her: A History of Jewish Women in America from Colonial Times to the Present.* New York: Basic Books, 2002.

Douglas, Ann. *The Feminization of American Culture.* 1st ed. New York: Knopf, 1977.

Gedge, Karin E. *Without Benefit of Clergy: Women and the Pastoral Relationship in Nineteenth-Century American Culture.* New York: Oxford University Press, 2003.

Greer, Allan. *Mohawk Saint: Catherine Tekakwitha and the Jesuits.* New York: Oxford University Press, 2005.

Griffith, R. Marie. *Born Again Bodies: Flesh and Spirit in American Christianity.* Berkeley: University of California Press, 2004.

———. *God's Daughters: Evangelical Women and the Power of Submission.* Berkeley: University of California Press, 1997.

Haddad, Yvonne Yazbeck, Jane I. Smith, and Kathleen M. Moore. *Muslim Women in America: The Challenge of Islamic Identity Today.* New York: Oxford University Press, 2006.

Hanks, Maxine, ed. *Women and Authority: Re-emerging Mormon Feminism.* Salt Lake City: Signature Books, 1992.

Higginbotham, Evelyn Brooks. *Righteous Discontent: The Women's Movement in the Black Baptist Church, 1880–1920.* Cambridge: Harvard University Press, 1993.

Hoy, Suellen M. *Good Hearts: Catholic Sisters in Chicago's Past.* Urbana: University of Illinois Press, 2006.

Hyman, E. Paula, and Deborah Dash Moore. *Jewish Women in America: An Historical Encyclopedia*. New York: Routledge, 1998.

Juster, Susan. *Disorderly Women: Sexual Politics and Evangelicalism in Revolutionary New England*. Ithaca, N.Y.: Cornell University Press, 1994.

———. *Doomsayers: Anglo-American Prophecy in the Age of Revolution*. Philadelphia: University of Pennsylvania Press, 2003.

Juster, Susan, and Lisa MacFarlane, eds. *A Mighty Baptism: Race, Gender, and the Creation of American Protestantism*. Ithaca, N.Y.: Cornell University Press, 1996.

Keller, Rosemary Skinner, and Rosemary Radford Ruether, eds. *In Our Own Voices: Four Centuries of American Women's Religious Writing*. 1st ed. San Francisco: HarperSanFrancisco, 1995.

Kern, Kathi. *Mrs. Stanton's Bible*. Ithaca, N.Y.: Cornell University Press, 2001.

Koehlinger, Amy. *The New Nuns: Racial Justice and Religious Reform in the 1960s*. Cambridge: Harvard University Press, 2007.

Larson, Rebecca. *Daughters of Light: Quaker Women Preaching and Prophesying in the Colonies and Abroad, 1700–1775*. 1st ed. New York: Knopf, 1999.

Lindley, Susan Hill. *You Have Stept Out of Your Place: A History of Women and Religion in America*. 1st ed. Louisville, Ky.: Westminster John Knox Press, 1996.

Morrow, Diane Batts. *Persons of Color and Religious at the Same Time: The Oblate Sisters of Providence, 1828–1860*. Chapel Hill: University of North Carolina Press, 2002.

Nabhan-Warren, Kristy. *The Virgin of El Barrio: Marian Apparitions, Catholic Evangelizing, and Mexican American Activism*. New York: New York University Press, 2005.

Nadell, Pamela Susan. *American Jewish Women's History: A Reader*. New York: New York University Press, 2003.

———. *Women Who Would Be Rabbis: A History of Women's Ordination, 1889–1985*. Boston: Beacon Press, 1998.

Orsi, Robert A. *The Madonna of 115th Street: Faith and Community in Italian Harlem, 1880–1950*. New Haven: Yale University Press, 1985.

———. *Thank You, St. Jude: Women's Devotion to the Patron Saint of Hopeless Causes*. New Haven: Yale University Press, 1996.

Painter, Nell Irvin. *Sojourner Truth: A Life, a Symbol*. New York: W. W. Norton, 1996.

Pesantubbee, Michelene E. *Choctaw Women in a Chaotic World: The Clash of Cultures in the Colonial Southeast*. Albuquerque: University of New Mexico Press, 2005.

Rayaprol, Aparna. *Negotiating Identities: Women in the Indian Diaspora*. New York: Oxford University Press, 1997.

Reis, Elizabeth. *Sinners and Witches in Puritan New England*. Ithaca, N.Y.: Cornell University Press, 1997.

Robert, Dana Lee. *Gospel Bearers, Gender Barriers: Missionary Women in the Twentieth Century*. Maryknoll, N.Y.: Orbis Books, 2002.

Ruether, Rosemary Radford, and Rosemary Skinner Keller, eds. *Women and Religion in America*. 3 vols. San Francisco: Harper and Row, 1981, 1983, 1986.

Ruether, Rosemary Radford, Rosemary Skinner Keller, and Marie Cantlon, eds. *Encyclopedia of Women and Religion in North America*. 3 vols. Bloomington: Indiana University Press, 2006.

Satter, Beryl. *Each Mind a Kingdom: American Women, Sexual Purity, and the New Thought Movement, 1875–1920*. Berkeley: University of California Press, 1999.

Sklar, Kathryn Kish. *Catharine Beecher: A Study in American Domesticity*. New Haven: Yale University Press, 1973.

Suh, Sharon A. *Being Buddhist in a Christian World: Gender and Community in a Korean American Temple*. Seattle: University of Washington Press, 2004.

Weisenfeld, Judith, and Richard Newman. *This Far by Faith: Readings in African-American Women's Religious Biography*. New York: Routledge, 1996.

Westerkamp, Marilyn J. *Women and Religion in Early America, 1600–1850: The Puritan and Evangelical Traditions*. New York: Routledge, 1999.

Contributors

Ann Braude is director of the Women's Studies in Religion Program and senior lecturer on American religious history at Harvard Divinity School. She is the author of *Radical Spirits: Spiritualism and Women's Rights in Nineteenth-Century America* (1989); coeditor of *Root of Bitterness: Documents of the Social History of American Women* (1996); and editor of *Transforming the Faiths of Our Fathers: Women Who Changed American Religion* (2004).

Catherine A. Brekus is associate professor of the history of Christianity at the University of Chicago Divinity School. She is the author of *Strangers and Pilgrims: Female Preaching in America, 1740–1845* (1998). She is currently writing a book for Knopf entitled *Sarah Osborn's World: Popular Christianity in Early America.*

Anthea D. Butler is assistant professor of religion and classics at the University of Rochester. Her forthcoming book for the University of North Carolina Press is entitled *Making a Sanctified World: Women in the Church of God in Christ.*

Emily Clark is assistant professor of history at Tulane University. She is the author of *Masterless Mistresses: The New Orleans Ursulines and the Development of a New World Society, 1727–1834* (University of North Carolina Press, 2007).

Kathleen Sprows Cummings is the associate director of the Cushwa Center for the Study of American Catholicism at the University of Notre Dame. Her teaching and research interests focus on the history of American Catholicism and the history of women and religion in the United States. Her publications have appeared in the *U.S. Catholic Historian, American Catholic Studies, Commonweal,* and *America.* At present she is at work on the forthcoming *New Women of the Old Faith: Gender and American Catholic Identity in the Progressive Era,* which will be published by the University of North Carolina Press.

Amy Koehlinger is assistant professor of religion at Florida State University. She is the author of *The New Nuns: Racial Justice and Religious Reform in the 1960s* (Harvard University Press, 2007).

Janet Moore Lindman is associate professor of history at Rowan University. She is the coeditor of *"A Centre of Wonders": The Body in Early America* (2001). She is currently working on a book entitled *Paradox of Piety: Baptist Community in Early America,* which will be published by the University of Pennsylvania Press.

Susanna Morrill is assistant professor of religious studies at Lewis and Clark College. She is the author of *White Roses on the Floor of Heaven: Mormon Women's Popular Theology, 1880–1920* (2006).

Kristy Nabhan-Warren is assistant professor of American religions at Augustana College. She is the author of *The Virgin of El Barrio: Marian Apparitions, Catholic Evangelizing, and Mexican American Activism* (2005).

Pamela S. Nadell is Clendenen Professor of History and director of the Jewish Studies Program at American University. She is the author of *Women Who Would Be Rabbis: A History of Women's Ordination, 1889–1985* (1998), which was a finalist for the National Jewish Book Award and a main selection of the Jewish Book Club; and *Conservative Judaism in America: A Biographical Dictionary and Sourcebook* (1988). She has edited *American Jewish Women's History: A Reader* (2003) and, with Jonathan D. Sarna, *Women and American Judaism: Historical Perspectives* (2001).

Elizabeth Reis is associate professor of women's and gender studies and history at the University of Oregon. She is the author of *Damned Women: Sinners and Witches in Puritan New England* (1997); and the editor of *Spellbound: Women and Witchcraft in America* (1998). She has also edited a collection of scholarly articles and primary documents called *American Sexual Histories* (2001) and her grandmother's memoir, *Dear Lizzie: Memoir of a Jewish Immigrant Woman* (2000). She is currently working on a book called *Impossible Hermaphrodites: Intersex in America, 1620–1960.*

Marilyn J. Westerkamp is professor of history at the University of California at Santa Cruz. She is the author of *Women and Religion in Early America, 1600–1850: The Puritan and Evangelical Traditions* (1999) and *Triumph of the Laity: Scots-Irish Piety and the Great Awakening, 1625–1760* (1988). She is at work on a book entitled *Sectarian Mysticism and Puritan Patriarchy: Engendering Puritanism in Old and New England.*

Index

Bederman, Gail, 32

Beecher, Catharine, 15, 25

Beecher, Maureen Ursenbach, 186

Bender, Thomas, 19

Bendroth, Margaret Lamberts, 234, 247

Bennett, Judith M., 3, 23

Bertrand, Sister Louis, 266

Bertrand, Sister Remigia, 266

Blackbourn, David, 298

Bonne, Julia, 97

Bordin, Ruth, 25

Błorresen, Kari, 298–99

Bow, Clara, 5

Boyd, R. H., 165

Boyer, Paul, 74–75

Bozell, Patricia Buckley, 234–36; *Triumph*, 234–35

Bradford, William, 77

Bradstreet, Anne, 52, 54, 234; on childbearing, 55; on death, 55–56; poetry of, 55–57; theology of, 55–57, 62; gender in writings of, 62; power of, 64; in historical narratives, 67

Bradstreet, Mercy, 55

Brandeis University, 241–42

Braude, Ann, 2, 8, 27–28, 31, 281, 283

Breen, Timothy, 118

Brereton, Virginia, 234

Broughton, Virginia, 162, 167

Brown, Anne S., 19

Brown, Peter, 260

Brumberg, Joan Jacobs, 25

Bryn Mawr College, 211, 222

Buckley, James, 234

Buckley, William F., Jr., 234

Buell, Samuel, 119, 123

Bugg, Lelia Hardin, 225

Bulkeley, Gershom, 86

Bulkeley, Peter, 61

Butler, Jon, 7

Butler, Judith, 11, 33, 272

Bynum, Caroline Walker, 272

Byrne, Julie, 10

Cadge, Wendy, 31

Calkins, Gladys Gilkey, 248–49

Campbell, Joan, 6

Capuchin missionaries, 95

Carmichael, Sarah, 191

Carr, Anne, 9

Carter, Minnie, 161, 164, 174–75

Casiano, Inez, 238

Catherine of Aragon (queen of England), 5

Catholic Church, American: and gender, 97, 253–73; and Americanist controversy, 207–9, 213–19; and immigrants, 208; and feminist movement, 234–40, 247; Mexican American women in, 294–313. *See also* Delille, Henriette; Girodeau, Felicité; Mary's Ministries; Ruiz, Estela; Sisters of Notre Dame de Namur; Sisters of the Congregation of the Presentation of the Virgin Mary, The; Trinity College; Ursulines; Vatican Council, Second; Virgin Mary

—African American women in, 92, 94–103, 255; baptism of, 96, 98–99; godparenting by, 96, 98–99

—and higher education, 210; of women, 206–26; fear of coeducation, 211–13, 215–18; fear of secular education, 211–13, 215–18; fear of "New Woman," 215, 218, 225

—historiography of, 92–93, 102; as immigrant church, 91–92; women in, 207, 257–60, 271–73; and Americanist controversy, 208; and Progressivism, 220, 226; women religious in, 258, 271, 273; institutional bias of, 296–97; Mexican Americans in, 296–97

—and women religious, 94–97, 206–26, 253–73; relevance of, 253–54, 257; critics of, 254; work in non-Catholic communities, 254–55, 263, 268; work among African Americans, 255–57, 260, 263–70; racial apostolate of, 255–

and African American women, 237–
38, 241–42, 245
—historiography of, 234; on secular
nature of, 234, 236, 239, 242, 245–47;
religion in, 234, 236, 241, 245–47;
ecumenical women's organizations in,
241; Protestant liberals in, 241, 245,
246, 248; exclusion of African Ameri-
can women from, 242; Mexican
American women in, 310–11
Fink, Rabbi Joseph I., 290
Fink, Toby, 290
Finney, Charles, 4
Fish, Joseph, 125, 130
Fortune-telling: and Puritanism, 85
Foster, Emma, 150
Foster, Lawrence, 186
Foucault, Michel, 10, 20, 33, 115
Fox, Ruth May, 188, 196
Franciscan Missionaries of Mary, 256
Frank, Ray, 282
Franklin, Benjamin, 110, 121
Frey, Sylvia, 103
Friedan, Betty, 237–40; *The Feminine
Mystique*, 233, 243–45; Jewish educa-
tion of, 243; religious response to,
243–45. *See also* National Organiza-
tion of Women
Frothingham, Ebenezer, 128
Fundamentalists: and women, 247–48;
and modernist controversy, 247–49
Furfey, Msgr. Paul Hanly, 236

Garrigan, Rev. Philip, 207, 210–12, 223
Gates, Susa Young, 191
Gaustad, Edwin, 6, 74
Gay, Peter, 111–12
Geck, Sister Mary Paul, 266
Geertz, Clifford, 18–19
Gender, 54, 97, 144; as category of anal-
ysis, 10–11, 32, 66–67, 260, 284–86;
social and cultural construction of, 11,
154, 207–8; and individual agency, 20,

33, 115–16; and Puritanism, 57–68, 75–
76, 87; and sexuality, 60; binary models of, 60, 260–61, 263, 272–73; as performance, 131; challenges to norms of,
131, 164; and Catholic sisters, 160–64,
271–73; and Mormon women, 185–
200; and nature, 192; and creation of
American Catholic identity, 208; and
racial hierarchy, 263–64; and Ameri-
can Judaism, 283–89
Genealogical Society of Utah, 185
General Theological Seminary, 242
Georgetown College, 218
Gibbons, Cardinal James, 212–19, 221,
223
Gifford, Carolyn, 246
Girodeau, Felicité, 94, 100–102; and his-
tory of American Catholicism, 100; as
godmother, 101–2; religious leader-
ship of, 101–2
Girodeau, Gabriel, 101
Global Ministries, 309
Goff, Philip, 7
Goldman, Karla, 285
Goodbeer, Richard, 75
Goody, Jack, 188
Gordon, Linda, 8
Gorton, Samuel, 66
Graham, Billy, 7
Graham, Richard, 238
Great Awakening: religious revivals of,
108, 114, 120, 122, 127; and rise of evan-
gelicalism, 114
Greenburg, Dan: *How to Be a Jewish
Mother*, 243
Griffith, R. Marie, 17
Guadalupanas, 296
Guyse, John, 120–21

Hackett, David, 14
Haener, Dorothy, 238, 241
Hall, David, 19
Hall, Timothy, 118

Hambrick-Stowe, Charles, 122

Hamer, Fannie Lou, 27

Hamilton, Alexander, 110

Hamilton, David: *The Private Christian's Witness for Christianity*, 120–21

Hanks, Maxine, 186

Hardesty, Nancy, 4

Hardy-Fantana, Carol, 311

Harmann, Susan, 289

Harris, Abigail, 142–43, 149–50; interactions with other evangelicals, 150; on marriage, 150; religious activity of, 150; writings of, 150–51; ecumenism of, 151; religious leadership of, 151; construction of religious self, 153–54

Harris, Barbara, 5–6

Harrison, Katherine, 85–86

Hart, R. E., 171

Harvey, Paul, 7

Haskell, Thomas, 9–10, 22

Hatch, Nathan, 4

Hazard, Paul, 110

Heaton, Hannah, 130

Hedgeman, Anna Arnold, 237–38, 241

Hempton, David, 114

Heresy: within Puritanism, 58; female heretics, 58–59; as feminine crime, 60, 66–67, 79–80. *See also* Witchcraft

Hewitt, Nancy, 25

Higginbotham, Evelyn Brooks, 162, 164, 180

Hijas de Marʲa, 296

Hildegard of Bingen, 129

Hill, Christopher, 63

Hill, Patricia, 247

Himmelfarb, Gertrude, 16

Hindmarsh, 114

Hine, Darlene Clark, 27

Historiography: and objectivity question, 9–10; social history, 18–19; cultural history, 18–20; of African American women, 27, 162–63, 180; of feminist movement, 27, 234, 236–37; of Puritanism, 51–52, 67, 73–75; of witchcraft, 74; of slavery, 92–94, 102–3; of Enlightenment, 109–17, 131; of evangelicalism, 113–14; of Mormons, 186, 191, 199–200

—of American Catholicism, 92–93, 102; as immigrant church, 91–92; women in, 207, 257–60, 271–73; and Americanist controversy, 208; and Progressivism, 220, 226; women religious in, 258, 271, 273; institutional bias of, 296–97; Mexican Americans in, 296–97

—of American Judaism: women in, 280, 283–84, 290–91; gender controversies in, 283–91; and mixed seating, 284–86; and embrace of modernity, 285

—American religious history textbooks: neglect of women in, 4–7, 143, 199–200, 232–33, 257–58, 279; Protestant bias of, 5, 14–15, 257–58; focus on public culture in, 14–18; agency in, 17–18, 20–21; attention to faith in, 162; social reform movements in, 258–59, 271; and race, 260; and gender, 260, 272–73

—American women's history textbooks: religion in, 24–28, 232–34, 237; African American women in, 27; feminist movement in, 27, 234, 236–37; Catholic women in, 257–58; social reform movements in, 257–58

Hobsbawm, Eric, 115

Hodgkin, Katharine, 153

Holifield, E. Brooks, 4

Holiness movement, 162–63, 165, 167–70, 173; and sanctification, 163–80; and ability to speak in tongues, 169; and Bible Bands, 170. *See also* Church of God in Christ; Pentecostals

Hooker, Thomas, 62, 84

Hopkins, Samuel, 109, 118, 119; *Familiar Letters, Written by Mrs. Sarah Osborn*

and Miss Susanna Anthony, Late of
Newport, Rhode Island, 118; Memoirs
of the Life of Mrs. Sarah Osborn, 118
Horkheimer, Max, 115
How, Elizabeth, 82
Hoy, Suellen, 256
Hudson, Winthrop, 6–7, 15, 34
Humanae Vitae, 236
Hume, David, 117
Hunt, Lynn, 10
Hunter, Jane, 25
Hutcheson, Frances, 113, 124
Hutchinson, Anne, 7, 52, 58, 60, 79, 86,
129, 234; theology of, 59, 62; power of,
64–65, 68; banishment of, 66; in his-
torical narratives, 67; on revelation, 78
Hyman, Paula, 280

Ines-Loya, Gloria, 300
Ireland, Archbishop John, 213–14, 219

Jacobs, Margaret, 10
Jacobson, Matthew Frye, 264
James, Henry, 245
James I (king of England), 61
Jefferson, Thomas, 110
Jewish Spectator, 289
Jewish Theological Seminary, 285, 288
Jews. See Judaism, American
Johnson, John: A Mathematical Ques-
tion, Propounded by the Viceregent of
the World; Answered by the King of
Glory, 124
Johnson, Mary Magrum, 176–77
Johnson, Paul, 14
Johnson, W. G., 176
Jones, C. P., 165, 170
Jones, Margaret, 59
Judaism, American:
—historiography of: women in, 280,
283–86, 290–91; gender controversies
in, 283–91; and modernity, 285
—women in, 279–91; and feminist

movement, 239–44; ordination of,
281–84, 286; and dissent, 283–84; and
mixed seating, 284–86; changing roles
of, 284–91; as historical actors, 286–
91; bat mitzvah, 287–88, 290; agunah,
288
Juschka, Darlene, 13
Juster, Susan, 8–9, 116–17

Kant, Immanuel, 110, 115
Kaplan, Judith, 288, 290
Kaplan, Mordecai M., 288
Karlsen, Carol, 75
Keane, Bishop John, 210, 213–14
Keller, Rosemary Skinner, 30
Kerber, Linda K., 24
Kern, Kathi Lynn, 28
King, Hannah T., 191, 198
King, Ursula, 154
Knapp, Elizabeth, 83
Koch, Adrienne, 109
Koehlinger, Amy, 28, 32
Kors, Alan, 114–15

Ladies of the Sacred Heart, 211
LaHaye, Beverly, 25–26
Landes, Joan B., 115
Las Hermanas, 296
Latitudinarianism, 113
Latrobe, Benjamin, 97–98
Latter-day Saints (LDS). See Mormons
Lawson, Deodat, 84
LeBeau, Henriette, 98
Lebeson, Anita Libman, 290
Lee, Ann, 2, 258
Lee, Jarena, 2, 5, 102
Leo XIII (pope), 215–16; Testem Benev-
olentiae, 208
Lerner, Gerda, 25, 283, 290
Lewinsky, Monica, 5
Lindley, Susan Hill, 3, 30
Literature: "culture of flowers" genre,
185, 188, 192, 199; Mormon women's

—and Enlightenment, 32, 109–10, 117; rejection of enlightened ideas, 119–22, 124, 131; attraction to Lockean empiricism, 123–25, 127, 132; attitude toward reason, 124; desire for certainty, 127–28

—writings of: memoir, 108; diaries, 108–9, 118, 120–32; *The Nature, Certainty, and Evidence of True Christianity*, 123, 128

Pace, Rev. Edward, 215
Paine, Thomas, 112
Painter, Nell, 27
Palmer, Phoebe, 7
Parham, Charles, 169
Parks, Rosa, 6
Parr, Susanna, 60
Pateman, Carole, 116
Paulists, 218
Pentecostals: and sanctification, 163–80 passim; Azusa Street revival, 169–70; theology of, 174; and speaking in tongues, 175, 304; marriage policy of, 178; influence on Catholics, 304
—African American women, 161–80, 247; testimony of, 161; construction of religious and social identity, 161–62; and sanctification, 163–80 passim; and agency, 164; and gender equality, 173; spiritual power of, 175, 180. *See also* Church of God in Christ; Holiness movement
Peters, Hugh, 59, 78
Phillips, Ulrich Bonnell, 93
Pius X (pope), 209
Pluralism, religious, 28–31, 118
Pocock, J. G. A., 112
Pomet, Felicité, 101
Porter, Roy, 111–12, 114
Pratt, Reba Beebe, 191
Prell, Riv-Ellen, 243
Presbyterians, 151, 165, 239

Priesand, Rabbi Sally, 279, 282
Proctor, Elizabeth, 52
Progressivism: women and, 208–9, 220; Catholicism and, 208–9, 220, 226; Progressive reform, 209; and expansion of women's higher education, 209
Promise Keepers, 309
Protestant Reformation, 112, 152
Protestants, American. *See specific denominations*
Puritans: historiography of, 51–52, 67, 73–75; and sexuality, 51–68 passim; and Quakers, 52, 61, 64–67; and Native Americans, 77
—and gender, 87; gendering of heresy, 58–60, 66–67, 79–80; cultural constructions of femininity, 60, 62, 73, 75–76; God as male, 62, 68; and class, 63
—and power: of women, 53–54, 63–66; subjectivity, 63–64; charisma, 64–65; in relationship to state, 65–66
—theology of: Half-Way Covenant, 52; popular, 54, 61; heresy, 58–60; egalitarian aspects of, 67, 75; sin, 73, 80–82; revelation, 76, 78, 80; salvation, 77, 79; predestination, 78, 84; confession, 83; hell, 84; magic, 85–87; role of religious certainty in, 113, 127; emphasis on experience, 114; rationalism, 114
—women, 51–68, 73–87; and witchcraft, 52; spiritual power of, 53–54, 63–66; and childbirth, 55, 57; female heretics, 58–59; understanding of female body, 61–62, 75
Putnam, Edward, 81

Quakers: Puritan treatment of, 52, 61, 64–66; feminization of, 66–67; women, 144–47, 151; and female leadership, 147
Quinn, D. Michael, 186

99, 302–7, 312–13; feminist critiques of, 296, 298–99; Marian shrines, 297–99, 301–3; and social action, 305–6; Virgin of Guadalupe, 312

Visitation Convent, 218

Voltaire, 110

Wacker, Grant, 7

Ware, Susan, 27

Warne, Randi R., 3, 9

Warner, Marina, 298–99

Watson, John, 92, 97

Wattleton, Faye, 246

Watts, Isaac, 120

Webster, Samuel, 119

Weisenfeld, Judith, 245

Weiss-Rosmarin, Trude, 289

Weld, Thomas, 80

Wellesley College, 211, 222, 224, 226

Wells, Emmeline B., 190–91, 195–96

Welter, Barbara, 25, 232

Wesley, John, 163

Westerkamp, Marilyn, 11, 32

Wheaten, Samuel, 117

Wheatley, Phillis, 5

Whitby, Daniel, 119

White, Deborah Gray, 27

Whitefield, George, 7, 18

Whitney, Orson F., 192

Wiesner-Hanks, Merry, 24

Wigglesworth, Michael, 55

Wilkinson, Jemima, 116

Willard, Frances, 2, 258–59

Willard, Samuel, 84

Williams, Abigail, 52

Williams, Roger, 64–66

Wilson, Lois, 245

Winer, Rabbi Gershon, 287

Winthrop, John, 54, 57, 61, 65, 77, 79–80; on revelation, 78

Winthrop, John, Jr., 86

Winthrop, Margaret, 56–57, 234

Wise, Rabbi Aaron, 289–90

Wise, Rabbi Isaac Mayer, 7, 285

Wise, Miriam, 289–90

Witchcraft, 52; and sexual deviance, 59–60; gendering of, 60–61, 73–74; and "monstrous births," 60–61, 79–80; historiography of, 74; socioeconomic dimensions of, 74–75; as challenge to providence, 76; and revelation, 76, 81; and secrecy, 81–86; and covenant with devil, 83; confession of, 83–85; and salvation, 84–85; and magical knowledge, 86. *See also* Heresy

Wolcott, Virginia, 176

Wollstonecraft, Mary, 116

Women: diversity of, 28–31; and witchcraft, 52, 59–61, 73–87; Quaker, 52, 64–67, 144–47, 151; African American, 91–103 passim, 161–80, 237, 241–42, 245; and Enlightenment, 109–10, 115–17, 128–31; evangelical, 109–10, 117, 128–31, 297, 311; Congregationalist, 118–20; and Holiness movement, 161–80; Pentecostal, 161–80, 247; in COGIC, 163–65, 167, 170–80; and sanctification, 163–80 passim; writings of Mormon, 184–200; and higher education, 209–11, 222–23; "New Woman," 215; Methodist, 237–39, 241, 243, 245, 248; and social gospel movement, 246, 248–49; and missions, 246–48; and social reform, 253–73; Jewish, 279–91; Mexican American, 294–313

—as authors, 123, 128; of diaries, 108–9, 118, 120–32, 142–53 passim; of poetry, 184–200

—Baptist: white, 142–44, 148–51; African American, 162, 164, 169–71, 173

—Catholic, 91–103; African American, 91–103; women religious, 94–97, 206–26, 253–73; higher education of, 206–26; Mexican American, 294–313

—Episcopalian, 144, 147–49, 238, 239; ordination of, 242–43, 245

—Puritan, 51–68, 73–87; and sexuality, 51–68 passim; and witchcraft, 52; spiritual power of, 53–54, 63–66; and childbirth, 55, 57; female heretics, 58–59; understanding of female body, 61–62, 75; and evil, 73; and devil, 75; and supernatural, 76; and revelation, 76, 80

—and second-wave feminism, 27, 233–49; Mexican American, 296, 298–99, 307–12

Women and Religion Task Force, 238–39

Women's Aglow, 309, 311

Women's history: and religion, 2–3, 24–28, 233–34, 245–46; methodology of, 8–13; objectivity of, 9–10; conservatism of, 10, 12–13; radicalism of, 13; and "mainstream" history, 23, 32–33; feminist influence on, 25–26, 246; and gender history, 260. *See also* Gender; Historiography

Women's League for Conservative Judaism, 280

Wood, Betty, 103

Wood, Peter, 93

World Council of Churches, 245

Young, Brigham, 189, 191

Young, Zina D. H., 188, 199

Young Ladies Mutual Improvement Association, 188

Young Woman's Journal, 191, 194

Young Women's Christian Association (YWCA), 241–42, 245–46

Zagarri, Rosemarie, 116

Zunz, Olivier, 18–19